Foreign Correspondence

Foreign Correspondence
The Great Reporters and Their Times

Second Edition

JOHN HOHENBERG

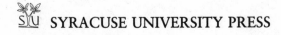 SYRACUSE UNIVERSITY PRESS

First Edition 1965
Second Edition 1995
95 96 97 98 99   6 5 4 3 2 1

Originally published by Columbia University Press in 1965.

The paper used in this publication meets the minimum requirements
of American National Standard for Information Sciences — Permanence
of Paper for Printed Library Materials, ANSI Z39.48 ∞™

Library of Congress Cataloging-in-Publication Data

Hohenberg, John.
    Foreign correspondence : the great reporters and their times /
John Hohenberg. — 2nd ed.
        p.   cm.
    Includes bibliographical references and index.
    ISBN 0-8156-2648-7 (cloth). — ISBN 0-8156-0314-2 (pbk.)
    1. Foreign correspondents. 2. Foreign news. I. Title.
PN4784.F6H6   1995
070.4'332 — dc20   94-37505

Manufactured in the United States of America

This book, which includes still more tales
of the great foreign correspondents and
their times, is gratefully dedicated to
JO ANN
because she encouraged me to persevere.

John Hohenberg, a distinguished journalist and political and diplomatic correspondent in New York, Washington, D.C., the United Nations, and abroad, was Professor of Journalism, Columbia Graduate School of Journalism, from 1950 to 1976. From 1954 to 1976, he also served as the Administrator of the Pulitzer Prizes and Secretary of the Pulitzer board. He is the author of *The Bill Clinton Story* (Syracuse University Press, 1994), *The Professional Journalist, Free Press/Free People,* and three books on the Pulitzer Prizes among others. He also holds a Pulitzer Prize Special Award for his services to American journalism.

Contents

Contents

The Strangest of Heroes

For a little more the 200 years, a small and tough-minded band of foreign correspondents has brought the story of war and peace to an often bemused public in the United States and abroad. Some have been captured or held hostage, others have been severely wounded or killed in action. But nearly always, these young men and a few courageous young women — plus a few older retreads in their always dangerous profession — have preserved their independence and their integrity whether they were under pressure from governments, military censors, or facing the fire of a foe.

In a lifetime of association with them after having been one of them in my younger years, I have always believed this to be the proudest part of their accomplishment. Thereby, they have kept faith with the open society that relies on them.

Nevertheless, their work has been challenged more often than not. On a trip to Vietnam in 1964, I remember landing in the middle of a brutal conflict between the American military and a handful of American correspondents who were reporting, even at so early a date, that that war was being lost to an elusive Asian foe.[1] Worse yet, these embattled youngsters were also being blamed for touching off the antiwar riots at home.

At the same time, a brilliant young general kept insisting to me, an older World War II type, that he and his command were winning the war despite the adverse views of the correspondents; and he came close to convincing me during a long interview across a luncheon table.[2] I shall never forget my surprise and my consternation, after leaving the general, when I returned to my hotel and found that a Vietcong soldier had bombed the lobby with destructive effect in the heart of the American stronghold in Saigon. That blast was the convincer.[3] I never again doubted the accuracy of the correspondents in Vietnam.

On the basis of such experiences, together with the generous critical reception given that same year to the original publication of *Foreign Correspondence: The Great Reporters and Their Times,* I have prepared this new edition for a new generation and a new century. If much of the story continues to deal with American and British correspondence, it is precisely because these nations have been the leaders in developing an independent foreign correspondence and tolerating its excesses for the sake of the undoubted benefits it bestows on a democratic people. In the never-ending conflict with the controlled press elsewhere in the world, the independent correspondents are still the leaders in their effect on both their governments and their peoples.

This, then, is an account of how these strangest of heroes came to be and how they have used their influence from the time of the semaphore and the carrier pigeon to the new era of the electronic superhighway. It is presented once again as the case for the foreign correspondent, that sometime myth and undiplomat-at-large, in a manner appropriate to the subject—honestly, not too reverently, but with respect.

John Hohenberg

Knoxville, Tennessee
September 1994

Foreign Correspondence

1 The First Foreign Correspondents

NEWS FOR AMERICA

Jared Ingersoll, coagent for Connecticut, sat in the House of Commons on a wintry day in 1765, listening to the droning discussion of a stamp tax for the American colonies. The honorable members, for the most part, were unimpressed and bored. After all, the stamp tax had a long history in England, and most of them felt, as Prime Minister George Grenville did, that the colonies "ought to pay something" for the privilege of belonging to the British Empire.

Ingersoll, a New Haven lawyer and an inveterate correspondent, took a few notes as Charles Townshend, speaking for the government, admonished the Americans that they were "children planted by our care, nourished by our indulgence . . . protected by our arms" and should therefore "contribute their mite." Then up stepped Colonel Isaac Barré, a Whig of the Pitt school who had fought under James Wolfe at Quebec, with a roar of protest that made Ingersoll's fingers fairly race pen over notepaper.

"They planted by your care?" Barré cried. "No! Your Oppressions planted 'em in America. . . . They nourished by your indulgence? They grew by neglect of 'em . . . whose behavior on many occasions has caused the blood of these *Sons of Liberty* to recoil within 'em."

It didn't matter to Ingersoll now whether the House was bored or not. He had a story for Governor Thomas Fitch and the New London *Gazette* in Connecticut that everybody would read. His account, written in London on the day of the debate, February 6, 1765, appeared in the *Gazette* on May 10 and was reprinted in the Newport (R.I.) *Mer-*

1

cury on May 27.[1] From New England, couriers carried copies of the papers to all other colonies, resulting in general publication. Barré's phrase, "*Sons of Liberty,*" became a watchword, a rallying cry, and the name of a radical organization of patriots whose agitation was the forerunner of American independence.[2]

It would be pleasant to report that this early example of the work and influence of an amateur foreign correspondent brought him honor and fame. But like many a professional who was to follow Jared Ingersoll in the next two centuries, his story backfired. He was among the first to fall afoul of those Sons of Liberty whose organization he had helped create.

Having been foolhardy enough to cast a shadow over his integrity as a correspondent by accepting the post of British stamp distributor for Connecticut, he was forced to resign by an indignant crowd of his fellow-citizens. "It is a time," wrote the sorrowful foreign correspondent, "when mankind seem to think they have a right not only to shoot at me with the arrow that flyeth by day, but to assassinate me in the dark."[3]

Ingersoll suffered the worst indignity that can befall any journalist even though he contended that his friend, Benjamin Franklin, had advised him that he could safely accept British largesse. Whether or not that was true, the Sons of Liberty came down hard on their London correspondent. He not only had to give up the distribution of the pernicious British stamps but also had to swear that he would thenceforth initiate no correspondence from the colonies to London unless it was first shown to and approved by a designated representative of the Sons of Liberty. To add to his disgrace, he was also made the victim of censorship—one of the earliest casualties in American history. In years yet to come, he would have a lot of company.

NEWS FOR ENGLAND

The London newspapers showed scant enterprise in their coverage of the American Revolution. In 1772, three years before the shot fired at Concord was heard round the world, the English press had won the right to publish the proceedings of Parliament—a good test of its strength. But for a distant war across the Atlantic, at a time when it took two months to send an American newspaper to London, the editors were content to republish their American news from the official London *Gazette* a day afterward.

The French Revolution, being closer to home, had to be handled differently mainly because the public was more concerned about it. But even here, since much of the news was copied from the French papers and the government sometimes directed the packets to friendly editors, what the public learned was chancy, days late, and often prejudiced about source.

It happened, however, that the London *Morning Post* had had the foresight to send an occasional correspondent to France that early summer of 1789; but through a lamentable error in judgment, he missed the fall of the Bastille on July 14, the beginning of the great revolt that transformed Europe. The gentleman correspondent, Arthur Young, had lacked the first quality of a professional journalist, patience.

"The whole business is over," he concluded, and went home across the Channel on June 27.[4] It was just as well, therefore, that a practical-minded coal dealer who had founded the *Times* in 1785, John Walter I, decided he needed a foreign staff to cover the nearby uprising. Although he complained bitterly about the cost and accused the government of routing his French newspapers to a rival in greater favor, he took a modest first step on August 27, 1792, by advertising: "Wanted immediately, A Gentleman who is capable of translating the French language."

Besides translators, Walter also took on agents in Paris and a few other foreign news centers, messengers to carry dispatches across the Channel, and the requisite office help needed for processing the new order of foreign correspondence.[5] With the rise of Napoleon, such foresight paid off. The alarm of the British public, intensified by the activities of the French conqueror, boosted the *Times*'s circulation. But Walter's independent operation also brought him into disrepute with his government.

By 1803, his son and successor, John Walter II, was accusing the Home Office of trying to intercept his correspondence from the "north of Europe," meaning Hamburg, the seat of the best available intelligence at the time of the Napoleonic wars. As if that weren't trouble enough for the *Times,* the younger Walter also complained that the government had seized papers intended for him and "the next day their contents appeared in the *Oracle,*"[6] a competing journal favored by the government. As a result, the angry proprietor told his foreign agents to address their dispatches to friendly merchants and bankers who let the *Times* use their offices as mail drops.

However, that also didn't solve the *Times*'s problem of beating the competition and the obstruction of a government that feared an independent source of news. The next step was foreordained. Young Walter turned to a 32-year-old lawyer he'd taken on as an editorial staffer two years before, Henry Crabb Robinson, and sent him to Altona, outside Hamburg, in January 1807.

Because Robinson was the first clearly identifiable representative of an important daily newspaper who was sent abroad to cover the news, he has often been called the first foreign correspondent. He wasn't. A number of other foreign newspaper people had been in Hamburg and Altona for some time before Robinson's arrival; but after almost 200 years, there is no way of determining who went there first to maintain watch on Napoleon's movements. Then, too, Robinson never pretended to be a reporter in the modern sense, a prime requisite of a foreign correspondent, but rather despised that aspect of the job. He was, in the old-fashioned British manner still observed from time to time on the news fronts of the world, a leisurely writer who sent letters on foreign affairs to his paper when he felt moved to do so.

Because of Nelson's victory over the French at Trafalgar in 1805* and the importance of Napoleon's continental system, news of Europe had become increasingly scarce in London. Not even the foreign papers were getting through to London regularly. In this extremity, the era cried out for active, energetic reporters at a time when Napoleon, the victor at Jena, was leading his armies eastward. That was when Robinson reached Altona.

Instead of chasing after Napoleon, a risky undertaking at best, the *Times*'s man, being fluent in German, made arrangements with the *Hamburgischen Correspondent* to use whatever information he wanted to forward to London. Therefore, it was six days before Robinson heard about Napoleon's victory at Friedland on June 14, 1807, and sent the news to London. He also picked up the story of the Peace of Tilsit on June 25, when Napoleon and Alexander I of Russia met at the Niemen.

Otherwise, the *Times*'s correspondent didn't perceptibly worry about covering Napoleon at long range but satisfied himself, as less-enterprising correspondents still do, by forwarding easily written pieces about the gossip and rumors of the era at Hamburg. And so Robinson didn't last long. In August, after he had been the *Times*'s man at Altona for a little more than six months, he was called home.

---

*The news of Trafalgar provides some idea of the manner and speed of news communication in 1805. The battle was fought on Oct. 21, the official British dispatch was dated Oct. 22, and the official London *Gazette* published it Nov. 2. The London papers picked it up next day with the news of Nelson's death "in the hour of victory." The French withheld the news until Napoleon lost power.

Despite his failings as a correspondent, however, Robinson turned out to have a first-rate editorial sense; he urged young Walter to establish regular correspondents in Paris, Vienna, Berlin and St. Petersburg, in addition to Altona, with instructions to do a roundup weekly piece on the news and its meaning from each of these bases. What was needed, considering the time and distance involved, he explained, was less "matters of fact men" but "men of letters" who could comment on the news.

For his sagacity and quick recovery from his failure as a correspondent, he was rewarded by being appointed foreign editor. And on January 25, 1808, he was writing to his brother that, upon Walter's direction, he was to be "known expressly as the Editor" of the *Times*.

Robinson didn't know when he was well off. He decided that he wanted to cover the British-Spanish-Portuguese effort to defeat Napoleon's forces in the Peninsular War and arrived at the northwest Spanish port of La Coruña on July 31, 1808, to report on the British occupation under Sir John Moore. The city already had achieved a place in history, first as the point of departure of the Spanish Armada in 1588 and ten years later as the target of Sir Francis Drake, who virtually destroyed it.

Having been seasoned in the field at Altona and in the office at the editor's desk, Robinson began a more businesslike operation as a correspondent by regularly forwarding letters from Spain on any British ship leaving La Coruña. Meanwhile, he passed the time, as he put it, by associating with the "grand ladies and noblemen" in the rebuilt city.

The *Times*'s correspondent apparently got along pleasantly enough until a quiet afternoon in January 1809 when he sauntered into the dining room of his hotel and found it deserted. "Have you not heard, sir?" a deferential waiter asked. "The French are come. They are fighting."

Robinson decided he'd better find out what was going on and walked out of town, remaining until dark. There, he heard cannonading which, he reported, appeared to come from the hills about three miles beyond the city. He also noted that British wounded and French prisoners were being brought in, but there is no indication in the available correspondence at the time that he knew of the British defeat or the death of Sir John Moore before boarding a British transport that night of January 16, 1809. The correspondent was safely back in London toward the end of the month.

Not long afterward, Robinson and Walter amiably parted company in an exchange of letters, and he resumed his career at the bar. The complications of management rather than any failings of his work as a correspondent, Walter assured him, had made the change necessary. For the rest of his life, Robinson and the *Times*'s publisher and his editors remained friendly, but he never again resumed his role as a pioneering foreign correspondent.[7] The law was much more comfortable.

NEWS FOR EVERYBODY

The great financial houses of Europe, the Fuggers in Augsburg and the Rothschilds in London, had been collecting information and quotations from important stock markets for some years before the *Times* and other London papers began assembling foreign staffs. The financiers used carrier pigeons to bring them news forwarded by their agents. The difference between them was that the Fuggers sometimes made their service available to clients, but the Rothschilds did not. And since there were no newspaper correspondents at the Battle of Waterloo and a Rothschilds' agent was first into London with the news, Nathan Rothschild made a fortune through his coup in consols out of his exclusive knowledge of Napoleon's defeat on June 19, 1815, well ahead of the official report.[8]

Although the French press after Waterloo had emerged from Napoleon's influence, it should not be imagined that these were days of hope for free journalism in Paris. On the contrary, there is abundant evidence to indicate that both the British and the French were extremely busy on both sides of the Channel, buying up as many papers, writers, and editors as possible. That, unhappily, was the way the system worked at the time.

While honest newspapers did exist, no paper and few writers, whatever their eminence, were spared accusations that they were being paid for their advocacy of a particular government or a cause of sorts. In some ways, the estate of the journalist, especially the few in the foreign service, was at its lowest point.

For this reason among many others, an innovator in the collection and distribution of news during that era required steady nerves, good health, and a stout heart. Such a one was Charles Havas, who then was in his early 20s, apparently a native of Hungary, and a dabbler in news, who had gone to Paris to make his fortune. What he sought to do was to emulate the private services of the Fuggers and the Rothschilds by starting his own news agency and selling his daily report to newspapers and other clients.

The French government at the time was collecting information by flashing messages between more than 200 steel towers, each equipped with black wooden slats that were used by agents employing a simple semaphore code between all major cities and Paris. On clear days, agents using telescopes atop the towers could get messages to Paris within a few hours.

What Havas did at the outset was to drive his horse and carriage near a busy tower, use a telescope to break the code and use whatever information was salable to his small and undiscriminating clientele. However, since most of the messages had to do with military data, Havas didn't do too well. It was only when he began collecting financial news and using carrier pigeons in the style of the Fuggers and Rothschilds that he was able to establish himself and his service in Paris. By 1835, he also was distributing stock-market quotations outside Paris with his pigeon flights, which was how he made his formal bow to the world as the proprietor of the Havas News Agency. When he bought out a rival service, the Agence Garnier, he reorganized his own headquarters in Paris with writers, translators, messengers, and clerks to serve his clients.[9]

Within five years, Havas had a virtual monopoly on the distribution of foreign news in France because few papers were then in a position to engage permanent professional correspondents abroad. Moreover, by 1850, Havas also had offices in London, Brussels, Vienna, and the principal cities of Germany as the first successful wholesaler of news — the originator of the agency business. The invention of the electric telegraph by Samuel F. B. Morse and its introduction in Europe in 1848 expanded Havas's report to such an extent that he reached out to the United States for more customers.

Two other developments helped solidify Havas's position as the first disseminator of cheap, mass-produced news that was reasonably fast and reliable for the time. In 1849, Bernhard Wolff, an early employee of the Havas Agency, founded a German service with the *Berliner National Zeitung,* of which he was a director, as the nucleus. That was Havas's first continental alliance.

Havas's other acquisition, however, raised a great many questions. In 1856, he had purchased an advertising agency, Société Général des Annonces, and promptly obtained agreement from 200 provincial newspapers to give him a certain amount of advertising space on a preferred number of pages in return for his daily file of foreign and domestic news. He then proceeded to sell the advertising space to clients, collecting his fees from them as well as from the editorial side that used his news report. As he soon learned, it wasn't a practice that endeared him to either newspaper proprietors or their editors.

Honoré de Balzac became Havas's most prominent critic, denouncing him as "le maître Jacques" (Jack-of-all-jobs) among the press and charging angrily, "There is but one newspaper made by him." Another critic wrote sardonically that Havas was "the great, the indispensable middle man through whom French business and industry control the press." Despite such derogatory comments, the Havas Agency in due course became the means for gathering and transmitting of news throughout the world.[10]

————

Another great figure in the agency business, Paul Julius Reuter, was running a hand-to-mouth financial service in London when the laying of the Dover–Calais cross-Channel cable was completed on November 13, 1851.

It occurred to him that the cable, if properly used, would revolutionize communications between London and the European continent. And, since nobody else in the news business was moving to take advantage of the new opportunity, he became the first to offer the London financial district fast service with stock-market quotations from the major European stock markets. The London Stock Exchange became his first client. Once he showed he could deliver stock quotations quicker than any rival, he attracted a huge following among bankers, brokers, and their best customers.

Out of that beginning, the news agency bearing Reuter's name would develop into a symbol of British prestige exceeded only by the Crown and the Union Jack.

The London press was slower to respond to the new dispensation than the money men. Mowbray Morris, the *Times*'s manager, thought the Channel cable a "great bore" and loftily ignored the upstart news agency. It had been common knowledge in Fleet Street that Reuter, a political refugee from Germany, and his wife, a banker's daughter, had tried and failed in advance of their Channel enterprise with a financial quotation service in Paris and later in Aachen (Aix-la-Chapelle).

But this time, Reuter would not fail. In responding to his challenge, the *Times* finally got around to moving its special cross-Channel dispatch steamer from its terminus at Boulogne to Calais. However, James Grant, editor of the *Morning Advertiser*, wasn't so stuffy. In 1858, he was the first to accept a proposal for a two-week free trial of a new Reuter's service devoted to news, and if it proved satisfactory, he agreed to buy it for £30 a month.

Several other newspapers in London then agreed to the same proposal, but not the *Times*, although its rivals reported they would save at least £100 a month over their previous arrangements if Reuter could deliver. At any rate, while maintaining his regular financial operation, Reuter put out his first newspaper telegram for general news on October 8, 1858, as follows:

> BERLIN, OCTOBER 8TH, 4.7 P.M.
> THE OFFICIAL PRUSSIAN CORRESPONDENCE ANNOUNCES THAT THE KING, RECOGNIZING THE NECESSITY, HAS CHARGED THE PRINCE OF PRUSSIA TO ACT AS REGENT WITH FULL POWERS, ACCORDING TO HIS OWN VIEWS, UNTIL THE REESTABLISHMENT OF HIS (THE KING'S) HEALTH. THE NECESSARY PUBLICATIONS OF THIS RESOLUTION IS EXPECTED. THE CHAMBERS WILL PROBABLY BE CONVOKED ON THE 20TH INST.

More of such brief dispatches came pouring into the London newspapers, frequently ahead of the specials on the Continent, and after six weeks even the dignified and slow-moving journalists at the *Times* felt obliged to sign up.

On February 7, 1859, Reuter scored his first great beat. He asked for an advance on a speech which Napoleon III had planned to deliver that day before the French legislative chamber—a declaration that Europe awaited with apprehension because of rumors that France would help Conte Camillo Cavour expel the Austrians from Italy.[11]

The publicity-conscious French emperor agreed, but bound the Reuters agent in Paris not to begin filing over the land lines and Channel cable until he had begun speaking—the first known instance of a familiar journalistic procedure.* Accordingly, as soon as Napoleon III uttered his first words, the sealed envelope was opened in the Paris office of the agency. Since an hour's service had been purchased exclusively in advance, tying up the Channel cable, Reuters was able to deliver the French text to London in time, and the agency's translators did the rest. Within two hours, special editions of the London papers were on the street carrying Napoleon's warning to Austria.

As the war clouds gathered over Italy, Reuters stuck to its system of covering the news in brief bulletins from its correspondents at French, Sardinian, and Austrian headquarters instead of trying to compete for space and glamor with the specials from Paris, London, and even New York. Thereby, the agency usually was first with developments—an impartial blanket coverage of the conflict that was beyond the power of any special to emulate.

On all sides, the question arose, "Who is Mr. Reuter?"

---

*The agency dropped the possessive, calling itself simply Reuters. The style is followed here. When a possessive is used, it is Julius Reuter's.

The reason for public curiosity was plain enough. Any contract Reuter negotiated with newspapers included a provision that his name would be used at the end of every telegram that was taken from his service and published. Readers thereby learned the source of the news in their journals, but many were unsure how to pronounce the name.

A jingle in the *Pall Mall Gazette* celebrated his fame as follows in part of a longer effusion:

> His web around the globe is spun,
>   He is, indeed, the world's exploiter:
> 'Neath ocean, e'en, the whispers run
>   Of Reuter . . .
>
> Let praise arise in every land
>   To Thee, the student's guide and tutor:
> I bless theee here as Reuter and
>   As "Rooter."

For all his new-found fame, however, Julius Reuter, like the first John Walter, was finding that his foreign service was extremely expensive. Cable tolls were considerably more costly than pigeon feed, for one thing; for another, with his necessarily increased fees, his clients expected greatly expanded coverage from his service. He was no longer charging £30 a month. Within ten years, his fee for his London papers soared to £1,000 a year, and he still wasn't growing rich on it.

Then, too, Havas was providing stiff competition across the Channel and doing better financially because he had become, in effect, a semi-official organ of the state. Havas also had added to its continental alliance with Wolff in Germany by taking on an Italian agency founded by Guglielmo Stefani for an interchange of French-German-Italian news.

Reuter joined the pack in 1856 by agreeing to add English news to the combine in exchange for their continental service—the critical move that signaled the eventual creation of a worldwide cartel. Necessarily, the governments involved were keenly interested in the way their respective national agencies were operating because agency reports were already swaying a far larger public than any "special" or group of "specials," as nonagency correspondents are known.

The rapid extension of the cable and telegraph meanwhile was broadening the horizon of the agencies. The cable companies, by 1858, had gone as far as Africa and the Middle East and were pushing on toward India. Then, with the completion of the trans-Atlantic cable on the night of August 17, 1858, a message from Queen Victoria was delivered directly to President James Buchanan at the White House in Washington.

Unhappily, Cyrus Field's ocean cable went dead next day, and it was eight years before the cable ship *Great Eastern* was able to effect permanent repairs. The accident gave Reuter the opportunity to score a great beat. By using a fast tender to meet an incoming American mail ship, his regular procedure, and routing messages over a land line across Ireland from Cobh to Cork and Crookhaven, thence across the Irish Sea cable to England and London, Reuters led by two days in breaking the news of Abraham Lincoln's assassination on April 14, 1865.

No one now had to ask, "Who is Mr. Reuter?" He had been able to give the world the greatest news agency of his time — and a model for all his competitors for years to come.[12]

Toward the end of the Mexican War, New York City's major newspapers formed the New York Associated Press as the first of a series of cooperative newsgathering agencies bearing the AP logotype. In the words of Frederic Hudson, the managing editor of James Gordon Bennett's New York *Herald,* a participant, the formation of the service was agreed upon by a "Great Congress of the Republic of News" that met in the office of the *Sun.*

The heavy costs of special coverage of the Mexican War from 1845 on plus the swiftly lengthening telegraph wires, which already had reached Canada through Boston, had obliged the fiercely competitive New Yorkers to come to terms with each other. The pigeon fanciers, the pony express, and the railroad messengers now were suddenly out of date; even in Washington, the veteran L. A. Gobright, the first AP correspondent in the nation's capital, was running for the wire.

From the outset, the trouble with the American equivalent of Reuters, Havas, and Wolff was that the New York publishers tried to run their cooperative on a shoestring while offering their service to other publishers in Boston, Philadelphia, and elsewhere. The first "general agent" they hired, Dr. Alexander Jones of the *Journal of Commerce,* was paid $20 a week — so limited an income even then that he continued his medical practice by prescribing for colds and broken bones while handling incoming bulletins from Washington and abroad.

The earliest New York AP records show that Dr. Jones's office expense was less than $50 a week exclusive of rent, which was about $500 a year. His greatest expense was for telegraph tolls, most of it to bring in foreign news, which amounted to $25,000 to $30,000 a year at the outset. Under such circumstances, Dr. Jones quit on May 19, 1851, to go to the *Herald,* and a hard-bitten former pigeon fancier who brought in foreign news by way of Canada, Dan Craig, succeeded him.

Once Craig took over in New York City, it was evident that a new force was at work. He insisted on spending money for news, and the publishers let him have it. The new manager also won reduced rates from the Western Union Telegraph Company and spread his service to the nation. For all practical purposes, he soon had a virtual monopoly on foreign news distribution, which was as effective in the United States as the foreign services. Except for a few great papers that still maintained their own specials, the rest of the American press found that they had to depend on Craig for foreign coverage. They soon learned, however, that he tolerated neither dissent nor opposition to his policies, despite being subject to the will of the seven publishers in the cooperative experiment.

Even so, he prospered at first. By 1855, he was spending $40,000 to $50,000 a year on foreign and domestic news. His own pay was $3,000 a year, and he paid his key staff people a top of $35 a week. He won friends with his domestic report, but he was seldom satisfied with his foreign file. He thought it less timely than it should have been. He also wasn't satisfied to follow the crowd. Restlessly, he always sought better ways of gathering news from abroad and presenting it in brief but attractive form to his subscribers.

In 1859, he made the New York AP a kind of junior partner in the global news pact of Reuters, Havas, and Wolff, but it did him no good. In 1862, his Midwestern members revolted and formed the Western Associated Press under the leadership of Joseph Medill of the Chicago *Tribune.* Four years later, Craig was fired when it was learned that he was planning to set up his own service. The Western AP promptly hired him but only for a year. When the warring American publishers patched up an agreement in 1867, Craig was fired again—this time for good. He had attempted to force all publishers into an American monopoly— something they refused to accept.[13]

A new team took over. A former New York *Times* correspondent, James W. Simonton, was named the New York AP's director and another *Times* veteran, Alexander Wilson, became the first AP correspondent in London. It was typical of the service that Wilson's first big story was the victory of a new *Herald* publisher, James Gordon Bennett, Jr., in the $60,000 stake race of his yacht, Henrietta, against two rivals across the Atlantic.

What Wilson did that was much more meaningful was to represent the New York AP in the creation of a global "Four Power" news agency cartel in 1870, in which his organization and Reuters, Havas, and Wolff divided the world into zones. Within their respective zones, each was given the right to gather and distribute news exclusively as follows:

Reuters was given the British Empire, Turkey, India, and the Far East. Havas received France, Switzerland, Italy, the Iberian peninsula, Central and South America and, in association with Reuters, Egypt. Wolff got Germany, Austria, Scandinavia, Russia, the Balkans and the Netherlands. As for the New York AP, it was restricted to the United States, as were its affiliated regional organizations.[14]

The compact, which was to last half a century, was to have a profound effect on the shaping of world opinion and a decisive influence on the independent journalism of the 20th century. As Kent Cooper wrote later, "In precluding the AP from disseminating news abroad, Reuters and Havas served three purposes: 1) They kept out AP competition; 2) They were free to present American news disparagingly to the United States if they presented it at all; 3) They could present news of their own countries most favorably and without it being contradicted. Their own countries were always glorified. This was done by reporting great advances at home in English and French civilizations, the benefit of which would, of course, be bestowed on the world. Figuratively speaking, in the United States, according to Reuters and Havas, it wasn't safe to travel on account of the Indians."

The irascible Craig, in sum, made two mistakes in building the first cooperatively owned news service in the world. He overestimated his own power, which was fatal to his career. He underestimated the power of his foreign competitors, which came close to strangling the American cooperative movement. As a result, it was many years before the balance was righted in gathering and distributing news through the agency system. Meanwhile, every emerging small national news agency was drawn inexorably into the orbit of one of the giants that controlled the movement of world intelligence for public consumption.[15]

THE SPECIALS

Almost unnoticed beneath the disorderly turmoil of world events, a few pioneering foreign correspondents began molding a new journalistic tradition in the middle of the 19th century. A mere handful of public-spirited editors and publishers in the United States, Britain, and continental Europe supported them, although they were often troublesome, even impossible at times to direct, much less control.

In journalistic parlance, they were known as the foreign specials — correspondents affiliated with only one paper whose work might be syndicated, as contrasted with the broader services provided by news agencies. There were already a number of domestic specials, particularly in Washington, but those assigned abroad were far from numerous at the beginning.

Mainly, they worked outside their own countries for independent newspapers of substance and quality either on spot or roving assignments, were given considerable freedom in commenting on the news, and often spent more money than their proprietors thought necessary. Moreover, not all of them were on glamorous missions, such as wars, revolutions, and milder civic disturbances. Some turned out to be advocates of causes that were not always pleasing to their employers; others were essentially novelists, poets, or dreamers; and a few even made history in a larger sense.

The most famous scriveners of the era included such propagandists as the great Italian patriot, Giuseppe Mazzini, for one, and the New York *Tribune*'s London special, Karl Marx, for another. Then, there was the poet Heinrich Heine, whose name was more treasured than his work by the *Allgemeine Zeitung* of Augsburg, which used him as a special in Paris and dropped him when he admitted having received a "pension" from the French government. However, it matters not that he has been forgotten as a journalist; as the author of *Die Lorelei,* he is immortal.[16]

On the Continent, there were a few papers of quality that were deeply committed to the reporting of foreign affairs. Probably the outstanding publication of that kind outside England and the United States was the Swiss twice-weekly *Zürcher Zeitung,* a Zurich newspaper in its earliest manifestation, for which no less than Johann Wolfgang von Goethe was asked to recommend an editor. Goethe's choice was a German writer, Kaspar Riesbeck, whose Paris correspondent, Gottfried Ebel, covered the storming of the Bastille and wrote three days later for his Swiss readers:

"One saw with amazement how on this day (July 14) an almost naked and unarmed people, inflamed by boldness alone, attacked entrenched positions, armed itself with what it found and in ten minutes conquered the first fortress of the Kingdom."

The correspondent also covered the massacre of the Swiss Guard of Louis XVI by a Parisian mob on August 25, 1792, and gave the first report of Nelson's victory at Trafalgar but was a week late with the news of Napoleon's defeat at Waterloo. By 1820, however, the paper had to be overhauled for lack of readership and emerged as a new and important publication, the *Neue Zürcher Zeitung,* which was soon eagerly read in every European capital for its authoritative special coverage of foreign affairs. There weren't many like it. And when it became a daily on January 1, 1843, it served as a landmark in independent journalism.[17]

Bennett's New York *Herald* became the equivalent in America of the *Times* in London and the *NZZ* in Switzerland. The publisher became the first to exploit the steamship for faster news transmission before the laying of the trans-Atlantic cable. He also made the first eastward trans-Atlantic crossing on the British steamer *Sirius,* leaving May 1, 1838, and arriving at Falmouth in 18 days.

With other leading journalists, Bennett witnessed the coronation of Queen Victoria and reported it for the *Herald.* He also used the trip to consult the leading political and literary figures of the day, visited his old home in Scotland, and crossed the Channel to inspect Paris. Throughout, he sent dispatches to the *Herald,* drawing a lively picture of the Old World for his readers.

It was the response to his English and European correspondence that caused him, upon his return, to set up the first foreign staff to serve a single American newspaper. He engaged six correspondents to cover the main centers of Europe, with Dr. Dionysius Lardner, a learned Irishman and the editor of the *Cabinet Encyclopedia,* as his Paris correspondent. Others were in London, Glasgow, Berlin, Brussels, and Rome.

Still, Bennett was not content. He wanted worldwide coverage for the *Herald* and later expanded his chain of specials to Mexico City and the Republic of Texas, never doubting that they soon would have exciting stories to tell, and also to Canada, where an abortive rebellion had just been snuffed out. He also set up a syndicate for his foreign material, charging only those papers able to afford his service and giving it free to smaller dailies and weeklies outside his general circulation area. Thereby, he gained wide reprints with credit to the *Herald* and stimulated a flow of news from his clients to New York.

The result was tremendous. The *Herald* became the most prestigious paper in the United States and the best known overseas. Nor did Bennett neglect Washington in the expansion of his news report. With the pride of a veteran Washington correspondent, and perhaps the first of a long line of Washington columnists, he opened a *Herald* bureau there in 1841 with Robert Sutton, a shorthand man, in charge.

Bennett created his journalistic empire almost entirely through his own efforts. As an emigre from Scotland, he had landed in New York virtually penniless and managed to find a temporary newspaper job as a $5-a-week apprentice at the age of 28 in the winter of 1822–23. From that inauspicious beginning, he became a working newspaperman in New York and Washington for 12 years and twice tried and failed to start his own paper. But with $500 and the trust of a printing firm, he began the New York *Morning Herald* on May 6, 1835 in a one-room basement office with a plank resting on two barrels as his desk. He wrote everything in his four-page sheet and took in ads as well.

It was the era of the penny paper—the "penny dreadfuls" as they were called—and Bennett made the most of his opportunities. He established himself and the *Herald* with his coverage of the Ellen Jewett story—the slaying of a beautiful prostitute for which a wealthy admirer was tried and acquitted. After that, he raised his price to 2 cents and advertised the *Herald* "as the most sensational, salacious and sardonic newspaper in the whole world."

The promotion worked. Soon, the *Herald* was selling 20,000 copies a day and advertising soared. Bennett bought his own news boat so that he could meet incoming ships and get the latest journals from abroad for his quotient of foreign news. And thereafter, he decided on the trip abroad that made him the publisher of the best paper in the country at the time.

Bennett did not let personal abuse from his competitors deter him. He profited by every new invention, the telegraph and the trans-Atlantic cable most of all. During the Mexican War, he went into a combine with two other papers, but his war correspondence during part of the conflict became secondary to another trip to Europe, this one with his wife. In his correspondence during his second European visit, he wrote of such sensations as Lola Montez's love affair with the King of Bavaria, unrest in Europe on the eve of the 1848 risings, and his own reception at the court of King Louis Philippe of France.

Upon his return home, his foreign service scored beat after beat. The downfall of Louis Philippe was forecast a week before it happened. A California correspondent forwarded samples of ore that was assayed as gold of the finest quality, a finding that started the gold rush in earnest upon publication. Not long afterward, Bennett himself suggested editorially that the United States should open up Japan to trade, after which Commodore Matthew Calbraith Perry undertook an expedition to Tokyo.

While Bennett's *Herald* could not approach the *Times* of London in suavity and style, nor hope to match the authority of its pronouncements, it could and did exceed that great newspaper in asserting its complete independence of any commercial or governmental interest. The climax came when Bennett publicly rejected advertising that had been offered to the paper by the Treasury Department in the form of patronage. Thereby, the *Herald* established its integrity — the most precious quality of the journalist.[18]

───────

When President James K. Polk called for war with Mexico and Congress obliged him on May 13, 1845, a 37-year-old editor in New Orleans hurried to General Zachary Taylor's camp on the Rio Grande and attached himself to Captain Ben McCulloch's Rangers as a volunteer. In this manner, George Wilkins Kendall began a glamorous career as the most celebrated correspondent of the Mexican War and an eyewitness of the revolutionary wave that swept over Europe in 1848.*

As a Yankee printer who had headed south from New York City in 1832, he had founded the daily *Picayune* in New Orleans with a friend, Francis Lumsden, and become the paper's editor in 1837. Four years later, when he had joined a party of Texans to cover their invasion of New Mexico, he had been captured by Mexican troops with more than 300 others and survived a death march to Mexico City. A year later, in an act of clemency by the Mexican dictator, General Antonio López de Santa Anna, he had been freed with the rest. Hero-worshipping New Orleans had eagerly read the story of his captivity when he returned and made the *Picayune* the most popular and influential paper in the Crescent City.

Now, when American troops marched across the Mexican border, the editor was with them — a symbol of the supercharged, nationalistic atmosphere of the time. "Manifest Destiny," the phrase coined by another editor, John L. O'Sullivan of the New York *Morning News,* had been presented to the American public as a right bestowed by Providence "to overspread and to possess the whole of the continent," to use O'Sullivan's phrase.

When the fighting began, however, there was no time to worry about phrasemaking. There was a war to be covered; but in that era when Kendall was galloping about Mexican territory with McCulloch's

───────

*There were at least a score of other correspondents from New Orleans's nine newspapers alone. There was also a prior example of rudimentary war correspondence in the United States — the editor of the St. Francisville (La.) *Timepiece,* James M. Bradford, fought under General Jackson at the Battle of New Orleans in 1815 and sent dispatches to his paper when he wasn't shooting at the enemy.

Rangers, he was more the soldier than the war correspondent. The more sensible estate of the war correspondent as a noncombatant had not yet been established, so that Kendall emerged from an early skirmish against the Mexicans with a Mexican cavalry flag, which he sent to the *Picayune* along with his latest dispatch.

It was the fashion then for correspondents to prove their courage by fighting rather than watching unarmed, bound by international conventions that had not yet taken effect. One of Kendall's rivals, James L. Freaner of the New Orleans *Delta,* killed a Mexican officer at the Battle of Monterey and appropriated his horse. In addition, both Freaner and Kendall more than once acted as official dispatch bearers.

Of the eastern newspapers, only the New York *Herald* had a special in the field during a part of the war. The others depended in the main on rushing official dispatches north from New Orleans, something the *Herald* did in cooperation with the Baltimore *Sun* and the Philadelphia *Public Ledger.* Kendall's dispatches were regularly used in the New York *Sun,* which boasted at one point that it had been able to bring battle news north 18 days after an engagement through a combination of a ship across the Gulf of Mexico, a train, the pony express and the telegraph.

No earlier American war had been as thoroughly covered, and public interest was high throughout the land. On February 23, 1847, General Taylor defeated Santa Anna's superior forces at Buena Vista, but the news was more than a month getting through. In some fashion, rumors spread in Washington that Taylor had been crushed; but Kendall wrote to the *Picayune* at the end of March about the victory at Buena Vista and the official dispatch followed next day.

Still, mainly for political reasons, the principal action in the war had been entrusted to General Winfield Scott, President Polk apparently having suspected that General Taylor would be a formidable rival for the presidency at the next election. Once again, Kendall made history by volunteering as an aide to General William Worth under Scott's command. Day by day, he sent back dispatches written under fire — from Cerro Gordo on April 15, the fortress at Perote on April 22 and Jalapa on May 1. With Scott's troops, he sighted Mexico City on August 10. His stories had been studded with the names of young officers such as Robert E. Lee, a captain; Phil Kearny, a colonel, and Franklin Pierce, a general.

General Worth must have thought highly of the services of his volunteer aide because Kendall was mentioned twice in dispatches — the first time after "the fighting at Molino del Rey when he was cited for bravery and again for "conspicuous gallantry." In the final hours of the attack on the citadel of Chapultepec, Kendall repeatedly exposed himself to fire and was wounded in the knee by a bullet but carried on.

At Chapultepec, he wrote of his admiration for a young officer, Thomas J. Jackson, the immortal "Stonewall." Had the correspondent noticed a young lieutenant manning a howitzer that day, he would have seen Ulysses Simpson Grant in action. On September 13, the American forces stormed into Chapultepec, and next day General Scott entered Mexico City as Kendall reported:

"Another victory, glorious in its results and which has thrown additional luster on the American arms, has been achieved today by the army under General Scott—the proud capital of Mexico has fallen into the power of a mere handful of men compared with the immense odds arrayed against them and Santa Anna, instead of shedding his blood as he had promised, is wandering with his army no one knows where."

This lengthy account, published in the *Picayune* on October 14, 1847, and relayed to the nation, was the final victory and ended the war. Kendall was the most quoted correspondent of all, and his dispatches were the most often reproduced. After his return to New Orleans, the *Picayune* distinguished itself once more. It brought the news of the peace treaty to New Orleans in February 1848 by chartered steamer, beating the War Department's dispatches and making possible another extra edition with exclusive news. That was Kendall's finest feat of the Mexican War as one of the pioneers in foreign correspondence.[19]

The editor, however, was neither in need of rest nor content to stay at his desk. He arrived in Paris in time to witness the rising of its citizens at the barricades once again, this time to dispose of Louis Philippe. In sympathetic detail, he described the revolutionary scene day after day for the readers of the *Picayune*. Despite the lengthy time lapse caused by trans-Atlantic and overland travel for his reports from Paris, these accounts deeply interested New Orleans with its French heritage and served to increase the prestige of the *Picayune* and its roving editor.

When Kendall returned a few years later, he brought with him a French bride—Mlle. Adeline de Valcourt, daughter of one of Louis Napoleon's officers. The journalist at last was home from the wars, his roving days over.[20]

Some of the most celebrated specials of the mid-19th century worked for another newly established penny paper in New York City, the *Tri-*

bune, which Horace Greeley had founded on April 10, 1841, with a partner and $3,000. The editor, who was 30 years old at the time, had an indifferent history of labors as a sometime printer and editorial idealist plus a number of publishing failures. But with his championship of the cause of antislavery and Abraham Lincoln, he made the *Tribune* a great newspaper with circulation of his daily paper at almost 50,000 by the beginning of the Civil War in 1861 and a weekly that was selling 200,000 copies. Under Greeley's guidance, his specials challenged those of the *Herald* and the great foreign dailies.[21]

One of the best was Margaret Fuller, of whom Ralph Waldo Emerson said, "She poured a stream of amber over the endless store of private anecdotes, of bosom histories, which her wonderful persuasion drew forth, and transfigured them into fine fables." The description bore little resemblance to the work of the ordinary journalist, nor did Margaret Fuller consider herself one.

Miss Fuller was the daughter of a lawyer and in her early 30s when Greeley brought her to the *Tribune* after her first published work, a translation of Johann Peter Eckermann's *Conversations with Goethe.* She had taken part in and reported on the transcendentalist experiments of her day and had visited Brook Farm without being unduly impressed. On the *Tribune* at the outset, she did literary criticism, quite a change from the hopped-up murder and violence of "penny dreadful" journalism.

Later, as her interests expanded, she did three pieces a week on social matters that interested her, one being a sympathetic study of the lot of the prostitute, strong stuff for a puritanical America but one that Greeley applauded. When she first ventured abroad in 1845, the beginning of five years of distinguished foreign correspondence, she did a notable article on Goethe, interviewed others of literary and cultural importance, and contributed as well a number of travel sketches. In her work, she followed the general pattern of social and literary journalism that had been developed by her contemporary, Harriet Martineau of the London *Daily News.*

After Miss Fuller's marriage to one of Mazzini's associates, Giovanni, Marchese Ossoli, who was seven years younger than she, her correspondence took on a different note. She immersed herself in the revolutions of 1848 in Europe and in the following year wrote a lively and detailed description of the fall of Rome to the leaders of the Risorgimento and the founding of the brief Roman republic.

In that fateful battle, she served as a nurse as well as a correspondent while her husband fought under the command of Mazzini. Once that ended, she and Giovanni and their baby, Angelo, sailed from Leghorn for the United States. Off Fire Island, in July 1850, their vessel, the *Elizabeth,* went down in a storm and all abroad were lost.[22]

Another correspondent who did his best work for the *Tribune,* the poet Bayard Taylor, was only 19 when he persuaded Horace Greeley to use some of the articles he intended to mail from Europe beginning in 1845. The only instructions young Taylor received from the editor was a tart precaution: "No descriptive nonsense! Of that I'm damned sick!"

Subsequently, Taylor's career took him to less traveled parts of the world for the *Tribune.* In March 1853, under orders from Greeley to join the black ships of Commodore Perry on their pioneering voyage to Japan, the correspondent managed to get to Hong Kong ahead of the Perry expedition.

China, as he soon found out, was a big story, too, for the Taiping Rebellion was raging against the Manchu dynasty in Peking. The ascetic rebel leader, Hung Hsiu Ch'üan, a convert to Christianity, was fighting to overthrow the Ch'ing dynasty, curtail foreign privileges in China, limit the opium trade, equalize land ownership, and assert full sovereignty for China. Like so many correspondents from the West who would follow him, Taylor had neither the background nor even a basic knowledge of the Chinese language to grasp the importance of the story, but he knew many people were being killed and he ought at least to try to look into the revolt and its consequences.

However, the best he could do in preparing a few pieces for the *Tribune* was to visit Shanghai, obtain translations of some of the articles about the fighting in the local papers after he landed there, and put together what turned out to be the initial published account in the United States of the Taiping rebellion. It was in this manner that the *Tribune* reported the slaughter of 20,000 defenders of Nanking by the rebels and the public quartering of the Chinese viceroy.

When Commodore Perry's ships arrived in May, the relieved Taylor was glad to leave the Chinese rebellion behind him and head north after being sworn in as a master's mate in the US Navy. In that role, he witnessed the first test of strength between Japan and the United States when Perry's squadron anchored in Tokyo Bay on July 8, 1853. With obvious satisfaction over the Commodore's iron-willed methods, the correspondent wrote of the ultimatum that was delivered to a Japanese official who had demanded that the vessels move on to call at Nagasaki.

In his report from Tokyo Bay, Taylor went on: "He (the Japanese official) was told that we came as friends, upon a peaceable mission, that we should not go to Naugas-Aki, as he proposed, and that it was insulting to our President (Millard Fillmore) and his Special Minister (Perry) to propose it. He was told, moreover, that the Japanese must not communicate with any other vessel than our flagship, and that no boats must approach us during the night. An attempt to surround us with a cordon of boats . . . would lead to very serious consequences."

The Japanese gave in, as Taylor duly reported in his dispatches as Perry's Master's Mate. One of the chief counselors of the Japanese emperor, he wrote, received President Fillmore's message of peace and good will from Perry and replied in satisfactory fashion. Taylor's dispatch concluded:

"We had obtained in four days without subjecting ourselves to a single observance of Japanese law what the Russian embassy failed to accomplish in six months."

Taylor also noted the surprise of a Japanese official who asked permission to examine an American pistol and of his astonishment at a steam whistle. In the correspondent's indulgent and patronizing view of the Japanese, he seemed not to have weighed the consequences of the American opening of so powerful a Pacific nation to the outside world. He did not even wait for the conclusion of the first Japanese-American trade negotiations but set out forthwith for home, where he began writing the poetry he always had preferred to a continuation of his correspondence. A generation of American maidens loved his Bedouin Song ("From the desert I come to Thee . . . on a stallion shod with fire"). But of his correspondence, no memorable passage remains.[23]

A more professional approach to the necessities of foreign correspondence, more in the manner of Kendall rather than Taylor, came at the Battle of Solferino on June 24, 1859. In that unremitting slaughter of 30,000 soldiers on both sides that day on the plains of Lombardy, Henry J. Raymond was among the correspondents who watched the French-Sardinian effort to expel the Austrians from Italy.

As an experienced journalist, a copublisher and founder of the New York *Times* in 1851, he was sobered by the enormous casualties and the inhumanity of the conflict that actually decided nothing. However, there is no record that indicates he or any other working journalist was appalled by the incredible human suffering he had witnessed that day. Such a reaction was not to his discredit, for it was in accordance with the spirit of the era. As Horace Greeley had once said of Raymond, "Abler and stronger men I may have met, a cleverer, readier and more generally efficient journalist, I never saw."

The despoiling of the captured, the terrors of the wounded, the despair of the dying, and the terrible waste of human life testified to by the thousands of bodies strewn across the battlefield all had been taken for granted for as long as wars had been fought. But at Solferino, there was one observer, Jean Henri Dunant, a 31-year-old Swiss citizen and writer, who determined that day that such scenes as he had witnessed required an effort in one way or another to stir the conscience of an uncaring world.

Like the rest meanwhile, Raymond did what he had to do as a correspondent. Through the good offices of the *Times*'s Paris correspondent, Dr. W. E. Johnston, Raymond was permitted to send his Solferino dispatch with the same French military messenger who carried the official battle report to the French capital.

There, Mrs. Raymond was waiting. Through her husband's advance arrangements, she was able to travel directly to Liverpool with his story, place it aboard an American mail steamer, and get it to New York ten days ahead of everybody else. (The trans-Atlantic cable still was being repaired at the time.) It was the *Times*'s greatest beat under Raymond's management when it was published on July 12, 1859.

The huge casualties at Solferino caused Napoleon III to sue for peace in a subsequent meeting with Emperor Francis Joseph of Austria at Villafranca di Verona. Once the preliminaries were arranged, the Austrians eventually withdrew from Italy, although the withdrawal by no means disposed of the troubles of the Italian people.[24]

Dunant, the Swiss writer, took somewhat longer to publish his report. But when it appeared in 1862 under the title "Un Souvenir de Solferino" he accompanied his moving description of the suffering of the wounded and the dying on the battlefield with an appeal to reason—the creation of a voluntary, worldwide agency dedicated to non-partisan, international assistance to the victims of war.

In Switzerland, the idea of a neutral organization dedicated to global relief for the military and all other victims of hardship and disaster took hold at once. A welfare agency, the Société Genovoise d'Utilité Publique, brought together an international convention a year later that formed the International Committee of the Red Cross, with a red cross on a white field as a symbol of mercy—a tribute to Switzerland because the colors were the reverse of those in the Swiss flag that features a white cross on a red field.

Next, in 1864, the delegates of 12 nations signed the Geneva Convention for the Amelioration of the Condition of the Wounded and Sick of Armies in the Field. That document provided for the neutrality of medical personnel of the armed forces of combatants and of the Red Cross as well as civilians who voluntarily gave assistance to victims of war. It was the opening phase of an organization of mercy that exists today in more than 100 nations. The American Red Cross was organized by Clara Barton in 1881, still another outgrowth of the Dunant memorial to Solferino.[25]

In the end, Raymond and others who described the horrors of war that day on the plains of Lombardy may well have performed a greater service than they realized at the time by preparing public opinion for Jean Henri Dunant's generous proposal. Like the great *Times* of London special, William Howard Russell, whose reports of a half-starved, half-naked British army in the Crimea finally brought relief to the beleaguered troops, the correspondents at Solferino learned that some things are more important than being the first to proclaim a victory in battle.

————

During the latter part of the 19th century, in summary, three major forces were contending for control of the world's flow of news. Of these, the greatest was governmental authority with its legal and economic power over most communications, news sources, and the business side of the press. It was not challenged anywhere for a sustained period, and with any degree of success, except in Britain and the United States.

At a time of British dominance, the British press manifestly was the more important of the two globally. However, only a few great British and American independent papers and a scattering of others, nourished by a mercantile class that found it profitable to advertise, were able to create their own foreign services and lay the basis for a small corps of professional correspondents. Of these, the leaders were the *Times* of London, a model for the British press in its authority and its methods, and the New York *Herald* in the United States, which conducted a frantic scramble for news almost entirely out of self-interest. Elsewhere, representatives of the independent press, such as the *Neue Zürcher Zeitung*, remained small and had relatively little power despite the general excellence of their foreign coverage.

The development of the news agency system, with all its imperfections, covered the less fortunate but by far the largest area of the world press. Despite the occasional brillance of some of the great British and American specials, the agencies did more to create the nucleus of an informed public in what was to become the North Atlantic community.

With the exception of the Asian-Pacific fringe and the eastern shore of the Mediterranean, the origin and dissemination of news elsewhere remained scanty in the extreme.

Ruled by power-conscious entrepreneurs in Britain and Europe, who invariably kept one eye on the interests of their respective governments, and by anarchic rival groups of money-conscious publishers in the United States, the agencies were severely limited to terse, factual announcements.

The pattern was far from ideal; but then, it was far from an ideal world and the makers and movers of world news reflected its weaknesses far more than its strengths. News was handled as if it had been a commodity instead of a public trust. Unhappily, there was often little to choose between the bureaucrats of governments, the barons who made personal fiefs out of news agencies, and the often whimsical autocrats of the independent papers.

It was natural for them, whether they were rulers or proprietors, or both, to act in the tradition of power politics, to treat most of their employees like chattels, to bicker and bargain over news as if it were so much cheese to be sold to the highest bidder. It was an era when both public morality and private virtue were in short supply, particularly in journalism. But where good newspapers were able to exist, for however short a time, their influence was profound and their foreign service influenced a rising generation in the United States, Britain and much of Western Europe.

2 The Master Correspondents

RUSSELL AND THE CIVIL WAR

"Mr. Russell," said President Abraham Lincoln, "I am very glad to make your acquaintance and to see you in this country. The London *Times* is one of the greatest powers in the world — in fact, I don't know anything which has more power except the Mississippi. I am glad to know you as its Minister."[1]

In this manner, William Howard Russell was welcomed to the United States early in 1861 on the eve of the Civil War. To account for President Lincoln's solicitude, it had been common knowledge for months that the *Times* favored the South in the struggle over secession and the correspondent's forthcoming reports, therefore, were accounted a danger to the Union. What Lincoln was trying to do at the outset was to persuade Russell to pay some attention to the cause of antislavery, for which the North already was willing to fight.[2]

Russell was well aware of the sensitivity of his position. He also knew perfectly well that the North could and would blockade the South if the shooting began. That meant he couldn't get his dispatches out regardless of how much the home office wanted to appease British mercantile interests as the South's strongest foreign supporters. To preserve his freedom of action, therefore, he couldn't stray very far south and get caught there; whether the home office liked it or not, he had to maintain a secure base in the North, so President Lincoln's overtures were welcome.[3]

Russell was then in his 35th year — a big, hearty Irishman with ten years of war reporting behind him as the most celebrated of foreign correspondents. He had seen action from the Danish war over Schles-

26

wig Holstein, where he had suffered his first bullet wound, to the Sepoy rebellion in India; but it was in the Crimea that he had established himself as a powerful influence over British opinion.[4]

In the combined British-French-Sardinian effort to save the tottering Turkish Empire from destruction by an aggressive Russian army, Russell's dispatches from the Crimea had warned for months in 1854 that the British expeditionary forces had been crippled by disgraceful conditions in the field, that neglect, disease, and lack of supplies had cut an army of 35,600 men to only 16,500 who were able-bodied enough to fight.

When the Russians finally attacked before Balaclava in the Crimea on October 25, the result was disaster. It was here that the Heavy Brigade failed, and the charge of the Light Brigade swept across the battle-field in a last desperate attempt to save the day because "somebody blundered." And when the smoke from successive volleys of fire cleared the Russian lines, only 198 returned of the 609 who had tried in vain to turn the certainty of defeat into victory.[5]

This was the burden of Russell's dispatch that day, which led to the collapse of the government. But it was Tennyson who had the last word in his memorial to the "noble 600." With the passage of another year, the rise of a new government in London, the steady flow of relief supplies, and the work of Florence Nightingale and her nurses at the base in Scutari, the strength of the British army was renewed. And on September 14, 1855, after another great battle, the Union Jack floated in triumph over the Russian stronghold at Sebastopol.[6]

When Russell went back to London that fall, he was hailed by all England as the man who had saved an army. The *Times* proudly reported that he arrived "in a blaze of glory, to be lionized as no journalist had ever been before." He was received by the Prime Minister, given an honorary degree by his old college, Trinity in Dublin, and saluted, in the words of Sir Evelyn Wood, "for awakening the conscience of the British nation to the suffering of its troops."[7]

And so, six years later, Russell once again was on foreign soil preparing to cover a war, this time one on which the fate of a whole great nation would depend. With the election of President Lincoln as the great antislavery advocate, the South was defiant and up in arms. The North was prepared for the worst, which Lincoln had anticipated in New York City the previous year when he had stated the issue at Cooper Union in these uncompromising terms:

"Let us have faith that right makes might, and in that faith let us to the end dare to do our duty as we understand it."

As the war clouds gathered over Charleston, S.C., Russell headed south on the basis of AP reports that the Confederates were preparing for action against Fort Sumter. A relief expedition already had started from New York to deliver supplies and arms in the event of a long siege, and so it was fairly certain that war was not far off.

Early on the morning of April 12, 1861, Russell was close enough to make it into Charleston and view the Confederate guns pouring a relentless fire into the Federal stronghold in the harbor. Most of Charleston was on the rooftops for the day, watching The cannonading and waiting for a white flag of surrender to be hoisted. But Major Robert Anderson, the fort's commander, refused to give in.[8]

However, by noon next day, Sumter's guns had been silenced, a fire was raging within the walls of the fort, and further resistance would have been futile. Up went the white flag, and the Confederates had scored the first victory of the Civil War, as President Lincoln learned that night together with all the rest of the land. The AP and the specials had been prompt in covering the news as it broke, but the honors—if there were any in so stunning a defeat—went to a correspondent of the New York *World*, Bradley Osbon, who had sailed south with the Navy's relief expedition, witnessed the battle from inside the fort, and returned to the metropolis under naval escort with Major Anderson and the survivors from the fall of Sumter.

Osbon's story of the action inside Fort Sumter created a sensation in New York City when the *World* published it. Despite the shock of the first Northern defeat in the war, the *World*'s reporter had contributed his bit to history.[9] As for Russell, whose dispatch had to cross the Atlantic, there wasn't much in it that differed from the American accounts except for his sardonic comment:

"Never was such a victory, never such brave lads, never such a fight."[10]

Russell had better luck at his next engagement, the first battle of Bull Run, mainly because he was late leaving Washington and failed to get across the Virginia countryside in time to reach the battlefield at Manassas. There had been skirmishes between the opposing armies near Centreville, where the Confederates were drawn up in battle array on the south bank of Bull Run Creek. But before dawn on July 21, 1861, two armies, each nearly 60,000 strong, clashed in the first big battle of the conflict.

Groups of newspaper correspondents for both the Northern and Southern newspapers already were in the field, each attached to their respective command staffs, at a time when Russell left Washington and crossed Long Bridge in his two-horse carriage, followed by a groom and saddle horse. To stem the correspondent's hunger, he had with him a ham, bologna sandwiches, Havana cigars, a flask of Bordeux, a bottle of tea, and a bottle of water. The Crimea had never been like that.

The *Times*'s war correspondent never reached Manassas that day. The Battle of Bull Run had already begun, and some of the inexperienced and overly enthusiastic Northern correspondents were already rushing back to Washington with tales of what they believed to be a glorious victory. However, the first the veteran *Times* man knew of what had happened at Bull Run occurred when he was caught up late in the day in a swirling panic of retreating Union soldiers.

Russell fell in with the crowd and made it back to Washington shortly before 11 p.m. at just about the time that "Father" Gobright of the AP, seeing the unruly survivors swarming into the capital, put a quick add to an earlier dispatch reporting a Bull Run victory with an observation that there had been a "sudden change in affairs." It didn't do the AP or anybody else a bit of good, for War Department censors bottled up all news of a Federal defeat until the next day. Because nobody thought to stop them, only the Washington papers came out with the story of the defeat at Bull Run.

When the New York papers finally were able to tell the truth, Henry Villard in the *Herald* reported, "We were retreating in good order when a panic among our troops suddenly occurred and a regard stampede took place." Henry J. Raymond in the *Times* was just as frank. And Edward H. House in the *Tribune* reached the lowest point in his assessment: "All was lost to that American army, even its honor. The agony of this overwhelming disgrace can never be expressed in words."[11]

All this made the attack on Russell's account of the debacle all the more difficult for the London public to understand. He had put his story aboard a mail steamer that sailed from Boston on July 23, so it was weeks before the *Times* of London carrying his account of Bull Run reached the United States. But the storm that broke about him then was terrific because he had set down on paper some unpleasant, unpalatable but entirely accurate truths:

"The repulse of the Federalists, decided as it was, might have had no serious effects whatever beyond the mere failure — which politically was of greater consequence than it was in a military sense — but for the disgraceful conduct of the troops. The retreat on their lines at Centreville seems to have ended in a cowardly rout — a miserable, causeless panic. Such scandalous behavior on the part of soldiers I should have considered impossible, as with some experience of camps and armies I have never even in alarms among camp followers seen the like of it."[12]

Russell was denounced in the Northern press as a traitor — "the bilious LL.D., the snob correspondent of the London *Times*," "that Cassandra in breeches, Dr. Bull Run Russell," and "Bombast Russell." He wrote that he was the "best abused man in America, caricatured, insulted, threatened, shot at in the streets." A foreigner in a resentful land, he was no longer the admired "Balaclava" Russell but a villainous journalist from perfidious Albion. And in London, George Otto Trevelyan wrote slyly

> Stain not a spotless name with useless crimes,
> O, save the correspondent of the *Times*.[13]

Despite a weak and dispirited defense of the distinguished visitor in the New York *Times,* the storm did not subside. The *Times* in London even added fuel to the fire by assailing the Americans in the North and their press for "childish irritability."[14] For the duration of the Civil War, that was the position of the British and the Northern press except for the liberal London *Daily News,* which used the dispatches of Edwin Lawrence Godkin and the pro-abolitionist Harriet Martineau, who wrote its leaders in London.

Russell also was adversely affected by the seizure of the two Confederate commissioners, James Mason and John Slidell, from the British Royal Mail packet *Trent* by the USS *San Jacinto.* on November 8, 1861. It so happened that the distressed visiting journalist learned of President Lincoln's decision to release Mason and Slidell, then wired a friend with stock-market interests, "Enjoy your dinner." In some way, the New York *Herald* learned of this indiscretion, took the message as a code in stock jobbing at American expense, and once again gave Russell a drubbing. Even his editors in London were worried, but they ordered him to go to the front instead of bringing him home.

By that time the War Department had had enough of Russell and refused to accredit him. It was this rather than his paper's attitude, he insisted, that caused him to return home in mid-April 1862 and proceeded ruefully to watch the Civil War from afar as the proprietor of the *Army and Navy Gazette* and a pensioner at the *Times* with a stipend of £300 annually for life.[15]

The *Times* sent others to the United States during the fighting, but none did well except for Francis Lawley, who covered the South — a lost cause. Whatever the reputation of the *Times* among its own people, its editorial policy and Russell's failures and its pro-slavery attitude cost it totally the regard of American opinion for many years thereafter. In the Civil War, it had been influenced by pounds rather than principle.[16]

There were a few other scattered foreign correspondents in the United States during the war years, but only one left an imprint on the history of the era. He was a fiery little French physician turned journalist who recalled long afterward that he had entered Richmond five minutes before General Grant and had covered President Lincoln in the capital of the fallen South. He was the correspondent of *Le Temps* of Paris, Georges Clemenceau.

Having left France after a political scrape, he continued his spasmodic correspondence for *Le Temps* from New York after the end of the Civil War but had to teach French in a girls' school in Stamford, Conn., to make ends meet. When he went home to Paris in 1869, it was to begin a career that would lead him from a musty editor's office to the heights as savior of his country's honor in the Alfred Dreyfus case, twice premier of France, the indomitable Tiger whose spirit led the Allies to victory over Germany in World War I.[17]

HOW SMALLEY MADE HISTORY

From Russell to Clemenceau, the foreign correspondents who wrote under American datelines during the Civil War included some of the adventurers of journalism, but from all of the available evidence, they didn't stay very long. Of necessity, much of the information about the four-year conflict came from the same sources that covered for the American people, their own correspondents—about 300 in the North and another hundred in the South.[18] What they wrote for their papers in substance was picked up and spread to the world either through wire services or syndicated arrangements or simply copied with acknowledgments of source.

It wasn't a very good way of covering so important a conflict; but little else was available at the time, with the trans-Atlantic cable under repair and the telegraph lines limited in scope and often tied up by the military. Even train service was spasmodic and subject to interruption. Moreover, on the evidence of one of the ablest in the North, Henry Villard of the New York *Herald* and Chicago *Tribune,* relatively few correspondents were qualified by education, experience, temperament, and judgment to give their respective publics an accurate accounting of the fearful changes and hazards in the fortunes of war.

Villard's judgment was supported by Henry Adams, then in London, who wrote to the New York *Times* that the wild swings in information and the biased reporting of the Northern press was a grave handicap to their cause.[19] As for the South, despite Villard's compliments to the four papers in the rebel capital, Richmond, Va., at least one Southern editor late in the war complained bitterly that he was tired of reading of great Confederate victories only to learn the next day that the rebel forces had suffered another defeat.[20]

Under such circumstances, a single brilliant performance in the reporting of a key battle of the war became a remarkable exploit of journalism, especially when it was sustained by the judgment of history. Such a feat was credited to a comparative newcomer to war reporting, George Washburn Smalley, in his coverage of the great Northern victory at Antietam for the New York *Tribune* and its publication of his story in an extra edition hours ahead of the competition.

Then and later in his foreign correspondence from Europe as the head of the *Tribune*'s foreign staff, he distinguished himself in the reporting of the Franco-Prussian War of 1870, the first of three German invasions of France within 75 years. But it was in the Civil War that he proved himself against formidable opposition and under the most trying conditions. He was probably the greenest of the 20 *Tribune* correspondents in the field. The New York *Herald* had 30 to 40 war reporters and was spending more than half a million dollars on such correspondence. The New York *Times* had at least 20 specials. The New York *World,* Chicago *Tribune,* Cincinnati *Gazette,* Philadelphia *Press and Inquirer,* Boston *Journal* and a scattering of smaller papers were also making tremendous efforts to bring war news to their readers.

While the South couldn't match the North in numbers, the quality of the best below the Mason-Dixon line stood up well in most instances. And why not? Henry Watterson was covering for the Chattanooga *Rebel,* and like others among the standouts, would be writing under pseudonyms for papers in Nashville and Atlanta before becoming the renowned postwar editor of the Louisville *Courier-Journal.* Peter Alexander of the Savannah *Republican,* styled "the Prince of Correspondents" in the South, was also covering under aliases for other papers — a practice followed by Dr. William G. Shepardson of the Richmond *Dispatch,* Felix de Fontaine of the Charleston *Courier,* Samuel Chester Reid of the New Orleans *Picayune,* and Albert Street of the Mobile *Register.*[21]

Whether they wrote for the North or South, these were Smalley's opposition during the Civil War, all far more experienced and battlewise than he was. As a late comer to the conflict, little was expected of Smalley — certainly not the kind of war reporting that had made Russell's reputation as a master correspondent.

George Washburn Smalley was the son of a Congregational minister of Worcester, Mass., a graduate of Yale and Harvard Law School, the stroke of the first Yale crew to race against Harvard (a race Harvard won in 1852), a practicing lawyer in Boston from 1856 on. He was big and smart, strong and tough by reputation, amply fulfilling Lord Salisbury's classic definition of a war correspondent as "a man who combines the skill of a first class steeplechaser with the skill of a first class writer."

At the time the Civil War began, however, Smalley hadn't ever earned his keep as a journalist and neither acted, looked, nor even talked the part. He was a bit on the precious side, affecting a broad Boston accent and the airs of a country squire on holiday, which in a way, he was. Evidently, he hadn't done very well as a lawyer at the time he was married to the adopted daughter of Wendell Phillips, the Boston reformer, because Phillips turned him toward newspaper work by sending him to the managing editor of the New York *Tribune,* Charles A. Dana, who hired him before the onset of the Civil War.

On Smalley's first assignment, a series on Negro life in the South, he did well enough to qualify for a staff job but he was just another inexperienced reporter toward the bottom of the list of 20 who were sent into the field for the *Tribune* when Fort Sumter fell. He seemed to have progressed sufficiently by the time of the second Battle of Bull Run to be given a tough assignment, being attached to the Federal forces under "Little Mac," General George B. McClellan. And in the haze of a late summer's morning on September 17, 1862, he prepared for action at Antietam.[22]

The lovely Maryland countryside, though quiet, teemed with fighting men that day. Behind Antietam Creek, winding through green groves and soft meadows, lay 40,000 Confederate troops under the command of General Robert E. Lee in a massive drive northward toward the Pennsylvania line. He already was less than 50 miles northwest of Washington and even closer due east of Baltimore — a major threat to the panicky North.

McClellan had defeated Lee's rear guard three days before at South Mountain, 12 miles west of Frederick, Md., but now a sterner test loomed for the Northern commander and his 70,000 men of the Army of the Potomac. President Lincoln and a prayerful North counted on that disciplined fighting force to turn back Lee's first northern invasion.

The battle of the main forces of North and South began at dawn in what was, by all odds, the most critical engagement for both in the early stages of the war. Smalley, who had slept on the ground with his horse's bridle around his arm, had attached himself to Major General

Joseph E. Hooker's corps on the Federal right wing. The correspondent had heard that "Fighting Joe" had been ordered to attempt a flanking movement around Lee's forces. The general was already in the saddle ordering his troops forward toward a cornfield where the great Confederate general "Stonewall " Jackson and his veteran troops were waiting for them.

Smalley rode along with Hooker's staff, although nobody, including Hooker himself, seemed to know that a correspondent had attached himself to them as part of an assignment parceled out among the half dozen or so *Tribune* staffers in the field that day. When challenged and forced to identify himself, Smalley was promptly impressed into service as a dispatch rider between Hooker's command and the staff of the commander that day, General McClellan. The correspondent had no choice. He was to be in the thick of the action that day.

The battle developed into one of the bloodiest during the whole course of the Civil War. Each side was reported to have lost at least 20,000 men during the day-long carnage, but neither had gained any advantage at dusk. It was Hooker's misfortune early on, at around 9 a.m., to be shot in the foot by a rebel sharpshooter and carried from the field. At the time, Smalley was with McClellan's staff where, so the correspondent was told, the general was wavering in his plan of attack and his subordinates were asking the correspondent from Hooker's command whether that general could take charge of the action.

Little as he had known of war, Smalley realized any attempt to push aside a military commander in the thick of battle would be the grossest insubordination and said so. He was persuaded, however, to consult with Hooker and return as soon as possible with some word on how the struggle against Jackson's troops was going.

That was when, toward dusk, Smalley found Hooker in a farmhouse, in bed and obviously in pain. The correspondent reported what McClellan's staff people had told him — that the Confederates had broken off the action, and Lee was preparing to withdraw south of the Potomac River. Although there could be no certainty that the battle might be resumed on the morrow, the odds seemed against it. At that hour, it did appear that Lee's first drive northward had been halted and he was falling back possibly to regroup.

When Smalley suggested that Hooker might want to ride in darkness to consult with McClellan and his staff, the closest he dared come to a disclosure of the staff's rebellious mood, "Fighting Joe" flew into a rage, left his bed, but couldn't stand. When he was able to control himself, he explained that he was unable to travel any distance with his wounded foot.

That actually was the end of the fighting at Antietam Creek. By pre-arrangement, Smalley met with the other *Tribune* correspondents to obtain an overall review of the action that day, then set out on a long ride to Frederick, the largest town in the area with a telegraph office. Two horses had been shot out from under him that day and bullets twice had singed him, tearing his clothes, but he was unharmed.

At 3 a.m. on September 18, riding his third horse, he reached Frederick only to find the telegraph office closed and the operator not due to reopen it until 7 a.m. Even then, the telegrapher told the correspondent that he was under military supervision and couldn't guarantee that any message would be delivered to its destination. However, the weary correspondent begged him to try and, when the telegragher agreed, scribbled several pages of a battle summary addressed to the *Tribune* office in New York. As the telegrapher had feared, the battle summary was held up by censorship, routed directly to the War Department and then to President Lincoln — the first word that Lee had broken off the action at Antietam and retreated southward into Virginia.

Now, not knowing what else to do, the frustrated correspondent begged the military to let him proceed by train to Baltimore, hoping somehow that he could in the interim obtain the release of his summary to the *Tribune* and add to it. He was given no encouragement, however. It was after 2 p.m. when an engine came chugging by, pulling a few cars, bound for Baltimore, and Smalley scrambled aboard in the belief that he might begin writing a complete account of the fighting at Antietam the day before. Still, when the train reached Baltimore late in the day, he had not written a line because he had fallen asleep out of sheer exhaustion.

But when he was told that the Washington express bound for New York was due in ten minutes, he pulled himself together, caught the express, and at once began writing the complete report he had planned. With delays en route, together with the difficulty of writing while standing under a flickering oil lamp at one end of the car in which he was traveling, it was a miracle that he was able to walk into the *Tribune* office in New York City at 5 a.m. on September 19 with what he called "the worst piece of manuscript the oldest printer had ever seen."

In the extra edition the *Tribune* put out, the complete story ran to six columns — a thundering beat for the correspondent and his paper with a distinctive account of "the greatest fight since Waterloo," to quote his lead. By that time, the War Department also had forwarded the summary he had written at Frederick, but now it wasn't needed.

There was no time for congratulations, however, because Smalley insisted on heading back at once to the southern battlefields. As he wrote later in a rueful admission of failure, "I might as well have stayed in New York for I was soon invalided back again with camp fever and remained in the office to write war editorials."[23]

From Vicksburg to Gettysburg and from Chancellorsville to Appomattox, others carried on for the *Tribune* in the manner that Smalley had inaugurated. To at least two of his competitors, Henry Villard and Albert Richardson, Smalley's was the greatest individual reporting feat of the war. The way he conducted himself in the field and the manner in which he worked to get around censorship over wire copy, as well as the prominence given to his *Tribune* account of Antietam at home and abroad, was to have a profound effect on future foreign correspondence all over the world.

———

Once Smalley had regained his health, he was assigned abroad. To quote the *Tribune* of May 11, 1867, "Mr. Smalley sails for Europe today to act as Foreign Commissioner for the *Tribune,* resident in London."[24]

It was the beginning of a new era in foreign correspondence. With the trans-Atlantic cable back in service and the telegraph linking the major centers of Europe, Smalley proposed to operate all European correspondence out of London with a separate budget and authority to hire and fire, shift, and assign all his agents. He would be responsible only to the managing editor in New York, but he would also be held to account for significant news coverage throughout the Continent, Britain, and Ireland. The advantage, of course, was faster news transmission, greater mobility for the foreign staff, and a vastly improved daily file of foreign news. To make certain the *Tribune* would be well served, Smalley entered into a two-way arrangement with the London *Daily News* for an exchange of their files on major stories when the *Tribune*'s management decided to try his scheme.[25]

In the Franco-Prussian War of 1870, Smalley's foresight paid off. After using a pretext to provoke the French into fighting, Bismarck unleashed the Prussian army under Field Marshal Helmuth von Moltke in a great wheeling movement through northern Europe into France. At the battle of Gravelotte, fought on August 18, 1870, Smalley's Berlin correspondent was first into London and New York with the report of a Prussian victory. The Berlin man, Joseph Hance, had the foresight to ride six hours from the battlefield to the nearest telegraph station at Saarbrücken and Smalley paid $5,000 to cable it to New York for publication on August 21. Altogether, Smalley was reputed to have spent

$125,000 in cable tolls alone to stay ahead of the competition during the short conflict.[26]

Nevertheless, for the complete story of Gravelotte, the New York *World* was ahead and sold its story to the London *Daily News;* Smalley had to pay for the right to republish it in the *Tribune.* But he had his revenge with an exclusive on the major Prussian victory at Sedan on September 1. Two days after the battle, all London had received was a Reuters bulletin saying that the French had lost but giving no inkling of the extent of their defeat. By that time, Holt White had beaten the censors by reaching the *Tribune* office in London, where he wrote the first complete story of the defeat of the French at Sedan.[27]

Still another *Tribune* beat followed when one of Smalley's stringers, Gustav Mueller, was first into London and New York with the news of still another French defeat after the collapse of their fortress at Metz on October 28. One of Smalley's allies, Archibald Forbes of the London *Daily News*, wrote in admiration of the *Tribune*'s feat.

"In modern war correspondence the race is emphatically to the swift, the battle to the strong. The best organizer of the means for expediting his intelligence, he it is who is the most successful man — not your deliberate manufacturer of telling phrases, your piler up of coruscating adjectives."[28]

Suiting his action to his words, Forbes was first into London with the news of the Prussian bombardment of St. Denis,[29] a suburb of Paris, and with the inspection of the center of the fallen city itself directly after its surrender on January 28, 1871. After 18 hours on horseback inside the city, he filed his dispatch to the *Daily News* in London through Karlsruhe and his paper put it on the street on February 4, an eyewitness account of the tragedy of Paris in which he wrote:

" 'Paris is utterly cowed; fairly beaten.' So said the first Englishman I met and his opinion was mine. Yet, Paris was orderly and decent, and with a certain solemn, morose self-restraint was mastering its tendency to demonstrate. . . . The whole city is haunted."[30]

The New York *Tribune*–London *Daily News* alliance had dominated the coverage of the war from beginning to end through the daring of their correspondents and the manner in which the wires had been used. However, the *Times* of London managed to bring William Howard Russell out of retirement to report on the formal declaration of the German Empire under Prussian domination in the Hall of Mirrors at Versailles.[31]

From the German peace *Diktat* to the abdication of Napoleon II and the rise of the Paris Commune amid a bloody orgy of street fighting, most of the honors went to the *Tribune–Daily News* combine. Once again, Forbes got into Paris and emerged with another eyewitness account in which he wrote:

"Paris the beautiful is now Paris the ghastly, Paris the battered, Paris the blood-drenched. And this in the present century — Europe professing civilization, France boasting of culture and refinement, Frenchmen beating one another with the butt ends of their rifles, and Paris blazing to the skies! There needed but a Nero to fiddle."[32]

Between them, Smalley and Forbes were to transform the remaining procedures of old-fashioned war reporting beyond recall before the end of the decade. With their news organizations, they were sounding a wake-up call to a drowsy Europe that a mighty new German Empire was on the march with unforseeable consequences. The overwhelming tragedy of the era was not the fall of France in 1870. It was that Europe slept on and paid the consequences in the century yet to come.

"FIND LIVINGSTONE!"

Not all the foreign news cabled to America at fantastic rates for the era was of war. On October 17, 1869, Henry Morton Stanley left Paris for Africa with a two-word command from the imperious new publisher of the New York *Herald,* James Gordon Bennett, Jr.:

"FIND LIVINGSTONE!"[33]

David Livingstone, a Scottish missionary, had been missing for some time while on a pioneering African expedition for the Royal Geographic Society that began in 1866. It was the younger Bennett's assumption that the missionary might have fallen victim to foul play, although there was no proof. Nor had there been any recent word from Livingstone to show that all had gone well for him and his expedition. Thus, the abrupt command from the eccentric publisher in the royal manner affected by the wilder species of the breed in the latter part of the 19th century:

"Draw a thousand pounds now. And when you have gone through that, draw another thousand, and when that is spent, draw another thousand, and when you have finished that, draw another thousand, and so on. *But find Livingstone!*"

After that interview, which took place in the Bennett suite at the Grand Hotel in Paris. Stanley took off. He was then 28 years old, a wiry five-foot, five-inch Welshman who had been in all manner of danger as a Civil War correspondent for the *Herald* and later a reporter of the Indian wars in the American West.

For 15 months after receiving his orders from the despotic proprietor of the *Herald*, Stanley fulfilled his assignment and dutifully sent pieces from all the places he visited in Africa for publication in the *Herald*. Gradually, the public became fascinated with this unique exploit. And as the story caught on, the *Herald* began syndicating it. Still, there was no word from Bennett. The instructions still stood: "Find Livingstone!"[34]

Finally, Stanley reached Zanzibar on December 31, 1870, after having strayed off course as far as Bombay in India on the off chance that the missionary might have whimsically changed direction. However, not a clue to the supposedly missing man and his party had turned up in the long search.

Rumors filtering to Stanley's party from the African jungle variously had Livingstone lost, comfortably attached to an African princess, and dead. At the time he reached Zanzibar, Stanley had only $80 in gold; but his credit at the *Herald* remained excellent, and so an American consul helped him raise additional funds for still another trek in the jungle.

On March 21, 1871, he left the coastal town of Bagamoyo with a little army of three whites, 31 armed freemen from Zanzibar, 153 porters, 27 pack animals and two riding horses. By May 8, he began the difficult ascent of the Usagara range, reached a village called Ugogo, and toiled on with his wagon train into the picturesque country called the Land of the Moon.

Actually, he had no true sense of direction or even a reportorial hunch. By that time in his long journey, he was traveling mainly by the seat of his pants. Everywhere he went, he asked for Livingstone; but nowhere in all the time he had been gone from Paris did he come across anything definite about the missionary's fate. He knew only that the Royal Geographic Society had asked Livingstone to try to locate the headwaters of the Nile but that uncertain clue had long since been exhausted.

Still Bennett had said, "Find Livingstone!" Nor had anything happened to date to countermand that instruction.

In Stanley's journey out of Zanzibar, he and his party were caught in a tribal war that held them up for three months. But once that was settled, he pushed on to Lake Tanganyika. Along the trail, he had heard a rumor, passed along by a native caravan, that a gray-bearded white man had been seen in a settlement called Ujiji, established in the lake country by Arabs. His hopes rose slightly, but he had been disappointed so often that he wasn't overly excited.

Yet when Stanley reached Tanganyika on November 10, 1871, a tall black man in a long white shirt hurried to greet the party and bowed to the roving reporter saying, "Good morning, sir."

Stanley was brusque. "Hello, who in the mischief are you?"

"I am Susi, sir. The servant of Dr. Livingstone."

Stanley was incredulous. "What! Is Dr. Livingstone here in this town?"

"Yes, sir."

Before Stanley could ask any more questions, the black man began running toward Ujiji, presumably to tell his master of the arrival of the Stanley party. Then followed the famous scene which is best told in Stanley's own words as he first wrote them for the New York *Herald* at the end of his account of the climax of his search:

"We have at last entered the town. There are hundreds of people around me — I might say thousands without exaggeration, it seems to me. It is a grand triumphal procession. As we move, they move. All eyes are drawn towards us. The expedition at last comes to a halt; the journey is ended for a time; but I alone have a few more steps to make.

"There is a group of the most respectable Arabs, and as I come nearer I see the white face of an old man among them. He has a cap with a gold band around it, his dress is a short jacket of red blanket cloth and his pants — well, I didn't observe.

"I am shaking hands with him. We raise our hats and I say:

"Dr. Livingstone, I presume?"

"And he says yes."

The first word to the New York *Herald* of the success of Stanley's mission was flashed through London on July 2, 1872, to the general effect that Livingstone was safe and Stanley had found him.[35] Stanley's own account, somewhat embroidered with colorful details of the first confrontation, including the missing observation of the trousers (they were gray tweed), was published on August 10 with tremendous fanfare. However, the opposition could have been counted on to raise doubts in England. One expert gibed, "Maybe it is Livingstone who has found Stanley."

On March 14, 1872, Stanley and his party had left Ujiji and reached Zanzibar 54 days later. On August 11, when the *Herald* sent Livingstone enough supplies to keep him going for two years at Stanley's request, the missionary plunged back into the bush country with a new party of 57 men completely outfitted. Upon returning to London, Stanley was hailed as a hero, and Bennett silenced further doubts by splashing a letter of thanks from Livingstone across the top of page 1 of the *Herald* as a tribute to both the publisher and his man, Stanley.[36]

There was a final touch from Stanley that particularly pleased Bennett. Livingstone, it appeared, had been impressed because he had been "found" by a caravan bearing the American flag.

On February 25, 1874, Livingstone died at Ilala near Lake Bangweolo, and Stanley replaced him as an African explorer by courtesy of both the New York *Herald* and the London *Daily Telegraph,* which were delighted to publish his later effusions. He was elected to Parliament, knighted, married late in life, and settled down as a country gentleman on a Surrey estate. When he died in London at the age of 63, there were services for him at Westminster Abbey with burial in Surrey.[37]

Just as Smalley and Forbes changed the nature of foreign correspondence by their daring and their successful efforts to quicken transmission, Stanley broadened the substance with which it dealt. He was the founder of a hard-riding troop of glory — men who sought adventure for its own sake in the jungles, deserts, and mountain fastnesses, in the bleak white midnight of the polar ice and the restless blue of the seven seas, and finally in the weightless emptiness of space itself.

Such larger concepts of life on this small planet brought knowledge of the power of the atom to humankind and illuminated the history of the species over the millions of years since the first anthropoid decided to walk on two limbs instead of four.

THE CRUSADERS

On the confused and shadowed stage of the 19th century, the journalist played many roles both inside and outside his native land and spoke in many voices. He was at once a chronicler and mentor, preceptor and guide, diplomat and adventurer, and even, on occasion, a warrior in his own right. At his worst, he was a mere echo of all the vices that beset humankind; at his best, he was its conscience.

There is little doubt that the 19th-century journalist played one of his most colorful roles as a seeker after fame and glory, a standard-bearer for the cause of empire. Such a one was a small, shrewd Bohemian, Henri Stefan Opper de Blowitz, the diplomatic correspondent of the *Times* of London, who obtained exclusively for his newspaper the publication of the treaty under which the Congress of Berlin in 1878 redrew the map of southeastern Europe mainly for the benefit of Germany and its allies.[38]

But for a cherished few in the journalism of the Western world, glory and empire meant little when a chance presented itself to right a grievous wrong, to raise the standard of truth against error. It was in such roles as these that the journalist made a more lasting impression on the history of his time.

The crusading instinct had been present at the very beginning of foreign correspondence — with Jared Ingersoll and the unwitting impetus he gave to the formation of the Sons of Liberty in the American colonies, Heinrich Heine and his attacks on German autocracy, Georges Clemenceau amd his correspondence as a political exile in the United States. Had it not been for the conscience of William Howard Russell, a British army would almost certainly have perished in the Crimea. Had it not been for the brilliant reporting of Januarius Aloysius MacGahan, a country boy from Ohio who worked for the New York *Herald,* the barbarities of Turkish rule in Bulgaria might never have been exposed.[39] And the cause of Italian freedom would have been the poorer had not the cause attracted a beautiful English girl, Jessie Meriton White Mario, who began as a war correspondent for British and American papers during Giuseppe Garibaldi's march on Rome but remained in her adopted country thereafter. "A great woman to whom Italians owe a great debt," in the words of Giosue Carducci, Italy's poet-patriot and Nobel Prize winner.[40]

Few such crusading lives were foreordained. So noble a purpose was far from the thoughts of Theodore Herzl when he became the Paris correspondent of the *Neue Freie Presse* of Vienna in 1891. He wrote to his parents, delighted with his good fortune as a journalist, "The position of Paris correspondent is a jumping board from which I shall swing myself high to your joy, my dear parents."

Herzl was then 31, the image of a dedicated man of letters. Wherever he went, his black-bearded, austere figure commanded both attention and respect. Those who knew him well realized that his restless, piercing eyes were constantly, fiercely probing beneath the surface of Parisian life, that his keen intellect was forever alert for a greater challenge than the recording of the news. Such a man needed a cause for fulfillment, a cause worth dying for.

One afternoon in 1894, while he was at work over his writing in his room at the Hotel Bastille in the Rue Cambon, he became deeply disturbed. An infuriated mob, surging along the street below his window, was shouting, "Death to the Jews!"

If this had been Poland or Russia or even his native Hungary, Herzl might have accepted what he heard with a bitter equanimity. But this was Paris, home of the rights of man; France, a nation founded on the principles of liberty, equality, fraternity. It seemed incredible to Herzl that the murderous incitement to Jewish mass destruction should have been heard amid such surroundings, almost as incredible as if such an outcry had been raised in Germany where the Jewish community felt so comfortable, even superior, in its seeming security.

Then, all at once, Herzl began to understand. In Paris at that time, a respected French officer who was Jewish, Captain Alfred Dreyfus, had been arrested and called a traitor; therefore, whether he was guilty or innocent, the mob even in liberty-loving France already had concluded that he must die and all Jews must die with him. Here, in the heart of the freedom-loving Western world, the savage anti-Semitism of Eastern peoples had taken root, and it would not easily be exorcised.

Amid such feelings, which grew more intense day by day, Herzl covered the Dreyfus trial for the *Neue Freie Presse,* the great newspaper that had always been so carefully read by the large and seemingly secure Jewish population of Vienna. But more important than anything he wrote for his newspaper about Dreyfus was the idea that had come to him as he listened with increasing concern to the testimony in the case — an idea that had caused him to begin making notes for the book of a lifetime.

As Herzl wrote to his friend, Arthur Schnitzler, the playwright, in Vienna, this book he had undertaken was "a mountain of granite. Perhaps it is because I am still so shaken that this apparition glows in me, frightening me." The book was *Der Judenstaat* (The Jewish state), which appeared for the first time in 1896.

Chaim Weizmann, then a student in Berlin, called it a "bolt from the blue" because it revealed to him a "historic personality" as well as a formidable concept of both the future and the responsibility of Zionism. *Der Judenstaat* became the fountainhead of world Zionism through the Zionist Congress, of which Herzl became the head. He thereafter gave up his cherished post as a journalist in Paris and spent the rest of his life rallying support for a Jewish national homeland in Palestine, but never lived to see it established.

Worn out through his efforts on behalf of his people, he suffered a heart attack at his Vienna home and died on July 3, 1904, at the age of 44.[41] Forty-four years later, the State of Israel was declared in Palestine and successfully fought for its life against four invading Arab armies after Hitler's Germans had carted off six million Jewish victims to die in his ovens during World War II.

Captain Dreyfus, whose plight had inspired Herzl's epic work, survived him. In his case, too, world opinion played a major role because the energies of French liberalism were refreshed and strengthened thereby. From the day that Emile Zola published his celebrated "J'accuse" in Georges Clemenceau's newspaper, *L'Aurore,* on January 13, 1898, journalists all over the world took up the challenge and republished it. This was no mere Jewish reaction; it was an expression of world outrage against a colossal injustice in France. As a result, more than 30,000 letters were sent to France in response. From an insignificant circulation, *L'Aurore* began selling 300,000 copies of every issue that dealt with the Dreyfus case.

Zola was promptly prosecuted for criminal libel, convicted in 35 minutes by a jury vote of 8 to 4 and, seeing his appeal would be hopeless, went into self-imposed exile in London. Strangely enough, no less than Queen Victoria interested herself in the Dreyfus case. In a confidential inquiry she sent to her grandson, Kaiser Wilhelm II, she asked if Dreyfus had been trafficking with the German espionage service, the charge on which he had been convicted. The answer was no.

The Dreyfusards, as they became known, surged to the attack, with Clemenceau directing their strategy, after Captain Dreyfus was convicted of high treason by a military court on October 15, 1894, and sent to Devil's Island the following February 21. He was still there while the struggle to prove his innocence continued year after year. His accusers all seemed supremely confident that the truth would never be known, but they did not count on the fury that Clemenceau and Zola had been able to arouse against French justice throughout the civilized world.

On August 30, 1898, in a sudden break in the case, one of Dreyfus's principal accusers, Major Hubert Henry, was arrested for forging evidence and killed himself by slitting his throat with a razor. Henry's friend, Major Count Ferdinand Walsin-Esterhazy, who had been tried and acquitted of the crime for which Dreyfus was convicted, then fled without luggage to London. Marquis Mercier du Paty de Clam, who had sworn that Dreyfus had written a confidential document recovered by French intelligence from the Germans, retired. Premier Henri Brisson's cabinet fell. The High Court of Appeals decided to hear arguments on the revision of the verdict against Dreyfus.

At this juncture, the *Times* of London came up with the great beat that at last cleared up the disgraceful conspiracy against an innocent soldier. On June 3, 1899, the *Times* published the signed confession by Esterhazy that he had written the confidential document that became the chief evidence against Dreyfus, the so-called *bordereau.* On the same day, the High Court ordered a new trial for Dreyfus. When it opened at Rennes on August 11, 1899, with the long-suffering captain still proclaiming his innocence, hundreds of foreign correspondents swarmed in and about the court, all awaiting the verdict. The French general staff, still determined to ride roughshod over world opinion, closed the doors on the foreign press, still another mistake. They reaped the whirlwind when they voted 5 to 2 to find Dreyfus guilty but softened his penalty to ten years in prison due to "extenuating circumstances."

It was inevitable that world opinion would prevail no matter what the French general staff might have done to try to preserve itself. When the indignation of free societies at last reached the conscience of France, Dreyfus was pardoned on September 19, 1899, and left prison through what President Emile Loubet, rather ironically, called an "act of mercy." On July 12, 1906, the High Court wrapped up the case by setting aside the guilty verdict of the Rennes court.

The Chamber of Deputies decorated Dreyfus and his military defender, Georges Picquart, who became a brigadier general. As a lieutenant colonel, Dreyfus fought in two major actions of World War I — at the Chemin des Dames and at Verdun. June 1, 1930, he received a letter signed by Louise von Schwarzkoppen, wife of Infantry General Max von Schwarzkoppen, who had been the German military attaché in Paris at the time the case began. Frau von Schwarzkoppen enclosed her late husband's diary, saying that "his wish had been to testify in the monstrous trial of which you were the central figure and victim. For reasons which his memoirs clearly indicate, this was impossible for him to do."

Thus came final vindication for Dreyfus. When he died on July 11, 1935, he was a man who had outlived his time; but in the new era that had already begun, Adolf Hitler was preparing for a new war and an even greater crime. Still, there was inspiration enough in the Dreyfus story to cause Jean Jaures to write: "What matter the errors of fate and false directions in life? A few luminous and fervent moments are enough to give meaning to a lifetime." For the foreign correspondents who had worked so effectively on the Dreyfus case, Julian Ralph had written in the New York *Sun:* "You may say it was the unfinishable vitality of the truth which reopened his case, but the French knew very well that they had exiled truth and it found its opening in our foreign press."[42]

In the United States, the crusading spirit had already become an ideal for the liberal-minded journalist. Its leading practictioner at the time, Joseph Pulitzer, had been an immigrant born April 10, 1847, in Mako,

Hungary; a Civil War soldier, mustered out of service well-nigh penniless in 1865; a reporter, legislator, civic leader in St. Louis, and eventually, the publisher of a small struggling newspaper, the St. Louis *Post-Dispatch*.

Once the *Post-Dispatch* became a success, Pulitzer's restlessness and ambition caused him to invade New York City, where he bought the *World,* a paper that had fallen on hard times. In one of his most remarkable crusades, when he learned no provision had been made for the exhibition of Bartholdi's Statue of Liberty, he used the *World* to raise the money through which it was brought to New York and placed on her pedestal in the harbor.

As he had written upon acquiring the *World:* "There is room in this great and growing city for a journal . . . that will expose all fraud and sham, fight all public evils and abuses, that will serve and battle for the people with earnest sincerity."

By carrying out this credo, Pulitzer became one of the dominant journalists of his time, famous and wealthy and unafraid of combating some of the best among American presidents if he thought they were wrong.[43]

In 1895, at the height of the Venezuelan border crisis in which President Grover Cleveland had pushed the United States to the brink of war with Britain, Pulitzer had published an editorial in the *World* on December 22 saying:

"President Cleveland's message to Congress on the Venezuelan matter is a grave blunder. It is a blunder because it is based on, a wrong conception, because it is not sustained by international law or usage and because it places the United States in a false position. The President assumes that the policy of Great Britain in Venezuela involves a menace to this country. . . . The assumption is absurd. And with it falls the structure of ponderously patriotic rhetoric reared upon it by the President."

Under Pulitzer's leadership, the *World* embarked on a full-scale peace campaign that helped, in its own way, to reduce the tension. When the British backed down, there is little doubt that Pulitzer's peace crusade had had its effect on the White House. The Venezuelan matter went to arbitration and was successfully settled. Had Pulitzer taken a similar position in the tension that led to the Spanish-American War three years later, he would have been happier. As it was, he let the *World* get into a headline rivalry with William Randolph Hearst's boisterous New York *Journal* and forever regretted it.

Less than a decade later, he was drawn into a battle with President Theodore Roosevelt over the *World*'s allegations that $40,000,000 had been disposed of illegally in the negotiations that led to the construction of the Panama Canal.

When the Indianapolis *News* republished the *World*'s charges, President Roosevelt angrily rebuked the Indianapolis paper's publisher, Delavan Smith. The *World* then attacked President Roosevelt, accusing him of making "deliberate misstatements of fact in a scandalous personal attack on Delavan Smith" and demanded a congressional inquiry into "who got the $40 million." T.R. countered with a message to Congress on December 15, 1908, that both papers had committed a "string of infamous libels" and demanded federal indictments for criminal libel.

The New York indictment was obtained March 4, 1909, after T.R. had left the White House. Other indictments were voted in both Indianapolis and the District of Columbia. However, such actions at the time went against both law and custom since libel actions generally are brought under the jurisdiction of the states. In the Panama Canal case, the Attorney General's office fought the jurisdictional issue by arguing the *World* had been sold on government property at West Point and similar jurisdictional claims were made in the Indianapolis *News* indictment.

Still, Pulitzer fought the case with all the power of publicity, charging at one point that federal agents were searching the *World*'s mail. However, the indictments were thrown out of court on the ground of lack of jurisdiction. And the key question, "Who got the $40 million?" was never answered.[44]

Toward the end of his life, when he was severely ill and almost blind, Pulitzer's main interest was in the perpetuation of high standards of journalism and the elevation of those in letters, drama, music, and art. It was for this that he endowed the Pulitzer Prizes at Columbia University and established its journalism school, now the Graduate School of Journalism, with a $2 million bequest. He died October 29, 1911.

Through the annual awards of the Pulitzer Prizes, the spirit of Joseph Pulitzer remains a dominant force in American journalism, letters, and music as he had intended. To the end of his life, he also maintained his policy of drastic independence. That was his twin heritage to those who followed him. In his lifetime, he demonstrated that peace, too, has its victories and of these the victories of conscience are the greatest.

His creed was stated best in a message on his retirement on April 10, 1907, which has been published daily ever since on the editorial page of the St. Louis *Post-Dispatch*:

"I know that my retirement will make no difference in its (the *Post-Dispatch*'s) cardinal principles: that it will always fight for progress and reform, never tolerate injustice or corruption, always fight demagogues of all parties, never belong to any party, always oppose privileged classes and public plunderers, never lack sympathy with the poor, always remain devoted to the public welfare, never be satisfied with merely printing the news, always be drastically independent, never be afraid to attack wrong, whether by predatory plutocracy or predatory poverty."[45]

3 Reports from a Changing World

"OUR WAR"

On the night of February 15, 1898, F. J. Hilgert, AP correspondent in Havana, sent two bulletins within a few minutes:

THERE HAS BEEN A BIG EXPLOSION SOMEWHERE IN THE HARBOR MAINE HAS BEEN BLOWN UP AND HUNDREDS OF SAILORS HAVE BEEN KILLED

Upon arriving home that night, William Randolph Hearst heard the news by telephone from his New York *Journal* and exclaimed, "Good heavens! What have you done with the story. . . . Have you put anything else on the front page?"

"Only the other big news," was the measured response.

"There is not any other big news. Please spread the story all over the page. This means war."[1]

Long afterward, when James Creelman was under no requirement to cheer whenever Hearst raised his hand, he wrote realistically of his old boss, "The outbreak of the Spanish-American War found Mr. Hearst in a state of grand ecstacy. He had won his campaign and the McKinley administration had been forced into war."[2]

The equally critical Willis J. Abbot, also a former Hearst editor and later the editor of the *Christian Science Monitor,* remarked wryly, "Hearst was accustomed to refer to the war, in company with his staff, as 'Our War.'"[3]

Perhaps it was, in a realistic sense. The California-born Hearst, then 35 years old, had set New York City agog with his campaign in his *Journal* to get the United States into a war with Spain. He had depicted

49

a 17-year-old Cuban, Evangelina Cisneros, as a Cuban Joan of Arc who had been cast into a dungeon for defending her chastity against a rapacious Spaniard. He had even directed her rescue from a Havana prison by an enterprising reporter, Karl Decker, who had thoughtfully bribed the guards and produced her at a Madison Square Garden rally in New York City.

When the unfortunate Spanish minister, Dupuy de Lome, had sent a letter critical of President McKinley to a friend in Havana, it had turned up on page 1 of the *Journal* under a banner:

THE WORST INSULT TO THE UNITED STATES IN ITS HISTORY.[4]

Dupuy de Lome resigned. Hearst, in short, had done everything he could think of, in his rivalry with Pulitzer's New York *World,* to exacerbate relations between the United States and Spain — and he had no apologies to make.

In fact, when the *Journal* came out on February 17, 1898, its most sensational headline read:

THE WARSHIP MAINE WAS SPLIT IN TWO

BY AN ENEMY'S SECRET INFERNAL MACHINE[5]

Hearst, of course, had not been the only one in that era of yellow journalism to agitate for war with Spain. The *World* had done its part. And Theodore Roosevelt, no yellow journalist, had demanded after visiting the White House and learning President McKinley still wasn't sure what to do:

"Do you know what that white-livered cur up there has done? He has prepared two messages, one for war and one for peace, and he doesn't know which one to send in!"

When the president asked Congress to decide, the Senate voted 42–35 for war on April 19, 1898, while the House whooped it up, 310–6.[6] Hearst now took charge of a fleet of 10 dispatch boats and a band of 25 roving foreign correspondents to cover the war with Creelman as his star and the artist Frederic Remington to provide the illustrations from the first battle between the United States and Spain on Cuban soil.[7]

Unfortunately for Hearst, the first battle news came from the Philippines by way of Hong Kong when Commodore George Dewey's Asiatic Squadron destroyed the Spanish fleet in Manila harbor and the New York *Herald* came through with the beat.[8] However, when the navy refused confirmation, rumors spread that Dewey must have taken heavy casualties. He hadn't.[9]

Six days after the battle, on May 7, an amateur correspondent aboard the navy's dispatch boat *McCulloch* filed the first battle message ahead of the offical report:

ENTIRE SPANISH FLEET DESTROYED. ELEVEN SHIPS. SPANISH LOSS THREE HUNDRED KILLED FOUR HUNDRED WOUNDED. OUR LOSS NONE KILLED SIX SLIGHTLY WOUNDED. SHIPS UNINJURED. (SIGNED) HARDEN.[10]

Edward Walker Harden of the Chicago *Tribune,* who also represented the New York *World,* had gone to the Far East on the *McCulloch* with John T. McCutcheon, a Chicago *Record* cartoonist. Together, they had gone to Hong Kong to file on the Pacific cable with Joseph L. Stickney of the New York *Herald,* the only bona fide war correspondent in the fleet who had seen the battle from Dewey's flagship, *Olympia.* At the toss of a coin, Harden was able to file first to confirm the early report in the New York *Herald.*

That was how the *World*'s extra reported Dewey's victory in New York while Hearst was preparing for action in Cuba.[11]

After a preliminary skirmish at Las Guasimas on June 24, 1898, in which he lost one of his correspondents who fell with bullet near his spine, Hearst now swung into action with a 3,000-word piece for the *Journal* of June 29 on the military situation before Santiago, a prime American objective.[12] Just two days later, the icy-calm six-foot, two-inch publisher and Creelman were together under fire at the battle of El Caney,[13] while Richard Harding Davis of the New York *Herald* was following the fortunes of war with Roosevelt's Rough Riders up San Juan Hill.[14] These were the climactic battles before Santiago de Cuba, and Davis was the opposition correspondent Hearst most respected.[15]

The small, black-bearded Creelman, a revolver in his holster, had dashed inside a Spanish fort at one point, saw a Spanish flag lying in the dust, and watched the American troops pick it up, cheering. Most of the garrison was dead, but a young Spanish officer was ready to surrender the rest. Just then, however, a Mauser bullet hit Creelman's arm, and he went down. Faint from heat and loss of blood, he lay helpless for some time. He recounted what happened next a considerable time afterward:

Some one knelt in the grass beside me and put his hand on my fevered head. Opening my eyes, I saw Mr. Hearst, the proprietor of the New York *Journal,* a straw hat with a bright ribbon on his head and a note-book in his hand. The man who had provoked the war had come to see the result with his own eyes and, finding one of his correspondents prostrate, was doing the work himself. Slowly, he took down my story of the fight. Again and again, the zinging of Mauser bullets interrupted. But he seemed unmoved. The battle had to be reported somehow. He said:

"I'm sorry you're hurt but" — and his face was radiant with enthusiasm — "wasn't it a splendid fight? We must beat every paper in the world."[16]

Creelman wasn't the only reporter-hero that day, nor was Hearst the only other correspondent under fire. Richard Harding Davis and the *Herald* made Theodore Roosevelt famous for leading the charge of his Rough Riders up San Juan Hill. The reporter wrote:

"I speak of Roosevelt first because . . . Roosevelt, mounted high on horseback, and charging the rifle pits at a gallop and quite alone made you feel that you would like to cheer. He wore on his sombrero a blue polkadot handkerchief . . . which, as he advanced, floated straight behind his head like a guidon."[17]

In a letter home later, Davis also made a confession of his own smaller part in the battle of San Juan Hill: "I got excited and took a carbine and charged the sugar house (on San Juan Hill). If the men had been regulars, I would have sat in the rear as (Stephen) Crane did but I knew every one of them — had played football and all that sort of thing, so I thought as an American I ought to help."[18]

It was, all in all, rather difficult to decide which correspondent deserved the honors in the field that day — Davis or Creelman or Crane or Hearst.[19] But there was no doubt whatever about who had captured the fancy of the American people as a soldier. The name was Theodore Roosevelt, and it rocketed across the land in the nation's newspapers with the reports of the action before Santiago that July 1.[20]

But on Sunday, July 3, an even greater sensation broke. Admiral Pascual Cervera y Topete tried to run his fleet of six ships out of the blockaded Santiago harbor. Rear Admiral William T. Sampson was caught on land at the American base at Guantanamo. But the alert Commodore Winfield S. Schley, who was chatting on the bridge of the USS *Brooklyn* with an AP correspondent, George E. Graham, heard the lookout bawl, "The enemy ships are coming out!"

Schley seized his binoculars and saw the Spanish fleet in column, led by the flagship *Maria Theresa,* racing from Santiago harbor. "Come on, my boy," he cried to the reporter, "we'll give it to them now!"

It was just 9:35 a.m. on a hot and cloudless Sunday. In response to Schley's signals, the American fleet pounced on the Spaniards with murderous fire, while Graham recorded the battle scene beside the commander.

Two of five AP dispatch boats darted into the thick of the battle. On one of them, *Wanda,* a veteran correspondent, John P. Dunning, rescued a Spanish officer and eight sailors from a sinking enemy destroyer and was enthusiastically kissed on both cheeks by the officer. Dunning also boarded the USS *Gloucester* and interviewed the defeated Cervera after he had been picked out of the water near his disabled flagship.

The battle off Santiago was over at 1:30 p.m. that Sunday. While *Wanda* and other press boats were racing to file the story of the latest American victory at the cable station at Kingston, Jamaica, Admiral Sampson took advantage of his position on land that day to flash the White House directly as soon as he learned of the end of the fighting. Both President McKinley and Secretary of the Navy John D. Long, therefore, became the first to receive the news.

By lucky chance, Matthew Tighe of the Hearst newspapers alone was covering the White House that day. When he saw Long leaving the executive offices late that day, the reporter as a matter of course asked the navy chief whether there was any news from Cuba. Long drew Sampson's message from his pocket and said: "I've just received this message from Admiral Sampson saying the fleet under his command has engaged and destroyed the Spanish squadron. I have just shown it to the President. Perhaps it will be of some interest."

Tighe ran for the wire, scoring a two-hour beat. The admiral, who had been conferring with General William R. Shafter ashore during the action, had evidently seized the opportunity to get the victory message through American headquarters at Guantanamo. For many years, it was a Washington legend that Hearst was so grateful that he guaranteed Tighe a job for life. In any event, Tighe died in the Hearst service.[21]

Amid all the shouting and scrambling and posturing, the shooting and fighting and dying in that short war, the United States became a major world power at Spain's expense. One of its authors, Hearst, established his New York *Journal* as a leader with the New York *World* in the dizzying competition that was typical of the way journalism then was conducted in New York City.[22] Hearst himself, like him or not, now was one of the most formidable forces in the land. Only one other man who had wanted this war achieved more in the few months it lasted—Theodore Roosevelt.

YOUNG LION OF BRITAIN

Toward the end of the Boer War in South Africa, a very young correspondent exclaimed in despair, "Alas! The days of newspaper enterprise in war are over. What can one do with a censor, a 48-hour delay and a 50-word limit on a wire?"[23]

The reporter was Winston Spencer Churchill, serving in the dual role of lieutenant in the South African Light Horse and correspondent for the London *Morning Post* at £250 ($1,250) a month. As he put his position, "It is better to be making the news than taking it, to be an actor rather than a critic."[24]

Churchill's beginnings as a correspondent went back to the second Cuban war of independence in 1895, when José Marti was leading a hopeless revolt against Spanish rule.[25] Covering for the London *Daily Graphic,* as his father once had done before him in another war, the 21-year-old Britisher chose to observe on the Spanish side. It was just as well. The uprising didn't last long. Toward the end of that year, Marti died at the battle of Los Rios and the revolution collapsed.[26]

After that, Churchill was in India with the 4th Queens Own Hussars in 1897 to subdue a native leader known as the Mad Mullah. Instead of sitting in the barracks with the rest of the troops, the newcomer chose to go to the front as a correspondent for the London *Daily Telegraph,* but once again, that conflict was quickly ended through the force of British arms.[27] In the following year, he was in the Sudan as a lieutenant in the 21st Lancers and a correspondent for the London *Morning Post.*[28] This time, the war took an ugly turn when 55,000 screaming dervishes flung themselves at a British expeditionary force under Lord Kitchener. But once again, the soldier-correspondent was able to fight, cover the story, and survive.[29]

In the war against the Boers, which had begun on October 12, 1899, Churchill learned with indignation upon his arrival at Cape Town from England that the British forces everywhere had been thrown on the defensive. Colonel Robert Baden-Powell and his troops were besieged in Mafeking. Kimberly was under attack. Ladysmith was about to be invested.[30]

The conflict was only five weeks old, and Churchill had been at work for only two weeks when he was slightly wounded and captured by the Boers.[31] That day, November 14, he had gone on an armored train which everybody in camp had called a "death trap," to reconnoiter toward Chieveley in Natal. A patrol of about 100 Boers derailed some of the cars, using field guns, then settled down to pound away at the scouting party with shells and rifle fire.

Churchill, with the permission of the commanding officer, called for volunteers to clear the track and get the engine free for a run from danger. For more than an hour, he and the husky soldiers tugged and heaved at the jammed rolling stock, under fire all the while. The engine meanwhile pushed ahead and backed up fruitlessly.

But through a lucky break, the engine was freed of obstacles at last, and Churchill jumped aboard with as many others as the engine could take, including wounded, but it was too late. Three Boers opened fire, and one bullet slightly nicked the soldier-correspondent's hand. He gave up and was taken to Pretoria, where an AP correspondent, Richard Smith, interviewed him and reported he was well.

The New York *World,* which had been using his copy when it was forwarded from London, twinned the story of his capture with a report of the shooting of a major *Morning Post* correspondent, Edward Frederick Knight, who lost an arm in battle at Belmont. The *World*'s headline:

WORLD CORRESPONDENTS SUFFER FATE OF SOLDIERS[32]

Churchill was not one to suffer such a fate for long. On the night of December 12, when the sentries' backs were turned, he scrambled over a wall and into an adjoining garden, waited there for about an hour and when he determined he hadn't been missed, calmly strolled along the crowded streets of Pretoria into the suburbs. At a bridge at the edge of town, he sat down and took stock — £75, four slabs of chocolate, and it was 300 miles to Lourenço Marques and Portuguese territory to the north.

What to do? Find the Deluga Bay Railway. How to judge directions? Follow the stars. It worked. Within a short time, the future prime minister was in a freight car buried under empty sacks covered with coal dust. He fell asleep, exhausted after his adventure. When he awoke, it was nearly dawn and he jumped from the moving train, fearing discovery with the coming of daylight. He landed in a ditch, shaken but unhurt. Nearby, he found a pool of clear water and drank his fill.

For the next five days, he took refuge in the wooded countryside during the oppressive heat of the day and walked steadily north by night. He became aware all too soon that he was a much-wanted prisoner, for the Boers had circulated a poster:

Englishman, 25 years old, about five feet eight inches high, indifferent build, walks a little with a bend forward, pale appearance, reddish hair, small moustache hardly perceptible, talks through his nose, cannot pronounce the letter S properly and does not know any Dutch.

On the sixth day of his escape, desperate after subsisting on nothing but his chocolate bars, he spotted a freight train at the Middleburg station and buried himself under sacks, this time stuffed with soft merchandise. "The hard floor was littered with gritty coal dust and made a most uncomfortable bed," he later wrote. "The heat was almost stifling.

I was resolved, however, that nothing should lure or compel me from my hiding place until I reached Portuguese territory."

The Boers searched the train at the border, but they didn't probe deeply enough. After 60 hours of misery, Churchill arrived at Lourenço Marques, a hero the whole length and breadth of Britain.[33] As he wrote triumphantly of his exploit in the *Morning Post* on December 21:

> "I am very weak, but I am free.
> "I have lost many pounds, but I am lighter in heart.
> "I shall also avail myself of every opportunity from this moment to urge with earnestness an unflinching and uncompromising prosecution of the war."[34]

For the other correspondents, there also were mishaps, good luck, and tragedy. Richard Harding Davis, determined as an American journalist to leave the British side and go over to the Boers who were more popular in the United States, made it with his bride in a cart. He was taken to Pretoria and shown every courtesy by General Christian DeWet. But once on the Boer side, Davis showed a different aspect of his character — a touch of steel under the cotton candy popular approach to the fortunes and misfortunes of war.

"As I see it," he wrote of the Boers, "it has been a Holy War, this war of the Burgher crusader, and his motives are as fine as any that ever called a Minute Man from his farm or sent a knight of the Cross to die for it in Palestine. Still, in spite of his cause, the Boer is losing and in time his end may come and he may fall. But when he falls he will not fall alone; with him will end a great principle — the principle for which our forefathers fought — the right of self-government, the principle of independence."

That wasn't all. Davis attacked Rudyard Kipling for writing about a "good killing" and assailed Churchill for reporting, "We had a good bag today, 10 killed, 17 wounded." Worst of all, he made the British furious by questioning their sportsmanship. For this he was cast into outer darkness by being expelled from the Garrick Club in London. He responded by founding the Order of Pretoria for Americans who had fought for or reported from the Boer side. He, too, was a worthy opponent.[35]

There was an epilogue. After finishing the war by marching with Lieutenant General Ian Hamilton's column for 400 miles from Bloemfontain to Pretoria, Churchill was elected to Parliament and lectured in the United States in defense of the British role in the Boer War. Davis publicly refused to serve on the official reception committee. But because of his friendship and admiration for the new bright hope of the Conservatives in Britain, Davis went to Churchill's hotel to give him a warm private welcome. "That same evening," Davis wrote, "three hours after midnight, he came in, in a blizzard, pounding at our door for food and drink. What is a little war between friends?"[36]

NEW TIMES IN THE FAR EAST

Some of the leading correspondents of the early 20th century were covering the Russo-Japanese War from the Imperial Hotel in Tokyo and hating every moment of it. As the position was described by Willard Straight of the AP:

"The air of the Imperial Hotel was a bright blue from early morn to golden sunset. Famous journalists, veterans of countless campaigns, were held up, bound hand and foot by the dapper little Orientals whose attitude throughout has been greatly wondered at. . . . The situation was unique in the annals of journalism. A government holding the rabid pressmen at a distance, censoring their simplest stories, yet patting them on the back, dining them, wining them, giving them picnics and luncheons and theatrical performances and trying in every way not only to soften their bonds and to make their stay a pleasant one, but siren-like to deaden their sense of duty and their desire to get into the field."[37]

No army had ever taken such strenuous measures before to protect its rear from the prying of journalists, especially foreigners. It was a deadly pattern that was to be emulated in every war that was to follow, leading to countless lamentations over the decline of war correspondence.

Inevitably, the frustrations produced incidents. The pugnacious Jack London, forgetting his Marxian sympathies for the downtrodden, slugged a Japanese groom and had to be extricated from the clutches of Japanese authorities by the fast-talking Richard Harding Davis, backed up by a cable from President Theodore Roosevelt. John Fox, Jr., a proper Harvard man at the beginning of the war, was trailed on suspicion by a Japanese Yale graduate, who unfeelingly tossed him into jail overnight as a spy. Fox was freed next day, forever resolved not to take lightly the counterespionage activities of Yale graduates, Japanese or not.[38]

The correspondents had gone to Tokyo in a rush with the unexpected Japanese triumphs over the Russians at the onset of this latest conflict in which Admiral Heihachiro Togo had attacked Port Arthur on February 6, 1904, two days after Tokyo severed relations with

Russia, and bottled up the Asiatic Russian fleet in the harbor of the Russian base in Siberia.

The correspondents, however, had a surprise of their own for the British-trained Japanese sea champion. The *Times* of London and the New York *Times* had joined forces to put a British correspondent, Lionel James, in charge of the first wireless-equipped ship to cover a naval action, the *Haimun*. James had put his craft off Port Arthur on April 13, when the Russian flagship, *Petropavlovsk*, tried to make it out of the harbor to take on Togo's ships but hit a mine and sank with the loss of most of its crew of 600.

James got his flash through first, inaugurating the era of radio reporting at sea, but the honors that day went to a patient Russian stringer for the AP, M. Kravchenko, who had been sitting on a hilltop overlooking Port Arthur harbor with a spyglass for days on end waiting for just such a move on the part of the desperate Russians. The AP's story was heavily played in the United States despite James's brief moment of glory, a stark reminder that ideas, words, and images that can be communicated to mass publics inevitably dwarf the technical means of communication.

Worse still, after that action in which the remainder of the Russian Asiatic fleet was rendered useless and Port Arthur was doomed, Admiral Togo complained that the *Haimun*'s radio had interfered with his own transmissions and refused to let the big dispatch boat anywhere near his fleet. So did the Russians, smarting from their first defeats both on land and sea.[39]

All through the rest of the spring and summer of 1904, most of the correspondents were kept in Tokyo waiting for the Japanese to move them into Manchuria, where the Japanese army was giving a good account of itself against the heavily favored Russians. Toward the end of July, when Richard Harding Davis and some others at last were mustered aboard an old bucket, the *Heijo Maru*, and promised they could witness the imminent fall of Port Arthur, they were routed north by their captors while the key battle of Liao Yang was being fought in Manchuria. On the night of August 27, 1904, a Japanese briefing officer (also a new invention along with the military censor) reported the Russians obligingly had moved out of Liao Yang without firing a shot and were in flight toward Mukden.

In high dudgeon, Davis and his colleagues were landed at the cablehead at Chefoo so that they could transmit the Japanese announcement of the fall of Liao Yang. While the American veteran was writing his story, a Chinese clerk, learning his identity and importance, murmured, "I congratulate you."

"Why?" Davis asked.

The Chinese bowed and smiled as he was handed the opening of Davis's story about Liao Yang, saying, "Because you are the only correspondent to arrive who has seen the battle of Liao Yang."

Davis protested weakly, "But there was no battle. The Japanese told me themselves they had entered Liao Hang without firing a shot."

The Chinese, apparently delighted to embarrass the Japanese press officer, said, "They have been fighting for six days."[40]

It turned out that Davis's informant was right. The battle at Liao Yang, one of the most critical of the war, had been fought from August 25 to September 4 and finally was reported first not by any harassed foreign correspondent but by the great Japanese newspapers — *Asahi, Mainichi,* and *Jiji,* all of which had their own war correspondents in the field and had been given an exclusive by the considerate Japanese military, always ready to take care of their own at a time of triumph.

Every time from then on when there was a Japanese victory, the great national dailies in Japan put out extras. At one point, Asahi Shimbun, emulating American methods, chartered a fast ship to speed its reports from the field to the nearest land wire. Mainichi broke a first-person story of the battle of Nanshan from one of its correspondents who had gone under fire as a coolie attached to the 11th Japanese divison.

The disgusted Davis, who was being paid $1,000 a week for his war correspondence at the turn of the century, poured out his frustrations on paper after being shut out at Liao Yang: "Six months we had waited only to miss by three days the greatest battle since Gettysburg and Sedan. And by a lie!"

The American specials continued to be bottled up and led around by the nose, and so the foreign agencies, especially the AP, turned to the use of English-speaking Russians to cover the war from the Russian side. The Russian writer Nemirovich Danchenko, for example, rode the last train out of Port Arthur in order to cover the battle at Liao Yang for the AP. Another of the AP's Russians, Nicholas E. Popov, writing under the name of Kirilov, was sending back dispatches while the battle was in progress, courtesy of the uncensored Russian military, when a Russian officer sent the AP this explanation for an interruption in the transmission: "M. Kirilov . . . was shot through the right lung while standing by our battery and fell back suffering intense agony. . . . Yet, he insisted on being placed on a horse so he could get to Liao Yang to file this dispatch."[41]

And so it went throughout the disastrous fall and winter for Russian arms with the Japanese victorious by land and sea. On January 2, 1905, Port Arthur surrendered. And at Mukden, in a battle that lasted from

February 20 to March 9, the Russian army was annihilated by the Japanese commanded by General Prince Iwao Oyama.

It became evident then the the Russian Baltic fleet of 42 ancient "battle wagons" was the czar's last hope. Under Vice Admiral Zinovi Petrovich Rozhestvensky, a proud and able officer, the fleet steamed around Africa, across the Indian Ocean, and past Singapore with wire services reporting its progress until it turned north into the Pacific and headed for Tsushima Strait, where Admiral Togo was waiting for them. The world watched and wondered, knowing a decisive battle at sea was inevitable, but all means of spot coverage had been blocked off, and even the first wireless dispatch ship had been sent back to Hong Kong.

The first news came out of Tokyo from Martin Egan of the AP, who had gotten a seemingly harmless dispatch through the Japanese censors:

TOKYO, MAY 28, 9 P.M. (AP) — TRANSMITTABLE INFORMATION CONCERNING TODAY'S HISTORIC EVENTS IN THE NEIGHBORHOOD OF THE TSU ISLANDS IS LIMITED TO THE BARE FACT THAT ROZHESTVENSKY'S MAIN FLEET . . . APPEARED IN THE STRAITS OF KOREA. ALL OTHER INFORMATION IS WITHHELD.

Two words, "historic events," were the tipoff, and the AP was soon able to confirm the Japanese victory at sea from the few Russian ships that had escaped Togo and reached Vladivostok. Howard N. Thompson, the AP correspondent in Moscow, was the first to give the bad news to Czar Nicholas II. At the end of an awesome display of human agony, Rozhestvensky had said, "We weren't strong enough and God gave us no luck."

The rise of Japan as a major world power was complete. In 31 hours, Togo's warships had destroyed the Russian fleet that had sailed halfway around the world to its doom.[42] Thenceforth, Japan would become the foremost rival of the United States in the Pacific. The sneak attack at Pearl Harbor would come 36 years later; the American atomic blasts over Hiroshima and Nagasaki in 40 years.

But in 1905, President Theodore Roosevelt acted as the mediator who brought peace to the empire of the Rising Sun and the slowly dissolving empire of the Czar at Portsmouth, New Hampshire. The first great international peace conference ever held on American soil was successfully concluded when Russia acknowledged Japan's claim to the Korean peninsula, and the Japanese gave up their demand for a huge indemnity that had been the crux of the negotiation.

The climax came on the last day of the Portsmouth conference, September 5, 1905. At 11:50 a.m., when many correspondents believed the American mediation had failed and the war might be renewed, the door to the conference room flew open and the chief Russian negotiator, Count Sergei Yulyevich Witte, gravely confronted the correspondents. "Gospoda, mir," he said in Russian. "Gentlemen, peace."[43]

Because Count Witte had obtained unexpectedly generous terms from the Japanese, Czar Nicholas called him to St. Petersburg at once to try to settle the workers' revolution of 1905. Partly caused by the war, it had been raging since January 22, 1905, "Bloody Sunday," when the Czar's police had shattered a peaceful workers' delegation bound for the Winter Palace to appeal for more considerate treatment.

Witte succeeded in temporarily easing the Czar's troubles by producing a document called the October Manifesto, the creation of a parliament, the Duma, with what turned out to be an illusory freedom of action in behalf of a distressed people. By December, the Czar already had limited the Duma's power, the remnants of the returning army had put down the insurrection, and hundreds of people had been executed under the rule of a new premier, Piotr Arkadevich Stolypin.

Just as Japan's power was expanding and bringing new times to the Far East, the Russian Empire was sinking. To the British correspondent Henry W. Nevinson, Count Leo Tolstoy confided his bleak vision of Russia's future in an interview at his great country house, *Yasnaya Polyana* (bright plain), near Tula, toward the latter part of 1905:

> You are a young man and I am old, but as you grow older you will find, as I have found, that day follows day, and there does not seem much change in you, till suddenly it is found that the age has become old. It is finished, it is out of date.
>
> The present movement in Russia is not a riot; it is not even a revolution; it is the end of an age. We ought to aim at something entirely different from your worn-out methods of government.[44]

Vladimir Ilich Ulyanov, better known by his pen name of Lenin,* was already plotting that "something different" with his Communist colleagues in Moscow through which he would ascend to power in place of the Czar in only a little more than a decade. That, too, was a part of the consequences of the war that had brought new times to the Far East.[45]

---

*He never used "Nikolai" Lenin as a pen name, but did sometimes sign himself as "N Lenin." "Nikolai," however, immediately suggested itself to many people as a Russian name beginning with N, and he became Nikolai Lenin in many minds.

THE STAR-SPANGLED CARTEL

A slender, thin-lipped stranger from Chicago called on Baron Herbert de Reuter in London on St. Patrick's Day, 1893. He was Melville Elijah Stone, the first general manager of the newly organized Associated Press of Illinois. No hard-pressed prime minister ever approached a foreign potentate with a greater need for an immediate alliance.[46]

Baron de Reuter, despite his scholarly appearance, was an eminently practical agency manager and knew perfectly well that Stone desperately needed Reuter's foreign service. The old New York AP had just collapsed, and most of its members had gone to a rival agency known as the United Press (no connection with a later agency of the same name). The remainder had rallied around Victor Fremont Lawson, who with other Midwestern publishers had incorporated the old Western AP as a new organization, the Illinois AP, with Stone in charge.[47]

With scant discussion, the baron laid down his terms, take it or leave it. There would be a 10-year alliance between the new AP and Reuters, Havas, and Wolff, with a self-renewing ten-year extension. It would be, in the Baron's view, "a close alliance for the exclusive interchange with each other, outside their respective territories, of all telegraphic news received by them." The annual fee to be paid to Reuters, $17,500, was nominal, but Stone realized that the service commitment was enormous. Still, he had to have the foreign news that Reuters and its allies could provide. Without argument, he signed and thereby once again wrapped the Stars and Stripes about the grand cartel.[48]

The new AP thereupon cleaned up, persuading the most powerful newspapers in the United States to join, with only a few exceptions, and electing Lawson as its first president. The hard-working Chicagoan had proved himself a super-salesman once the organization was assured of a dependable foreign service file out of London. As a result, the old UP went into receivership in 1897.

However, three years later, the Supreme Court of Illinois denied the right of the new AP to withhold its services from a rebellious member, the Chicago *Inter Ocean,* or to any other newspaper that applied for it. At one stroke, Lawson and Stone found themselves out of the agency business. But the resourceful Stone quickly organized a new committee and obtained permission in New York to form the Associated Press of New York as a new organization on May 22, 1900.[49]

In that way, the AP at last had achieved the status of a legal, national newsgathering cooperative which was ruled by its own membership. Although Frank B. Noyes of the Washington *Evening Star* was named as its first president, it was Stone as general manager who was the real power in the organization. He saw to it that certain rules were liberalized to avert what had proved to be a fatal defect in the Illinois charter. In effect, therefore, the new AP in New York sought to preserve the rights of each member in his franchise and protected him against rivals in his territory who also wanted membership in the organization.[50]

Stone wasted no time on self-congratulation. As soon as the agency's business was on a firm base in New York, he took the first significant step to ensure that the AP would always have at least a minimal foreign service of its own. It was delicate work. He could not do anything to offend Reuters, Havas, or Wolff. Yet, he realized that his members would not long be content to take merely what news the British agency and its European allies were willing to send to the United States. The tradition of American independence in journalism was too strong.

"From the beginning," Stone wrote, "the AP had only one foreign agency and that was located in the British metropolis. It was from a British news agency or through English dispatches that we derived all our European news. True, there were interesting letters from the continental capitals, but long before their arrival or publication the story of any important event had been told from London and had made its impress on the American mind — an impress that was not easy to correct. . . . Thus, British opinion in large measure became our opinion."[51]

Stone did not have to make any similar observation about the foreign contributions of the Havas Agency to his membership because some of its intergovernmental operations were notorious and its critics, inside and outside France, were legion.

In due course, he moved directly after the Spanish-American War to make a modest expansion in the AP's foreign service. He made three trips abroad, first opening a Paris office and another in Berlin with the agreement of the respective governments. In Italy, both King Victor Emmanuel III and the 93-year-old Pope Leo XIII agreed to receive an AP correspondent for Rome and the Vatican, Salvatore Cortesi, known far and wide as the *Commendatore*.*

Stone also visited Czar Nicholas II at the Winter Palace in St. Petersburg to tell him bluntly that "a wall has been built up around (Russia) and the fact that no correspondent for a foreign paper can live and work here has resulted in a traffic in false Russian news that is

---

*Cortesi's wife, Isabelle Lauder Cochrane of Boston, was the first New York *Times* correspondent in Rome. His son, Arnaldo, was the paper's correspondent there, off and on, until his retirement in 1963.

most hurtful." The Czar agreed to let an AP correspondent work in his capital.

In this way, the American news agency was able to bring news from some of its own correspondents into its own file for the first time. Admittedly, the coverage from Paris, Berlin, and Rome was thin at first, and the grand cartel had to forward coverage of London and all other foreign points of consequence. But after more than half a century, the American point of view at least had been recognized abroad in the agency business. That was Stone's unique contribution to foreign correspondence — something of increasing importance as the United States continued to grow as a major world power.[52]

———

As long as everything went well, nobody could question Reuter's methods. Yet, it was perfectly clear to Stone and others in the agency field that the baron was letting his agency lag far behind the times. In the age of the wireless and the airplane, the telephone and the automobile, Reuters was still in the horse-and-buggy era.

As early as 1872, the firm of E. Remington in the United States had put out a typewriter (The laptop computer hadn't even been thought of at the time). But a decade later, Reuters was still doing everything by hand. It didn't really give up what amounted to quill pen journalism until the Boer War.

Similarly, the Baron was highly suspicious of the telephone, for which Alexander Graham Bell had taken out his first American patent in 1876. A year later, the Boston *Globe* had received the first news from a reporter 18 miles away. But to Reuters, it was a sensation when in 1882 a telephone was used for the first time to notify London subscribers of the bombardment of Alexandria. It also was many years before Reuters gave up its gray-uniformed messengers who delivered confirmation of copies of everything sent by electronic devices. When blinding speed was required, bulletins for years still were delivered by messengers in hansom cabs.[53]

Even so, Reuters's dominance in foreign news gathering and transmission was still so great that no rival domestic agency was interested in competing with the giant. For a few anxious years in the 1890s, the *Times* of London for its own reasons had tried to weaken the agency and reduce its foreign coverage by backing a new agency known as Dalziel. That effort failed, too. The most any rival was able to do at that stage in the grand cartel's operations was to reduce Reuters's role in the immensely profitable field of financial reporting, which is what happened when the Exchange Telegraph began a rival service.

Reuters didn't really start modernizing until the last years of the 19th century and then only through the cooperation of the British domestic agency, Press Association (PA), which had been organized as a membership cooperative on the style of the AP. Through a joint special service, PA and Reuters began offering subscribers a faster service that would be paid for by the word by any paper desiring it in addition to the regular Reuters general file.[54]

After that, the grand cartel itself became a major problem despite the division of the world into zones that supposedly guaranteed a Reuters monopoly in agency coverage of some of the most important foreign news of the day. Realistically, it became impossible to separate Havas, Wolff, Stefani, and even the smaller Austrian Korrespondenz Bureau in Vienna from the influence of their respective governments.

Wolff, for example, was under the control of Bismarck, who was jealous of the power and influence of Havas and also suspected Reuters of opposing German interests. Stefani, as an Italian agency, took its news from Havas but its orders from Rome. The same was true of the Austrian agency in Vienna. It was a threadbare myth that a news agency could operate in Europe with complete independence of its government under all circumstances. If Baron de Reuter had ever believed it, and it is doubtful that he did, he was quickly disabused.

Despite the political stability Baron de Reuter managed to preserve in his agency at home and abroad, he was continually plagued by the greatest weakness of the agency business, the enormous expense of gathering news and the reluctance of subscribers to face the economic facts of foreign correspondence. Reuters twice tried Havas's remedy, the creation of a special branch to solicit and place advertisements, and twice failed.

Instead, Reuters tried a remittance business and created a bank to handle it. Primarily because telegraphic remittances were profitable, Reuters reserves rose from £30,000 in 1900 to £100,000 in 1910. The upshot was the transformation of the Reuters Bank in 1912 into the British Commercial Bank with a paid-up capital of £500,000 in Reuters ownership and public subscription permitted at £10 a share. But with World War I looming on the horizon of Europe, the fate of this venture—and Reuters itself—was anything but bright as expenses mounted.

This was primarily the reason for American concern about unusual influences affecting Reuters, Havas, and Wolff that so often disturbed both the AP management and its membership. Kent Cooper of the AP put the position this way:

"Actually, the story is that, after the turn of the century, interna-

tional bankers headed by the Rothschilds became interested in the ownership of all three agencies. Certainly, they were important customers.
Whether or not they were owners, they were credited with influence
with all three agencies second only to the influence of their respective
governments."[55]

Yet, because the AP had made its agreement with the European agencies in 1893, it had to put up with this messy state of affairs or get out
of the grand cartel with complete responsibility for its own news-gathering operations. The cost would have been too great; and so the AP
was stuck for the time being, even though it was now selling its service
to Canada in violation of its pledge to its three great European associates.

By all odds, Havas presented the greatest embarrassment when it
came to influence peddling. Regardless of political advantages and personalities, every French government that came to power regarded cooperation with Havas as a priceless advantage. That worked both ways, of
course. The result was the granting of subsidies in one form or another
by the government to the agency that eventually reached Fr. 30,000,000
annually.

This is what Pierre Lazareff, a leading French newspaper publisher
and a scathing critic of Havas, had to say about the agency:

> Havas handled the publicity for foreign governments, for big business
> enterprises, financial publicity, both private and official [the French bud-
> get]. In addition, Havas handled propaganda campaigns on behalf of var-
> ious French products as well as stocks and bonds. Through its grip on the
> distribution of news and advertising, the Havas Agency was able to exert
> control over the biggest newspapers in France and gradually acquired an
> actual interest, either direct or indirect, in those properties. No other ad-
> vertising agency could possibly offer any serious competition. Nor was
> any other news agency ever able to organize effectively in France.[56]

The truth is that outside the United States and Britain, it was difficult
then—and even more troublesome today—to find any independent
newspaper or group of newspapers that were prosperous enough to pay
the huge assessments necessary to operate a true global news service for
an agency or a syndicate. Whether those assessments were in the form
of membership fees or payments to a profit-making corporation, the
ultimate result was about the same.

Moreover, it remained true that the relatively few rich newspapers
with foreign staffs were the ones that also had to support the cost of
global news-gathering by an agency. For all its seeming advantages,
therefore, the grand cartel, with its star-spangled cover that gave a

world-news monopoly to a few agencies, was at best an uneasy alliance. If there were doubts about the honor and independence collectively represented in the partnership, how could there be universal public confidence in agency news?

The doubts about the system were mounting as World War I approached with all its strains on the governments of Europe.

A new American wire service, the United Press Associations, was incorporated on June 21, 1907, with contracts to sell its daily report to 369 newspapers. It was operating on a shoestring and had returned a profit of only $1,200 in its first full year of operation in 1909; and so it didn't seem to be much of a threat to the global agency cartel, much less to the AP, with its more than 800 members and an expense budget for 1910 of $2,700,000.[57]

Still, UP's founder, Edward Wyllis Scripps, had a record of accomplishment that could not be disregarded. At 53, when he incorporated the UP, he had run $80, a scanty education, and a lot of gall into a multi-million-dollar newspaper chain; and now he was looking for a general manager to play hell with the AP. The best man he could find, Roy Wilson Howard, turned up as the New York manager of the UP at 25.

Scripps and his partner, Milton McRae, had put together the Scripps-McRae chain of newspapers by making each new acquisition profitable before buying another. None was outstanding individually, but they proved to be impressive as a money-making unit. Scripps also had put together three small agencies — the Scripps-McRae Press Association, the Scripps News Association, and the Publishers Press Association — into the new UP. Howard, having been the $33-a-week manager of the New York bureau of the Publishers Press Association, had to stand inspection before Scripps at his California ranch, Miramar, soon after joining UP.

The publisher had seemed sufficiently impressed with his New York bureau manager to confide that he never had wanted to stay with the AP. "I'm not interested in just making money out of the United Press," he told Howard. "I believe there must not be a news monopoly in this country. At one time, I would have gone into the AP but it would have limited my own operations and it would have put into the hands of the board of directors of the AP the fate of any young man in America who wanted to start a new newspaper. I believe that any bona fide newspaper in the country should be able to buy the services of the UP."

It developed that Scripps had always wanted to build a wire service on the ruins of the old UP, which had long since gone out of business; and he gave these instructions to Howard, who was presently to be elevated to the presidency of the UP:

> "Always see that the news report is handled objectively as far as it is humanly possible. You must not be biased or take sides in controversies. You won't always succeed in being completely objective but you must always try to tell both sides of any dispute.
>
> "And second, never make a contract to deliver news exclusively to one newspaper in any territory."
>
> "Not even in cities where you have newspapers?" Howard asked.
>
> The answer was, "Never."[58]

Scripps meant to operate by the AP's rules, except that he would charge fees for service rather than membership rates. And this is what Howard set out to do as the UP's president beginning in 1908, after the death of his predecessor, John Vandercook, in Chicago.

Regardless of what happened to UP when it fell on hard times toward the end of the 20th century, it began as a first-rate news agency under Howard's management, with a report of 10,000 to 12,000 words a day, hard-hitting reporting by a few veteran professionals, and a number of bright but underpaid youngsters who were out to make a reputation. Being well aware of the enormous cost of a fully developed foreign report, Howard was careful not to attempt too much.

As his first foreign staff, he put Ed L. Keen in London after Keen scored a beat on General Emilio Aguinaldo's revolt in the Philippines, William Philip Simms in Paris, and Henry Wood in Rome. Even with limited resources, Howard made such an impression that Baron de Reuter invited him to London in 1912 to consider entering into an alliance with Reuters, Havas, and Wolff, replacing the AP.

The offer came during one of the grand cartel's periodic maneuvers in which each member usually tested the intentions of the others. In any event, even though Howard did go to London and meet with the Baron on the basis of a vote of approval by UP's board of directors, nothing came of the suggested replacement of the AP in the grand cartel. Nor was the AP unduly worried.

In retrospect, Howard cooled off considerably about the prospect then or later that UP might join such a global cartel. He finally realized that, if he did so, he would be bartering away the one advantage the UP had to offer its subscribers in the United States and elsewhere — its independence.[59]

There was one other news agency in the United States at the time, Hearst's International News Service (INS), but INS never was a threat to any other group in the field, certainly not to the AP. Even Hearst himself was never enthusiastic about INS saying, "The trouble is that feeling a loyalty to the AP and having newspapers in its membership, I am competing with myself by having to operate another press association."

Few Hearst editors had much respect for INS at the beginning, but it managed to exist primarily on the costs that were levied against the Hearst papers that couldn't get the AP, the prosperous New York *Journal* among them. Even though Hearst could have bought UP at that time, he was reluctant to do so because it was the offspring of the competitive Scripps McRae chain (later Scripps-Howard). It was years before sheer necessity forced him to overcome his dislike.

Long before that, however, INS was in deep trouble. During World War I, the British and French governments barred the Hearst agency from the use of their cables. While charges against Hearst of pro-German sympathy undoubtedly motivated the Allied governments, the immediate cause was what the British called "continued garbling of messages and breach of faith." INS denied it, but the prohibition was enforced.

When INS continued to operate from Britain and France, the AP investigated, formally accused INS of news piracy, and won an injunction restraining INS from using AP material—a judgment that was upheld by the Supreme Court. That was a long step toward the establishment of a property right in the news, for which Baron de Reuter also had been fighting in contesting news piracy against Reuters in Britain.[60]

Late in the century, UP finally absorbed INS, but the combined United Press International (UPI) service by that time was no longer a threat either to AP or to the foreign agencies. And the grand cartel itself had seen its best days, no longer being able to control the vigorously expanding Americans in their drive to dominate the gathering and distribution of foreign news on a global basis.

THE PRINTER FROM KNOXVILLE

Adolph Simon Ochs, a 38-year-old printer from Knoxville, Tennessee, decided one spring day in 1896 that he wanted to buy the New York *Times,* which, so he had heard, was on the verge of bankruptcy. Caught between prestige papers like the *Herald* and *Sun* on one side and the sensational *Journal* and *World* on the other, the *Times* in a quiet and gentlemanly way seemed about to pass from the turbulent metropolitan scene to which it had at one time contributed so much.

In 1871, it had saved the city from financial disaster by exposing the multimillion-dollar grafting of Tammany's Boss William Marcy Tweed and his corrupt political gang. Ten years later, the paper saved the US Treasury millions of dollars in exposing contractors and their political cronies who were looting the post offices in what came to be called the Star Route Mail Frauds — deliveries made by private carriers on remote mail routes.

But now, the newspaper could not even save itself in the grip of bankers who were about to throw it into bankruptcy. If Ochs or anybody else believed the newspaper worth saving, immediate and decisive action was necessary.

And so, on a quiet evening a few days later, the editor of the *Times*, Charles R. Miller, received Ochs as an unexpected caller at the editor's home in mid-Manhattan more or less as a courtesy. Actually, Miller saw little hope in the small, dark-haired Tennessean with the courageous blue eyes who had intruded on him just as he was about to leave for the theater.

But then, Miller didn't know anything about Adolph Ochs. He had been born March 12, 1858, a son of a German-Jewish immigrant who lived in modest circumstances in Knoxville. At 14, he had begun as a printer's devil on the Knoxville *Chronicle*. A year later, he left school and became a printer. At 20, he made a down payment on the Chattanooga *Times* nearby with $250 cash, which he had borrowed, and a lot of nerve; in a few years, he had made good and paid off the remaining $5,500 of the purchase price.

Still, that was Chattanooga. This was New York.

Ochs must have seen how greatly Miller doubted him. Yet, with characteristic enthusiasm, the printer turned journalist began talking about the *Times* and his plans for it. The suave, polished Miller listened to this direct, rough-hewn Tennessean who had become a small city newspaper proprietor. And the more he listened, the more interested he became. He sent his wife and children to the theater without him. When they returned, his mind was made up.

With the support of the editor of the *Times*, Ochs presented his case next to the dubious bankers who were looking for a buyer. The newcomer said he realized the *Times* had only 9,000 circulation, $300,000 in debts, and continued weekly losses of $2,500, but he went on confidently:

"I know that I can manage the *Times* as a decent, dignified and independent newspaper and still wipe out the deficit. I'm sure that I can make it pay 5 per cent a year interest. I could change your $100,000 a year loss into at least a $40,000 a year surplus."

The bankers were impressed. One said, "We're prepared to pay you $50,000 a year to do just that."

Ochs rejected the offer, explaining, "I simply will not take the job for merely a fixed salary, not even if you offer me $150,000. I am not looking for employment. Unless you offer me eventual control of the property — based, of course, on my making good — there is no sense in keeping on with these negotiations."

The bankers dithered, and the *Times* went into receivership. But when Ochs raised $75,000 by risking everything he owned and obtained another $125,000 from others, he won his prize, and Miller became his life-long associate. In this inauspicious manner, Ochs laid the groundwork for the creation of one of the world's dominant newspapers and an independent foreign service second to none.[61] He did so well that within a year he was in possession of 51 percent of the *Times*'s stock, added to the paper's circulation and advertising, and injected new spirit in his small, downcast staff.

But as the Spanish-American War developed and the sensational *Journal* and *World* blanketed the story with their phalanxes of correspondents, Ochs saw that he could be wiped out if he didn't do something fast. All that was available to him was to drop the newsstand price of the *Times* to one cent, denounce yellow journalism with steadiness and vigor, and print all the AP copy he could get about the war.

It was an impossible position for a paper that became the acknowledged leader in the publication of world news a half-century later, but it was the best Ochs could offer. "It is the price of the paper, not its character, that has changed," the *Times* explained loftily to its readers. None other than Andrew Carnegie agreed. Being a hard man with a penny, the Scotsman sent word that it was "the best cent's worth in the world." And on page 1, the *Times* plastered its slogan that has remained there ever since: "All The News That's Fit To Print."

By September 1899, the *Times* was selling 76,260 copies a day, and advertising was up. While it wasn't one-tenth the circulation revved up during the war by Pulitzer and Hearst, Ochs began dreaming of an uptown building in a spot that he wanted to call Times Square, and he bargained with the *Times* of London to buy its foreign service.[62]

In all truth, Ochs's early preoccupation with foreign news was one of the most practical concepts of the kind of newspaper the *Times* would have to be if it was to rise to worldwide fame and affluence. Never mind that the American public was neither informed nor even interested in the general run of foreign news, except when the country was at war; in a great city such as New York or Chicago at the turn of the century, tens of thousands of immigrant peoples from Europe who had come to America to seek a better life still wanted to pay their one, two, or three cents a day to learn whatever they could of conditions from which they had fled.

Joseph Pulitzer knew that, having been an immigrant from Hungary. And Ochs knew it, too, as the son of an immigrant from Germany. That was a part of their strength in building a solid base for their circulation, war or no war. As a stunt, Ochs even spent $50,000, in association with his brother, George, the general manager of the Chattanooga *Times,* to issue the first international edition of the New York *Times* at the Paris Exposition of 1900.

Four years later, when the 375-foot Times Tower was completed at Broadway and 42d Street, later called Times Square, Adolph Simon Ochs stood with a great crowd outside his own building. He listened to his 11-year-old daughter, Iphigene, standing with silver trowel over the newly-laid cornerstone that January 18, 1904:

"I dedicate this building to the uses of the New York *Times.* May those who labor herein see the right and serve it with courage and intelligence for the welfare of mankind, the best interests of the United States and its people, and for decent and dignified journalism, and may the blessing of God ever rest upon them."[63]

The printer from Knoxville, who had become the publisher of the New York *Times,* would devote the remainder of his life to the kind of service for which his daughter had just prayed. It would not be long before his newspaper would replace the hallowed *Times* of London as the standard-bearer of independence in the dissemination and interpretation of foreign news. He, Adolph Simon Ochs, would become a power in the journalism of his country and of the world. In so doing, he would inevitably clash one day with the foreign news cartel of his time — and the cartel would be the loser.

It so happened, as the New York *Times* was reviving in strength, that the *Times* of London was in drastic decline.

Arthur Fraser Walter, the hereditary proprietor of the London paper, had tried to keep up appearances at all costs since the turn of the century, but to no avail. The *Times* was sinking.

And yet, the fourth Walter still had enough spirit to put down the arrogant Lord Northcliffe, who wanted to add the *Times* to his vast holdings. The *Times*'s proprietor not long before had flung a contemptuous challenge at the Napoleon of Fleet Street:

"What would you do with the *Times?*"

With silken scorn, Northcliffe had given as good as he received: "I should make it worth threepence, Mr. Walter."[64]

Now, however, Walter could no longer afford to taunt the newspaper peer. After a century and a quarter of enormous prestige, the *Times* had become an expensive luxury at best; a bore at worst. Its foreign service, maintained at great cost, was draining off its life blood.

Such mistakes as the long and costly effort to ruin Charles Stewart Parnell, the "uncrowned king of Ireland," had damaged the newspaper's prestige and cost it public support. A decision to run a book club in conjunction with the paper, a fantastic effort to recoup its losses, had gone sour. The hundred or so stockholders, finding that they were receiving little or nothing on their investment, had begun a rebellion against the management as early as 1898. Finally, on July 31, 1907, it was all over. That day, the Chancery Court ordered the dissolution of the *Times*'s partnership and the sale of the newspaper.

Northcliffe, who had won a fortune and a peerage out of publishing cheap, popular journals and establishing his journalistic authority by founding the London *Daily Mail* in 1896, was ready to take over. On March 16, 1908, he won the court's approval for the purchase of the *Times* for £320,000. He let the *Times* stagger along for four years until he put his own man, Geoffrey Dawson, in the editor's Chair (always spelled with a capital *C* at the *Times*) on September 24, 1912.[65]

As it turned out, Northcliffe was his own editor both on the *Times* and on the *Daily Mail,* and he dabbled in his popular mass-circulation *Mirror* whenever he took a notion. He was possessed that war with Germany was imminent and began receiving reports directly from the *Times*'s foreign correspondents. He brought in Wickham Steed as foreign editor of the *Times* and asked both the *Times* and the *Mail* correspondents in Berlin for long, confidential messages.

Northcliffe even set up a German War Emergency Fund of £20,000 for the use of his editors to gather news when the conflict broke, ordered more background pieces for European points, of interest, and shook up the *Times*'s foreign staff. He wanted no more stately journalistic think pieces from the leisurely, mostly old-fashioned *Times* correspondents. Instead, he ordered short, sharp news stories, and after a time, he began getting them from his newer men. It would take a long time, however, to modernize the *Times* (it was not until May 3, 1966, that the paper put news instead of ads on its front page).[66] To be sure, The *Times* still had the influence of its great name and its historic past, but — as it was put at a later date in its official history — the paper "wasn't in it" with the kind of foreign news staff that was being assembled even then by the New York *Times*.

Ochs and Miller meanwhile were working hard to catch up with Pulitzer and Hearst in New York. One of Ochs's enthusiasms, the news of science and exploration, became a prime weapon to help him advance the cause of the New York *Times* later in the century. But at the outset, the paper failed dismally — along with the rest of the American press — to recognize the coming of flight.

When the Wright brothers flew their awkward aircraft for 59 seconds for the first time on December 17, 1903, near Kitty Hawk, N.C., only the Norfolk *Virginian-Pilot* took notice of it. The AP filed merely a brief account. The New York *Times* didn't record the event until Christmas Day, when it reported the Wrights wanted to sell their invention to the government.[67]

In Europe meanwhile, Northcliffe as early as 1902 had noted that he had driven to Monte Carlo in his "steam-traveling carriage," one of the first automobiles, to watch a young Brazilian, Alberto Santos Dumont, fly a dirigible balloon. But there is no record that the *Times* was interested in flight that early, even though Northcliffe was urging his editors at the *Daily Mail* to go after the story. He had grasped the importance of flight quicker than anybody else in the business on both sides of the Atlantic. When Santos Dumont flew 250 yards in a heavier-than-air machine in 1906, the newspaper peer rebuked his *Daily Mail* editors for not featuring the event.

To one unfortunate, Norchliffe bawled, "Don't you realize, man, that England is no longer an island?"

To whet public interest in flight, Northcliffe offered £10,000 for the first aviator who would fly from London to Manchester and was laughed at for his pains. It happened in 1910, when Louis Paulhan did it. Another Northcliffe prize for £1,000 for the first flight over the English Channel was won by the Frenchman, Louis Bleriot, on July 25, 1909, when he landed near Dover Castle after a 37-minute flight from France and surprised the *Daily Mail*'s reporters who were still asleep at the time.[68]

It was Northcliffe's furious promotion of flight in the *Daily Mail* that helped jar the Americans into action. In 1910, the New York *Times* stole a beat on a Pulitzer Prize flight, which the New York *World* had sponsored from Albany to New York. When the *World* ignored a young flier named Glenn H. Curtiss, the *Times* followed him and was the first to report that he had flown 150 miles along the Hudson River at an average speed of 54.18 miles an hour on March 29.[69]

Unlike the automobile, which had gained acceptance slowly, the airplane eventually was presented to the world in a wild burst of enthusiasm on both sides of the Atlantic. The newspaper reading public loved it. The more papers the airplane sold, the greater were the prizes that were offered. And quietly, in the war offices of a swiftly arming Europe, military leaders studied the possibilities of this extraordinary new weapon. They did not have to do a great deal to develop the airplane. Private aviators and companies — and the newspapers — did it for them after a slow start.

The New York *Times* had the satisfaction of sponsoring the 1908–9 North Pole expedition of Commander (later Admiral) Robert E. Peary, USN. Having advanced $4,000 to help outfit Peary for his long trek, his eighth over a period of 23 years, and obtaining the exclusive rights to his story, the *Times* was tipped on what was to come when Peary flashed a prearranged code — "OP," meaning "Old Pole."

Then followed this message flashed from Indian Harbor, Labrador:

I HAVE THE POLE APRIL 6TH (1908) EXPECT ARRIVAL AT CHATEAU BAY SEPTEMBER 7TH (1969). SECURE CONTROL. WIRE FOR ME THERE AND ARRANGE EXPEDITE TRANSMISSION. BIG STORY. PEARY.[70]

However, there already had been a previous claimant for the honor of being first to the North Pole, Dr. Frederick A. Cook, a Brooklyn surgeon who had accompanied Peary in 1891 and 1902 on two failed expeditions, also another failure in 1897–98 by a Belgian group. (In all, more than 500 attempts had previously been made to reach the North Pole.)

A distinguished correspondent for the London *Daily Chronicle*, Philip Gibbs, had already interviewed Dr. Cook, who claimed to have reached the North Pole April 1, 1908, and expressed skepticism because Cook's story didn't seem to stand up under questioning. In fact, at the time the AP flashed Peary's claim to have reached the North Pole, Dr. Cook had been given the Danish Royal Geographic Society's gold medal for his accomplishment at a ceremonial dinner in Copenhagen.

When told about Peary's telegram, the rival explorer commented, "That is good news. I hope Peary got the pole. . . . We are rivals, of course, but the pole is good enough for two."

Once again, Gibbs interviewed Dr. Cook at the dinner at the Tivoli Gardens and came away even more convinced that Dr. Cook was a liar.[71]

The AP, nervous about the whole business in view of Dr. Cook's $25,000 contract with the New York *Herald* for his story, sent a wireless message to Peary querying him for details. His reply:

> REGRET UNABLE DISPATCH DETAILS. MY DISPATCH STARS AND STRIPES
> NAILED TO NORTH POLE AUTHORITATIVE AND CORRECT. COOK'S
> STORY SHOULD NOT BE TAKEN TOO SERIOUSLY. THE TWO ESKIMOS
> WHO ACCOMPANIED HIM SAY HE WENT NO DISTANCE NORTH AND NOT
> OUT OF SIGHT OF LAND. OTHER MEMBERS OF THE TRIBE CORROBORATE
> THEIR STORY. PEARY[72]

For four days, from September 8 through 11, the New York *Times* played Peary's own story at length and syndicated it all over the world at a profit to the explorer of $12,000. In subsequent inquires Peary's story was accepted; Cook's wasn't.[73]

Gibbs, whose articles were also carried in the New York *Times,* had his anxious moments. But with the support of the Danish explorer Peter Freuchen and others, he shook confidence in Dr. Cook to such an extent that the University of Copenhagen eventually rejected his claim and canceled his honorary degree. Gibbs commented, "Looking back on it, I marvel at my luck."[74]

Through the New York *Times,* the wireless, and the work of a great correspondent, Gibbs, Peary earned the accolade of history. In the rapid evolution of foreign correspondence as the basis for an enlarged public participation in world affairs, it turned out that all three were important.

―――――

There was one other news crisis before World War I in which the New York *Times* played a key role. It began on a quiet Sunday night in the spring of 1912 in the Boston bureau of the AP. J. D. Kennedy, the night telegrapher, was on his dinner hour in the cluttered supply room where he had rigged up a crude wireless set. He was, in the slightly derisive term applied to radio amateurs, a ham—and an enthusiastic one. As he fiddled with his homemade tuning device, he froze. The White Star liner *Titanic,* billed for months as the unsinkable *Titanic,* was flashing a wireless distress call:

COME AT ONCE. WE HAVE STRUCK BERG. IT'S CQD* OLD MAN. POSI-
TION 41–46 N 50–14 W

The AP put out a bulletin:

CAPE RACE N.F., SUNDAY NIGHT, APRIL 14 (AP) AT 10:25 O'CLOCK
TONIGHT THE WHITE STAR LINE STEAMSHIP TITANIC CALLED CQD TO
THE MARCONI STATION HERE AND REPORTED TO HAVE STRUCK AN ICE-
BERG. THE STEAMER SAID THAT IMMEDIATE ASSISTANCE WAS REQUIRED.[75]

It was 1:20 a.m. Monday, April 15, when the bulletin reached the
New York *Times*. Carr Vattel Van Anda, the saturnine *Times* managing
editor, hesitated not a moment. With the next edition deadline only
minutes away, he discarded the myth that the *Titanic* was unsinkable
and slapped the story in the most prominent spot he could make on
page 1. Other papers hedged. The White Star offices in New York were
insisting the *Titanic*'s safety compartments couldn't be breached.

However, the *Times* had been handling and using wireless news from
the earlist days of the Russo-Japanese War. In 1905, the paper had
reported the first wireless distress call from the storm-battered Nantucket *Lightship* in common with the rest of the American press. With
the Chicago *Tribune*, the *Times* also had shared a wireless message
from the liner *Cymric* reporting the rescue of 37 of 51 crewmen from
the freighter *St. Cuthbert*, afire off Cape Sable on February 2, 1908.
And then, there had been the great story of chunky little Jack Binns, the
wireless operator of the White Star liner *Republic*, who on January 23,
1909, sent the CQD that resulted in the rescue of all but six of the
ship's 1,600 passengers after she was rammed off Nantucket by the
Florida.

Wireless communication had proved itself, and Van Anda and the
Times were going with it, regardless of the White Star Line's protests. It
was big news.[76]

All too soon, tragically, the final AP bulletin and the dreaded final
flash came piling in that April night in 1912:

SINKING. CANNOT HEAR FOR NOISE OF STEAM ENGINE ROOM GET-
TING FLOODED.

Then — the flash:
SOS . . . SOS . . .

Shortly after 2 a.m., the *Titanic*'s wireless fell silent. All Kennedy
could hear over the air in his headphones was the frantic signaling of

---

*Usually, preliminary to an SOS.

other ships racing to the scene, trying to raise the *Titanic*'s wireless room. It was no use. And Van Anda, along with all save the *Sun* in New York, had to conclude that the *Titanic* had gone down.

How many had died of the more than 2,000 passengers and crew aboard the big ship, nobody could know for perhaps days.

The list of notables on her maiden voyage was therefore run without comment — Colonel and Mrs. John Jacob Astor; Mr. and Mrs. Isidor Straus; Frank D. Millet, the old war correspondent turned artist; W. T. Stead, the British editor; Major Archibald Butt, President Taft's military aide-de-camp; and many, many others.

The spluttering of the wireless at sea next day spelled out the story of the disaster in unmistakable terms. The Cunarder *Carpathia* reached the last location given by the *Titanic* at dawn on April 15 and found only crowded lifeboats and the wreckage of the unsinkable ship. The White Star liner *Olympic* wirelessed Cape Race that the *Carpathia* was steaming to New York with about 655 survivors. And at last, at 8:20 p.m., P. A. S. Franklin of the International Mercantile Marine conceded that probably only those aboard the *Carpathia* had survived the *Titanic*.[77]

The rest of the story was told by local reporters in New York who shoved their way through a shrieking crowd of 30,000 on the night of April 18 to get aboard the *Carpathia* as she docked along the North River. Despite the enterprise of the *Herald,* with a woman reporter aboard the *Carpathia* who wirelessed her account, the *Times* once again was ahead.

The ever-resourceful Van Anda had enlisted the cooperation of Guglielmo Marconi himself. Because all wireless operators then were part of the Marconi company, the inventor was among the first aboard the *Carpathia* after she docked and took *Times* reporters with him. It was then that the *Times* came out with the story of Harold Bride, the *Titanic*'s wireless operator who survived. He told how the great ship went down with the band playing, some women staying aboard to die with their husbands, and all the doomed singing the Episcopal hymn, "Autumn."

It was then, too, that the New York reporters learned of the great ones who had perished — Colonel Astor, the Strauses, Millet, Stead, and the rest of the 1,517 who had perished with the ship while only 706 had been saved.[78]

Once again, the New York *Times* had made history in more ways than one. It had established the reliability of wireless communication as the world approached the war years of the 20th century. And it also had shown that it would be a worthy successor to the leadership that once had been exerted in so magnificent a manner by the old Thunderer, the *Times* of London.

The printer from Knoxville had kept his word: "I know that I can manage the *Times* as a decent, dignified and independent newspaper and still wipe out the deficit." Adolph Simon Ochs and his descendants one day would dominate New York to a greater extent than Pulitzer or Hearst, Greeley and the two Bennetts, father and son, by giving all the news that's fit to print.

4 The Challenge of World War I

HOW WAR CAME

Robert Atter, chief of the Associated Press bureau in Vienna, prepared for a routine job on a hot and dusty summer Sunday in 1914. Archduke Francis Ferdinand, heir to the throne of Austria-Hungary, and his Duchess were making a ceremonial visit to the capital of Bosnia, a benighted town of 80,000 called Sarajevo, to impress the restless populace. Bosnia, with Herzegovina, had only lately been added to the many and ill-assorted lands gathered under the dual monarchy, much to the displeasure of the neighboring Serbs. The visit was intended to quiet matters.

While the Archduke and Duchess were driving to the Town Hall for a reception, a bomb was hurled at him, and he warded it off with his arm. The blast injured two of his entourage and six spectators. The Archduke exclaimed angrily at the Town Hall: "Herr Bürgermeister, it is perfectly outrageous! We have come to Sarajevo on a visit and have had a bomb thrown at us!"[1]

Atter began filing. But before he had gone very far, more shocking news broke. This was the AP bulletin:

SARAJEVO, BOSNIA, JUNE 28 — ARCHDUKE FRANCIS FERDINAND, HEIR TO THE AUSTRO-HUNGARIAN THRONE, AND THE DUCHESS OF HOHEN-BERG, HIS MORGANATIC WIFE, WERE SHOT DEAD TODAY BY A STUDENT IN THE MAIN STREET OF THE BOSNIAN CAPITAL, A SHORT TIME AFTER THEY HAD ESCAPED DEATH FROM A BOMB HURLED AT THE ROYAL AUTOMOBILES.[2]

The details of the crime of the student, Gavrilo Prinzip, and his fellow-conspirators came in swiftly to Vienna, where the official Telegraphen Korrespondenz-Bureau made them available. The correspondents who had not left Vienna, as well as those at the scene, kept the cables clogged with messages all that day. But in all the accounts, not a reference was made to war by any responsible correspondent.

At Kiel that sunny Sunday, Frederic William Wile, then on the staff of the London *Daily Mail,* was covering Kaiser Wilhelm II and the annual yachting festival which Germany had designed to try to outdazzle the British Cowes Week. His roommate, Otto von Gottberg, the correspondent of the Kaiser's mouthpiece, the Berlin *Lokal-Anzeiger,* burst in on him exclaiming: "The Archduke Franz Ferdinand and his wife were assassinated today at Sarajevo!"

"Good God!"

Von Gottberg went on: "It's a good thing."

The Kaiser's racing schooner, *Meteor* V, received the news by wireless and turned. A destroyer approached, taking the Kaiser from the schooner and transferring him to his royal yacht, *Hohenzollern.* Soon, the royal ship broke out a signal flag meaning: "His Majesty is aboard but preoccupied."[3]

In Paris it was the day of the Grand Prix at Longchamps, the climax of a brilliant social season. President Raymond Poincaré and the majority of the French cabinet occupied boxes. The crowd was never more gay. But as the news came to the President's box, spectators saw Poincaré's face turn grave. He squinted up at the blue, cloudless sky, abruptly arose, and left Longchamps with his cabinet. The Quai d'Orsay would be busy far into the night.[4]

Wickham Steed, who had returned from Vienna as the *Times*'s correspondent, spent that day outside London on a holiday and didn't return until seven that night. He found the *Times* office in turmoil. "Until early on Monday morning, I worked without a break," he wrote.[5]

In the United States, the New York *Times* reprinted the translated account of the Vienna *Neue Freie Presse,* with other details from the London *Daily Mail,* under a four-column headline in moderate half-inch type:

HEIR TO AUSTRIA'S THRONE IS SLAIN

WITH HIS WIFE BY A BOSNIAN YOUTH

TO AVENGE SEIZURE OF HIS COUNTRY

The New York *Times* was perturbed, but not unduly excited. Its eight-column headlines were invariably reserved for events it believed to be world-shaking.⁶ To those who were only casually interested, the *Times*'s policy seemed to be the right one. The excitement over Sarajevo evaporated quickly. In fact, some of the dispatches from Vienna seemed far more concerned over the effect of the double murders on the health of the octogenarian Francis Joseph than on the fate of the world.

Yet, in Berlin, there now began an extraordinary three-week game of hide-and-seek, a deadly diversion, in which suspicious foreign correspondents called daily, and sometimes twice daily, at the Wilhelmstrasse to try to divine Germany's course toward Austria and the Balkans. It had been no secret to them that Francis Ferdinand had been the major roadblock in the Kaiser's effort to acquire greater influence over Austrian foreign policy. With the Archduke now removed, the correspondents could only guess at the extent to which the Wilhelmstrasse would dictate policy to the Ballhausplatz.

The Kaiser did not attend Francis Ferdinand's funeral. He came down conveniently with a slight case of lumbago, obviously a diplomatic illness, and the Austrian court helped out by announcing that no foreign guests were expected to attend the rites. Next, he sought to lull world opinion still further on Monday, July 6, by taking off in the *Hohenzollern* for a quiet cruise in the fjords of Norway. The Berlin *Lokal Anzeiger* and the rest of the German press dutifully pointed out that the Kaiser's cruise signified that there was no reason for concern over the shaky situation in the Balkans. Yet, the day before, the Kaiser and his Chancellor, Theobald von Bethmann-Hollweg, had given Austria full assurance of German support in punitive measures against Serbia. It was the infamous "Blank Check," the most fateful of all the decisions that were taken in secret that tragic midsummer. For from it, all the others flowed.

The German government, no less than the statesmen of both its allies and enemies, were under the impression that the foreign correspondents could not know what was going on. But, even if this was so, the livelier and shrewder correspondents could not be prevented from raising questions based on their suspicions, their guesses, and very likely their prejudices. That is what happened in Berlin. The foreign correspondents kept after Privy Counsellor Hammann, the gloomy chief of the press section of the Foreign Office. But whatever their questions, his invariable answer was a pious assurance that Germany wanted peace and was not at all concerned by the gravity of the position between Austria and Serbia. The line put out by the German Press Bureau, which the foreign correspondents did not buy at all, was that if difficulties did develop between Austria and Serbia they could be localized.

By July 15, stocks were dropping on the Berlin and Vienna bourses. There were rumors that Austria had decided on a partial mobilization and that Serbia was acting accordingly. Actually the Austrian decision to present an ultimatum to Serbia was not taken until July 19, and the note was not drafted until the next day; but the stock markets, the most sensitive of barometers, were reacting to a mood. So were the foreign correspondents. Yet, they could not convince their editors. The Berlin and Vienna correspondents of the British dailies, almost to a man, found most of their dispatches played down and sometimes discarded.

Despite a virulent Austrian press campaign that was raging in Vienna, which should have been a signal to sophisticated British opinion that something was up, the *Times* of London chose to ignore it. Instead, the newspaper editorially advised Serbia to cooperate with an inquiry into the Archduke's murder which "will do much to put herself right with outside opinion." The editorial went on: "Austria-Hungary has acted with self-possession and with restraint hitherto. We earnestly hope she will continue so to the end."[7]

The Austro-Hungarian ambassador to Britain, Count Albert Mensdorff, took heart at this favorable development, published on July 16. Certainly not by coincidence, Max Goldschneider, the correspondent of the *Neues Wiener Tageblatt,* held a dinner the next night for some influential correspondents. Wickham Steed of the *Times* attended, as did M. Condurier de Chassaigne, president of the Foreign Press Association in London, and others. It was no secret that the Austrians, through their subservient correspondents, were trying to court British public opinion as much as they dared.[8]

The line which Dr. Hammann had been handing out at the Foreign Office finally appeared in print for the first time in a German newspaper when his most faithful echo, the *Norddeutsche Zeitung* in Berlin, proposed in a rather vague way the "localization" of war in its issue of July 19, a Sunday. The Austrian press promptly picked up the statement, with attribution to its source, which meant a great deal to the nervous and highly suspicious Steed.[9] But he was almost alone on Fleet Street in his well-nigh frantic mood, although next day stocks on every exchange in Europe began to drop precipitously.

The British press registered no alarm. It was full of the magnificent review of the British fleet off Spithead, which began on July 19, with King George V on his royal yacht cruising among 230 warships manned by 70,000 officers and men.

As for the French press, it was crowded with the details of the trial of Mme. Henriette Caillaux, wife of Joseph Caillaux, once Premier of

France, for the fatal shooting of Gaston Calmette, the editor of *Figaro*. Calmette had attacked Caillaux's private life, and Mme. Caillaux had provided a typically French solution for her husband's troubled affairs. What foreign correspondent in Paris could think of war with so juicy a story to cover? They flocked to the courtroom, nearly 150 strong, and some reputedly paid as much as $200 or more to be certain of a seat. To be sure, there was an item in some of the papers that President Poincaré and Premier René Viviani were on the way to St. Petersburg for a ceremonial visit. But what of it? Maybe they wanted the trip!

The press campaign in Vienna was intensified. In Berlin, the German Press Bureau was more evasive than ever, and the Kaiser's holiday cruise was over. In St. Petersburg, there was genuine alarm, and as the world was to learn later, renewed assurances were exchanged with the visiting French statesmen of the strength of the Franco-Russian alliance. And in London, Count Mensdorff took the extraordinary step of inviting Wickham Steed to lunch on July 21. The Austrian ambassador for the first time took the gloves off with a hostile correspondent, evidently acting under instructions. "Serbia," Mensdorff said, "must be punished. But if the *Times* will give the lead, the rest of the press will follow. British opinion will remain friendly to us and the conflict may be localized."

Steed, who like Wile had been predicting for years that Germany would go to war, forgot he was a correspondent and began lecturing the Ambassador in the most extreme manner. "I am too good a friend of Austria," he replied, "to help her commit suicide. . . . You can certainly crush Serbia if you are left alone to do it. . . . But that is not what will happen. At the first shot you fire across the Save, Russia will cry, 'Hands off.' Germany will summon Russia not to intervene, Russia will refuse. . . . Germany will then mobilize and will bolt through Belgium into France; and when England sees German troops in Belgium, she will intervene against Germany and against you."

The ambassador flared back, "You will never intervene. . . . I have assurance that you will not intervene."

"You do not know the strength of English public feeling."

"Then you will not help us?"

"On no account whatever."

The thoroughly alarmed and shaken Steed now drove to the Foreign Office to try to report at once to Sir Edward Grey, the Foreign Minister. But the best he could do was to talk with an under official who listened to his tale and remarked, "You're off your head."[10]

Steed rushed off to alert Northcliffe, with the result that the *Times* next day carried a leading article, "A Danger To Europe," which was intended to convey a warning to both Germany and Austria. But even Northcliffe feared to exaggerate the danger of war at this stage, causing the editorial to be couched in such vague terms that it could scarcely have disturbed the leaders of the Central Powers, who were convinced that Britain would remain neutral.[11] On July 23, Austria handed Serbia a 10-point ultimatum with a 48-hour time limit for reply. Wile sent a bulletin on it to the London *Daily Mail* at 7 p.m., Berlin time, several hours before the official announcement.[12] Still, the German Press Bureau kept saying nobody wanted a war, least of all Germany.

At 8:30 on Saturday night, July 25, however, the government mouthpiece, the Berlin *Lokal Anzeiger,* was the first to put a black bulletin in its windows, "Serbia Rejects Austrian Ultimatum!"[13] Of course, the Serbs had done no such thing. They had given in to eight out of the ten Austrian demands. But to the Wilhelmstrasse, as well as to the Ballhausplatz, that was a rejection. Suddenly, frighteningly, the fierce passions of a German street mob let loose and thousands streamed through Berlin yelling, "*Krieg! Krieg!*" ("War! War!") The sight was not lost on foreign correspondents, who transmitted such stories to newspapers all over the world. If nothing else brought home the danger to other peoples, that did.[14]

In London next day, Sunday, July 26, Sir Edward Grey learned that Russia would come to the aid of Serbia, if Serbia were attacked, and that France would fight with Russia. Treaties were being invoked. The cards in the stacked deck of war were falling into place.

The London *Chronicle* received a brief dispatch from its correspondent in Austria-Hungary, Martin H. Donohue, on July 28, reporting that three gunboats in the Danube had fired on Belgrade. The correspondent was arrested, then expelled.[15] He had reported the first shots of World War I. And in Paris, Mme. Caillaux was acquitted, but few correspondents in Paris bothered to send much about her. In London, the excitement over the Home Rule Bill and the latest Irish shootings also sank back in the consciousness of press and public. The war correspondents began taking off, many for Paris, and a few doughty ones for Berlin and Vienna.

On July 29, news came from St. Petersburg that Germany had warned Russia that Russian mobilization inevitably would be followed by German mobilization. Next day, Russia ordered mobilization. And the *Times,* almost coincident with German diplomatic efforts to buy British neutrality with a pledge not to take French or Belgian territory, came out with an editorial that could have been written by the Foreign

Office, but wasn't: "If France is menaced, or the safety of the Belgian frontier which we have guaranteed with her and with Prussia by treaties that Mr. Gladstone's government in 1870 confirmed, we shall know how to act. We can no more afford to see France crushed by Germany, or the balance of power upset against France, than Germany can afford to see Austria-Hungary crushed by Russia and that balance upset against Austrian and Hungarian interests."[16]

But the British press by no means spoke as one. The Manchester *Guardian* and the London *Daily News* wrote against war. And the London *Chronicle* protested against attempts to "dictate" to Sir Edward Grey. Whereupon, in another extraordinary attempt to influence British public opinion, two members of the House of Rothschild — Lord Rothschild and his brother, Leopold — presented their own ultimatum on July 28 to the financial editor of the *Times,* Hugh Chisholm. Lord Rothschild bluntly warned Chisholm that the *Times* must change its tone because it was "hounding the country into war." The banker demanded a policy of British neutrality. Northcliffe himself turned the Rothschilds down when they later carried their proposal to him.[17] The City plunged into near panic as stocks plummeted. That night, Germany gave the Russians twelve hours to demobilize or face war. That night, too, Germany would send the British no assurance that the neutrality of Belgium would be respected. And next day, August 1, the *Times* boldly proclaimed, while the British government hesitated: "We dare not stand aside . . . our strongest interest is the law of self-preservation."[18] That same day, the *Daily News* accused the *Times* of having "paved the way to this stupendous catastrophe," and the gentle Henry Nevinson assailed the *Times* for trying to drag the country into "abominations."

Northcliffe called a conference at his office, no less intense and no less dramatic than the many other conferences that were taking place in the chancelleries all over Europe. "I have trustworthy information," he announced, "that the government are going to 'rat.' We have taken a strong line in favor of intervention on behalf of France and Russia. What do we do if the government give way?"

The well-nigh hysterical Steed demanded that, if the government backed down, the paper would have to go "bald-headed against it."

"Would you attack the government at a moment of national crisis?" Northcliffe demanded.

"Certainly!" Steed snapped.[19]

Although it was the August Bank Holiday weekend, a traditional vacation time, the conferees agreed to put out an extraordinary Sunday paper if it became necessary. And most of them decided in advance that it would be necessary. That night, Germany declared war on Russia and, in the west, invaded Luxembourg. The Germans still had given no answer to the British request for a guarantee against the invasion of Belgium, but the invasion of Luxembourg should have been a sufficient reply. It wasn't. Both the British and the French were far more conscious of the care with which they had to clothe their every action than were the reckless Germans and their sword-rattling Kaiser. The Germans seemed to have paid no attention whatever to the sensitivities of neutral opinion.

The *Times*'s Sunday edition carried the deadly news of German aggression, as did every newspaper that was published that day around the world. Reuters needed only to use the news exactly as it happened. Havas had to do nothing more than follow suit. The Germans did try once more to influence British opinion. At the *Times*'s Sunday editorial conference, a typed letter bearing the name of Albert Ballin was forwarded from the London office of the Hamburg-American Line, of which he was president. Later, a telegram came addressed to the Wolff Bureau instructing it to send the Ballin text verbatim to Berlin as soon as the *Times* published it. This was the gist:

"I hear with astonishment that, in France and elsewhere in the world, it is imagined that Germany wants to carry on an aggressive war, and that she has with this aim brought about the present situation. It is said that the Emperor was of the opinion that the moment had come to have a final reckoning with His enemies; but what a terrible error that is. . . . He has not wanted war; it has been forced upon Him by the might of the circumstances. . . . Russia alone forces the war on Europe."[20]

The letter wasn't published at that time. Northcliffe was in no mood to present the Kaiser with an apologia in the *Times*. For on that Sunday the British cabinet voted to guarantee the French coast against attack, but waited to see what the Germans intended to do in the west. Before that day passed, they knew. Germany had demanded permission to cross Belgium without opposition and had promised in return not to retain any Belgian territory after the war was over. The ultimatum had been sent in a sealed envelope to the German ministry in Brussels on July 29 with orders that it was not to be opened until telegraphic instructions arrived. The decisive wire came on the night of August 2, and Belgium's equally decisive answer was given in a matter of hours by its king, Albert I. It was, "No!"[21]

Now, with the German war machine already in motion, Berlin tried to clothe its aggression with an appearance of righteousness. There were German reports that the French were invading Belgium, that the French had crossed the German border, that French dirigibles had dropped bombs on German territory. All were untrue, and the foreign correspondents quickly learned that the Wilhelmstrasse could not be trusted, if they didn't already know it. The truth was that the French, anxious to avert all blame for this war and to ensure complete British support, actually ordered a 10-kilometer withdrawal on July 30 along the German frontier from Luxembourg to Switzerland.[22] On the next day, August 3, Germany declared war on France and began the invasion of Belgium, thus executing the plan perfected as early as 1906 by the then Chief of Staff, Count Alfred von Schlieffen. It was, Schlieffen argued, the only way to envelop and defeat France quickly, a concept which was developed by his successor, General Helmuth von Moltke, the nephew of the conqueror of 1870.

In Berlin, the crazed crowds were still cheering the coming of war and snapping up the first war extras put out by the controlled press. For the edification of the foreign correspondents, the Wilhelmstrasse issued its official White Paper, which blamed the war on everybody else, almost as soon as German troops crossed the Belgian frontier.

London, by contrast, was sober, quiet, apprehensive. At three o'clock on that historic August 3, Sir Edward Grey rose before a packed House of Commons and placed before the honorable members the issue and the choice — support of Belgium and support of France, "these obligations of honor and interest." The House broke into prolonged applause. Back at the Foreign Office, waiting for the decision, Wickham Steed was talking with Sir Arthur Nicolson, the Permanent Under-Secretary, when a secretary ran in with a news dispatch.

"They have cheered him, sir!" the secretary exclaimed.

Sir Arthur replied, "Thank goodness!"

When the speech was over, Lord Onslow joined them, having come directly from the House. "He has had a tremendous success, sir. The whole House is with him."

Steed saw Sir Arthur was greatly relieved and heard him say fervently: "Thank God! Now the course is clear, but it will be a terrible business."[23]

The British sent off a note to Berlin, demanding an end to the invasion of Belgium within twenty-four hours. It was foredoomed to failure. But out of it came another of those fatal German lapses that flashed around a shocked world, strengthening the Entente, and costing the Kaiser whatever hope he had of swaying neutral sentiment. Sir Edward Goschen, the British ambassador in Berlin, detailed his final interview with Bethmann-Hollweg in this manner:

"I found the Chancellor very agitated. His Excellency at once began a harangue, which lasted for about twenty minutes. He said that the step taken by His Majesty's Government was terrible to a degree. Just for a word—'neutrality,' a word which in wartime had so often been disregarded—just for a scrap of paper, Great Britain was going to make war on a kindred nation who desired nothing better than to be friends with her."[24]

The world would never forget that to Germany, bent on war, a treaty such as Britain's commitment to defend Belgium was "a scrap of paper." It was a story that sank deeply into the consciousness of the neutrals, that inspired the peace-loving Benito Mussolini to proclaim in *Avanti!* his loathing of Germany: "The neutrality of Belgium has been violated. . . . To be in direct or indirect solidarity with Germany means—at this moment—to serve the cause of militarism in its most insane and criminal expression."[25]

But Bethmann-Hollweg, in his arrogance, was to say things far worse than that before that day of August 4 was over.

The sad-faced, lanky Chancellor wasted no time with his war speech, and swept aside all sentimentality. "Our invasion of Belgium is contrary to international law but the wrong—I speak openly—that we are committing we will make good as soon as our military goal has been reached," he said.[26] He spoke of the German soldier "hacking his way through" to victory. He thundered that "necessity knows no law."[27]

The Reichstag applauded Bethmann-Hollweg as he concluded with clenched fist: "Our army is in the field! Our fleet is ready for battle! The whole German nation stands behind them! Yea, the whole nation!"

Wile turned to Martin Schmidt, of the *B. Z. Am Mittag,* and muttered, "Supposing the Belgians resist?"

"Resist?" Schmidt was pitying. "Why we'll spill them into the ocean."[28]

At about that hour in London, Northcliffe and Steed exchanged a few words together. "Well, it's come," Northcliffe said. And Steed replied, "Yes, thank God!"[29]

Along the boulevards in Paris, as war came, there was quite as great a wave of patriotic destruction by mobs as there had been in Berlin. German-owned shops were demolished. Suspected German sympathizers were hounded and beaten. There were cheers for Britain, for Belgium, for the United States, and patriotic songs for the youth of France leaving for the front. As Wythe Williams and Walter Duranty went to the office of the New York *Times* in Paris on the first night of war, they saw a poster beside the Tricolor of France that draped the entrance to the newspaper, *Gil Blas:* "Every employee of this paper is of military age and therefore is now in the service of France. *Gil Blas* necessarily suspends publication, perhaps forever."[30]

As the foreign correspondents of the belligerents prepared to pull out of enemy capitals, leaving the neutrals to cover for them, many were detained temporarily as spies. Eventually, all were permitted to go home. None of them were able to capture in a few words the feeling that was expressed by Sir Edward Grey as he stood at the window of the old Foreign Office on the night of August 4, watching the lamplighters in St. James's Park: "The lamps are going out all over Europe. We shall not see them lit again in our lifetime."[31] Yet, those same foreign correspondents already had cost Germany the war for world public opinion. Nothing that Germany could do in the next four years would wipe out the spiked-helmet image of the Kaiser in his "shining armor," brandishing in his "mailed fist" the "scrap of paper" that guaranteed the freedom of a small nation.

FRONTLINE REPORTING

"The entrance of the German army into Brussels has lost the human quality," wrote Richard Harding Davis from the Belgian capital on August 21, 1914. That was the beginning of Davis's most celebrated single piece of war correspondence. In it, he likened the German invaders to "a force of nature like a tidal wave," adding, "when they passed, the human note passed with them."[32]

The "hero of our dreams," as a youthful H. L. Mencken called him, was then 50 years old and at the height of his fame. He had just been married for a second time to a vivacious beauty half his age, Bessie McCoy, the "Yama Yama Girl" of the Ziegfeld Follies. He was reporting the war for the newspaper clients of the Wheeler Syndicate at $600 a week, plus $1,000 an article for *Scribner's,* and he had left Bessie in London to wait for him.[33] If he had planned to send for her, as he had escorted his first bride into Boer territory some fourteen years before, the first sight of the German army changed his mind.

Virtually a German prisoner in Brussels, he managed nevertheless to get his story out through a young Britisher, E. A. Dalton, who risked his life to reach Ostend and board a Channel boat to Folkestone. When Davis himself tried to get away, he was picked up by a German officer, who threatened to have him shot as a British spy. The American minister, Brand Whitlock, interceded for him.[34]

Although the French and British had refused to accept correspondents at the outset, a number of them dashed to the front anyway, despite lack of credentials, as Davis did. There were other Americans at the front, including Irvin S. Cobb for the *Saturday Evening Post;* William G. Shepherd for *Collier's;* Harry Hansen of the Chicago *Daily News;* John T. McCutcheon, the cartoonist, for the Chicago *Tribune;* and Arno Dosch-Fleurot of the New York *World.* Some of them, unexpectedly reunited with Davis as prisoners, were thrust into a troop train loaded with captive French and British soldiers and headed toward the German border.

On August 27, as the troop train pulled into Louvain, Davis saw flames consuming the ancient city, its university, and its library which had been founded in 1426. He quickly learned that the Germans had begun burning the city two days before, charging that Belgian snipers had killed fifty Germans. Davis was horrified. Once he was out of German hands and back in London on August 30, he wrote the story of the burning of Louvain: "For two hours on Thursday night, I was in what for six hundred years has been the city of Louvain. The Germans were burning it, and to hide their work they kept us locked in the railroad carriages. But the story was written against the sky, was told to us by German soldiers incoherent with excesses; and we could read it in the faces of women and children being led to concentration camps and of citizens on their way to be shot."[35]

Davis's was not the only voice raised against German *Schrecklichkeit.* Newspapers all over the world denounced the crime. And Romain Rolland, a wartime contributor to the *Neue Zürcher Zeitung,* wrote in an open letter to the German dramatist, Gerhart Hauptmann, "Are you descendants of Goethe or Attila the Hun?"

At the time the Germans were putting Louvain to the torch, the British were waiting complacently for the first victories of their tiny expeditionary force, the "Old Contemptibles," who had gone forward to Mons. It was representative of the British state of mind that three elderly gentlemen — Bennet Burleigh, Henry W. Nevinson, and Frederick Villiers — should be out riding in Hyde Park on fine mornings, getting themselves in shape to cover the war. They had always gone out on horseback, and they could not conceive that this war would be any different. Then the terrible news came in from Mons, where the Germans shattered the British forces. Arthur Moore, a war correspondent for the *Times* of London, and Hamilton Fyfe, a correspondent for the London *Daily Mail,* wrote their stories at Amiens on August 29. Moore's story, the celebrated Amiens Telegram, was published in the *Times* next day, with Fyfe's following, both having been passed through censorship by a considerate official, F. E. Smith, later to be Lord Birkenhead. "We have to face the fact," wrote Moore, "that the BEF . . . has suffered terrible losses and requires immediate and immense reinforcement. The BEF has won indeed imperishable glory, but it needs men, men, and yet more men."[36]

The French were bracing for their first stand on the Marne, and all the world watched and wondered. Wythe Williams of the New York *Times* saw the old Paris taxicabs, each crowded with French soldiers, puttering off to the northeast, where the big guns were thundering on the Marne.[37] He understood then what General Joseph Simon Gallieni, the military governor of Paris, had meant when he had vowed that he would defend the city to the last man. The taxicab army of only 6,000 men was the final resort.

Then, miraculously, the French held. The Germans were flung back. The correspondents were permitted at last to go out to the Marne by the censorship officials. But instead of being able to tell the great story, they were, almost to a man, rounded up by suspicious French officers, forcibly detained overnight, and told they were being held as spies.

It was futile, trying to be a correspondent under such circumstances. Williams joined the first American ambulance unit, determined to do something useful, and served under fire at Amiens until Christmas, 1914, when he finally was given permission by the French Government to go to the front. Nevinson offered his assistance to a Quaker ambulance unit at Dunkirk for a few months. Philip Gibbs was luckier, being one of six correspondents officially recognized for accreditation to the front. The only American with such official accreditation from the British authorities during the early years of the war was Frederick Palmer, a correspondent for *Collier's* and a veteran war reporter who served all American wire services and newspapers. As for the rest, they scratched for what they could get, and most of that never passed censorship. Now and then, as the war progressed, a reporter performed some heroic feat and attracted attention. But by and large, the agony and the effort and the risk and the sheer staying power required of all reporters in war zones was very largely unrecognized after the opening weeks.

Wilbur Forrest, who went to Europe early in the war for the United Press and later achieved a certain amount of fame as a correspondent, wrote a bitter and cynical denunciation of the system.

> A heavy defeat in the field was often described as a strategic withdrawal, or even more boldly, the occupation of a new position in accordance with plan. Communiques minimized defeat and exaggerated

victory. They did so rightly, because in a struggle of world magnitude it was a vital function of the communique writers to keep the people at home in an optimistic frame of mind. . . .

The war correspondent of 1914–1918 was nevertheless a sort of glorified disseminator of official military propaganda. . . . The critical correspondent was outflanked, decimated, routed.[38]

The even more knowledgeable Frederick Palmer put it this way on the basis of his frustrating experiences from the outset of the war: "My personal story is a thread, running through the familiar background, knotted with moments of acute consciousness of the double life I led—when I was cast for the part of a public liar to keep up the spirits of the armies and the peoples of our side."[39]

Palmer and Elmer Roberts, the chief of the Paris bureau of the AP, were able to see the Marne battlefields only because they were foresighted enough to persuade Senator Paul Doumer, afterward President of France, to escort them. But on his return to London, Palmer found the British raising so many objections to his projected trip to join their armies that he went instead to Berlin. There, he found the victory-flushed Germans only too willing to let the press representatives of the great neutral, the United States, see how easily they were crushing the enemy. The winning side never objects to having its story told by correspondents it deems "objective," meaning either too polite or too lazy to look below the glossy surface of immediate success. Eventually, when Palmer and his few associates were received by the British forces in France, much to the disturbance of French headquarters, it was with several distinct reservations:

> There was not the freedom of the old days, but there can never be again for the correspondent," Palmer wrote. "We lived in a mess with our conducting officers, paving for our quarters, food and automobiles. I do not recall ever having asked to go any place without receiving consent. Day after day we sallied forth from our chateau to different headquarters and billets for our grist, and having written our dispatches, turned them over to the officers for censorship. We rarely had our copy cut. We had learned too well where the line was drawn on military secrecy. The important items were those we left out; and these made us public liars![40]

Here was the basis for another new concept of foreign correspondence either during wartime or under conditions similar to war. The correspondent was told the rules, given all assistance, treated as if he were the very prince of good fellows, and trusted to be his own censor because he had "learned too well where the line was drawn." Just in case he forgot, the censor was there to take care of him. And in Britain, there was an added refinement under the Defense of the Realm Act (DORA), when British newspapers cheerfully accepted government suggestions against publishing certain things that might help the enemy.

This meant that any rebellion would have to start at the top, not at the level of the correspondents, if it was to be effective, and that is precisely what happened. Provoked by what he considered government laxity in not providing the British army with high explosive shells in sufficient quantity, Northcliffe soon began moving against Lord Kitchener's regime in the War Office. When Colonel Repington managed to cable the *Times* through censorship on May 15, 1915, that "the want of an unlimited supply of high explosive was a fatal bar" to the success of a British attack in France, Northcliffe threw off all restraint. On May 21, in the *Daily Mail,* he wrote and published a devastating editorial, "Kitchener's Tragic Blunder," blaming the great soldier for the shell shortage. The *Daily Mail* lost 238,000 circulation. Both the *Mail* and the *Times* were burned on the Stock Exchange. Northcliffe, however, was obdurate; in part, he was responsible for the fall of the Liberal Asquith cabinet in May 1915 and the rise of a coalition which, while retaining Asquith and Kitchener, brought in David Lloyd George as Munitions Minister.[41]

The same thing happened in France. Despite even more severe press restrictions, the snarling old Tiger, Georges Clemenceau, kept up an unceasing fire against government laxity despite the war. He had only a small paper, *L'Homme Libre,* but in it he disclosed that wounded French soldiers transported in a dirty freight car (Quarante Hommes, Huit Chevaux) had contracted tetanus. *L'Homme Libre* was suspended for a week, whereupon Clemenceau immediately put out a supposedly new paper called *L'Homme Enchaine.* When that, too, was suppressed, he printed private copies and sent them out to the Deputies with pitiless attacks on the supreme military commander in France, General Joseph Joffre, and others.[42] The Government didn't have the nerve to arrest him; through his little paper, in fact, he eventually became the government and, with Generalissimo Ferdinand Foch and the heroic poilus, the savior of France.

The coverage of the war on the western front settled down to an exhausting, nerve-wracking routine. Reuters had 115 men on active duty in all theaters, but mostly in the west; and of the total, fifteen were killed and several others were accounted as missing. The AP and the UP had smaller but no less expert staffs, headed respectively by Elmer Roberts and William Philip Simms. The correspondents who eventually were permitted at British headquarters included such veterans as Philip Gibbs and Frederick Palmer, Percival Phillips of the London *Morning Post,* W. Beach Thomas of the London *Daily Mail,* H. Perry Robinson of the *Times* of London, and Herbert Russell of Reuters.

There were many others who were active, including such major Paris-based correspondents as Wythe Williams of the New York *Times,* Paul Scott Mowrer of the Chicago *Daily News,* Sisley Huddleston of the *Christian Science Monitor,* Arno Dosch-Fleurot of the New York *World,* Stoddard Dewey of the New York *Evening Post,* who was dean of the corps, and Frederic Villiers, the war artist.[43]

Frequently, the newer correspondents were the ones who caught the greatest share of attention. Will Irwin, the author of a famous story about the San Francisco earthquake of 1906, wrote the most devastating account of the German use of poison gas at Ypres on April 22, 1915, published in the New York *Tribune.* He was much admired, also, for his detailed reconstruction of the battle from the British side.[44] Herbert Bayard Swope, the mercurial correspondent of the New York *World,* interviewed General Paul von Hindenburg after the German victory over the Russians at Tannenberg, toured the Somme on the German side, and wrote a story of the fighting there that helped him win a Pulitzer Prize.[45] Edgar Ansel Mowrer, younger brother of Paul Scott Mowrer, broke into journalism as a war correspondent and later toured occupied Belgium with Herbert Hoover's relief commission.[46]

Not all the work was a battle against censorship. At strategic times, all censorship would be removed to let news of inestimable benefit to the Allies flow freely. Such a day came on May 7, 1915, when the *Lusitania* was sunk off the Irish coast. On the Cunarder's departure from New York, an ad signed by the Imperial German Embassy in some New York papers had warned passengers not to board the ship, but the warning had been disregarded. When Wilbur Forrest heard the first rumor of the sinking in the UP London office, he quickly confirmed it by telephoning the British Admiralty. He was told that the great ship, with 1,924 persons aboard, had gone down off Old Kinsale Head after being hit by two torpedoes from a German submarine. There had been no warning. Survivors were being landed at Queenstown (Cobh).

The UP flash went out all over the world, as did the AP flash which originated with James Ryan, its resident correspondent at Queenstown. Within hours, Forrest and other correspondents, British and American, were at Queenstown, talking with survivors; and it was there, finally, that the tragic story unfolded. A total of 1,153 persons, including Americans, had lost their lives, among them Alfred Gwynne Vanderbilt,

Elbert Hubbard, Charles Frohman, and Herbert Stone, son of the AP general manager, Melville Elijah Stone.

Forrest alone sent 7,000 words of skeletonized cable copy on the *Lusitania* story, which was just a fraction of the flood that British censorship permitted to flow over the world's communications systems. "Perhaps [Forrest wrote later] these words contributed something to a growing sentiment in the United States which eventually brought us into the European War."[47]

Forrest, of course, was right. The factual reporting of German folly in wartime, in itself, was a powerful factor in swaying American public opinion. First Belgium, then the *Lusitania,* began hardening American sentiment against Germany despite everything that blundering German agents and fanatical German-Americans could do. It was something more than a mere passing incident when David Lawrence of the AP was able to report exclusively the resignation of William Jennings Bryan as Secretary of State in the Wilson cabinet, soon after the *Lusitania* sinking.[48] That, in itself, was a symbol of the power and the effectiveness of the press despite the suppression of much news under wartime censorship.

There was another, even more potent, symbol — Richard Harding Davis, crusading in the last weeks of his eventful life for American participation in the war on the Allied side. Whatever his colleagues may have thought of him with his tailor-made correspondents' uniforms, his D'Artagnan posturing, and the wealth that rolled in on him from his plays and his novels, there was no doubt of his hold on the American public. In his lectures, in his war books, in his correspondence, he hammered away at the theme of intervention with the singleness of purpose that William Allen White was to display a quarter-century later during World War II.

After returning from a visit to the war fronts in Europe, Davis was working at his home, Crossroads Farm, in Mount Kisco, N.Y., on the evening of April 11, 1916, on a piece about preparedness. Martin Egan, the old AP correspondent who had covered the Russo-Japanese war, talked with him briefly by telephone that evening and recalled that the conversation ended abruptly. Davis's stout heart had failed, but he had left behind a final appeal to his countrymen which he had written that night:

"That France and her Allies succeed should be the hope and prayer of every American. The fight they are waging is for the things the real, unhyphenated American is supposed to hold most high and most dear. Incidentally, they are fighting his fight, for their success will later save him, unprepared as he is to defend himself, from a humiliating and terrible thrashing. And every word and act of his now that helps the Allies is a blow against frightfulness, against despotism, and in behalf of a broader civilization, a nobler freedom, and a much more pleasant world in which to live."[49]

Soon afterward, the British naval victory at the battle of Jutland gave added support to the Allied cause. The news was reported first by the regular correspondents, based on the official communiqués. But afterward, Rudyard Kipling functioned once again as a journalist and wrote his own account of the events of May 31, 1916, for the London *Daily Telegraph*.[50] Philip Gibbs reported another milestone in the art of making war when he described the birth of the tank on the Somme in 1916: "Our soldiers roared with laughter, as I did, when they saw them lolloping up the roads. On the morning of the great battle of September 15 the presence of the tanks going into action excited all the troops along the front with a sense of comical relief. . . . Men followed them laughing and cheering." H. G. Wells, who had dreamed of this monster, could scarcely add anything to the reality of it in his own piece for the London *Daily Chronicle*. All he could say was: "They were my grandchildren."[51]

The most moving stories of the war, to neutral America as well as to others, were those written about Verdun by Gibbs, Wythe Williams, Paul Scott Mowrer, and their associates. No writer on the Allied side, standing in the presence of a generation of dead Frenchmen who had purchased a terrible victory with their sacrifices, could fail to be affected and transmit his feeling to his readers. Williams, returning from Verdun, quoted Joffre at the Grand Quartier General, Chantilly, "I do not speak of the wounded. At Verdun, our losses were 460,000 killed, and the Germans 540,000. It is a field of a million dead."[52]

The Allies desperately needed the United States now. Italy, the reluctant ally who had come into the war in 1915, was not doing well. The news from the Russian front, never good from the beginning, was growing alarming. And at the Dardanelles, site of the worst British setback of the war outside the western front, there was a burial of dead hopes and brave men. Winston Churchill, who had had such hopes for the Dardanelles campaign, was dropped from the cabinet and went to France as a soldier, but only for a short time.

The public learned soon enough of the Dardanelles failure. But one correspondent, Ellis Ashmead-Bartlett, who tried to circumvent censorship to tell the story in its darkest colors, was caught, sent home, and blacklisted by all commands. Nevinson, who also covered the losing campaign and might have been expected to protest, dismissed the Ash-mead-Bartlett case with these quiet words: "It might be argued that a correspondent is justified in breaking his pledged word for what he considers to be the highest interests of the country, but there is no question that the man who is discovered doing it has to go."[53]

And yet, censorship was circumvented successfully on another Allied secret which was not, however, of quite such strategic importance. Toward the end of 1916, Wythe Williams sent a message to Carr V. Van Anda, the managing editor of the New York *Times,* asking him to read a recent piece in *Collier's* by Alden Brooks. It was about the hero of Verdun, General Henri Philippe Pétain, who had said within earshot of alert journalists at a critical moment, "They shall not pass!"

Van Anda knew, of course, that Williams wanted to use the article as a code and cabled back: "Does Brooks's man want a job with us?"

"Yes," Williams replied. "We are dickering for him now."

Van Anda guessed a change of command was coming. His next message was: "Is Brooks's man to have only the French branch house or the entire firm?"

There was a considerable exchange over this, and the censors were none the wiser, until Williams finally came through with two messages within hours of each other. The first was: "Brooks's man wants too much. Think it best to consider his assistant." Then came this one: "Assistant accepts."

The New York *Times,* as a result, ran a story under a Washington dateline, as protection for Williams, announcing that General Robert Georges Nivelle would succeed General Joffre as the French commander. The same code was used a little later to announce General Petain's elevation to succeed General Nivelle. The *Times* kept its secret despite a lot of official prying.[54]

Northcliffe, meanwhile, was playing a powerful role in unmaking another cabinet in Britain. When David Lloyd George came into power as Prime Minister at the end of 1916, he asked Northcliffe to call on him at 10 Downing Street, but the press lord curtly refused. The two men had quarreled bitterly, and Lloyd George had said at one time: "I would as soon go for a sunny evening stroll around Walton Heath with a grasshopper as try and work with Northcliffe." But they did work together. And eventually, another pet hate of Northcliffe's, Winston Churchill, came back into the cabinet and occupied the War Office post that Kitchener had filled until he went down with the torpedoed HMS *Hampshire.*[55]

There was, however, no king-making at the front. Sickened by the horrors of trench warfare, the tank and gas and heavy artillery attacks, the enormous loss of life to gain a few feet of ground, the correspondents turned with a kind of relief to write of the air war, and the censors permitted them great liberty. True, the *Zeppelin* and the primitive bombing plane had done damage in the cities of Europe, but wholesale death had not yet begun to rain from the skies. Such Allied fliers as René Fonck, Georges Guynemer, Albert Ball, W. A. Bishop, and, later, Eddie Rickenbacker, were pictured as knights of the air. Even the Germans, Oswald Boelcke, Max Immelman, and Manfred von Richthofen, were given the qualities of generous foes. They were romanticized almost beyond recognition even by the grimmest realists among the war correspondents, creating an image that long persisted in the public mind.

Nobody thought of writing about the submarine war in the spirit of "well-played-old-chap." It would have been an incredible affront both to the American and to the Allied publics. The Germans, suffering under the effects of the British blockade, began unrestricted submarine warfare early in 1917 and thus threw away the last chance they had to keep the United States neutral.

A nervy 29-year-old Chicagoan, Floyd Gibbons, dramatized that fatal policy with the support of his newspaper, the Chicago *Tribune,* in one of the strangest exploits of the war. Fresh from the Mexican border, where he had reported the pursuit of Pancho Villa for the *Tribune,* Gibbons booked passage for Britain on the Cunarder *Laconia* when he was assigned by his paper to combat reporting overseas. He could have gone on a neutral ship with a good chance of getting through safely, but he actually looked for a ship likely to be torpedoed. When he went aboard, the *Tribune* saw to it that he was provisioned with a special life preserver, flasks of brandy and fresh water, and several flashlights. This was one reporter who was prepared to survive a torpedoing if he could.

The *Laconia* left New York February 17, 1917. She was sunk by a German submarine on February 25, but most of the 73 passengers and 216 crew members were saved, only 13 aboard being lost.

After six hours in lifeboats, the survivors were picked up by rescue vessels. On February 26, the same day President Wilson told Congress that Germany had not yet committed an overt act in the submarine war, Floyd Gibbons's story was distributed by the Chicago *Tribune* to newspapers throughout the United States, and realists knew it was just a matter of time before the United States entered the war.

Two nights later, on February 28, Secretary of State Robert Lansing, who had succeeded Bryan, invited Edwin M. Hood, the AP correspon-

dent at the State Department, to come to his house. There, Lansing told
the astounded Hood about a hitherto secret document that gravely in-
criminated Germany in hostile action against the United States. The AP
was offered the document exclusively but only on condition that the
source was kept secret.

Hood consulted his superiors, who agreed to Lansing's conditions
and sent a young reporter, Steve Early, for the document. The result
was an international sensation:

> WASHINGTON, D.C., FEB. 28 — THE ASSOCIATED PRESS IS ENABLED TO
> REVEAL THAT GERMANY, IN PLANNING UNRESTRICTED SUBMARINE
> WARFARE AND COUNTING ITS CONSEQUENCES, PROPOSED AN ALLIANCE
> WITH MEXICO AND JAPAN TO MAKE WAR ON THE UNITED STATES, IF
> THIS COUNTRY SHOULD NOT REMAIN NEUTRAL.
>
> JAPAN, THROUGH MEXICAN MEDIATION, WAS TO BE URGED TO
> ABANDON HER ALLIES AND JOIN IN THE ATTACK ON THE UNITED
> STATES.
>
> MEXICO, FOR HER REWARD, WAS TO RECEIVE GENERAL FINANCIAL
> SUPPORT FROM GERMANY, RECONQUER TEXAS, NEW MEXICO, AND ARI-
> ZONA — LOST PROVINCES — AND SHARE IN THE VICTORIOUS PEACE
> TERMS GERMANY CONTEMPLATED.

This was the celebrated Zimmermann telegram — a coded message
dated January 19, 1917 — which, it was later learned, had been intercepted by British Intelligence, decoded, and turned over to the American
authorities. The note was from Dr. Arthur Zimmermann, the Kaiser's
new Foreign Minister, to the German embassy in Washington, and it was
intended for Heinrich von Eckhardt, the German ambassador to Mexico.
Von Eckhardt was supposed to propose the deal to the Mexicans.

Coming so soon after the *Laconia* story, the effect of this journalistic
disclosure was stunning. As a wave of anger swept over the United
States, hardheaded journalists crowded into Lansing's office to find out
what they could about the AP's beat. Lansing would not talk. The reporter pinned down the reluctant Secretary.

"Mr. Secretary, did you know the Associated Press had this story last
night?

"Yes."

Did you deny its authenticity?"

"No."

"Did you object to the Associated Press carrying the story?"

"No."

Seymour Beach Conger, the AP correspondent in Berlin, soon cabled
Dr. Zimmermann's admission that the note was authentic, together

with this classic excuse: "The instructions were to be carried out only after the declaration of war by America."[56]

When the United States entered the war on April 6, 1917, as a result of Germany's continued submarine warfare, the Allied press leaders clearly displayed their relief. Thus, the *Times* of London wrote that "America has no sordid interests involved. . . . She has come forward to defend the right and overthrow the wrong." *Le Matin* proclaimed: "President Wilson's message has changed the face of the war." And *Le Petit Parisien* published a large American flag on its front page with the headline: "America enters the struggle to defend the rights of humanity."[57]

The change in the face of the war, envisioned by *Le Matin,* was painfully slow in coming. The Allies' vaunted spring offensive came to naught. The Italians bogged down on the Isonzo. And in the east, the Russian front collapsed. As the world watched apprehensively, the Red flag was raised over Russia.

THE BIRTH OF THE SOVIET UNION

It was no secret to any informed statesman or journalist in Petrograd that the Tsar's Government was tottering in the autumn of 1916. The only question was when it would fall and what would happen afterward, but the Allied publics were carefully sealed off from events. One of the most knowledgeable correspondents, Robert Wilton of the *Times* of London, wrote privately to his home office on November 16: "I hear that the Allied ambassadors have made very strong representations in high quarters including the Emperor himself who was told in very plain language by H. E. [Sir George Buchanan] that the dynasty was in peril." Like the rest of the Allied press, the *Times* chose to ignore these and other warnings, evidently on patriotic grounds. Instead, the *Times* published an overly optimistic Reuters report from Russia on December 11 and headed it: "Russia Firm and United." It wasn't true, as the public learned.[58]

The conspiratorial monk, Grigori Rasputin, who dominated the weak and foolish Czarina, Alexandra, was assassinated on December 31, 1916, by Prince Felix Yousoupov and a group of fellow-aristocrats. At a hint from the Foreign Office, however, the *Times* published only the barest details. Everything else Wilton passed on to Wickham Steed, the foreign editor, was suppressed. In addition the grave shortages of food and labor and the disorganized railroad transport, fully known in the Russian capital, did not become news that was publishable in Allied capitals. But the Germans, of course, were well aware of it.

Yet, Wilton faithfully persisted. As a Russian-speaking Britisher of long experience, he had worked under such handicaps for many years. Correspondence from Russia had always been difficult. When Charles Dickens had sent George Augustus Sala to Russia in the 1850s for a weekly called *Household Words,* Sala had used Giuseppe Mazzini's device of inserting a single human hair in his letters home to show if they had been opened.[59] Of course they had been. Later, in 1891, when Harold Frederic had toured Russia for the New York *Times* and emerged with a shocking series on the persecution of Jewish minorities, he had been barred from the country.[60]

It was to just such a circumstance as this that Wilton owed his appointment as a Moscow correspondent for the old Thunderer. A predecessor, D. D. Braham, had been expelled in 1903 for writing about the Kishinev pogrom. Wilton, also the correspondent for the Glasgow *Herald,* served from then on as a stringer. For three years the *Times* refused to send in another man, insisting on Braham's return. But finally, as a part of a diplomatic formula, the Russian Government on December 15, 1906, announced that the "administrative measures" against Braham had been "recalled." Thereupon, the *Times* named Wilton formally as its correspondent.[61]

Wilton's first major story after that was the announcement of the British-Russian alliance of August 31, 1907, which ended nearly eighty years of conflict between the two nations. It also eased his own position appreciably. But as the Russian Revolution cast its shadow over the desperate land, he delivered the most earnest warnings to his paper. On January 17, 1917, he wrote privately to Steed:

"Things have been allowed to drift so long that only a very strong and capable government could possibly hope to deal with it satisfactorily. Under present conditions there is no such hope. It is perhaps time for us to speak out. The young Empress and her clique of women have evidently got the reins entirely into their own hands, and the Emperor is being blindly driven into acts that will sooner or later precipitate grave disorders unless a palace revolution averts a general smother. I do not think I am exaggerating the state of affairs."[62]

Two days later, the alert correspondent informed his office that he had heard "from all sides" of a plot to get rid of the Czar and Czarina.[63] On March 15, amid strikes and riots and the mutiny of troops in Petrograd, Nicholas II abdicated in favor of a provisional government supported by the Duma. In this manner, the sensational news burst on a world that was largely unprepared for it. In Zurich, where a group of Russian revolutionaries was living in exile, Lenin refused to believe the news until he had read it in the Swiss newspapers. His associate, Leon Trotsky, who then was publishing a radical sheet in New York, wrote of the Bolsheviks: "The revolutionary explosion they had so long and so tensely awaited caught them unaware."[64]

The provisional Government of Prince George Lvov, which included Professor Pavel Miliukov as Foreign Minister and Alexander Kerensky as Minister of Justice, sought to keep Russia fighting against Germany. Curiously, when Joseph Stalin reached Petrograd on March 28 and took control of *Pravda,* the party newspaper that had been founded in 1912, he published a manifesto: "The mere slogan: 'Down With The War,' is absolutely impractical. As long as the German army obeys the orders of the Kaiser, the Russian soldier must stand firmly at his post."[65]

The Germans weren't worried about Stalin at that point. Matthias Erzberger, the Catholic Centrist leader who was the Kaiser's chief propagandist, and General Max Hoffman, the chief of the German general staff on the eastern front, both agreed that Lenin and his party should be sent to Russia through Germany to stir up all possible trouble for the shaky new Russian regime.[66]

On April 8, 1917, Lenin and his party of Bolsheviks, including the sardonic journalist, Karl Radek, boarded a train at Zurich and were sealed into their compartments. Lenin seemed not to hear the cheers of his supporters, the playing of the "Internationale," or the abuse showered on him by his opponents who howled that he was nothing but a German spy. He kept staring toward the distant Alps as the train rolled toward the German border. Radek remarked in a burst of irreverence, "Vladimir Ilich is imagining himself as premier of the Revolutionary Government." Lenin said nothing, but smiled.[67] The trip did not attract attention in the world press, at the time, and the *Neue Zürcher Zeitung* waited an appropriate period before publishing a sarcastic observation on the "loving support of Lenin from German Imperialism."[68]

It was April 16 before Lenin and his party arrived at the Finland Station in Petrograd, to be hoisted on the shoulders of his supporters and given a bouquet of flowers, to which he replied, with some difficulty: "The Russian Revolution, achieved by you, has opened a new epoch. Long live the world-wide Socialist Revolution."[69] It was April 20 before Reuters reported Lenin had passed through Stockholm on his way to Petrograd and April 30 before the Finland Station demonstration reached the British papers, an indication of the difficulties of communication through censorship.[70] Wilton, attacked for his dispatches both at home and in Petrograd, was ill in London at the time. Arthur Ransome of the Manchester *Guardian* was having trouble getting through. Isaac Don Levine, the foreign news editor of the New York *Tribune,* was so bemused by the situation he saw in the Russian capital that he believed Lenin's attacks on the provisional government had "alienated the large following" he once had. Yet, despite the confusion, Levine was shrewd enough to see that the situation was "fraught with extreme danger."[71]

Lenin's hammer blows against the Menshevik war policy kept up all summer in the Petrograd soviet and echoed elsewhere in Russia. One by one, his exiled associates rejoined him for the struggle they all knew was coming with the moderate government. The most important of all, Leon Trotsky, who for years had wavered between the Bolshevik and Menshevik wings, left his newspaper, *Novy Mir,* in New York and boarded a Swedish-bound ship in Brooklyn. He was taken off at Halifax by British Intelligence officers but told a fellow-passenger, Ulrich Salchow, an AP correspondent bound for Sweden, that he would be in Stockholm soon. Within three weeks, he called on Salchow, as he had promised. Asked how he had done it, he remarked: "Easy. I merely told them how I was going back to Russia to end the revolution and throw the force of Russia back into the war wholeheartedly against Germany." He went to Petrograd to do exactly the opposite.[72]

As the Lvov Government wavered, the Bolsheviks under Lenin's urging launched an attack in mid-July in an effort to seize power. The attempt was premature. After it failed, Lenin fled to Finland and Trotsky was thrown into prison. The principal result of the first test of strength was to bring Alexander Kerensky to power as premier. Within a short time, he had to dismiss the Russian commander-in-chief, General Lavr Kornilov, who then advanced on Petrograd with an army in September to overthrow the government. Trotsky was released from prison. Kerensky had to depend on the Bolsheviks to help him turn back Kornilov and became, in effect, their prisoner.

It was at this juncture that the most eloquent non-Russian witness of the revolution, John Reed, arrived in Petrograd with his beautiful but eccentric bride, Louise Bryant. Reed was 30 then, had been a journalist for six years, and was deeply attracted to the Soviet cause. His background was anything but proletarian — a member of a well-to-do family in Portland, Ore.; graduate of Harvard as a classmate of Walter Lippmann and T. S. Eliot; dabbler in the drama as a member of the Provincetown group, which had staged one of his short plays with another by his friend, Eugene O'Neill. Nor was his Louise a born revolutionary. She had been the wife of a Portland dentist until she and Reed had fallen in love, but she was scarcely absorbed in him. Her roving eye had caught and held O'Neill at Provincetown until she had tired of him. Still, Reed hadn't seemed to mind and had brought her to Russia with him.[73]

During his wandering in Mexico as a war correspondent covering Pancho Villa and his border forays against the American forces, Reed had had a ready market for his pieces in *Metropolitan* magazine and other publications. But his expedition to Russia was something else again. American editors, wary of his radical outbursts, steered clear of him and he had to accept the rather impractical sponsorship of the *Call,* a struggling left-wing paper in New York; the *Masses,* a radical magazine; and *Seven Arts* magazine. From the day he arrived in Russia, he was not a reporter but a partisan and made no secret of it. "Already, I have thousands of comrades here," he wrote home.[74]

There is no doubt that Reed was on top of the story. Even though he did not know Russian, he and Louise made certain they were always with Americans or others who did. He and Louise received much of their information from Alexander Gumberg, a Russian with close ties to the revolutionaries, who was translator and handyman for Colonel Raymond Robins, nominally a Red Cross representative. They also had help from others like Albert Rhys Williams, Bill and Anna Shatoff, and Bill's brother, Zorin, all of whom were sympathizers. All through October 1917, the Bolsheviks met incessantly and laid their plans with Reed as a trusted observer. He wrote home to Boardman Robinson on the New York *Call:* "It is possible that the proletariat will finally lose its temper and rise; it is possible that the generals will come with fire and sword. . . . It looks like a showdown soon." And for Kerensky, whom he interviewed, there was this chilling prediction: "Life is hideously swift for compromisers here."[75]

Events were now racing toward a climax in Petrograd. At the Smolny Institute, the Petrograd soviet began holding all-night meetings early in November. There was no doubt that the Bolsheviks now had a majority. Reed listened to their debates. Then, he would go up to the top floor of the Smolny where the Military Revolutionary Committee was meeting and see how coolly the Soviets were preparing to make their bid by force of arms. On November 6, with Lenin and Trotsky urging them on, the Bolsheviks made their decision. On November 7, they struck with all the force at their command.

Reed and Louise picked up Albert Rhys Williams that morning and walked to the Winter Palace, where Kerensky had his office. He wasn't there. Soldiers and sailors and Red Guards were everywhere on the streets. Barricades were being thrown up. But although tension was high, nothing had happened yet. Reed and his two friends walked to the Smolny Institute, where they saw that fourteen out of the twenty-five members of the presidium of the All-Russian Congress of Soviets were Bolsheviks. The moderate Mensheviks and the Social Revolutionaries attacked the aggressive policy of the Bolsheviks, were voted down, and finally walked out amid hoots and curses. Lenin now was staking everything on his strike for power.

Reed's party, now increased to five by the arrival of Gumberg and Bessie Beatty, another visiting journalist, left the Smolny Institute, were given passes and rode to the Winter Palace in time to see the Red Guards, soldiers, and sailors swarm to the attack. The takeover was so swift that Reed and Louise were able to wander around inside the Winter Palace. He even picked up a jeweled sword as a souvenir and smuggled it out with him.

On the next evening, Reed was at the Smolny Institute when Lenin, short and stocky in his ragged clothes, stood before the Congress of Soviets, accepted their ovation, and shouted, "We shall now proceed to construct the Socialist order." He read the Bolshevik program: immediate talks to arrange for peace, no indemnities or annexations, publication of secret treaties, and a three-month armistice.[76]

Reed heard it all.[77] But neither he nor any other correspondent was able to get much through Soviet censorship. On November 8, Reuters had sixteen lines from Petrograd saying that naval forces had seized a few points in the city but otherwise things were "normal." On November 9, it was clear that the Bolshevik coup d'état had been successful. Wilton, who was then in London, put together a column of news out of telegrams to the *Times* from various sources.[78] But on November 12, Wilton's information from Petrograd was so uncertain that he had a story in the paper headed, "Lenin Losing Control."[79] The *Times* hastily called James David Bourchier from the Balkans as a temporary replacement, but he evidently could learn little during all the disorder and soon left.

The mob soon turned on the correspondents, always a ready target in any such situation. Charles Stephenson Smith, the AP bureau chief in Petrograd, was knocked cold by a soldier swinging a rifle butt, and another member of the AP staff was shot in the knee by a sniper.[80] Guy Beringer, the Reuters correspondent, escaped with his wife to Finland but didn't know when he was well off. He came back, was thrown into prison for six months, and barely escaped execution.[81]

Reed was just about the only foreigner who could work effectively at this period. He cabled a short statement from Lenin to the American

Socialists on November 15. Six days later, he filed his first complete story of the revolution and had it cleared through censorship. It ran in the New York *Call* under a seven-column banner.[82] The Bolshevik victory was then complete. Kerensky escaped, but most of his associates in the Provisional Government were jailed. Lenin was the commissar who headed the Council of People's Commissars. Trotsky was the commissar for foreign affairs; Stalin, the commissar for national minorities. This was the government that concluded an armistice with Germany on December 3, 1917, and took Russia out of the war with the signing of the Brest-Litovsk Treaty of March 3, 1918.

Far from removing the steely grip in which the czars had held Russia for so many centuries, the new masters of Russia merely replaced the old imperial repressions with their own. Their excuse was the necessity for the security of the state; as a result, they instituted a tighter form of state-controlled journalism. One of its manifestations was strict censorship, another the deliberate falsification of the news when that was believed necessary. When local Soviet leaders executed the Czar, Czarina, and their children on July 16, 1918, at Ekaterinburg (Sverdlovsk), fearful that they might be liberated by anti-Bolshevist forces, the official Government paper *Izvestia* announced three days later that the Tsar had been shot, but that "the wife and son of Nicholas Romanov were sent to a safe place." The world did not really know the truth for many months, although rumors of the executions spread widely. Then, a young former UP correspondent in Berlin, Carl W. Ackerman, reached Ekaterinburg with the Czech Legion, formed out of former Austrian war prisoners in Russia, and verified the tragic end of the Romanovs. He published his story in the New York *Times*.[83]

At about the time of the Czar's execution, John Reed was back in the United States, defending Russia with all his strength. He was indicted for sedition as a result of his antiwar activities, but nothing came of it. Instead, he returned to Russia with Louise Bryant and worked in the Soviet propaganda bureau, an enthusiastic convert to state-controlled journalism. When he died of typhus in 1920, he was buried with the heroes of the Soviet Union inside the Kremlin wall.

American opinion on Russia, so vital a force in world affairs in the years to come, also was significantly affected by the work of a variety of other commentators and correspondents, among the most important being George Kennan, then 72 years old, in the *Outlook;* Professor Samuel Northrup Harper in the *Christian Science Monitor;* Harold Williams, correspondent for the New York *Times;* Louis Edgar Browne, correspondent for the *Chicago Daily News;* Colonel George Harvey, former ambassador to the Court of St. James's, in the North American Review's *War Weekly;* Max Eastman in the *Liberator;* Oswald Garrison Villard in *The Nation;* and Walter Lippmann in the *New Republic.*

Kennan, one of the leading authorities on Russia in his day, was one of the proponents of intervention, however cautious, in Siberia and thereby anticipated the Wilson administration's eventual action. Professor Harper, who also had a deep firsthand knowledge of Russia, was for economic aid plus moral support of the Russian people, but did not necessarily oppose the use of military force in this connection. Colonel Harvey wanted all-out intervention, using Japanese troops, principally, in Siberia, as a counterweight to any possibility that the new Russian regime might give aid and comfort to the German war machine. Villard and Eastman both favored recognition of the new Soviet regime, with the former taking a strong line against intervention. Lippmann, so soon to become one of the strongest journalistic voices of his time, also opposed intervention, basing himself on Wilson's one-time position against interference in Russia's internal affairs.

Yet, despite the importance of the times and the issues, there was a crucial shortage of authentic, firsthand information from Russia in some of the leading news agencies and newspapers in the world.* The most dramatic was the refusal of the *Times* of London to send in a permanent correspondent from the time that Wilton returned home in 1917 (Bourchier served briefly and temporarily) until relaxation of censorship made it possible to send a staff man to Moscow in 1939 to cover the abortive talks on an Anglo-Soviet Pact. The *Times* depended mainly on wire services and its own man in Riga, R. O. G. Urch, who had once been imprisoned by the Bolsheviks for two months. During the period between the enforced departure of the AP Petrograd staff in 1918 and the end of the intervention period, the AP also was without a staff man in the capital. Mrs. Marguerite Harrison of Baltimore, who had been a reporter for the Baltimore *Sun* in 1916 and a war correspondent with the AEF in France, tried to act as an undercover correspondent for the AP in Petrograd during the interim but was caught, jailed for a short time as a suspected spy, and thereafter desisted. The AP reported Russia from its perimeter, as did a number of other newsgathering organizations. Foreign Commissar Maxim Litvinov's refusal

---

*Walter Lippmann and Charles Merz, in a supplement to the *New Republic* of Aug. 4, 1920, showed the ineptitude of American press coverage by pointing to the many false reports of the overthrow of the Bolshevik regime.

to grant visas to correspondents whose views were not "of known sympathy" with Soviet rule made it impossible for a time to get foreign correspondents inside Russia.

In this respect, the Soviet regime merely continued the Russian tradition of the czars. The new masters of Russia were against a press they could not wholly control. When Lenin ordered the merger of the Petrograd Telegraph Agency and the Soviet Press Bureau in 1918 to form the Russian Telegraph Agency, Rosta, he also saw to it that a special section called Agit-Rosta was organized to get out propaganda for party workers. In 1925, Rosta became the Telegrafnoie Agenstvo Sovietskavo Soyuza, the Telegraphic Agency of the Soviet Union, or, to use its familiar name, Tass.[84]

The basic attitudes toward the press in general and foreign correspondence in particular that were so apparent at the birth of the Soviet Union became a pattern for the future. On some occasions, foreign correspondents were treated with indulgence and permitted some leeway; on others, they were held in the tightest restraint. But at no time for many years were there to be large numbers of them inside the Soviet Union.

THE UNITED STATES AS A WORLD POWER

General John J. Pershing, then a major general, marched off the Cunarder *Baltic* at Liverpool with a small group of officers on June 8, 1917. For the thoughtful ones among the knot of correspondents who gathered on the pier, it was a symbolic act — the arrival of the United States as a world power. And yet, there was an air of improbability about the whole business, as if nobody was quite willing to take America's lofty aspirations seriously. The welcoming British military mission did the honors for General Pershing, then one of them asked, indicating the American's modest entourage: "General, is this your personal staff?" The grim-faced Pershing replied, "No, this is my general staff."[85] Next, to make everything seem completely homey to the Americans, there was a fine censorship foul-up. The British censors had forbidden mention of Pershing's port of debarkation, which caused the impish Floyd Gibbons to draft the following cable to the Chicago *Tribune* and see it cleared:

PERSHING LANDED AT BRITISH PORT TODAY AND WAS GREETED BY LORD MAYOR OF LIVERPOOL[86]

Pershing, with a military man's simple directness, had decided he would be able to control the press by limiting the numbers of correspondents and by getting the best man he could find to handle censorship matters. The limit of a dozen correspondents was soon exceeded. Before the war was over. there were sixty Americans who had been officially accredited to the AEF as correspondents and a number of others, including such imposing figures as Herbert Bayard Swope and Westbrook Pegler, who weren't on the rolls of the military in any form. As for the chief censor, he turned out to be the veteran Frederick Palmer, who gave up an estimated $40,000 a year and a new job as the New York *Herald* correspondent at the front to become a lowly public relations major at $175 a month, with nothing to look forward to except incalculable abuse.

Palmer was then 44 years old. He had been newspapering since he had written about a Fourth of July parade for the Jamestown (N.Y.) *Morning Post* at the age of 15. At 22 he had gone to London and Paris to do pieces for the New York *Press*. Then, working for *Collier's* and various newspapers, he had covered a long string of big and little wars — the Greek-Turkish war, the Spanish-American War, the Philippine insurrection, the Boxer Rebellion, the Russo-Japanese war, and the Mexican border war, among others. Palmer, without doubt, was one of the most experienced of living war correspondents. Yet, it scarcely qualified him for censorship, as both he and General Pershing were to discover ultimately.[87]

The new chief of the AEF censors should have known better, of course, but no one is more ferociously military than a journalist who is put into uniform and given a command. He decreed that all correspondents, uniformed by General Pershing's orders, would have to be herded together like a party of tourists wherever they went. All copy was to be cleared by his office — and his office was unyielding on protests. There were a lot of other rules, many of them irksome and some unnecessary. The upshot was that long before the first American troops arrived at the front, the unruly and independent-minded American war correspondents decided they didn't like the system and had distinct doubts about their old colleague, Major Palmer.

Floyd Gibbons took off from the correspondents' bivouac in France and busied himself with some mysterious assignments in Paris. A large and rumpled New York *Tribune* correspondent, Heywood Broun, also had a bad habit of deserting the Palmer establishment and eventually had his accreditation suspended — which bothered him not at all. Still others poked around in odd places and found out things they shouldn't.

And those who were beaten on stories invariably protested heatedly that they had abided by the rules and lost out to less gentlemanly but more competitive comrades. "This," wrote the despondent Palmer, "is worse than war."[88]

His trials as a censor had only begun, however. When the first American troops, units of the 1st Division, arrived in convoy at St. Nazaire on June 26, the American correspondents were out in force against their natural enemies, the censors. Major Palmer decreed that nothing could be printed until the last ship bearing the last troops in the convoy made port. There was a lot of grumbling, succeeded by the usual scheming. But to the surprise of Major Palmer, and the discomfiture of the American correspondents, the big news was published first by their Allies. It so happened that a French censor at *Ce Soir,* Paris, efficiently killed the story of the American landing in page proof but forgot to kill the headline. Accordingly, *Ce Soir* came out with a blank column under these words in large type on page 1:

LE PREMIER CORPS EXPEDITIONNAIRE AMERICAIN EST ARRIVE A SAINT-NAZAIRE.

The British correspondents didn't bother to wait for Major Palmer's stamp of approval but forwarded their copy directly to London by courier. For once, the British censors were less efficient than their American counterparts. It was Reuters, therefore, that carried the first news to the United States of the landing of the modest AEF contingent in France.[89] American editors and correspondents, who aspire to a high degree of sophistication except when they are beaten on a story, particularly by the British, reacted with a first-rate display of journalistic rage, but it didn't do them much good. The determined Major Palmer refused to turn any American dispatches loose until July 1, when the last ship of the convoy reached port.

This was distinctly not the way a great power was expected to handle its affairs. The United States was at war; and yet, despite everything the State Department, the War Department, and the Creel Committee on Public Information could do, the press was conducting business pretty much as usual. Every editor and correspondent swore wholeheartedly that he would be the last to give aid and comfort to the enemy, but few would agree to sit on any piece of war news for very long. This was in the old, independent tradition of American journalism. In consequence, an ever greater strain was placed on the principle of freedom of the press.

To add to Major Palmer's woes, there were unintended excesses of reporting that were caused by sheer enthusiasm. One of the most famous incidents occurred on July 4, 1917, when the American correspondents, having nothing better to do, traipsed out to Little Picpus Cemetery on the outskirts of Paris to watch General Pershing lay a wreath on the tomb of Lafayette. Major Charles E. Stanton, the AEF paymaster, one of the early speakers, was an old-time country orator. As the general stood by, the major wound himself up to a pitch of oratorical fervor, ending his remarks with a ringing, "Lafayette, we are here!" General Pershing, who followed him, muttered as he laid the wreath on the tomb of Lafayette that the paymaster had spoken for all Americans. In the confusion and hubbub, the correspondents, who were some distance off, gained the impression that Pershing had spoken the historic words. Floyd Gibbons, among others, cabled them home in an effusive July 4 story. Major Palmer wrote sorrowfully of the incident that Pershing was no orator: "He was not a phrase-maker, except the 'Lafayette, we are here! of Paymaster Stanton, which was credited to him, and led to false expectations."[90]

It was a talented but unruly crew that Palmer tried to discipline. To have to handle a young Heywood Broun and a young Westbrook Pegler at the same time would have been a sufficient chore for any censor. In addition, he had to keep tabs on, among others, Damon Runyon of the New York *American,* Irvin S. Cobb of the *Saturday Evening Post,* a hard-boiled, 28-year-old Virginian; Edwin L. (Jimmy) James, of the New York *Times;* Junius Wood, a Chicago *Daily News* man who operated as if he were back at City Hall; wily Fred F. Ferguson, of the UP, and Raymond Carroll, a loner known as the "Hermit Crab" who wrote for the Philadelphia *Public Ledger.* There was usually a publisher around, as well. When Floyd Gibbons got into trouble, as he frequently did, he would bring in a doughty major, Robert R. McCormick, the publisher of the Chicago *Tribune.*[91]

To transmit sensitive war news to such a crew, to say nothing of the regulars in Paris, would have tried the talents of a Theodore Roosevelt. Major Palmer had grave forebodings when he led his charges toward the front on October 23, 1917. They were bound for the town of Bathelemont, on the Lorraine front, where it was expected the first American gun crew would go into action that day. As they halted some miles from their destination, a battery of American artillery passed them with a familiar figure draped on a caisson. The always alert Runyon yelled, "Hey, there's Gibbons! How the hell did *he* get there?" Gibbons and Raymond Carroll saw the first shot fired from a French 75 by the Americans that day. Gibbons got the shell case and was persuaded with difficulty to give it up so it could be presented to President Wilson. Then he and Carroll, as a penalty for their unwarranted enterprise, were placed under arrest for forty-eight hours, but were permitted to send their stories after the rest.[92]

The other "firsts," so dear to the hearts of American newspapermen, were soon disposed of—the first wounded American, the first to be killed in action, the first German prisoner (who was bayoneted after he was disarmed, a detail that was quickly censored).[93] Palmer, after some months of such trials, was relieved. The military succeeded him, but without improvement in an altogether trying situation for both correspondents and censors.[94] Life for the correspondents in the American sector continued to be every bit as frustrating as that under the British and French. The censors had to bear down. It was in the nature of modern war and of the modern state fighting for self-preservation, as even the veteran Wythe Williams discovered. When he evaded censorship by mailing an article to *Collier's* giving the detailed reasons for the failure of an Allied offensive, his credentials were immediately suspended, and he was nearly expelled from France in disgrace. The man who saved him was Georges Clemenceau, the Tiger, who had come to power that fall and who, even as premier of France, remembered his first profession and his friends.[95]

In a situation of this kind, there was only one way to stay ahead of the opposition, and that was to use the quickest (and the most expensive) cable services to bring in the official news. Carr V. Van Anda of the New York *Times* was among those who realized it. As soon as the massive Ludendorff spring offensive began on March 21, 1918, on the western front, Van Anda kept cabling Walter Duranty, a young Britisher in the *Times*'s Paris office, to send everything at the "double urgent" message rate. That was 75 cents a word. It enabled the *Times* to print news of the current date from the battlefield, when it was officially released. In effect, this was a mere process of expediting official communiqués, although Edwin L. James did send some firsthand stories of Americans in action as they began to make themselves felt.[96]

It was the courageous Gibbons, always disregarding his own safety, who nearly lost his life by going into combat. On June 6, 1918, he entered Belleau Wood with the U.S. Marines and was hit three times by machine gun bullets, one gouging out an eye. Lieutenant Oscar Hartzel, a former New York *Times* man, helped him to safety, an exploit for which the correspondent received the Croix de Guerre and the famous patch over his left eye that was his trademark. The soldier was mentioned in the newspaper reports.[97] There was less glory still for the newspapermen who stayed in the ambulance corps. One of them, a young man from the Kansas City *Star,* Ernest Hemingway, was thankful he was able to survive the Italian campaign.[98]

It was Clemenceau, the old journalist, who dominated the final stages of the war. He had begun his second term as premier on November 16, and, as the Germans smashed forward in their final offensive he rallied his people: "I shall fight before Paris, I shall fight behind Paris. The Germans may take Paris but that will not stop me from carrying on the war. We shall fight on the Loire, we shall fight on the Garonne, we shall fight even on the Pyrenees. And should we be driven off the Pyrenees, we shall continue the war from the sea. But as for asking for peace, never!"

The biggest news now emanated from the headquarters of the Generalissimo, Marshal Ferdinand Foch, as the Allies held the Germans at the second battle of the Marne. But once more, the American correspondent reached for competitive advantage. Fred Ferguson of the UP learned of the projected American offensive at St. Mihiel and prepared a series of bulletins, with the time left blank, announcing the achievement of each objective. He turned these over to Captain Gerald Morgan, the field censor at Nancy, and asked him to release them when he could. Morgan agreed. Next, Ferguson hired an auto and kept James Howe of the AP and Hank Wales of International News Service out of headquarters for hours. When they returned, Ferguson had sheafs of congratulatory telegrams; his rivals had rockets, as angry inquiries from the home office are known.[99]

It was simply in the nature of such correspondents to compete, regardless of censorship, and whatever the ultimate cost might be. For just as Ferguson was able to bring the first news to the United States of the St. Mihiel offensive, Wales gained journalistic fame for an exploit of his own. His was the most eloquent report of the execution of a Dutch dancer, Gertrud Margarete Zelle, and through it he helped create the twentieth-century legend of the femme fatale, Mata Hari, as she called herself when she was not selling military secrets to the Germans.[100]

The pendulum of interest swung briefly from the advancing Allies to New York on September 16, 1918, when the New York *Times* published an editorial on Austrian peace feelers that had been put out to avert total defeat. The *Times*'s editorial was deliberately done; written by the editor, Charles R. Miller, on the basis of news dispatches that had been read to both him and Adolph S. Ochs, the publisher, by Van Anda. Miller dictated the piece to the office from his home in Great Neck but did not clear it with Ochs, who up to that time had trusted his judgment implicitly.

"Reason and humanity," said the editorial, "demand that the Austrian invitation be accepted. The case for conference is presented with extraordinary eloquence and force, a convincing argument is made for an exchange of views that may remove old and recent misunderstandings. . . . We cannot imagine that the invitation will be declined. . . . When we consider the deluge of blood that has been poured out in this war, the incalculable waste of treasure, the ruin it has wrought, the grief that wrings millions of hearts because of it, we must conclude that only the madness or the soulless depravity of someone of the belligerent powers could obstruct or defeat the purpose of the conference."

The uproar that had greeted Northcliffe's attack on the British government earlier in the war for failing to send enough high explosive shells to the British troops was a mere murmur compared to the devastating protest that now descended on the New York *Times*. It was almost as if President Wilson's Fourteen Points for a peaceful settlement had been repudiated, which was certainly not the *Times*'s intention. The President himself was upset. So were some members of the *Times*'s own staff, who thought their newspaper was "running up the white flag." Even more criticism flowed from Allied capitals. Northcliffe, who had been a member of a British wartime mission to the United States, was thoroughly out of sympathy with the New York *Times*. The newspaper lost circulation that took it years to recover and unfairly gained a reputation for being pro-German.[101]

Nor was the *Times* alone in facing such criticism. William Randolph Hearst was attacked throughout the war as pro-German. One reason was Hearst's unwise decision to hire William Bayard Hale, the former New York *Times* correspondent whose pro-German sympathies were known, and send him to Germany. Although Hearst did not know it, Hale was being paid by the Germans at the time. Even more damaging was Hearst's visiting with Paul Bolo Pasha, a Levantine merchant who was reputed to be the financial power behind the Paris newspaper, *Le Journal*. It later developed that Bolo was being heavily paid by the Germans to influence Allied opinion. He was tried and shot as a traitor, as were some of his associates. It did not make Hearst give up his anti-British line, however; for he was one of the most vigorous champions of the Irish patriot, Sir Roger Casement, who was executed because the British accused him of holding secret talks with the Germans.[102] The effort of Hearst's enemies to make him appear to be a traitor never got very far, in any case.

In the final days of the war, the tension among journalists became almost unbearable. Each watched the other for a sign that the news for which the whole world hungered, the end of the war, might be close.

Censorship was tighter than ever on all fronts, as a result. Nobody wanted to let down. In this strained atmosphere, Roy W. Howard, the jaunty little president of the UP, left Paris on November 7, 1918, to go to Brest and board an Army transport for home. He knew, of course, that the armistice terms had already been agreed on by the inter-Allied conference. Consequently, when he walked into the office of Admiral Henry B. Wilson, commander of U.S. Navy forces in French waters, he was not particularly surprised when the Admiral handed him a telegram reporting the good news. All Brest was celebrating.

"The armistice has been signed," Admiral Wilson said.

Howard asked, "Is it official?"

"Official, hell, I should say it *is* official. I just received this over my direct wire from the embassy. It's the official announcement."

The wire had been cleared by the Admiral for posting in the office of the Brest newspaper, *La Depeche.* Outside, the crowd in the streets was cheering.

"I beg your pardon, Admiral," Howard asked, "but if this is official and you've announced it to the base and have given it to the local paper for publication, do you have any objection if I file it to the United Press?"

"Hell, no. This is official. It is signed by Captain Jackson, our naval attache in Paris. Here's a copy. Go to it."

This was the message Howard filed, countersigning the name and official press card number of his French bureau chief, William Philip Simms, as required by regulations:

UNIPRESS NEW YORK — URGENT ARMISTICE ALLIES GERMANY SIGNED ELEVEN SMORNING HOSTILITIES CEASED TWO SAFTERNOON SEDAN TAKEN SMORNING BY AMERICANS.

HOWARD
SIMMS

In New York this became a bulletin under a Paris dateline that incorporated other material. Why not? Wasn't it Howard, the boss himself, who had in some miraculous fashion achieved the greatest beat of the entire war? No wonder the UP put out this triumphant lead:

PARIS, NOV. 7 (UP) — THE WAR IS OVER. GERMANY AND THE ALLIES SIGNED AN ARMISTICE AT 11 A.M. TODAY, HOSTILITIES CEASING THREE HOURS LATER. AS MARSHAL FOCH'S TERMS ARE KNOWN TO INCLUDE PROVISIONS WHICH WILL PREVENT RESUMPTION OF HOSTILITIES, THE GREATEST WAR OF ALL TIME HAS COME TO AN END.

The news touched off a roaring, jubilant, unrestrained celebration throughout the United States. It could not be stopped for hours, even though many an editor viewed the beat with skepticism. A number of papers didn't publish it. The AP issued a note to its editors:

AT THIS HOUR THE GOVERNMENT AT WASHINGTON HAS RECEIVED NOTHING TO SUPPORT THE REPORT THAT THAT ARMISTICE HAS BEEN SIGNED AND WE HAVE RECEIVED NOTHING FROM OUR CORRESPONDENTS ABROAD TO SUPPORT IT.

Several hours passed. There was still no confirmation from Washington, London, or Paris. Carl D. Groat, the UP correspondent at the State Department, asked about his boss's exclusive, remarked sourly that it was "too damned exclusive." At 2:15 p.m. on that maddening day, the AP finally put out this bulletin:

WASHINGTON, NOV 7 (AP) — IT WAS OFFICIALLY ANNOUNCED AT THE STATE DEPARTMENT AT 2:15 O'CLOCK THIS AFTERNOON THAT THE GERMANS HAD NOT SIGNED ARMISTICE TERMS.

In Brest at about that hour, a courier located Howard and told him Admiral Wilson had had a second message from the embassy in Paris. That message said the original telegram was now "unconfirmable." Howard was thunderstruck. He filed a correction, but with the cables clogged it didn't get through for many hours. The UP rode with his bulletin to a journalistic disaster.

Howard next cabled his alibi, a statement issued by Admiral Wilson:

"The statement of the United Press relative to the signing of the armistice was made public from my office on the basis of what appeared to be official and authoritative information. I am in a position to know that the United Press and its representatives acted in perfect good faith, and the premature announcement was the result of an error for which the agency was in no wise responsible."

The indignation against the UP was great, but the most moral papers were the ones that happened to be among the greatest rivals of the Scripps-Howard organization. Thus, the New York *Tribune* said editorially: "The statement of Admiral Wilson is an amazing one. It only intensifies the mystery of what must now rank as one of the greatest hoaxes of newspaper history." The mystery of who actually issued the news on which the telegram to Brest was based never was solved. With the signing of the armistice on November 11, 1918, the incident passed into history.[103]

Thus, the wartime challenge to the independent press to choose be-

tween freedom and security was, for all practical purposes, left unre-
solved. Government regulation and censorship were merely tolerated by
the press of the Allied nations, never fully accepted. Once the big guns
fell silent, the press of the West reverted to its old anarchic habits and,
ever so briefly, the press of Germany experienced the dizzy sensation of
freedom. But in Russia, state-controlled journalism set out to provide its
peoples only with information of which the government approved. And
this, by all odds, was the greatest challenge and the greatest danger to
the continued growth of a free and uninterrupted exchange of foreign
information for public consumption.

5 Not So Brave . . . Not So New

"OPEN COVENANTS . . ."

When Woodrow Wilson arrived in Paris for the peacemaking on December 13, 1918, many a correspondent, with a myopia strange to a querulous profession, actually expected that there would be "open covenants . . . openly arrived at." It was the catch phrase the President had used in his Fourteen Points speech of January 8, 1918. Unhappily, it had been a mere expression of his philosophy, a figure of speech. For when the Council of Ten met on behalf of the Allied and Associated Powers, one of its first decisions was to exclude the press.

The red-headed and violent Herbert Bayard Swope of the New York *World,* known as "Wilson's paper," was chairman of the committee of correspondents, which protested vigorously. The Council relented, but only a trifle. A few meek and well-behaved correspondents were admitted to selected plenary sessions, not Swope. The ever-resourceful gentleman from the *World* attired himself tastefully in top hat, morning coat, and striped trousers, hired the longest and shiniest black limousine he could find, and had himself driven to the conference scene. His welcome befitted that of any potentate. His story next day was great. Whereupon his angry associates drew up a petition demanding his removal as chairman of their committee. In a light moment, he signed the petition — and killed it.[1]

The exploit was important only as an illustration of the temper of the correspondents. Since they were determined not to be counted out of the peace-making, they had to be dealt with. But the diplomats, dangerously underrating them, did not do a very thorough job, and the consequences were not long in coming.

In many ways, Versailles set the pattern for acquainting the public with the vast network of international negotiations that was to develop in the years to come. Sir George Riddle for the British, Ray Stannard Baker for the Americans, and Louis Aubert and sometimes André Tardieu for the French set up daily briefings for the press. So did the other delegations that sensed there was a press problem. But, too often, the briefing system became a source of misunderstanding, half-truths, propaganda pitches, and occasionally outright untruths. Now and then, a glamorous figure like Lloyd George would hold a press conference, in which he said little or nothing. Finally, rounding out the pattern of daily information, there were the inevitable wire-pullers who inhabited the half-world between diplomacy and journalism — Wickham Steed, André Geraud ("Pertinax"), commentator of the *Echo de Paris,* and Philippe Millet, foreign editor of *Le Temps.* It was a miserable system. Even Steed had to concede that "a thick mist veiled the peace conference from the British public."[2] As for the United States, things were even worse.

Swope worked with his own sources, as good reporters invariably do. He had the best. There was, first of all, Colonel Edward M. House, Wilson's confidant. Moreover, Frank I. Cobb, the *World*'s editor, and his young associate, Walter Lippmann of the *New Republic,* had written the commentary on Wilson's Fourteen Points — a document House read to an impatient Lloyd George and a scornful Clemenceau. These, too, were Swope's friends.[3] They all sought support for Wilson's views; but without publicity, how could there be support?

Colonel Stephen Bonsal, the old foreign correspondent who had been on Pershing's staff during the war and now was President Wilson's translator, worried about Wilson's aloofness from the press. He wrote, "I have gloomy forebodings. Not a few of the delegates will 'leak' to their favorite newspaper when the leakage promises to be helpful, and of course the burden of newspaper unpopularity under which the President suffers will be increased by what many have already called 'the revival of Star Chamber proceedings' by one who promised 'open covenants . . . openly arrived at.' "[4]

Thus, Wilson, by sealing himself up, virtually handed the advantage to the opponents of the League of Nations who made sure that the most adverse material would be "leaked" at the very worst time. Wire-service men, fighting for every scrap of news against the dominance of the specials, took everything they could get. Wilson's secrecy, the uninformative and sometimes dishonest briefings, and the wooden communiqués only spurred them on to seek news from his opponents.

In this manner, the all-important Article X of the Covenant got out prematurely and with damaging effect. Wilson's chief Republican foes, Senators William E. Borah of Idaho and Henry Cabot Lodge of Massachusetts, with the support of the Hearst newspapers, were raising questions about the enforcement of the Covenant. There had been reports out of Paris that Article X, if approved at Versailles and ratified by the American Congress, would pledge United States troops to fight for the League at the discretion of foreign powers. Nothing was more calculated to arouse the indignation of the superpatriots, plus the Republicans who needed a campaign issue. "What is Article X?" the League's foes demanded. "Will it destroy American sovereignty?"

Fred Ferguson, one of the United Press correspondents in Paris, began looking around for the text of the proposal. He asked Colonel House for it, but the Colonel refused to give it to him. But another member of the American delegation told him to go to a sixth-floor workroom of the Hotel Crillon at 2 a.m. after the guard had left. The door would be unlocked. No officials would be around at that hour. And inside, on a table, would be a draft of the entire Covenant as far as it had been developed.

Ferguson did as he was told. To make certain he would not be interrupted at his diplomatic second-story job, he walked up six flights of stairs at about 2 a.m., found the Covenant draft, copied out Article X, and put it on the cables as quickly as he could. He added no comment, no interpretation. There was no need for it. While the UP thus preserved its impartiality, Lodge, Borah, and Hearst supplied the adverse interpretation. The news beat created a sensation in the United States and aroused roars of protest. The American delegation, of course, tried to find out how the UP had obtained the Article X text, but Ferguson kept his secret. He had broken the story and that was all he cared about. What the result would be was not his concern.[5]

Scant wonder that Herman Kohlsaat, a Chicago publisher whom Colonel House regarded as a seer, wrote to Paris privately, "I think the great majority of our people are still behind the President. But I fear they are very far behind him."[6] House didn't relish the comment. He began sending out memoranda and private advices to Kohlsaat and other friends back home to try to turn the tide of public opinion that was running so heavily against Wilson. But such stuff wasn't easy to publish, and once published, it had no effect.

All this tied in with Swope's argument that the American delegation would have to make public some major news through sources that were bound to be favorable if the peace treaty and Covenant were to survive in the United States. He waved aside the communiqués, briefing sessions, and private advices as useless. What the journalists wanted was news — and if the news put the treaty and Covenant in a favorable light, so much the better. Wilson and House came around to the idea with painful slowness. They simply weren't used to this kind of a battle, in which every trick was employed to make an impression on the public.

Thus, the peace conference degenerated into a brawl. The victors, cocksure that the common menace of Germany had been removed, fought each other at the Council tables. Their adherents in the press vigorously took up the cudgels of national self-interest. And a thoroughly bewildered world public looked on without much comprehension.

The British press, led by the London *Daily Telegraph* and the London *Daily Express,* belabored Wilson. The French press almost uniformly jumped on Lloyd George, with Jean Herbette of *Le Temps,* Pertinax, and Andre Cheradame leading the attack. The American press, with the notable exception of the New York *World,* the New York *Times,* and a few scattered Democratic papers elsewhere, fired away indiscriminately at Wilson as well as his opponents.

Sisley Huddleston wrote that Wilson was "bewildered at the assault of the press, English, French and American, upon him."[7] Who could blame him? He had tried to impose his ideals on the world, only to find that the world didn't want them. He had ignored the opposition part at home, lecturing them on their duty instead of making them his partners in the peace making, and now they took their revenge.

At this unhappy juncture in world affairs, Swope finally had his way. As the leading correspondent of "Wilson's paper," he began publishing exclusively some of the major decisions of the conference. When the League Covenant was introduced at a plenary session, so intertwined with the peace treaty that the two could not be separated, Swope had a verbatim report of the proceedings. He also gave the first summary of the German reparations clauses of the treaty.[8] Finally, in early April 1919, he obtained an official summary of the amended and revised League Covenant in its final version, primarily through the assistance of President Wilson. The President told him to go to Colonel House's office, adding that the Colonel would not be there, but the document would be. It turned out exactly as the President had arranged. On April 9, Swope published the whole thing exclusively in the *World.*[9]

The Paris edition of the rival New York *Herald,* once the great organ of foreign correspondence, humbly republished the *World*'s account with this acknowledgment: "Mr. Herbert Bayard Swope, the special correspondent of the New York *World,* has scored the great journalistic success of the Conference by obtaining an analytical synopsis of the new document. By courtesy of Mr. Swope, the *Herald* is enabled today to reproduce the salient passages of the new version of the Covenant."[10]

After that, nothing stayed secret for very long. Wilson and his foes were joined in battle to sway public opinion, and all the unrealistic communiqué-briefing officer machinery was shattered. Paul Scott Mowrer obtained an unbound, printed copy of the entire peace treaty from "one of Wilson's professors," not otherwise identified, and cabled essential parts of it to the Chicago *Daily News.*[11] Not to be outdone, the Chicago *Tribune* produced a complete copy of the same document for Senator Borah,[12] who had it published in the *Congressional Record* for everybody's convenience. Whereupon the New York *Times,* even then eager for a full text, opened twenty-four telephone and telegraph lines from Washington and republished the treaty from *Congressional Record* proof sheets. The *Times* of June 10, 1919, was a monumental publishing job — sixty-two columns, nearly eight full pages, of Versailles Treaty text. The whole thing was now out in the open,[13] but the manner in which it had happened hurt Wilson rather than helped him.

All the haggling over territory, all the fury that was loosed against the Germans, all the idealism that went into the work of building the League of Nations were in vain. Even the defeated Germans plucked up courage when they saw — and read — of all the ill-will among the victors. On May 7, 1919, at the Trianon Palace Hotel, Count Ulrich von Brockdorff-Rantzau, the leader of the German delegation, furiously rejected the terms that were read to him by Clemenceau: "We are under no illusion as to the extent of our defeat. . . . We are asked to confess that we alone are guilty. Such a confession would be a lie."[14]

It was only a foretaste of what was to come from a nation that had been defeated but not crushed. That same day, when the terms of the treaty were first published in Germany, the whole nation stormed with protests. The Versailles Treaty became a *Diktat,* a weapon which the most dangerous elements in the Reich would soon use with a devastating effectiveness.

What was the *Diktat?* It limited Germany, the aggressor, to 100,000 army troops without a general staff, planes, or tanks, and a navy which could build no submarines or warships exceeding 10,000 tons. A reparations first payment of $5 billion was decreed. Alsace-Lorraine was given back to France. Belgium, Denmark, and Poland all were given back land taken from them by the Germans; and Poland, in addition, was given a corridor for access to the Baltic that split Germany. Finally, the Germans were saddled with responsibility for the war, which stirred them up more than anything else. But for all the rage displayed by a defeated but still powerful and completely united nation, the Germans were then powerless to resist. On June 28, 1919, in the Hall of Mirrors at Versailles, they were forced to sign the peace treaty—a treaty that settled nothing.

The scene shifted then to the United States, where on July 10, President Wilson submitted the treaty with its intertwined League Covenant to a suspicious, embittered, and coldly hostile Senate. The President would not plead. He could not persuade. Although many a correspondent suspected even then that he was ill, he set out on September 3 to try to sell the Versailles pact to the people of the United States over the heads of the opposition Senators.

It was a gallant but desperate twenty-one day tour that took the ailing President through seventeen states over an 8,000-mile route. On September 25, at Pueblo, Colorado, a sympathetic young UP correspondent, Hugh Baillie, noted Wilson's brave words to an enthusiastic crowd. "There is one thing that the American people always rise to, and extend their hand to, and that is the truth of justice and of peace. We have accepted that truth, and we are going to be led by it; and it is going to lead us—and through us the world—out into the pastures of quietness and peace such as the world never dreamed of before."

Baillie wrote of how President and Mrs. Wilson went for a long walk that day, a walk that "testified to his excellent health." But the next day, a mimeographed White House statement was distributed to the correspondents, announcing tersely that the President was ill, and the rest of the trip had been canceled. The "pastures of quietness and peace" speech was Wilson's last. The long walk, which had been ordered by his physician, Admiral Cary T. Grayson, was a final despairing effort to stave off the collapse of a President who had worked too hard and promised too much. Wilson returned to the White House on September 28. Four days later, he suffered a stroke that paralyzed his left side, but the press and the nation were kept in ignorance of his condition.

Yet, the correspondents sensed something was wrong. "The air of mystery surrounding Wilson's disappearance within the White House was so thick that all sorts of rumors were abroad—he was dead, insane, comatose," Baillie wrote. "Though we didn't know the truth about the President's health, we knew that he was sick—and that his great effort for the Treaty and the League had failed."[15]

The news struck Europe like a thunderbolt. In Berlin, the *Tageblatt* published a brief bulletin about Wilson's failure and his breakdown under date of September 27. That same day, the *Tageblatt*'s editor, Theodor Wolff, happened to meet Colonel Bonsal in a Berlin bookshop, and they gloomily discussed the outlook. Wolff said, with sadly prophetic insight, "At the Conference, the victors could have chopped Germany into fragments and remnants. That would have been a solution, although a bad one. Or the Allies, under the guidance of America, could have bound the Germans to them by a treaty of friendship, which might have resulted in peace and security for all. Unfortunately, the conference pursued neither of these courses."[16]

Germany, Britain, Italy, France, and Japan ratified the treaty in that order. All then watched the United States, where the hostile mood of the Senate was unmistakable. Wilson, desperately ill, was represented by Admiral Grayson and Mrs. Wilson as unalterably opposed to the slightest change in the commitment he had signed at Versailles. The reservations that had been drafted by Henry Cabot Lodge were rejected at the White House without consideration.

Through Colonel Bonsal, Colonel House now tried to win some kind of a compromise between Wilson and the Senate. But House's position at the White House had been undermined for many months because of his differences at Versailles with the way in which the President had chosen to operate. Bonsal had to go it alone. Yet, despite his handicaps, the old foreign correspondent-turned-diplomat was able to persuade Lodge to soften his reservations, which maintained the historic power of the Senate over foreign commitments. House was jubilant, but not for very long. Word came from the White House that Wilson would accept no compromise.[17] He wanted his own supporters to reject a treaty that was not entirely of his own making.

And so, Bonsal's effort failed. On November 19, the Senate rejected both treaty and Covenant. On December 11, the *World* — still "Wilson's paper" — blasted Colonel House as a traitor to Wilsonian ideals, with the result that the *Times* of London immediately rallied to the Colonel's defense. Thus, the long and dramatic struggle to bring peace to Europe and draw the United States into the shaping of a better world ended in a flurry of petty hostility between two newspapers of major importance.[18] It was not an edifying spectacle, either for the United States or its press.

The *World*, under Swope's dominant influence, made one more effort. It fought valiantly against the "return to normalcy" for which Warren Gamaliel Harding and the Republicans called in the presidential campaign of 1920. It tried, with all its resources, to bring about the election of James M. Cox, a kindly and liberal man, as Wilson's successor, hoping in that way to bring about a return to a Wilsonian peace. But Senator Harding, the publisher of the Marion (Ohio) *Star*, defeated Governor Cox, the publisher of the Dayton (Ohio) *Daily News*. The Republican tide overwhelmed "Wilson's paper" as well and all who stood with it. The United States chose the pathway of isolation and disaster. The voice of reason, the *World*'s editorial page, drew only hollow echoes for response.

Viewing the debacle from afar, many a correspondent who had struggled against frustration at Versailles could not have been blamed for wondering what might have happened if there had been, in truth, "open covenants . . . openly arrived at." The outcome could hardly have been worse.

THE PASSING OF THE OLD GUARD

Lord Northcliffe, the Napoleon of Fleet Street, embarked on a world tour in the latter part of 1921 and celebrated New Year's Day, 1922, by sending affectionate greetings to his principal associates. Less than two months later, he was in a violent rage. His world tour was canceled. He sped home. He had just seen a profit-and-loss statement for the *Times* of London, his expensive plaything, and it was awful. In his own view, he was "appalled."[19]

Northcliffe had been in a good mood at the Washington naval conference, where the grandees of European and Japanese diplomacy had persuaded the United States to sink most of its navy, while they retained their own. It was considered a very fine way, by everybody but the American people, to make a beginning on disarmament.

Then, too, the Anglo-Irish Treaty had finally been signed in London on December 6, 1921. With the formal recognition of the Irish Free State, not even Eamon de Valera's repudiation of his own negotiators had dimmed the *Times*'s rejoicing. This was something for which Wickham Steed had campaigned from the time of his appointment as editor of the *Times*. As the paper itself said of its Irish position, "The *Times* felt it had succeeded so far as its contribution was concerned and that circumstances outside the influence of any newspaper had intervened to perpetuate partition. But at least it may be said that by its leadership between 1919 and 1921, in the cause of dominion status for Ireland, the *Times* rendered compensation for its misjudgment in the case against Parnell in 1886–1890."[20]

Perhaps that had given Northcliffe pleasure at the time. But in the spring of 1922, he began a steady warfare against both Wickham Steed, whom he had appointed editor to succeed Geoffrey Dawson in 1919, and John Walter IV, the chairman of the *Times* board. At the Chief's insistence, Steed went to Genoa on April 10 to cover the economic conference there, knowing that it was a move to get him out of the way. If he had sat by idly, perhaps he might have escaped Northcliffe's wrath. But his weakness for playing the diplomat rather than the journalist once more got him into trouble. He cabled a story from Genoa on May 7 that Northcliffe's old foe, Lloyd George, had threatened in an interview with M. Louis Barthou, the French delegate, to end the entente between Britain and France. If the editor hoped to please the Chief with the story, he was quickly disabused; Lloyd George denied he had said anything of the kind, while Barthou issued a qualified denial.[21] It was the pretext for which Northcliffe had been waiting to get rid of the editor.

Steed was summoned to Northcliffe's apartment on the fifth floor of the Hotel Plaza-Athenee in Paris on June 11. He found the Chief in bed, wild-eyed and talking strangely. For several days he had been conducting business in a frenzy, arranging for the purchase of John Walter IV's shares in the *Times*, firing executives, putting on others, and acting generally like a man bereft of his senses. During a long and trying evening, Steed saw him waving a loaded revolver which he produced from under his pillow. Once he saw the shadow of his dressing gown hanging on the door and threatened to fire at it, mistaking it for an intruder. Steed managed to unload the revolver, called for medical assistance, and tried to persuade Northcliffe from going to Evian-les-Bains the following day. But Northcliffe persisted, and Steed went with him, although he had been told he was no longer editor but personal adviser to the Chief, who would assume the editorship.[22]

From then until the end on August 14, 1922, at his home in London, the affairs of the *Times* were administered in a kind of journalistic *Walpurgisnacht*. With Northcliffe incapacitated for all practical purposes, Steed hung on grimly as editor in fact if not in name, and Walter maintained his position as board chairman, although his status was in doubt. Necessarily, the completion of the sale of Walter's shares to Northcliffe had been delayed by the Chief's condition, but no successful contention was made that he had not been of sound mind at the time of the negotiations. Despite statements made by Steed and others in the official history of the *Times*, Northcliffe, according to Sir Thomas Horder, was never certified as insane. Sir Thomas, having attended Northcliffe during his last illness, certified that death was caused by malignant endocarditis, a type of blood poisoning that frequently induces delusions and hallucinations.[23] There was no doubt whatever that the Napoleon of Fleet Street had suffered from both in his last months of life.

The *Times* was sold to Major the Honorable John Jacob Astor, M.P., in association with John Walter IV, on October 23, 1922. Astor paid £1,580,000 for a paper which was piling up enormous losses and could no longer be said to be the leader in its field. With the coming of a new administration, the *Times* became somewhat of a journalistic monument.[24] Despite its achievements in helping settle the Irish crisis, its influence as a leader in foreign affairs long since had passed into other hands. Steed left the editorship, passing into journalistic limbo, and was succeeded by his predecessor, Geoffrey Dawson, under whom the *Times* lapsed into an arm of the "Cliveden set."[25] It was significant that both the office and the title of foreign editor, or its equivalent, were abolished. Dawson, forthwith, tried to run both his job and the foreign staff with consequences that could have been pointed out to him by the greenest correspondent.[26] The Thunderer became the Murmurer.

Like its distinguished British contemporary, the New York *Herald* also slid into a genteel decline during the early part of the twentieth century, yielding its preeminence in the field of foreign correspondence, and merged its identity in a new ownership. The younger James Gordon Bennett, who was even more flamboyant and eccentric than Northcliffe, turned out in the end to be far less capable. Bennett took close to $40,000,000 out of the *Herald*'s profits during the fifty years of his ownership, but put nothing back. From a high of 511,000 at the time of the Spanish-American War, the *Herald* dwindled in circulation to a mere 55,000 in 1920. It operated at a loss, and was sustained only by its colorful affiliate in Paris.[27]

The difference between the two papers was that the New York *Herald* lost its sense of direction while the Paris *Herald,* for all its zany characteristics, stood for something. It had not been the first English daily in Paris. Giovanni Antonio Galignani had started his *Messenger* as an English-language weekly in Paris in 1814 and had turned it into a daily in 1884. But the Paris *Herald* had put Galignani's *Messenger* out of business in 1904. Competition was too much for it.

The Paris *Herald* was Bennett's own link between France and the United States, which he had been obliged to leave for drunken and grotesque behavior. He published it as an act of faith in the destiny of France, and every English-speaking resident or visitor in Paris loved the *Herald* for it. In the earliest days of World War I, Bennett argued editorially that the United States would soon be in the conflict. When the

Germans surged to the Marne in 1914, the publisher, then in his seventies, worked in the city room in Paris and got out the paper. He never missed an issue, causing an old *Herald* man to report to his New York colleagues "Bennett is dead. In his place has come a Scotch miser."[28]

But Bennett was no miser when he proclaimed in 1914 to his staff: "Those of you who wish to quit may do so. This place will be under the protection of the Stars and Stripes and I will defy the Prussians to disregard it.

"If they come and you stay I will do what I can to ensure your safety. In any event, the paper comes out."[29]

Bennett had the satisfaction of seeing the Paris *Herald* on the street with the story of how the taxicab army had repulsed the Germans at the Marne. No other paper was published in Paris during those critical days. So that all the world would see that he was a changed man, Bennett at the age of 73 finally married on September 10, 1914, his bride being the widow of Baron George de Reuter, the former Maud Potter of Philadelphia. The groom worked each night at the *Herald* office in his shirtsleeves, this one-time millionaire who could fling himself into a monumental rage over a trifle. Now, his main battles were with the censors, and they were furious ones. Yet, he still saw to it that the *Herald* published each day on its editorial page a letter that had appeared for the first time on December 27, 1899:

TO THE EDITOR OF THE HERALD:
   I am anxious to find out the way to figure the temperature from centigrade to Fahrenheit and vice versa. In other words, I want to know, whenever I see the temperature designated on the centigrade thermometer, how to find out what it would be on Fahrenheit's thermometer.
                                        OLD PHILADELPHIA LADY.
                              Paris, December 24, 1899[30]

Through war and peace, affluence and poverty, bachelorhood and marriage, Bennett protected the Old Philadelphia Lady to the last, and nobody ever knew why he caused the letter to be printed in his newspaper 6,718 times. When the United States went into the war and American soldiers thronged into France, the *Herald*'s circulation soared from 12,000 to more than 100,000 despite the rivalry of the Chicago *Tribune*'s Paris edition, established July 4, 1917. The profits piled up in the bank because Bennett was now too busy to spend money with his onetime profligacy.

However, he did not live long enough to enjoy his new affluence or to celebrate the Allied victory. With the approach of his 77th birthday on May 10, 1918, he began to fret over the fact that his father had died of a stroke at that age. He imagined that he would go the same way and worked himself into a fearful state. On the morning of May 10, he was stricken with a massive brain hemorrhage while he was taking a short vacation at his villa at Beaulieu. On May 14, he died and was buried in a nameless grave in Passy, his headstone marked only with two small graven owls, in accordance with his instructions. The Old Philadelphia Lady vanished from the *Herald* two days later, never to return.[31]

On January 14, 1920, Frank A. Munsey, a grocery clerk who became a millionaire magazine publisher, bought the New York *Herald*, the New York *Telegram*, and the Paris *Herald* for $4,000,000 from the Bennett estate. To his utter astonishment, the parsimonious Munsey discovered that he had also taken over the Paris *Herald*'s bank account (the Paris paper had been thrown into the sale as an afterthought), in which reposed more than $1,000,000. He picked up an additional $1,000,000 when he resold the *Herald* in 1924 to Ogden Reid, the son of Whitelaw Reid, for $5,000,000. Reid, whose New York *Tribune* also had fallen on evil days and a circulation of about 25,000, put the two enfeebled giants together and produced a new and spritely paper, the New York *Herald Tribune,* with its reinvigorated Paris edition. Munsey then peddled the *Telegram* to the Scripps-Howard interests, among his other operations, leading William Allen White to publish this obituary of him eventually in the Emporia *Gazette:* "Frank A. Munsey contributed to the journalism of his day the talent of a meat packer, the morals of a money-changer and the manners of an undertaker. He and his kind have about succeeded in transforming a once-noble profession into an eight per cent security. May he rest in trust."[32]

The passing of the *Times* of London and the New York *Herald* from their long leadership in foreign correspondence coincided with other changes that vitally affected the field. Victor Fremont Lawson, the developer of the Chicago *Daily News* foreign service, died in 1925, but his business manager, Walter A. Strong, continued his policies. Edward Wyllis Scripps retired in 1920, elevating the fighting bantam of the UP, Roy W. Howard, to partnership with his son, Robert P. Scripps, in the Scripps-Howard Newspapers. By the time Scripps died in 1926, he saw the UP firmly entrenched in the foreign field as the greatest independent rival of the Grand Cartel. William Randolph Hearst, who lived like a nabob in California, had his wings clipped in the financial crisis of 1929, lost control of his papers and International News Service to a management group in 1937, and lingered on as a journalistic legend until 1951.

There was one newspaper collapse above all others that jarred even the most callous professionals—the death of the New York *World.* When Herbert Bayard Swope took over as executive editor soon after his return from Versailles, he saw that something drastic would have to be done to maintain the *World*'s leadership of liberal opinion. It was no longer possible to bring the United States into the mainstream of international affairs; moreover, the *World* no longer had the resources to maintain a large staff of foreign correspondents, although it did retain a few good ones.

Swope therefore led the *World* in such glamorous and effective crusades as the exposure and crippling of the Ku Klux Klan as it then existed, the elimination of the abuse of prison labor in Florida, and other domestic causes. But as the years of normalcy slipped by, it became clear that the *World* was no longer the newspaper that Joseph Pulitzer had created. Its summons to action in the greatest international cause of the 1920s, the Sacco-Vanzetti case, was not a trumpet call, but a frightened whimper.

Heywood Broun, the large and unkempt foreign correspondent who was also a sports writer, dramatic critic, and literary figure, raised his voice on the *World* in defense of Nicola Sacco, the shoemaker, and Bartolomeo Vanzetti, the fish peddler, on the ground that they had been wrongfully convicted in 1921 of a holdup-murder in South Braintree, Mass. "I am afraid," he wrote as the case reached its climax in 1927, "there is no question that a vast majority of the voters in the Bay State want to see the condemned men die. I don't know why. Clearly it depends upon no careful examination of the evidence. Mostly the feeling rests upon the fact that they are foreigners. Also, the backbone of Massachusetts, such as it is, happens to be up because of criticism beyond the borders of the State. 'This is only our business,' say the citizens of the Commonwealth, and they are very wrong."

Like the citizens of France at the time of the Dreyfus trial, the citizens of Massachusetts were outraged by the millions of words that were printed about them in the foreign press, most of them derogatory. But what a howl of rage went up when Broun concluded his column with the angry barb, "From now on, I want to know, will the institution of learning in Cambridge, which we once called Harvard, be known as Hangman's House?"

Expressions like these were too much for Ralph Pulitzer, the publisher. He accused Broun, by his excesses, of hurting the *World*'s effort to obtain a new trial for Sacco and Vanzetti. Finally, when Broun's continued criticism was omitted from the *World,* he resigned and found a species of welcome at the Scripps-Howard *Telegram*. Despite the furor, Sacco and Vanzetti were executed on August 27, 1927.[33] And young Eugene Lyons, a Tass employee in New York, sent the flash to Moscow.

Whatever Swope may have thought of Ralph Pulitzer's management of the *World* on this and other occasions, he made no public criticism. But in 1928, when he was independently wealthy through his investments in a booming stock market, the correspondent-turned-editor resigned. Three yeas later, at its nadir in influence, prestige, and income, JP's once-great newspaper, its younger brother, the Evening *World,* and their Sunday edition were sold to Scripps-Howard for $5,000,000 and became the New York *World-Telegram*. At a time when a free society had need of every strong and independent voice it could muster, one that had formerly been the most influential of all was gone beyond recall.[34]

Thus, the old guard passed on. Death, consolidation, financial stringency, and sheer disinterest combined to reduce the number of independent newspapers that considered it a duty to gather, evaluate, and disseminate foreign intelligence to their publics. Such services as the *Times* of London, the New York *Herald,* and the New York *World* had been able to provide at the height of their power could not easily be replaced. Moreover, few new ones were being developed in France, Britain, or the United States.

But in Italy, a newspaper founded during the war, *Il Popolo d'Italia,* had become the dominant journalistic voice, and it was spreading shivers of fear all over the Continent.[35] Its editor, Benito Mussolini, the one-time Socialist and pacifist, had marched on Rome in 1922 with his Fascists and was now the new leader, Il Duce. The great papers of Italy, the *Corriere della Sera, Stampa,* and *Giornale d'Italia,* no longer were the primary sources of foreign intelligence and the molders of public opinion. None of them took the trouble to tell the world exactly who Mussolini was — and the world did not find out for some time.

The great newspapers of Germany did not heed the lesson, any more than did the others. The *Berliner Tageblatt* and the *Frankfurter Zeitung* and the rest didn't even bother to take notice of a run-down, debt-ridden, anti-Semitic gossip sheet, known as the *Voelkischer Beobachter,* which had been published twice a week in Munich since 1920 by a peculiar little man, Adolf Hitler, who styled himself the Fuehrer of the National Socialist Party. The Nazis were almost universally regarded as crackpots, but in 1923 the *Voelkischer Beobachter* became a daily under the editorship of a shoemaker's son, Alfred Rosenberg, with Hitler's former army sergeant, Max Amann, as business manager. The great German papers still slept, although they could have guessed that the *Voelkischer Beobachter* was attracting substantial conservative business support and, quite probably, some of the Reichswehr's secret funds.[36] None of these agencies underestimated the potential of Adolf Hitler or his newspaper to shake the destinies of the world. Its theory was based on the authoritarian press system that now controlled the dissemination of all news, domestic and foreign, in the Soviet Union. In its practical application of the authoritarian doctrine, it would soon rise to challenge the established laissez-faire press systems of the democratic world.

THE END OF THE GRAND CARTEL

Baron Herbert de Reuter shot and killed himself at his estate near Reigate in England on April 18, 1915. He left a letter to his wife, who had died three days before, saying, "Life without you is insupportable and the loss of your cherished companionship and tender devotion has shattered my being."[37]

The suicide of the 63-year-old Baron intensified a financial crisis for the global news agency which his father had founded. The Reuters Bank, now known as the British Commercial Bank, was in trouble, partly because its assets had been frozen by war, partly by mistakes in management. Reuters' shares, which had been worth more than £12 before the war, now were half that and dropping fast. They reached a low of slightly more than £3.[38]

It was in this situation that the energetic 37-year-old South African manager for Reuters went to London to advance his claims to the management of the agency. He was the junior reporter of the Boer War, Roderick Jones, born and educated in England, and sent to Pretoria while still in his teens to live with relatives after his father's death. After the Boer War, he had won Baron de Reuter's favor during three years of service in the London office and had gone back to South Africa as the top man.

Jones had the rare good fortune, when he arrived in London after the Baron's suicide, to make an ally out of Mark F. Napier, the chairman of Reuters' board. Together, they raised £550,000 to buy the agency, disposed of the bank, formed a private company known as Reuters, Ltd., and entered into a wartime alliance with the British government. The government, by contributing substantially to the financing of Reuters' cable costs, eased the financial crisis of the agency. Reuters, by stressing the government's point of view, bolstered the British war effort. Moreover, by entering into an arrangement with the Press Association, which represented British provincial papers, the costs of supporting war correspondents were shared. The whole operation was so successful that plain Roderick Jones was knighted before he was 40 and became the dominant power in the grand cartel.

Sir Roderick made only one slip during his wartime rescue operation. While he was serving as managing director of Reuters, he was also British director of propaganda under Lord Beaverbrook, the Minister of Information. No matter how patriotic, this arrangement was severely criticized, and on July 31, 1918, the Select Committee on National Expenditure reported to the House of Commons, "During the last financial year, about £126,000 was paid for cables, mainly to Reuters. . . . The position of Sir Roderick Jones, who is both managing director of Reuters and also a high official of the Ministry of Information, is on principle open to objection." Sir Roderick gracefully withdrew from the government, "acting under urgent medical advice."[39]

Whether he was criticized or not, he saved Reuters. During the Versailles conference, he also saved the grand cartel by renewing relations with Reuters' old ally, Havas. Together, they took in more territory and left the defeated Wolff and Austrian Korrespondenz Bureau with nothing but their own truncated respective national territories. Then Reuters and Havas entered into a succession of formal compacts with a host of national news agencies, completing what was known as the National Agencies' Alliance.[40] To the victors went the spoils.

Melville E. Stone, the Associated Press's old general manager, watched all this in New York and saw that his agency was being pushed into a corner, but feared to protest. "I think it would be a disaster . . . for this organization to break with the combination," Stone told his board in 1920. "Their attitude is this: if we want to break with them, we can break. . . . They can get more money anyhow than we would pay them."[41]

What bothered Stone, of course, was the possibility that the grand cartel would deal with the fast-developing UP if the AP kicked up too much of a fuss, thereby cutting off much of the AP's foreign service. One of his younger associates, Kent Cooper, didn't believe the grand cartel would dare drop the AP and said so. But even in the unlikely event that it happened, Cooper told Stone, it would be no calamity. "It would result in freedom of action for the AP abroad," he said. "It would also benefit the AP because, in order to be different, the AP would more than ever intensify establishing its own independent news sources."[42]

Stone remained unconvinced. However, as a prudent manager, he developed more foreign offices and hired more foreign correspondents for the AP, thus creating the nucleus of a foreign service that could dispense as well as gather foreign news. Yet, he maintained good relations with the cartel and did not try to infringe on their territory.

Cooper bided his time, waiting until he would be able to rally more sympathy for his point of view within the AP management. He had been a working newsman for almost as long as he could remember. Born in 1880 in Columbus, Ind., he had carried newspapers as a delivery boy at 11, worked as a local reporter later during the summer, and gone to the Indianapolis *Press* at 19 as a reporter for $12 a week. Being an enterprising sort, he soon joined the Scripps-MacRae Association, one of the forerunners of the UP. There, he drew attention to himself by developing a method of telephoning his news budget to smaller papers at a cheaper rate than it could be telegraphed. Like his fellow-Hoosier, Roy W. Howard, he became one of the UP's pioneers; unlike Howard, he proceeded to talk himself into the AP's service in 1910 at $65 a week as a traveling inspector reporting directly to General Manager Stone.[43]

In 1914, Cooper, for the first time, began to question the worth of the AP's association with the grand cartel. At that time, Don Jorge Mitre, the director of *La Nacion* of Buenos Aires, cabled Stone for AP service because Havas had patriotically refused to transmit the official German war communiqués. "We are French," Havas had said. "We cannot do it." When Stone ignored Mitre's message, *La Nacion* signed with the UP. Cooper found out about it and promptly asked Stone for permission to bring the great Buenos Aires opposition paper, *La Prensa*, into the AP's camp. Stone put him off.[44]

Curiously, it was an abortive effort by the U.S. government to force the AP into a propaganda role during World War I that finally softened Stone's opposition and gave Cooper his chance. Stone reported to the AP's board in October 1917, that the government "was very anxious to soften the asperity toward us that was evident in South America." The State Department's proposition was to have the AP employ editors of leading South American newspapers as AP correspondents at "handsome salaries," whether or not they did any work. The government was to repay the AP. The board, shocked at the notion, turned it down.[45] A year later, Cooper was permitted to make an exploratory trip to Latin America.

Cooper persuaded Charles Houssaye, director of Havas, to give the AP a free hand in South America provided that Havas was reimbursed for any lost income there. Since the UP already had taken away many

Havas clients in South America, Cooper wasn't afraid of the bargain. He thought he could fight the UP without further injuring Havas, and so it turned out.[46] Three days after the signing of the Armistice in 1918, Cooper embarked on his selling trip. He bagged both *La Nacion* and Don Ezequiel Paz, the publisher of *La Prensa,* in Buenos Aires. In addition, he signed up a number of other South American newspapers.[47]

Emboldened by his success, Cooper extended his operations to Europe and in 1919 called on Sir Roderick Jones at his London office. Cooper was then the chief of the AP's traffic department, scarcely on a level with the tall, austere Briton. When he began describing his Latin American operations, Sir Roderick said coldly, "I am fully informed by our good friends of Havas." Cooper should have heeded the warning, but he was not the kind of man to back away from an opponent. He argued for a better break for the AP, but found himself ignored. After an embarrassing pause, he changed the subject and left.[48]

That was the beginning of the long AP revolt against the grand cartel, for as Cooper phrased it, Reuters "did sit at the crossroads of the world and control traffic."[49] His policy was simple and direct. He intended to break the foreign stranglehold on the AP and thereby enable it to compete in the world market on equal terms with the UP.

Cooper and Sir Roderick were well-matched as opponents. Cooper was 39, Sir Roderick 41. Both had come up the hard way in their respective organizations. Neither had benefited from inherited wealth or family influence, but had made their way in large part through their own efforts. They were thoroughly competent professionals, each with acquired loyalties and supporters.

It was in Japan that the break came between the AP and the grand cartel. Reuters had sent Japan its foreign news from 1870 on and, in 1913, had set up the Kokusai agency under the nominal control of Japanese businessmen. In 1916, the rival Nippon Dempo Tsushin Sha (Japanese telegraph news agency) was formed as a UP client and soon began serving 200 Japanese papers.[50] The AP began talking with both Yoshio Mitsunaga, president of Nippon Dempo, and Yukichi Iwanaga, director of Kokusai, but didn't get very far at first. The UP and the cartel were too strong.[51]

Changes in management occurred. Cooper became the AP's general manager in 1925. In the following year, Sir Roderick, now Reuters' majority stockholder, offered half his interest to the Press Association, representing British provincial papers, and the other half to the Newspaper Proprietor's Association, the organization of the London press. The Press Association accepted the proposal and nominally took over the direction of Reuters, but Sir Roderick remained as chairman and managing director.[52] The antagonists, Sir Roderick and Cooper, now were in a position to wield both power and authority.

The independent trend in Japan became unmistakable when, in 1926, Kokusai was replaced by a new association, Nippon Shimbun Rengo (Associated Press of Japan), with charter membership allotted to eight newspapers having 75 percent of the total circulation in Japan. Nippon Dempo remained in business, linked to the UP, but Rengo could not buy the AP service because of its affiliation with Reuters. In April, 1927, at length, the AP board of directors voted unanimously to denounce the grand cartel treaty. The purpose was to make a new arrangement between the AP and Reuters, Havas, and 27 other agencies, most of them purely national in character. Cooper was instructed to go to Europe for the negotiations.

This time, Sir Roderick received Cooper for lunch at Claridge's with the then British Foreign Minister, Sir Austen Chamberlain, in attendance. The AP's general manager also attended a news agency conference in Warsaw and a Conference of Press Experts of the League of Nations in Geneva, made some gallant speeches about freedom of information, but nothing happened. All the grand cartel offered was the cancellation of a fee the AP had been paying for thirty-four years as a differential between the news it received from abroad from the others and the news it offered them. Reuters, in addition, demanded to know what the AP was going to do about the inroads the UP was making in Reuters territory in the Far East. Cooper wryly replied that he could do nothing about the UP.

In 1929 and 1930, the AP's board sent Cooper to see Sir Roderick twice more on fruitless errands. Reuters would not budge. Meanwhile, Rengo had completed a contractual arrangement with the AP, to be whipped into final shape when the AP obtained its release from the bonds of the grand cartel. It was 1932 before partial relief finally came, with Sir Roderick at least modifying the four-agency agreement to permit the AP to enter Japan and China. However, when Cooper dramatically made public his AP contract with Rengo in 1933, Sir Roderick made no attempt to disguise his wrath. He denounced the arrangement as an unfriendly act and, finally giving the AP exactly what it wanted, served formal notice severing relations with the American agency upon the expiration of their contract. The AP lost no time in agreeing.

For a short time, there was confusion in the news centers of the world. Reuters tried to tempt the UP into replacing the AP in the cartel, but Roy Howard didn't intend to be caught. He had his own bureaus abroad. He was selling his service to foreign newspapers at profitable terms. He and his associates didn't make any serious reply, therefore, to Sir Roderick's suggestion. What they did do, as a kind of impudent gesture, was to enter into an agreement with the AP—a kind of treaty of mutual defense—guaranteeing that neither would enter into an agreement with a foreign agency to the disadvantage of the other. The pact was just a showpiece and was soon allowed to lapse.

Sir Roderick gave up gracefully. On February 12, 1934, at the offices of the AP in New York, he signed a contract for an exchange of news between Reuters and the AP which gave both the right to serve newspapers and news agencies wherever they wished. The AP gained the right to make a direct contract with the Press Association, and it also insured the same freedom of operation to the Canadian Press. The policy of separate two-party contracts was carried out with Havas; the Deutsches Nachrichtenburo (DNB), which had replaced Wolff; Stefani; Tass; and a host of other agencies.

The entire character of the global news agency operation changed. Yet, however devotedly he had labored to liberate the AP and put it into a sound competitive position against the UP, Cooper could not insure his ideal of free access to news sources everywhere and free interchange of news between countries. Freedom had been wiped out in Germany and in Italy. It had never existed in Russia. It was tottering in Japan. Much more than the chatter of news agency tickers would be needed to preserve a free society from the challenge of totalitarian dictatorships of the Left and the Right.[53]

THE GROWTH OF THE NEW YORK *TIMES*

Adolph S. Ochs, the one-time printer's devil from Knoxville, Tenn., traveled to Paris in 1922 to ask a question. How much, he wanted to know, would it cost the New York *Times* to build up its foreign staff and provide the best foreign service of any newspaper in the world? Edwin L. James, the audacious little European news manager for the *Times,* shot back an answer that would have made any other publisher wince: $500,000 a year. Ochs evidently expected it. He simply told James to develop a plan for expanded coverage of foreign news which, eventually, was approved.[54] While neither he nor James could anticipate it, they soon would be spending much more on foreign news. The *Times*'s two-man bureau in Moscow alone would be costing upward of $100,000 a year.

The decision to try to take over the preeminent position of the *Times* of London, which still had a fine foreign staff but no longer could undertake new adventures at great cost, was characteristic of Ochs. In the first quarter-century after he had brought the New York *Times* out of bankruptcy and low estate in 1896, he had made it a journalistic bible. From 9,000, its daily circulation had soared to 323,000; from 2,227,000 lines of advertising annually, the total had gone to 23,447,000 lines. Profits had exceeded $100,000,000 on an original investment of $75,000, a thumping vote of confidence from readers and advertisers alike, and all but 4 percent of it, or less, the rate of dividends, had been reinvested in the paper.[55] Ochs truly believed in a newspaper that would "give the news impartially, without fear or favor," and he meant to print foreign news as it had never been done before.

Fortunately, he had editors with ideas and a staff bubbling with energy and talent to which newcomers were added. Instead of concentrating on the traditional areas of diplomatic coverage, which had caused Northcliffe on occasion to rant that the *Times* of London was little more than a stuffy court gazette, the New York *Times* now boldly plunged into the colorful reporting of high adventure and exploration; science and medicine; and, most thrilling of all, aviation. James Gordon Bennett's ideas were exploited at a higher level. True, the slow-paced minuets of diplomacy were still described in sometimes painful detail, but *Times* correspondents concentrated less on worn and faded figures than on the raucous new leaders who were about to make world history. It was a pattern, all in all, that was generally favored by American papers and wire services in the post-World War I era, as well as by the British to a far more limited extent; but the virtue of the New York *Times* was in its superior execution of the design.

As early as 1919, Henry Charles Crouch of the *Times*'s London bureau, who preferred reporting on golf, was writing about Professor Albert Einstein and his theory of relativity (with a distinguished assist from Sir Arthur Stanley Eddington). In 1922, after the AP had reported the discovery of the tomb of Tutankhamen, the New York *Times* sought out the most authoritative journalist in the field, Sir Harry Perry-Robinson of the *Times* of London, and contracted for exclusive rights to his work, beginning with a four-column account on December 21 in which he told of entering the 3,000-year-old resting place of the Egyptian monarch.[56]

Alva Johnson, a New York *Times* reporter, won a Pulitzer Prize for directing the world's attention to the splitting of the atom. Other staff men told of pioneering experiments in rockets and space and television, of the oceanic explorations of William Beebe, the experiments of Professor Auguste Piccard in the stratosphere, of ventures that took men deep into South American and African jungles, adrift on polar ice, and high into white mountain fastnesses. It was a magnificent outburst of journalistic enterprise.[57]

The outpouring of foreign news was so great, and so much of it was printed to the appreciation and even delight of a growing audience of knowledgeable and sophisticated New Yorkers, that the *Times* in 1924 opened its own radio station for the receipt of press messages direct from Europe and, soon afterward, from elsewhere in the world. It was the first newspaper to operate in this way. Moreover, it set the pattern for the cooperative operation of Press Wireless, Inc., in which it participated with a number of other newspapers and wire services.[58]

If the *Times* had contented itself with mere volume and emphasis on the picturesque, however, it could not have attained its dominant position in the foreign news field. Something extra, a sense of history, a grasp of the meaning of the flow of events, had to be conveyed through its columns; otherwise, its file of dispatches could have become a confusing mélange.

A small, red-headed woman, Anne O'Hare McCormick, who tried her hand at submitting free-lance articles to the *Times* after World War I while she was traveling in Europe with her husband, Francis J. McCormick of Dayton, Ohio, had that "something extra" to a superlative degree. Mrs. McCormick seldom wrote news stories. As the *Times* gained confidence in her work, she talked with and wrote about people and princes, and events and their meaning, wherever she went. On June 21, 1921, Arnaldo Cortesi, the son of the Commendatore and like him an AP correspondent at the time, got her into the Italian Chamber of Deputies to hear King Victor Emmanuel III. She wrote in the *Times* magazine on July 24: "More interesting than the speech of the King was the sudden emergence of the new party of the Extreme Right—the small group of Fascisti. Benito Mussolini, founder and leader of the Fascisti, was among the parliamentary debutants, and in one of the best political speeches I have ever heard, a little swaggering, but caustic, powerful and telling."

In Mussolini, said Mrs. McCormick with great conviction, Italy "has heard its master's voice."[59] The future Duce, whose role seemed so foreordained to Mrs. McCormick, did not make such an impression on his other journalistic colleagues. In January 1922, at the abortive Cannes conference, Mussolini was covering for his paper, *Il Popolo d'Italia*. As distinguished a correspondent as Webb Miller of the UP wrote later, "For my part, I would never have known of his presence among the two hundred correspondents . . . but for an incident in the lobby of the Carlton Hotel." Lord Riddell, the British briefing officer, referred at that time to the Fascists as "a gang of hooligans," whereupon another correspondent pointed out Mussolini, saying, "Careful, that man's the head of it." To which Miller added, "Mussolini trotted around with the rest of us, carrying his notebook and pencil; nobody paid any attention to him at all."[60] They paid attention when he marched on Rome later that year.

The rise of Hitler, which was slow and painful in its early stages, was not accompanied by a similar outburst of journalistic prescience, although Cyril Brown, a *Times* correspondent in Germany, did observe as early as November 20, 1922: "The Hitler movement is not of mere local [Munich] origin or picturesque interest. It is bound to bring Bavaria into a renewed clash with the Berlin government as long as the German Republic goes even through the motion of trying to live up to the Versailles Treaty."[61] Marcel William Fodor, the erudite correspondent of the Manchester *Guardian* and the New York *Evening Post* in Vienna, and Edgar Ansel Mowrer, the Chicago *Daily News* correspondent in Berlin, were more aware than their colleagues of the threat that Hitler represented almost from the beginning. The *Times* of London, of all the great English language newspapers, was the most complacent. And the great German newspapers, the *Vossische Zeitung,* the *Berliner Tageblatt,* the *Frankfurter Zeitung,* and the *Deutsche Allgemeine Zeitung* were blind to the evil force that coiled its strength before them. The virtue of the New York *Times* correspondence from Germany was that it carefully and consistently reported the tragic course of events in daily detail during the 1920s. Although its correspondents could not exercise Mrs. McCormick's intuitive insight, neither were they as bland as the *Times* of London nor as uncomprehending as the Germans themselves. As for the French and their largely venal press, that was, of course, another story.

In Moscow, the *Times* was fortunate to have Walter Duranty, the young Englishman whom Wythe Williams had hired for the Paris office at the outset of World War I and sent to cover the French front later. It was Duranty's destiny to be the most imposing of all the foreign correspondents who worked in the shadow of the Kremlin between the wars. Yet, he did not spring to journalistic perfection overnight, even though, as a young and inexperienced correspondent covering the counterrevolution from Riga, he wrote with a clear vision on January 13, 1920, "An interrogation of Red prisoners, in which the New York *Times* correspondent took part a couple of days ago, reveals the Bolshevist system in its true light as one of the most damnable tyrannies in history. It is a compound of force, terror, and espionage, utterly ruthless in conception and execution."[62]

Duranty was molded by many, but perhaps the most important of all was the brilliant South African who began life as Bill Ryall and ended it as William Bolitho (his full name was William Bolitho Ryall). After fighting at Ypres and the Somme during World War I as a British junior lieutenant, Bolitho became the Manchester *Guardian*'s correspondent in Paris. The grateful Duranty, who worked with him — and against him — in Paris for two years, wrote of him, "I have never met anyone who could see further through a brick wall than he could, or who was better, to use a newspaper phrase, at 'doping out the facts' of any situation."[63]

It was Duranty's misfortune, when he reached Moscow in 1921, to be installed as the New York *Times* correspondent without Bolitho as a colleague and with a tough operator like Floyd Gibbons working against him. The story of the year was the great famine of the Volga, in which nearly a million Russians were said to be dying. The Lenin government was pleading for the assistance of the United States on the one hand and refusing permission to American correspondents to enter the stricken area on the other.

While Duranty meekly waited in Moscow for permission to move, Gibbons, the foreign director of the Chicago *Tribune,* flew into Riga with his associates, George Seldes and Ambrose Lambert. Seldes learned that Maxim Litvinov, the Soviet ambassador, was holding off swarms of correspondents who were clamoring to get into Russia and warned Gibbons to try some other way. Gibbons, never at a loss, marched into Litvinov's office, threatened to precipitate an international incident by flying across the border, and dared Litvinov to stop him. It was a bluff, of course; but Litvinov, knowing how his regime was counting on American relief, couldn't take a chance. He rode with Gibbons into the Soviet Union on the next train.

Duranty himself described what happened: "The Volga famine was the biggest story of the year, but we sat there in Moscow fighting vermin and Soviet inertia whilst Floyd Gibbons of the Chicago *Tribune* was cabling thousands of words a day from the Volga cities, beating our heads off and scoring one of the biggest newspaper triumphs in postwar history. Every day we received anguished and peremptory cables from our home offices about the Gibbons exploits, and all we could do was to run bleating with them to the [Soviet] press department and be told, 'We are making arrangements; there will doubtless be a train for you tomorrow.' It was an agonizing experience, but there was nothing we could do about it but gnash our teeth and wait."[64]

Eventually, Duranty and some other correspondents in Moscow were permitted to reach the Volga area on a selective basis and confirmed every horror of which Gibbons had written. More than 30,000,000 Russians were destitute. The American Relief Administration, the Red Cross, and the Quakers fed daily rations to more than 27,000,000 persons, sufficient to keep them alive. While perhaps fewer than 1,000,000 persons died of actual starvation, more than 5,000,000 were the victims of the epidemics that followed. This was the price of the victory of the Communists in Russia, as Duranty saw it. For its emergency work, the American Relief Administration received no thanks from Soviet historians; moreover, Herbert Hoover's experiences during the ARA campaign were accounted by Duranty to have enforced his determination not to recognize the Soviet Union after he was elected President of the United States.[65]

Duranty stayed in Russia while most others, both the eminent and the workaday figures of journalism, came and went. He reported the sequence of events as they unfolded in Russia: the death of Lenin on January 21, 1924; the rise of Joseph Stalin, the man of steel; the fall of Trotsky; the first of the treason trials that shocked the West; the procession of five-year plans; the initial Russian failure to introduce a successful Communist regime in China; and the membership of the Soviet hierarchy that was involved in each. Many a first-rate correspondent analyzed the progress and the failures of the Soviet Union — Paul Scott Mowrer of the Chicago *Daily News,* William Henry Chamberlin of the *Christian Science Monitor,* Eugene Lyons and Henry Shapiro of the UP, Jim Mills and Eddy Gilmore of the AP, Samuel Spewack and Arno Dosch-Fleurot of the New York *World,* Louis Fischer and H. R. Knickerbocker of the New York *Evening Post,* among the Americans, and a host of equally expert British, French, and Germans. Among them there were perhaps better reporters than Duranty in grinding out the daily grist of the news. But none surpassed him in the ability to do what he admired so much in his friend, Bolitho, to "see through the brick wall" of Soviet plans and purposes and correctly interpret the course of events for the West. It was this, rather than mere length of service, that made him one of the most influential correspondents of his day and helped lift the New York *Times* foreign service out of the commonplace.

Even after he lost a leg in a railway accident in France in 1924 and Bolitho counseled him to quit daily journalism, Duranty returned to his post in Moscow. He loved the "novelty, variety and fantasy of Russian life."[66] If anybody rivaled him in expertness as a Moscow correspondent in his day, it was Paul Scheffer of the *Berliner Tageblatt;* but Scheffer's work was not generally known in the English-speaking world. It was from Duranty, therefore, that the West learned that Russia could never again be ignored as a world force. Few who knew Duranty ever recalled any great world beat as an index of his stature. It was his incalculable influence on his fellow-correspondents and on the collective public opinion of the West that distinguished him.

There was still another *Times* correspondent who exercised an influence far beyond the bounds of the post to which he was assigned. He was Clarence Streit, a young Montanan who enlisted in the AEF during World War I and later returned to Europe as a Rhodes Scholar. His assignment was the League of Nations at Geneva, once he joined the *Times* after having served from 1921 on as the Philadelphia *Public Ledger*'s correspondent in Rome and in the Greek-Turkish War.

Streit was one of hundreds of correspondents who covered the League at one time or another between the wars. He was by no means the best known, even of the Americans. Nor was his work the most closely read. He did not have the grace of Paul Scott Mowrer of the Chicago *Daily News,* who could favor American participation in the League even if he recognized that its lack of force would prove fatal both to it and to world peace.[67] Nor did he have the ruthlessness of Sisley Huddleston of the *Christian Science Monitor,* who saw the League collapsing and said so.[68] He was no hard-boiled journalist who went to Geneva in search of news, not sentiment, like the UP's Henry Wood, the AP's Joseph Sharkey, and the enterprising Henry Wales of the Chicago *Tribune.* Nor was he a distinguished analyst like Robert Dell of the Manchester *Guardian,* Jules Sauerwein of *Ce Soir,* "Pertinax" of *Echo de Paris,* and Georg Bernhard of the *Vossische Zeitung.* Streit had the one thing these distinguished journalists did not have — a messianic urge to improve the world, to bring mankind to its senses, to force a change in the age-old initiatives of individual nations insistent on working their sovereign will. Such a view was unusual among the Geneva journalists; among New York *Times* correspondents, it was almost without parallel.

Streit was fair. He was reasonably objective, in the *Times*'s sense, as a League correspondent. But nothing could prevent his international outlook from showing through. Eventually, he stepped out of his daily journalistic routine and became more widely known as the author of a book, *Union Now,* which was published on the eve of World War II in 1939. It called for a union of the North Atlantic democracies in common citizenship, defense, customs, money, communications, and postal services. He lived to see the North Atlantic Treaty Organization come into being under different circumstances and in different form.[69]

If individual correspondents were undoubtedly important to the New York *Times* in its foreign expansion, the teamwork of editors with the foreign service was the most crucial factor in the success of the great experiment. In 1925, when Carr Van Anda retired, he was succeeded by a fussy little goateed Britisher, Frederick T. Birchall, who began almost at once to push the paper's superiority in the reporting of exploration and aviation. A staff man, William Bird, wrote an exclusive account on May 10, 1926, of the successful flight of Richard Evelyn Byrd's three-engine Fokker aircraft to the North Pole and back. Next day, another staff correspondent, Russell Owen, flashed the takeoff of the dirigible *Norge* from Kings Bay, Spitzbergen, for a flight over the North Pole to Point Barrow, Alaska. On May 12, Frederick Ramm, a Norwegian, reported the success of the *Norge* expedition in reaching the pole. Ramm's radioed bulletin reached the newspaper after seven hours of relays.[70] It had taken Admiral Peary 153 days to send his own polar story.

An even greater exploit was now in the making—the solo flight of Captain Charles Augustus Lindbergh across the Atlantic from New York to Paris. The St. Louis *Post-Dispatch* had turned down the rights to the Lindbergh story, its icy managing editor, Oliver Kirby Bovard, saying that he would not "gamble on a man's life for the sake of a piece of newspaper promotion."[71] But when Lindbergh flew into Curtiss Field in his single-engine Ryan monoplane, the *Spirit of St. Louis,* two *Times* reporters had no such qualms. They were Lauren D. (Deak) Lyman and Russell Owen, and they convinced Birchall that Lindbergh could do it. Arthur Hays Sulzberger, Ochs's son-in-law and eventual successor, authorized paying the tall, blond, 25-year-old former airmail pilot $5,000 for his story if he made Paris.[72]

Lindbergh winged away into the sunrise at 6:52 on Friday, May 20, 1927, flying by a periscope that projected over his blind cockpit, at a hundred miles an hour. He sped past Cape Breton Island at 4:05 that afternoon into the darkness that crept over a stormy sea. No newspaperman will ever forget the growing suspense that day and the next. Lindbergh and the *Spirit of St. Louis* were swallowed up in silence. The *Times* alone received 10,000 telephone calls about him. The radio babbled on incessantly, but had nothing new to report. No flier had ever attracted public interest so deeply; few men, whatever their mission, had ever stirred up so many hopes and prayers for a brief time.

At 10 p.m., in the darkness at Le Bourget Field outside Paris on Saturday, May 21, a four-man *Times* staff plunged hopelessly into a mob of 100,000 excited Frenchmen and women as they heard an airplane engine faintly in the distance. They were Jimmy James, the boss, and his henchmen, Carlyle MacDonald, P. J. Philip, and Harold Callender. They had been told by their home office, "Isolate Lindbergh." After one glance at the crowd, they knew they would be lucky to keep him away even from the New York *Herald Tribune,* which was also out in force along with every other newsgathering organization in Paris. When the landing lights of the field flashed on and Lindbergh landed at 10:24 p.m., the expected happened. The French took over in a madly exciting, noisy, jubilant celebration.

The *Times* had Lindbergh's story, but it lost him in the crowd. When Carlyle MacDonald finally found him, carefully tucked away at the American Embassy, he had to share him that night with Ralph Barnes of the Paris *Herald,* Freddy Abbott of INS, and C. F. Bertelli of Universal Service. The rest had to fill in as best they could by telephone. But next day, when Lindbergh's own story appeared under his by-line in the *Times,* those who wanted it had to pay for it. In St. Louis, it was the *Globe-Democrat* and not the *Post-Dispatch* which ran his story. It earned Lindbergh more than $60,000.[73]

As surely as Bleriot's hop across the Channel had signaled the end of British security, Lindbergh's flight across the Atlantic showed that the United States could no longer live in isolation behind its own ocean barriers. Fourteen years would pass before the United States would pay the penalty at Pearl Harbor for failing to learn the lesson.

The *Times* sponsored many other flights, establishing its leadership in aviation coverage. When Byrd went to the Antarctic, Russell Owen accompanied him in 1928–29 on an assignment without a parallel in journalism. The Admiral's departure on his first flight to the South Pole on November 28, 1929, was Owen's story alone. Nobody else could touch it, and the *Times* made the most of it. Byrd himself sent the radio bulletin announcing his arrival at the South Pole, and Owen recorded his arrival back at his Little America base on November 29 after a flight of eighteen hours and fifty-nine minutes. It was a triumph of enterprise, both for aviation and for journalism.[74]

At the end of 1929, the *Times*'s circulation soared to 431,931 daily and 728,909 Sunday. In advertising it led the world's newspapers with 32,162,870 lines annually. Adolph Ochs's foreign news policy had paid handsome dividends. There was no doubt about the *Times*'s leadership in the field. But the world in which that leadership had been established was now gone beyond recall, shattered by the stock market collapse of October 29, 1929.

The news from New York radiated all over the world with an almost paralyzing effect: "Stock prices virtually collapsed yesterday, swept downward with gigantic losses in the most disastrous trading day in the market's history. Billions of dollars in open market values were wiped out as prices tumbled. . . . Hysteria swept the country and stocks went overboard for just what they would bring at a forced sale."[75]

Such was the news the *Times* printed on October 30, 1929. From that day on, it would no longer be sufficient for American newspapers and news agencies to bring the world's news to the United States. The world—and not merely Britain and France and Germany—now would have to pay greater attention to the news from America, as well.

THE YOUNG FALCONS

Colonel Robert R. McCormick, the tough and strong-minded ruler of the "world's greatest newspaper," as he called the Chicago *Tribune*, told Floyd Gibbons, after World War I, to build up a foreign service. The ebullient Floyd needed no urging. Within a few years he collected a spirited group of high-flying young falcons—Frazier Hunt, Larry Rue, David Darrah, Vincent Sheean, Richard Henry Little, George Seldes, and one of the finest of all women correspondents, Sigrid Schultz. Then, by his own irrepressible example, he showed them what he expected of them.

It was, in Westbrook Pegler's phrase, the "age of wonderful nonsense" and the *Tribune* had its share in the work that was done abroad. In 1923, because Rudolph Valentino had created a sensation in a movie, *The Sheik,* Gibbons organized a camel caravan to cross the Sahara. The objective, on cabled instructions from Chicago, was to "obtain true picture sheiks and their appeal Anglo-Saxon and American women." For three months and five days, Gibbons and his party struggled across the scorching desert for 2,000 miles from Colomb Bechar to Timbuktu. At the end of this odyssey, he reported disappointedly: "I never encountered the type of dashing, handsome, love-making sheik made famous in fiction and movies as a romantic conqueror of the hearts of beautiful Anglo-Saxon girls in the desert. Real sheiks . . . are very unromantic."[76]

Such exploits were bound to have an effect on pliant young correspondents, particularly uninhibited romantics like Jimmy Sheean, who had joined the *Tribune*'s staff in 1922. In the fall of 1924, he vanished into the Rif mountains of Morocco and interviewed Abd-el-Krim, who had been leading a rebellion of 5,000 tribesmen against Spanish rule. Out of this exploit came the Romberg operetta, *The Desert Song,* and some romantic newspaper pieces. But alas for fame, Sheean was later fired from the *Tribune* for taking what his indignant superiors thought was too long a time over dinner—a base canard, of course.[77]

Yet, Sheean's luck held. When he reached New York to look for another job, he ran into Merian Cooper of the New York *Times,* whom he had known for some years. The aggressive Cooper helped him sell a book about his Rif journey and introduced him to the North American Newspaper Alliance, for which he returned to the Rif and more adventure. Now, instead of working for one newspaper, and an ungrateful one at that, he was to appear in a number of leading American journals, including the New York *World,* and some of the British press, as well.

The second expedition to the lair of the Rif patriot was somewhat less than romantic. The French, by this time, had been drawn into the fighting because Abd-el-Krim had had the bad judgment to send his tribesmen on raids across the border into Algeria. The musical comedy was over. The unsentimental Marshal Henry Philippe Pétain went after Abd-el-Krim with French bomber aircraft, machine guns, and the latest thing in artillery. Sheean survived air bombardment and other hardships. But when he returned to the outside world this time, nobody was waiting to scatter roses in his path and put book contracts in his eager hands. The *Journal des Debats* in Paris called him "le press agent attitre d'Abd el Krim." Of course, he had the satisfaction of being beatified in the columns of the New York *World,* which gave his report a dazzling display. But by 1926, the story was all over. Pétain, with scant ceremony, crushed the Rif and sent Abd-el-Krim into exile.

Sheean wrote a disenchanted postscript before he went on to examine the more humdrum aspects of foreign affairs: "That imperialism was murderous and hypocritical was no discovery. . . . You could not be immersed for years in political journalism without getting to know the nature of the beast. But until these journeys to the Rif, I had not realized its awful stupidity—the ghastly wrongheadedness with which it sacrificed the time and the lives of its best men for the enrichment of its worst. . . . So, as all know, the French empire in Morocco was preserved from danger, and the Spaniards returned to that strip of land out of which Abd el Krim had driven them."[78]

A more philosophic Chicagoan, William Lawrence Shirer, another new foreign correspondent who was working at that time for the Chicago *Tribune* in Paris, put it differently: "The Paris that I came to in 1925 at the tender age of twenty-one and loved, as you love a woman, is no longer the Paris that I will find day after tomorrow—I have no illusions about that."[79] But there were few like Shirer, realistic enough to know that new leaders sometimes make deceptive music in their hideaways. It was to be his fate to record the rise and fall of the Third Reich.

There were few, too, like Dorothy Thompson, the Methodist minister's daughter from Lancaster, N.Y., who set out for Europe in 1920 at the age of 26 with nothing but her courage and $150 to sustain her. Following her graduation from Syracuse in 1914, she had been a women's suffrage organizer, done advertising and ground out social service publicity. In London, she patiently applied for work and finally sold a few stories to INS, one about a Zionist convention and others about the Irish rebellion. What she earned wasn't enough to sustain her, so she went back to publicity, this time for the Red Cross in Paris.

The Philadelphia *Public Ledger* at about this time was just embarking on a foreign service venture, in which the New York *Evening Post* later shared, both papers being owned by Cyrus H. K. Curtis, the publisher of the *Saturday Evening Post*. Miss Thompson resolved to keep trying and wrote a piece about czarist refugees in Paris who were doing menial labor. With it, she invaded the *Ledger*'s Paris office. There, she encountered the ever-gallant and ever-generous Sam Dashiell, who was bureau chief, and who promptly bought the story. Dashiell did even more. Out of sheer friendliness for the young and the penniless — there were literally hundreds whom he helped in one way or another — he took the determined young woman with the fair hair and the bright blue eyes to his chief, Wythe Williams, and recommended her.

It was another break for Dorothy Thompson. Williams, the old New York *Times* correspondent who had done an unpleasant hitch with the Northcliffe papers, was now busy developing the *Ledger*'s service with Carl W. Ackerman, back from his exploits in Berlin and Siberia and newly installed in London as its chief European correspondent. It wasn't long before Miss Thompson was the *Ledger*'s correspondent in Vienna. There, fortunately, she came across another sympathetic colleague, M. W. Fodor, whose training worked wonders. In 1922, she obtained an exclusive interview with Emperor Karl in Budapest after the failure of his putsch and sent it through censorship by a sleeping-car porter to Fodor in Vienna, with whom she shared the story.

Soon afterward, when Fodor tipped her at a party that Marshal Josef Pilsudski was marching on Warsaw intent on a revolutionary seizure of power, she borrowed $500 from Sigmund Freud and took off by train for the Polish border, still in evening gown and satin slippers. About fifty miles outside Warsaw, the train halted because the tracks were mined. Floyd Gibbons, Karl Decker, and other correspondents aboard the train rounded up automobiles to take them to the Polish capital. Out of consideration for Miss Thompson, who seemed quite regal in her party dress, they bowed her to a big, shiny Daimler. But with the frugality of most women correspondents, she refused to pay the $60 rental charge on the Daimler and took an old Ford instead. Virtue was rewarded. The Daimler was riddled with machine gun fire before it reached Warsaw. Miss Thompson got through in her jalopy, walking the last few miles in high heels. Through Fodor's training, she knew how to circumvent the Polish censors, just as she had the Hungarians. Once more, her copy came through nicely, and the honors were principally hers.

It did not take long to make a seasoned correspondent out of Dorothy Thompson. By 1925 she was the chief of the Philadelphia *Public Ledger*–New York *Evening Post* bureau in Berlin, a title long on prestige but lamentably short on salary. It paid only $50 a week. Fodor inherited the *Ledger-Post* bureau in Vienna, which he filled with distinction for many years along with his responsibilities for the Manchester *Guardian*. He watched with interest the development of the most brilliant of his many protégés, particularly her rivalry with Edgar Ansel Mowrer of the Chicago *Daily News,* Sigrid Schultz of the Chicago *Tribune,* and Joseph Shaplen of the New York *Times* in Berlin.[80] With her other friends, he worried over the failure of her four-year marriage to a young Hungarian, Josef Bard.

Nobody, as it turned out, had any need to worry about love and Dorothy Thompson. Shortly after she received her divorce from Bard, she attended one of Gustav Stresemann's press conferences in the German foreign ministry on July 8, 1927, and met a lanky, freckled, red-headed friend of H. R. Knickerbocker's. The newcomer was Sinclair Lewis, who wouldn't let her out of his sight. She invited him to a party for her thirty-third birthday next day. When he arrived, he wore a Rotary button in his lapel and carried a Bible in his rucksack. He proposed to her that night, his first wife, Grace Hegger Lewis, already having determined on a divorce.

Miss Thompson didn't take him seriously at first. But he was persistent. And she soon saw that he was in earnest. On July 18, 1927, when the Socialist workers' riots broke out in Vienna and the Palace of Justice was burned to the ground in the heart of the city, Miss Thompson flew in to help Fodor with the story. Sinclair Lewis came along. Humbly, he wrote his impressions of the scene, merely because she asked him to do so, and let her cable the story to the *Public Ledger* syndicate, the first and last time it ever carried a spot news foreign story written by a major American novelist at far less than the going rate.

From then on, Lewis went wherever Dorothy Thompson was. He even followed her to Moscow on November 29, when she was sent there on a Russian assignment. This was the celebrated occasion on which she and Theodore Dreiser talked separately to Anna Louise Strong, the Communist journalist from Seattle, and later wrote pieces that strongly resembled each other textually. This was the cause of a one-punch fight later between Lewis and Dreiser. Dreiser won.

To nobody's surprise, Miss Thompson and Lewis were married in London on May 14, 1928 at St. Martin's Registry Office in London. It was, without doubt, the literary marriage of the year. The new Mrs. Lewis, abruptly interrupting her career, followed her husband and indulgently humored him in his peculiar, alcoholic ways, although she saw from the outset that she would have to make all the sacrifices to keep the marriage going. She made the effort, explaining that she loved him: "Why else should I have married him, considering my own position when we met, except because of that pull of his genius and my faith in his almost agonized protestations, at times, that he *needed* me?" But neither love nor pity, Lewis nor marriage, were to keep her forever from the life she had ordained for herself as a journalist in 1920.[81] Knickerbocker took over from her as the *Ledger-Post* correspondent in Berlin and in 1931 distinguished himself by doing a Pulitzer Prize-winning series on Russia.

The Chicago *Daily News,* meanwhile, was building up a foreign staff that was the finest of the era for its size. Hal O'Flaherty in London, Paul Scott Mowrer in Paris, Junius Wood in Moscow, Edgar Ansel Mowrer in Berlin, Hi Moderwell in Rome, A. R. Decker in Vienna, and Constantine Brown in Turkey were all authorities in their areas. In some ways, these knowledgeable correspondents eclipsed the kind of men who for generations had been representing the *Times* of London in key spots of the world. The New York *Times* was able to compete with individual correspondents of such brilliance only by the sheer force of numbers and greater financial resources.

To join this group of experts, younger men flocked to Europe by every device that is known to the local reporter who wants to become a foreign correspondent. Upon his graduation from the University of Michigan in 1925, William H. Stoneman lived with a Swedish family and learned the language while he worked for three years for the *Daily News*'s local staff. Then, quite calmly, he sailed for Stockholm, notified his office that it had a new Swedish-speaking correspondent, and was rewarded with the appointment for his daring. Negley Farson, who came from the University of Pennsylvania, recommended himself to the *Daily News* foreign service by traveling from the Netherlands to

Rumania by canal and riverboat and writing pieces as he went. John Gunther, who was no less ingenious, applied for the foreign service almost as soon as he was graduated from the University of Chicago as a member of Phi Beta Kappa. A few years later, as a $55-a-week *Daily News* reporter, he simply walked off the job, sailed to England, and was hired by the newspaper's London bureau. However, he didn't have Stoneman's luck and was fired as soon as his first by-line appeared in the paper. After doing six months' penance on the UP, he was taken back by the *Daily News,* gravitated to Vienna, where he became another of Fodor's protégés, and eventually developed into the author of a staggering number of "Inside" books on the great nations and continents of the world.[82]

The *Christian Science Monitor,* too, was developing a formidable foreign service with the accession of Willis J. Abbot, the old Hearst executive, as its editor in 1921. Until Abbot went to the *Monitor,* its correspondents sometimes were more colorful than expert. Demarest Lloyd, who liked newspapering despite his wealth, was accustomed to cover assignments in London in a chauffeur-driven Rolls-Royce. Abbot used a more conventional journalist in London, John Sidney Braithwaite, who headed the European service, and the crotchety veteran, Sisley Huddleston, in Paris. On Russian affairs, in addition to the informed comments of the University of Chicago professor, Samuel N. Harper, the *Monitor* used William Henry Chamberlin as resident correspondent from 1922 on for 14 years. At the League of Nations in Geneva, the coverage was more conventional, the correspondent being Hugh Spender, a British journalist of the old school. He made little impression on Erwin Dain Canham, of Auburn, Maine, a graduate of Bates College, who appeared at Geneva in 1926 during a vacation from Oxford, where he was a Rhodes Scholar, to assist him. It was the first foreign assignment for the *Monitor*'s future editor. The *Monitor* also brought to American readers the political dispatches of the liberal British editor, H. W. Massingham, and the British critics, V. S. Pritchett and Harold Hobson, among others.[83]

Another American newcomer to the European field was the Baltimore *Sun,* which in 1924 decided to open its own London office after having used the Manchester *Guardian*'s foreign service for a considerable time. John W. Owens, its first correspondent, was the forerunner of a number of competent experts who gave the *Sun* papers a broader outlook on foreign affairs.[84]

The newest, and yet in a sense the oldest, of all the American foreign services was that of the New York *Herald Tribune,* which contrived to put together a group of seasoned correspondents and youngsters, soon after the merger of the two old newspapers, to compete with the more powerful New York *Times*. Wilbur Forrest, the old dependable, was in charge of the Paris office, with Leland Stowe, then only a few years out of Wesleyan, to help him. Arthur Draper was in London, John Elliott in Berlin, and John T. Whitaker in Rome. But there was a constant ebb and flow of newcomers on the Paris *Herald,* as the European edition of the *Herald Tribune* continued to be known, and some became outstanding correspondents. A typical case was Ralph Barnes, whose first big foreign story was Gertrude Ederle's successful swim across the English Channel in 1926. In the excitement Barnes, who had suffered the excruciating pangs of seasickness during the crossing, plunged overboard from his rowboat and managed to get to a telephone with his story.[85] Among others were Bert Andrews, who was to become chief of the newspaper's Washington bureau; Will Barber, who would be a star for the Chicago *Tribune;* Rex Smith, later to be editor of *Newsweek;* and Elliot Paul, a picturesque character who would write nostalgic books about Paris.

At least one of the *Herald Tribune*'s raw recruits varied the usual pattern by sidestepping the Paris *Herald*'s dubious training and beginning, instead, on a more conventional Paris newspaper, *Le Matin.* She was Sonia Tomara, a slim young Russian refugee who spoke nine languages. She arrived in Paris after World War I by a circuitous route with only 150 francs and a flaring ambition to make something of herself as a journalist. For six years, she served her apprenticeship as secretary to Jules Sauerwein, one of the distinguished editors of *Le Matin.* Then, the ever-alert Leland Stowe hired her away for the *Herald Tribune* and launched her on an adventurous career.[86]

There is, of course, no way of knowing how many young American journalists were nurtured on the thriving English language press in Paris during the 1920s. Only fading memories and tattered books of reminiscences provide the total record, and they are, by and large, uncertain accountings. Nor can there be any proper estimate of the influence that was exerted on the young, the eager, and the enthusiastic ones by the colorful, careless, and often irresponsible Paris *Herald* and its rivals, the Paris edition of the Chicago *Tribune,* the Paris *Times,* and the continental edition of the London *Daily Mail.* All flourished, to the extent that is possible for English-language newspapers in France, during the 1920s. But after the debacle of 1929, when the grand American binge in Paris was over and most of the frolicking young Americans had to go home, the *Herald* alone survived as an American publication in France. While its appearance began to conform to the handsome dress of its parent newspaper, it did not really change its careless and casual ways between the wars. Moreover, it continued, rather defiantly, to present as one of its trademarks the semi-literate maunderings of its ancient sports columnist, Sparrow Robertson, to a vague audience of good companions whom he called his old pals.[87]

There were a few other independent American newsgathering organizations that maintained a semblance of a foreign service in the 1920s. The New York *World* got by with such veterans as Arno Dosch-Fleurot, such newcomers as John L. Balderston, a graduate of the soldiers' newspaper, *Stars and Stripes,* and such distinguished commentators as William Bolitho. The New York *Sun* took on an occasional correspondent, too, one being a youngster on the China coast, Edgar Snow, who had an intense curiosity even then about the Chinese Communist movement. Many other newspapers sent correspondents overseas either for limited periods or for single assignments, in much the same manner as the infant American radio networks and news magazines at first tried to fill their foreign needs. But basically, except for the foreign services of the New York *Times* and its principal rivals, American newspapers were able to get what little foreign news they published from their wire services — the AP, the UP, and the Hearst services, INS and Universal Service. An America in isolation basically wanted foreign news that was compounded either out of crisis or curiosity, sometimes both, and that is what was generally in the wire service foreign file in that era.

The wire service correspondent was, by and large, a generalist picked on the basis of his ability to get a story and wing it into the cablehead quicker than his rivals. If he had any ability as a linguist, or if he knew something more about the background of his assignment at first than the average college junior, it was purely accidental. And yet, some of these correspondents very quickly developed a familiarity with Europe that was the equal of any Reuters correspondent of standing, enabling them to compete successfully with the great British wire service. Such AP correspondents as James A. Mills could pick up a telephone in Paris and summon King Carol of Rumania for an exclusive interview at the other end of the line in Bucharest. Such UP correspondents as Ed L. Keen in London and Webb Miller in Paris were regarded as authorities in their areas. And despite their many weaknesses, the Hearst services could put up a good front on big stories by using their stars, of whom Karl H. von Wiegand was a prime example in Germany, Russia, and eastern Europe. The youngsters came and went in the wire service offices, too, although not quite on the same scale as on the English-language newspapers in Paris; the wire services wanted a little more responsibility for their money, although their pay, also, in those days, was disgraceful.[88]

There were some, of course, who went into journalism in Europe merely to sustain themselves while they worked hopefully on the great American novel, musical composition, or painting. But it was relatively easy for the professionals to tell at a glance who was seriously interested in the work of foreign correspondence, regardless of talent or lack of it, and who was not. Wilbur Forrest, of the New York *Herald Tribune*, remarked after brief observation of the husky young man who represented the Toronto *Star* at the Genoa conference in 1922: "He didn't give a damn about it, except that it provided some much-needed funds and gave him an association with other writers."[89] The Toronto *Star*'s correspondent was a 23-year-old native of Oak Park, Ill., Ernest Hemingway.

In fairness to Hemingway, he gave much more thought and effort to his work as a journalist, limited though it was, than did his fellow novelist, Stephen Crane; but, of course, he never wrote as consistently for any newspaper as did Harold Frederic for the New York *Times* or even Mark Twain for the New York *Herald*. Hemingway was serious enough about newspaper work when he broke in on the Kansas City *Star* in 1917, for he labored industriously on a mountain of trivia before he took off for Italy in the summer of 1918 as a Red Cross ambulance driver and canteen assistant with the rank of lieutenant.

It was his misfortune to be riddled with fragments of an exploding Austrian trench mortar on July 8, 1918, near the Italian village of Fossalta, two weeks before his nineteenth birthday and only a week after he had gone into the trenches. There is a legend that, like Richard Harding Davis, he was firing at the foe although he was a noncombatant, but it has never been proved.[90] In any event, when he returned to New York on January 21, 1919, his arrival as a wounded ex-newspaperman was recorded by the New York *Sun* with a sympathetic 500-word piece, which certainly didn't discourage his interest in journalism. It was perfectly natural for him, therefore, to seek work at the Toronto *Star*, to which friends directed him, and persuade the *Star* to let him be its stringer in Paris when he returned there in 1922.

For about two years, while he was working on his short stories and his first novel, *The Sun Also Rises*, Hemingway supported himself by turning out a mélange of features, spot news, and interpretive articles for the *Star*. If he wasn't serious about continuing in journalism,

as Forrest and others said, he was at the very least a serious and con-
scientious journalist. At Genoa, he wrote of Fascist psychology: "The
Fascisti make no distinction between Socialists, Communists, Republicans, or members of cooperative societies. They are all Reds and
dangerous."[91] And of Georgi V. Chicherin, the Soviet Commissar for
foreign affairs, he observed at the same conference: "Chicherin rose and
his hands shaking spoke in French, in his queer, hissing accents, the
result of an accident that knocked out half his teeth. The interpreter
with the ringing voice translated. There was not a sound in the pauses
except the clink of the mass of decorations on an Italian general's chest
as he shifted from one foot to the other."[92] He interviewed Mussolini:
"Mussolini is a big, brown-faced man with a high forehead, a slow-
smiling mouth, and large, expressive hands. . . . His face is intellectual,
it is the typical 'Bersagliere' face, with its large, brown, oval shape, dark
eyes and big, slow-speaking mouth."[93]

There was a lot more of this, equally competent as the work of a
young journalist abroad, so that Hemingway had a right to expect reasonably considerate treatment when he went to Toronto to work on the
Star in the fall of 1923. He was given short shrift and quit after four
months, the final blow being the destruction of some confidential official documents he had shown an arrogant desk man in connection with
an interview with a visiting foreign dignitary. It was the end of him as a
day-to-day working journalist, although he would be drawn back into
the profession for limited periods in years to come.[94]

Such was the manner in which American foreign correspondence
began to flourish in Europe in the 1920s, and such were the young
journalists who gave up precious years to work in the field, some temporarily, some for just a lark, but most of them for the rest of their
lives. If the Americans achieved a certain preeminence over their British
and European rivals in a limited area, it was primarily a triumph of
superior drive and energy at first. Elsewhere in the world, American
coverage of Asia was sketchy, and the reporting from other areas not
commonly covered was based on either crises or stunts. The young falcons would have to mature before they could achieve the leadership
they sought.

6   The Darkening Horizon

STORM CLOUDS OVER CHINA

Demaree and Dorothy Bess, who worked for the United Press in Peking, were awakened before dawn on September 18, 1931, by a telephone call. William Henry Donald, the Australian journalist who was public relations adviser to Generalissimo Chiang Kai-shek, announced excitedly: "The Japanese are seizing Mukden and I wanted to tell you that we are appealing to the League of Nations."

There was no more sleep for Demaree Bess that night. The 40-year-old Missourian, who had been in the Far East for seven years and now was North China bureau manager for the UP, knew he had a major story. Donald wasn't one to bluff about danger. In Sun Yat-sen's 1911 revolution, the Australian, then a correspondent for the New York *Herald,* had fired the siege guns that blew open the gates of Nanking. He knew more about what was going on in China, perhaps, than anybody except Chiang himself. His information had to be taken at face value.

Within a short time, Bess confirmed the Japanese attack. He learned that the Japanese army in Manchuria had begun punitive action against the Chinese for allegedly blowing up a small section of track on the South Manchurian Railway at Mukden. Marshal Chang Hsueh-liang, who was allied with Chiang Kai-shek, was withdrawing his Manchurian troops south of the Great Wall. The richest part of China was being left to the marauding Japanese.

This was the so-called Mukden incident which, although Bess couldn't foresee it, was the first in a chain of small wars that would lead to World War II. All the correspondent knew at the time was that he had to find some way of covering. By a stroke of luck, Martin Sommers, a first-rate New York newspaperman and graduate of the Paris

157

Herald, was in Peking, and Bess quickly arranged to send him north as the UP's man. In a few years, Sommers, as the foreign editor of the *Saturday Evening Post,* would be assigning Bess as a correspondent, but this time it was the other way around. By the time Sommers reached Mukden three days later (the train trip normally took one day, but the Japanese created difficulties), the New York headquarters of the UP was supremely uninterested in the Mukden story.[1]

Yet, it was clear that the Japanese were not likely to pause after their easy conquest of Manchuria. The League of Nations was powerless to stop them. Henry L. Stimson, the Secretary of State, did little more than hurt their feelings by refusing to recognize their rule over Manchuria. Moreover, despite their initial defeat, the Chinese were showing signs of fight. They were clamping an economic boycott on Japan. The Chinese Nineteenth Route Army was bracing itself in Shanghai for a bold stand.

To any alert independent newspaper and news agency, the danger signals were almost painfully apparent. And yet, among the old China hands and the youngsters who then were covering for the foreign press either as regulars or stringers, there were few with the experience to handle a crisis like this. China was thinly covered at best and correspondents moved in and out, few staying for very long. Two of the better ones, George Sokolsky, who had edited the *Far Eastern Review* and corresponded for London and New York dailies, and Relman Morin, a 25-year-old graduate of Pomona College who had worked on the Shanghai *Evening Post,* had just gone back to the United States. Reinforcements had to be brought in.

The Japanese finally moved to the attack on January 28, 1932. They landed 70,000 troops in the Hongkew area of the International Settlement of Shanghai and began lobbing shells into the Chinese army of about 45,000 in the native sector. H. R. Ekins, a tall, fair-haired minister's son who was the UP correspondent in Shanghai, walked past the Japanese lines wearing a fedora and swinging a gold-headed cane as if it were the most natural thing in the world to be out taking the air. Within a few minutes, he walked right into the field of Chinese rifle fire. The walk ended abruptly. Bud Ekins flung himself into a ditch and began crawling to safety. Eventually, Chinese soldiers pulled him out, brushed him off, and took him to their commander. They had tea together which was, as Ekins observed later, a strange way to cover a war.[2]

Ekins was far from alone. Floyd Gibbons, who had been earning a good living as a broadcaster, was in Shanghai as a war correspondent, this time for International News Service. It was his seventh war. His colleagues were saying, with wry humor, that no war was really official until Gibbons appeared. From the twelfth-story roof of the Hotel Cathay in Shanghai, the veteran somberly watched the Japanese war planes bombing a railway station in which Chinese troops were holding out.[3] Most of them were killed, but their companions in the Nineteenth Route Army fought on. And Gibbons filed his stories to the United States, day by day, to a large and relatively unconcerned audience. Americans just didn't believe Shanghai was their concern.

Among the younger men who underwent their baptism of fire as war correspondents in Shanghai was Edgar Snow, then a 27-year-old correspondent for Consolidated Press, a syndicate which included the New York *Sun* and the Chicago *Daily News*. Daily he walked through the shattered streets with his friend and mentor, John Benjamin Powell, the editor of the *China Weekly Review* and the correspondent of the Chicago *Tribune*. Snow had gone to Shanghai in 1928 with a letter of introduction to Powell from Walter Williams, dean of the University of Missouri School of Journalism. Now, after four years of training, he could write with sickening precision of the "smell of smoking flesh slapped against the steel sides of a bombed troop train" and the "rag-doll men in their rough cotton-padded blue gowns hanging where the Japanese had left them after using them for bayonet practice."[4] It was, he assured himself, "real" war at last, not the chase and occupation he had witnessed in Manchuria.

There was still another newcomer who was being introduced to the ferocity of war — 27-year-old Christopher Chancellor, who had taken a "first" in history at Cambridge and had come out to the Far East as Reuters chief correspondent. One day, he would head the entire service. Now, he was a particular target of the Japanese despite his youthful years. Their intelligence reports, as it was later learned, credited him with strange extracurricular activities: "It was said in foreign circles that Chancellor's wife had connections close to the British court, while he himself had made a career as a news agency man only because he was in close contact with British Secret Service circles and had offered his fortune and his wife's to Britain."[5]

Had the Japanese realized it, there was a real spy — the most dangerous of his era in the Far East — operating right under their noses in Shanghai at that time. He was a big, brown-haired correspondent for the German *Soziologische Magazin*, Dr. Richard Sorge. Nobody thought much of him as a correspondent; he seemed, to both the Japanese and his colleagues, to be a crazy, drunken, woman-chasing Nazi. In reality, he was the organizer of the most efficient Communist spy ring in the Far East and even then was recruiting the members of his apparatus with his chief of staff, Ozaki Hozumi, a special correspondent of the Osaka *Asahi*.[6] But nobody suspected either of them.

Few among the correspondents, particularly the latest arrivals, knew very much about the complicated relations between Chiang, the Russians, and the Chinese Communists—and cared less. That was the crucial failure in much of their work. All they saw before them was stricken Shanghai, with Chiang obviously reluctant to rush reinforcements to the embattled Nineteenth Route Army. His hesitation was costing him friends everywhere.

Actually, as the better correspondents realized, Chiang was caught between three foes—the Japanese invaders, the Chinese Communists, who had set up a Soviet regime in Kiangsi in 1931, and the remaining independent war lords. If he moved against anyone, he weakened himself in fighting the others. He was still convinced, of course, that the Chinese Communists eventually would be his most dangerous foe.

The Chinese Communists had organized in Shanghai in 1921, one of the original members being a round-faced farm boy, Mao Tse-tung. In 1927, after a long period of temporizing, Chiang had broken with them. He had swept them from the Yangtze Valley, captured Nanking in a savage onslaught, and forced his political and military advisers from the Soviet Union, headed by Mikhail Borodin, to flee. He had tried in vain to exterminate the Chinese Communists in Kiangsi; now, seemingly, he had decided to wait, safeguard his own forces, and let the Shanghai tragedy take its course.

It was this position that brought him so much criticism from the foreign correspondents who covered the Japanese assault in Shanghai.[7] Unwittingly, the Chinese Communists, far removed from the scene of the battle, were the beneficiaries as far as public sentiment was concerned. The Nineteenth Route Army, after 34 days of heroic resistance centered in the Chapei area, had to withdraw from Shanghai, half its strength gone. On May 5, the Chinese ended their boycott and agreed to a demilitarized zone about the International Settlement. Chiang Kai-shek broke up the remainder of the Nineteenth, distributing its troops. At the first opportunity, he resumed his attack against his "first and worst" foes, the Chinese Communists.

Japan took advantage of the civil war, creating an "independent" nation, Manchukuo, occupying Jehol, and advancing south of the Great Wall. There was little doubt of what the Japanese meant to do in the minds of such correspondents as Hallett Abend of the New York *Times* and Victor Keen of the New York *Herald Tribune,* both Asian veterans.

One of the outstanding feats of the entire campaign was the investigation by Edward Hunter of INS of reports that Japanese troops had massacred Chinese peasants. He risked his life to obtain the evidence and documented it so well that it became a part of the League of Nations records. However, when the League, on May 27, 1933, finally adopted the Lytton report, incorporating the Stimson formula of nonrecognition of Japanese conquests, Japan withdrew from the League. By that time, the ranks of foreign correspondents in Asia had been thinned again by momentous occurrences elsewhere. In the United States and in Europe, the public gave up worrying about the unsettled Far East.

When Edgar Snow of the *Saturday Evening Post* sought out Mao Tse-tung and Chou En-lai in distant Yenan three years later and told the story of the fantastic "Long March" of 6,000 miles that saved the Chinese Communist Party from Chiang Kai-shek's annihilation campaign, it was regarded as a sensational journalistic feat. Only a few specialists, however, noted Mao's stinging references to the failure of the Soviet Union to help him in 1927 when the Kuomintang-Communist alliance collapsed, and Chiang opened fire on the Reds. They wondered at it but concluded in the main that it was double talk. Few in the West would have taken any stock then in a Communist split between Russia and China. And even fewer would have prophesied that a chain-smoking, long-haired Chinese with an amiable smile and ruthless revolutionary policy would one day be the master of a billion Chinese.[8]

FIRE IN BERLIN

Flames burst from the Reichstag in Berlin at 10 p.m. on February 27, 1933. Members of the foreign press corps who gathered outside the building knew without being told that it was the end of the Weimar Republic, that brief and feeble moment of German liberty. On January 30, 1933, Adolf Hitler, the one-time Austrian paper hanger, had been named Chancellor by President Paul von Hindenburg with the support of both the German army and the nation's most conservative elements. All Hitler needed was a pretext to make himself dictator. And this was it.

At 11:30 p.m., after the fire had been extinguished, the foreign correspondents' suspicions were confirmed in a strange way. They had expected the Nazis would raise the cry of "Red terror," against which Hitler alone could lead the defense. They had learned that the Nazis had arrested a 20-year-old Dutch Communist, Marinus van der Lubbe, and obtained a confession from him. But what they hadn't expected to find, once they were permitted inside the gutted Reichstag, was about twenty bundles of incendiary materials scattered through the building. Even the cautious *Frankfurter Zeitung* was to report on March 1: "There is some doubt as to whether the imprisoned man could have done it all himself."

The world was not to know until the Nuremberg trials that Nazi storm troopers had scattered gasoline and self-igniting chemicals in the Reichstag that night and used the supposedly demented Dutchman as a dupe. But such correspondents as Edgar Ansel Mowrer of the Chicago *Daily News,* and others, broadly intimated in their dispatches that the Nazis had set the fire themselves.[9] They were not in the least taken in by Hermann Goering's order the night of the Reichstag fire to Rudolf Diels, the new chief of the Gestapo: "This is the beginning of the Communist Revolution! We must not wait a minute. We will show no mercy. Every Communist official must be shot where he is found. Every Communist deputy must this very night be strung up."

The somber story of Hitler's takeover was quickly told in the foreign press. On February 28, all guarantees of individual and civil liberties were suspended. On March 5, the last democratic election in a dozen years gave the Nazis 288 seats in the Reichstag which, with 52 Nationalists' seats, provided a slender majority of 16. On March 23, by 441 to 84, the Reichstag voted itself out of power and gave all its authority to the cabinet. Thus, Hitler became the German Fuehrer, while the Nazi deputies shouted the "Horst Wessel" song, and many millions began the tragic journey to death on the battlefield, in the concentration camps, or in the crematories.

It scarcely mattered that Ernst Torgler, Georgi Dimitroff, and two other Communists were acquitted after a trial and the Dutchman, van der Lubbe, alone was convicted and decapitated. By that time, it was too late for any German to do anything about Hitler and the Nazis. Germany, as Edgar Ansel Mowrer wrote, had put the clock back.

Dr. Paul Joseph Goebels, the Nazi propaganda minister, dealt swiftly with the German press — the "lap dog press," he called it contemptuously. When he demanded that his controlled journalists be a little brighter, Ehm Welk of the Ullstein *Gruene Post* made a mildly sarcastic comment and was packed off to a concentration camp. The *Voelkischer Beobachter* became the principal party paper, with Dr. Goebels issuing his program through the *Angriff* and Marshal Goering taking over the Essen *National Zeitung.* The Wolff Agency and the old Telegraphen Union merged into the new national propaganda wire service, the Deutsches Nachrichtenburo (DNB). The *Vossische Zeitung,* founded in 1704 and numbering Frederick the Great among its contributors, suspended publication. It had been owned by a Jewish firm, Ullstein Verlag. The *Berliner Tageblatt* and the *Frankfurter Zeitung,* both Jewish-owned, were taken away from their proprietors, and continued publication as mere shadows of themselves. The radio and the motion pictures, too, became adjuncts of the State.

Journalists became licensed servants of the government. To practice the profession in Germany, one had to be a German citizen, more than 21 years of age, and neither Jewish nor married to a Jew within the meaning of the Civil Service Law (all with Jewish grandmothers were excluded).[10]

The inevitable reaction was that fewer newspapers were bought and read, greater demand was evident for foreign newspapers, and the work of foreign correspondents, accordingly, was carefully scrutinized. Edgar Ansel Mowrer was told that, because of his outspoken opposition to the Nazi regime, he would have to resign as president of the Foreign Press Association or it would be officially ignored. He tried to quit, but the foreign correspondents triumphantly kept him in office for a short while longer. Threats and pressure eventually forced him out of Germany, the first of the foreign correspondents to go.[11] He won a Pulitzer Prize for his German correspondence.

For those who remained, conditions became increasingly difficult. Telephones were tapped, mail opened, associates were interrogated, correspondents themselves were trailed. A card file was kept on each in Goebbels' ministry. German associates of the correspondents were pressed into service as informers.[12] The whole apparatus of the police state was brought to bear on all those who were obliged to work under the sign of the swastika. Conditions were scarcely worse in Moscow.

It was particularly hard on the wire service correspondents, who were responsible for getting news from Germany quickly and accurately, but most of them managed to stick it out. Dorothy Thompson was not so favored. On August 25, 1934, she hastily left the German capital, having been given twenty-four hours to depart. Her book, *I Saw Hitler,* had made her unpopular.[13] Moreover, the Nazis didn't care too much for one of her friends, H. R. Knickerbocker, who had switched to INS in Berlin, and was presently replaced by the more phlegmatic Pierre J. Huss. However, Ward Price, the monocled British correspondent of the London *Daily Mail,* was popular in Berlin and had a series of interviews with Hitler. A sample of Hitler's pronouncements in the *Daily Mail:* "War will not come again. . . . Germany's problems cannot be settled by war."[14] *Le Matin,* in Paris, ran the same stuff, but no realistic foreign correspondent believed it.

About a hundred of the foreign press corps jammed the conference room of Dr. Goebbels's propaganda ministry in Berlin on March 16, 1935. The little propaganda chief excitedly read off the text of a new law which, as the correspondents immediately realized, wiped out all the military prohibitions of the Versailles Treaty against Germany. The Third Reich was rearming forthwith. Universal military service was restored. Twelve army corps, 36 divisions, would be the beginning. As for the end, any correspondent could guess.

The wire service men jumped up — Louis Lochner of the AP, Edward W. Beattie Jr. of the UP, Pierre Huss of INS, and Gordon Young of Reuters. Before Goebbels finished, they were on the telephone to their offices, and the bulletins were going out to an apathetic world. Norman Ebbutt of the *Times* of London and Pat Murphy of the London *Daily Express* walked up the Wilhelmstrasse later with William L. Shirer, who was the Universal Service correspondent in Berlin at the time and didn't have to file for afternoon papers. Ebbutt kept trying to reassure his colleagues that it was not news — that the Germans had been building up their armies for some time in secret.

Shirer knew better. In his diary he wrote: "Hitler, I learn, acted with lightning speed, apparently on the inspiration that now was the time — if ever — to act and get by with it, and it looks as though he will." With a correspondent's dichotomy over the quick dispatch of bad news, he added: "To bed, tired, and sick at this Nazi triumph, but somehow professionally pleased at having had a big story to handle, Dosch [Fleurot] being away, which left the job to me alone."[15]

The correspondents sounded the alarm in Germany, clearly and faithfully, just as they had in China. And still, France, Britain, and the United States slept. Paul Scott Mowrer wrote: "Most people just couldn't believe that the things the Nazis were doing were true."[16] They would soon pay heavily for their neglect. The reoccupation of the Rhineland, the annexation of Austria, and the rape of Czechoslovakia would be the consequences of a foreign hope of "peace in our time."

THE WEAKNESS OF FRANCE

Philippe Barres, Berlin correspondent of *Le Matin* of Paris, waged an aggressive campaign in the 1930s against the rearmament of Germany. He was one of the few on *Le Matin* who did so; the paper, by and large, sided with the conservative elements that had a sneaking admiration for the way Hitler was doing things. But Barres persisted in his disclosures until he found that *Le Matin* was using his material to dazzle its readers with German might instead of preaching the cause of a stronger France. Then he quit, going over to the opposition Paris *Soir*.[17]

Maurice Bunau-Varilla, the proprietor of *Le Matin* and brother of Philippe Bunau-Varilla, who had helped arrange the Panama Canal land grab, saw virtue in the Germans, as did the French rightist press generally. The Germans, in their own way and for their own purposes, appreciated M. Bunau-Varilla's fine qualities. They even took the trouble to send a German chemist to him to praise a pharmaceutical compound known as Synthol, in which he had an interest, and which he presented to visitors on the slightest excuse.[18] It was certainly no surprise, therefore, when one or the other of *Le Matin*'s directorate, but not all, made trips to the shrine of Nazidom in Berlin.

Nor was *Le Matin* alone of the major French newspapers in gingerly approaching a policy of appeasement at first, then becoming bolder as the Germans gained strength. The respected *Le Temps* had much the same leanings. The rightist press was, of course, outspoken. Pierre Guimier's *Le Journal, Le Jour, Gringoire, Candide,* and *L'Action Fran-çaise* all seemed to desire the death of the French Republic more than they did the defeat of Hitler. And then, too, there was a new service called the Prima Press, which distributed news and pictures of obvious Nazi origin to the French press free of charge.[19]

Otto Abetz, Hitler's chief agent in France, was having a rather easy time, all in all, gently leading his distinguished French friends along the path that one day would drop them off the precipice in Vichy. Paris *Soir*, among others, was fighting back. *Le Petit Parisien,* despite a certain fondness for Mussolini, would have nothing to do with Hitler. Henri de Kerillis, in *L'Epoque,* was denouncing Abetz and his French crowd of appeasers. So was André Geraud ("Pertinax") in *L'Europe Nouvelle* and *L'Ordre*. But Geneviève Tabouis, one of the wisest and most courageous of all diplomatic correspondents, was obliged to share honors in *L'Oeuvre* with two French pacifists, Georges de la Fouchardiere and Marcel Deat, who opposed her.[20] It went without saying that strange things were going on in the background of French journalism in the years when Hitler was building his war machine.

As every seasoned foreign correspondent in Paris knew, it had always been difficult for an honest and competent French journalist to make his way. The miracle was that so many of them survived the system that produced them and labored, despite all difficulties, to try to produce decent newspapers and a responsible press. In 1931, Robert Dell, the Paris correspondent of the Manchester *Guardian,* wrote: "There has been corruption in the French press as long as I have known France, but it is worse now than it ever has been before."[21] An even gloomier observer, Al Laney of the Paris *Herald,* estimated that the news columns were for sale in all but one or two of the more than a hundred Paris dailies. It was, he wrote, the "most venal press the world has known."[22]

There were, of course, few specific details. Such charges can seldom be documented. But Dell and Laney both expressed the belief that much of the French press in the 1930s was subsidized by powerful interests, of which Havas was still the most potent because it controlled the flow of advertising. However, the correspondents also were convinced that foreign money was involved in seeing that there was favorable publicity. German money could scarcely have been excluded from so lamentable a situation, although it was traced to relatively few traitors.

Remarking on what he believed to be the general philosophy of much of the French press, Laney wrote: "The owners and directors of daily papers . . . even took the position that any article, pointed in this direction or that, should be paid for. Favorable criticism of the arts was figured at so many francs a line in practically all the papers dealing with these subjects and was cheerfully paid for by the artists. Paid publicity was made to pass . . . as bona fide, impartial statement of fact. The hidden sources of revenue in the leading French dailies were enormous." As for Havas, he continued, "Havas had correspondents in all parts of the world, and the news they supplied it was often, if not always, bent to fit its enormous volume of advertising. It enjoyed a practical monopoly and it could and did control news anywhere in France."[23]

Nor did first-rate French journalists themselves fail to protest the insidiousness of the system. Pierre Denoyer, New York correspondent for *Le Petit Parisien,* told a Princeton audience in 1930: "To alienate Havas may mean for a newspaper the loss of practically all its advertising revenue. This power of one advertising agency is of tremendous importance for the press and for the public, for it is known that in several cases advertising patrons have objected to editorial policies and interfered directly or indirectly with them, stopped campaigns and tabooed topics."[24]

Yet, who in France could denounce Havas? Pierre Lazareff, who edited *Ce Soir* before World War II, pointed out the consequences of an attack on the system, however much he deplored it, saying: "A mere dispatch from Havas was enough to start a panic on the Bourse, or to set in motion a movement in the Parliament which might lead to the Government's fall, to rioting, or even to war. Who, then, would have dared to attack these evils? Who was in a position to denounce them? Of all the poisons which exerted their influence on French public opinion, the Agence Havas was surely one of the most virulent. And this poison often fell on favorable grounds."[25]

The weakness of the French system, as it then existed, was that the factual newsgatherer, as distinct from the editor or commentator, had no standing and received the barest subsistence pay. Like the newspapers in Germany, much of the French press consisted of journals of opinion rather than fact. The mere reporter, consequently, was looked down upon; the commentator, having more freedom to bestow his favors, was eagerly sought after and rewarded in a variety of ways.[26] Moreover, because a number of French journalists accepted what amounted to bribes to publish certain material, it was assumed in France that the same procedures could be used against foreign correspondents. Obviously, the game couldn't be played that way in very many instances. But the suspicion was raised now and then, which annoyed and sometimes even embarrassed the foreign press corps in Paris.

By and large, the condition of the French press was symptomatic of the general malaise that was attacking the nation itself. The Stavisky scandal, which rocked the French Republic to its foundations in 1934, was one aspect of this fatal illness. Serge Alexander Stavisky, a Bayonne swindler, sold millions in worthless bonds, fled to Chamonix when he was threatened with exposure in December 1933, and there either committed suicide or was killed the following month. Fascists and Communists alike charged the Radical Socialist government of Camille Chautemps with corruption, although Chautemps himself was later cleared. But the reputation of the French press suffered once more when it became known that Stavisky had spread Fr. 3,000,000 in two years to bribe newspapers and journalists.[27]

Efforts to suppress the story failed. The foreign correspondents jumped on it with vigor. The new premier, Edouard Daladier, ruthlessly repressed extremist riots in Paris on February 6–7, 1934, and clapped a censorship on cables to halt outgoing news. For some reason, he forgot about the telephones, which were promptly used by both British and Americans to get their news through to London. Daladier fell, being replaced by a national unity cabinet under Gaston Doumergue, who also failed to maintain himself in office for very long. The Stavisky affair, consequently, shook France with unparalleled violence.

It coincided with a stepped-up campaign by Otto Abetz to win greater sympathy for Hitler's aims in France. A number of French journalists were invited to Berlin, among them Count Fernand de Brinon, a political ally of Pierre Laval. When de Brinon returned to Paris, it was with an appeal from Hitler for cooperation between French and Ger-

man war veterans—a document that was duly published in *Le Matin.*
The French veterans sent a deputation to Berlin, received excellent treat-
ment, and came home in a glow of new understanding for the Third
Reich.

Not all of Abetz's Nazi promotions came off so well. Once, he arranged for an exclusive interview for Bertrand de Jouvenel, a correspondent of *Ce Soir,* with Hitler. It was at a time when the Chamber of
Deputies was debating the ratification of the Franco-Soviet pact. Hitler,
in the Jouvenel interview, offered France a 25-year nonaggression treaty
provided France scrapped its arrangements with the Soviet Union. The
story was not published in *Ce Soir,* however, to avoid prejudicing the
Chamber debate; instead, it appeared in the smaller allied paper, *Midi.*
Abetz complained: "Everything has been ruined. You've made a
Franco-German alliance impossible."[28]

Through it all, the French people, like those in Britain and the United
States, simply could not comprehend their danger. As Eric Sevareid
wrote: "They were no more capable of taking preventive action based
on a rational analysis of the facts than the American people were of
attacking Japan prior to Pearl Harbor or than the British were of getting down to serious business prior to Dunkirk. They were sickened by
the chauvinist's use of 'la gloire' as we, as university students, were of
'patriotism,' and they were unable or unwilling to believe that their
personal lives and the life of their country were mutually incompatible,
until their own patriotism was put to the test. Because of their geographic fate, when the test came for the French, it was too late."[29]

"AVANTI!"

During the peaceful and pleasant spring of 1935 in England, Webb
Miller reluctantly decided that Italy meant to go to war with Ethiopia.
As the European news manager for the UP, he alerted his organization
and began shifting his men to cover all eventualities. He was not alone
in his foresight. Nobody, not even the procrastinating diplomats at the
League of Nations, could have had much doubt about the intentions of
Benito Mussolini, who had the morals of a jackal and the ambitions of
a Caesar. Yet, when he thundered his command, "Avanti!" the world
would bow before him.

All that lazy spring and summer, while Britain and France tried various devices to appease Il Duce, the newsgathering organizations, large
and small, made their preparations. The veteran war correspondents
were called up—Miller, Jim Mills of the AP, Sir Percival Phillips of the

London *Daily Telegraph,* and the most celebrated of all, Floyd Gibbons. As reinforcements, there were far more than the usual number of solemn, wide-eyed youngsters, among them a recent bridegroom who represented the Chicago *Tribune,* Will Barber; a clear-eyed, fine-looking AP sports writer, Edward F. Neil; and a tall, gangling, ex-secretary-stenographer, Herbert Lionel Matthews of the New York *Times.*

Among those who swarmed to Rome and Addis Ababa to file the first war bulletins, there was overwhelming sympathy for Emperor Haile Selassie of Ethiopia, the Conquering Lion of Judah, and his people. Nobody made a secret of it. Mussolini, despite the certainty of his coming conquest, had no admirers among the dependable correspondents of an independent press, which disconcerted only a few Fascist-minded editors and publishers. As for the Italian and German correspondents, it was perfectly obvious by this time that they were paid propagandists who wrote what they were told to write. Outside their own circle, no one respected them.

Webb Miller, perhaps, expressed the feelings of most of the foreign press corps when he wrote: "My emotions were tangled and conflicting when the question of going to witness another war arose. I was disgusted by the hypocrisy, two-faced maneuvering, and double-dealing of the British, French, and Italian statesmen and by the prospect of watching the aggression of a nation with all the modern resources for slaughter upon an ignorant, backward, comparatively defenseless people."[30]

Mussolini had been planning this war for years. As far back as 1925, he had placed the Italian colony of Eritrea on a defensive alert against the spear-carrying warriors of neighboring Ethiopia. In 1932 he had sent one of his earliest supporters, the fumbling General Emilio de Bono, to Eritrea to inspect the Ethiopian frontier and told him subsequently to start building roads and creating an African army. De Bono's mission wasn't noticed, although it was an important step on the way to empire, Mussolini style.[31] When Il Duce was almost ready, finally, a small clash between a few Ethiopian and Italian soldiers on December 5, 1934, at Ualual, in disputed frontier territory, gave him a pretext for action. He demanded reparations and an apology. Haile Selassie, thoroughly concerned, appealed to the League of Nations. Two days after the Ethiopian plea was received on January 3, 1935, Pierre Laval, the French Foreign Minister, arrived in Rome and was widely accused there after of having given Il Duce a free hand in Ethiopia, although both, of course, denied it.[32]

In any event, Italian troops began arriving at their colonies bordering Ethiopia within a month. By midsummer, nearly 250,000 soldiers and adjunct work forces were in position. Britain and France, finding that Mussolini was deaf to appeals for territorial "arrangements" to accommodate him in Africa, began to talk of invoking sanctions before the League of Nations. Winston Churchill delivered an eloquent warning in London: "To cast an army of nearly a quarter-million men, embodying the flower of Italian manhood, upon a barren shore two thousand miles from home, against the good will of the whole world, and without command of the sea, and then in this position embark upon what may well be a series of campaigns against a people and in regions which no conqueror in four thousand years ever thought it worth while to subdue, is to give hostages of fortune unparalleled in all history."

If he heard or read Churchill's warning, Mussolini was completely unimpressed. He told a London *Morning Post* correspondent that he already had spent two billion lire, about 100,000,000 prewar dollars, and demanded, "Can you believe that we have spent this sum for nothing?"[33] He refused to be dismayed by the power of the British fleet in the Mediterranean or the size of the French army. As for the League of Nations, it hadn't stopped the Japanese. Why should it stop him?

Haile Selassie had one more card to play. Francis M. Rickett, a British promoter representing large British and American financial interests, was in Addis Ababa negotiating for exclusive rights to Ethiopian oil and mineral exploitation. Of the correspondents who were swarming about the Ethiopian capital in August, only two seemed interested in Rickett — Mills, the sardonic, gray-haired AP veteran, and Phillips, one of the best in British journalism. Finally, to keep them from following him, Rickett agreed to give them his story exclusively if they would leave him alone. On August 30, he made good. The AP and the London *Daily Telegraph* together scored a world beat which impressed nearly everybody but Mussolini.[34] It meant nothing to Il Duce that the Negus had handed over half his kingdom to British and American financiers. The preparations for the invasion went ahead relentlessly.

Webb Miller had been in Rome since August 27, trying with a number of others to obtain permission to join the Italian army in Eritrea. The Ministry of the Press, through which Mussolini exerted his control, had arranged to permit 14 foreign correspondents to sail for Eritrea in mid-September aboard the *Vulcania,* but Miller fully realized that acceptance of such Italian support would be fatal to his own freedom of movement. Moreover, he had learned that Gibbons was already on the way to Eritrea for INS and NBC. Mussolini, an admirer of the Hearst newspapers, had provided the irrepressible Floyd with an Italian army airplane for the trip.[35] Miller had no such influence working in his favor, but somehow he managed to get "Press Card No. 1" out of the Italian Ministry of the Press. Then, he talked his way aboard a ship to Alexandria, an Imperial Airways plane to Khartoum, and an Italian air liner to Asmara. He and Gibbons were the only two American or British correspondents with the Italian army at the outset, and the invasion, as they could see without trouble, was only a short time off.[36] Their principal rivals would be cooped up on the *Vulcania* until it pleased the Italians to put them ashore.

Gibbons was then 48 years old, Miller 44. Both had grown up in the rough and tumble of Chicago journalism. Miller, a farm boy from Pokagon, Mich., had begun on the Chicago *American* at $12 a week at the age of 21. Gibbons, who had been born in Washington, D.C., was working on the Chicago *Tribune* at that time at slightly more money, having had five years of experience in Minneapolis. Both covered the miniature U.S. border war against Pancho Villa in 1916, Gibbons for the Chicago *Tribune* and Miller as a UP stringer. Both were correspondents in World War I. As Miller wrote when he saw Gibbons in the press headquarters shack, the Ufficio Stampa, at Asmara, "Old war correspondents never die. They just fade away."[37]

While they were waiting for D-Day, Gibbons and Miller each were favored with a ride in a bombing plane piloted by Count Galeazzo Ciano, Mussolini's son-in-law. It was a three-engine Caproni with an 11,000 foot ceiling, but it was, of course, better than anything the Ethiopians could get. As a further demonstration of Italian good will to the correspondents, both were driven to the Ethiopian frontier in an Italian military car with an Italian escort on a two-day scouting expedition. When they returned, Miller began what amounted to an advance story on the invasion. Much to his surprise, it was passed through Italian censorship:

> WITH ITALIAN ARMY ON MAREB STOP IMPORTANTEST REPEAT IMPORTANTEST DEVELOPMENTS IMMINENT MY PERSONAL IMPRESSION RESULT TWOHUNDREDFIFTY MILE TWODAY MOTORTRIP WITH COUNT DIBOSDARI THROUGH CONCENTRATION AREA.[38]

The roar of many columns of motor trucks awakened Miller at dawn on October 2, the signal that the Italian army was moving up. At press headquarters, where the Italian, a few French, and one Polish correspondent clamored for news, Count di Bosdari obligingly announced that the invasion was set for 5 a.m. October 3. Naturally, the news couldn't be sent, although Miller tried to tip Rome and was blocked.

Well before dawn, on the brow of a mountain overlooking the broad

Asamo plain, Miller and Gibbons were both ready. They sat astride a parapet of sandbags, their typewriters in front of them. Beside them was their telegraph operator, working a military wire that had been strung to their observation post. He was to send five 20-word bulletins for each correspondent, no more. Nearby, a motorcycle courier waited to take their detailed stories 60 miles to the radio station at Asmara. The Italians were so sure of a great triumph that they took every precaution of which they could think to advise the world.

Miller and Gibbons waited for dawn, their first bulletins ready to go. Both were old hands at this kind of thing and had made their own preparations. Miller's first message, addressed urgently to his offices in New York, Paris, Rome, and London, was:

ITALIANS COMMENCED INVASION ETHIOPIA FIVE AM

Exactly on the hour, with dawn casting a pale glow over the martial scene, the operator sent the opening bulletins for the Americans and their continental rivals. Then, as the sun mounted, the correspondents watched the troops wading across a river at the border and saw the Caproni bombers roaring off in the direction of Adowa, scene of a disastrous Italian defeat by the Ethiopians in 1896. From time to time, they filed their 20-word bulletins.

At 9:30 a.m., with the temperature at 118° in the shade, an Italian staff officer told Miller and Gibbons abruptly to have their detailed stories ready within 15 minutes or the motorcycle courier would go without them. Miller had left a lot of descriptive matter behind him in Asmara to be filed when the invasion began, and Gibbons doubtless had done the same. But now, hot and tired as they were, they had to pump out a rounded beginning for the whole effort. Miller wrote about 600 words of cablese in the time allotted to him. Gibbons did about the same. Both delivered their copy in time, then confessed themselves exhausted.

When all the returns were in, Miller had a beat although Gibbons was not far behind. Both, of course, were into New York far ahead of the AP, which had to rely on the official Italian dispatches as they came into Rome. The UP triumphantly claimed a five-hour advantage over its old rival with the first news of the Italian invasion. From the Italian side, as *Newsweek* summed up the whole business, it was "history's best-advertised war."[39]

It was quite different in Addis Ababa that October 3. There, a panicky Haile Selassie received word of the bombing of Adowa and the first skirmishes between his primitive warriors and Mussolini's tanks. He called for a general mobilization, ordering the ceremonial beating of a five-foot lion's-hide drum. The group of correspondents scattered to file what little they had, taking the trouble as they went to fill in Will Barber, the Chicago *Tribune*'s correspondent, who was ill of malaria in the Seventh Day Adventist Hospital. Barber dictated his story from his sickbed, describing the pathetic efforts of the Ethiopians to resist the cruel might of a modern aggressor. It was his last effort. Robinson Maclean, correspondent of the Toronto *Telegram,* cabled the Chicago *Tribune* the story of Barber's death on October 6. He was buried on a hilltop overlooking Addis Ababa next day. He was 32 years old and had been married less than a year. His father, Frederick Courtenay Barber, who had also been a war correspondent, wrote his obituary.[40]

The heat, the enormous exertion, and the sheer exhaustion of trying to keep going at altitudes of 8,000 and 9,000 feet soon told on other correspondents. Gibbons, who had been an iron man until he went on the Ethiopian campaign, teamed up again with Miller to try to reach Adowa following its capture by the Italians, but had to drop out. Miller pushed ahead, hiking about 30 miles to the native village and part of the way back, to share the story with his friend and colleague. But Gibbons couldn't stay much longer. He had to give it up and go on to philosophize about the Holy Land, which was easier.[41] Miller himself suffered a physical collapse after two months, with John T. Whitaker of the New York *Herald Tribune* and William W. Chaplin of Universal Service using high-handed methods to commandeer an official Italian car to evacuate him. It was the end of the war for the UP man, also.[42]

On the Ethiopian side, the durable Jim Mills kept going, although most of the youngsters were felled. Mills was caught in an Italian bombing raid on Dessye December 6, in which 84 persons were killed and 363 wounded, but escaped without a scratch. Soon afterward, Haile Selassie ordered all correspondents back into Addis Ababa and kept them there until the end of the war, which cut news from the Ethiopian side to a trickle.[43]

The League of Nations went through the motions of branding Italy an aggressor on October 7 and four days later imposed sanctions. But nothing happened. Mussolini was more annoyed because the Ethiopians would not stand still and fight than he was by the reluctance of the democracies to do business with him. The news from Geneva, too, dribbled off after that.

It just became a matter of time, on the Italian side, until modern weapons could be brought into play against a sufficient number of Ethiopians to end the war. By the time 1936 began, only three American

correspondents and one British were left with the Italians — Reynolds
Packard of UP, Eddie Neil of AP, Christopher Holme of Reuters, and
Herbert L. Matthews of the New York *Times.*[44] Of this quartet, which
whiled away the hours playing bridge when there was nothing better to
do, Matthews saw little reason to go on with the assignment. On New
Year's Day, 1936, he cabled Edwin L. James, who had become the
managing editor of the *Times,* asking to be recalled. James cabled back:
"Remain for present."[45] It was the only reason why Matthews was on
hand to write three columns about his first major battle, Amba Aradam, called Enderta by the Italians, which was fought on February 10–
15, 1936.

Matthews was then 36 years old, a New Yorker by birth rather than
adoption, a graduate of Columbia College, and a seasoned member of
the New York *Times* staff. He had begun there as secretary-stenogra-
pher in 1922 and worked his way through the ranks as reporter, copy
editor, and foreign correspondent to reach his current assignment. He
recorded the events of Amba Aradam between bridge games, as did
the others, because the Italian commander, Marshal Pietro Badoglio,
shelled the Ethiopian positions most of the five days and used tear gas
and there was little else to report. But at last, 70,000 Italian troops
backed by artillery and aircraft were able to close in on the positions
stubbornly defended by 50,000 Ethiopians. At the end, the Ethiopians
were routed. The way to Addis Ababa was open. On the afternoon of
May 5, 1936, Matthews and his companions rode into the Ethiopian
capital with Marshal Badoglio and the Italian army: "The setting was
an imperial capital in ruins — buildings still burning, the stinking dead
still lying about the streets, gutted houses and stores gaping blackly and
emptily at us as we drove by."[46] Such was the manner in which the
glories of Italian civilization were brought to Ethiopia, which for all its
faults had managed to exist independently in the East African highlands
for 4,000 years.

"Mussolini, like the sorcerer's apprentice, had set in motion forces
which he could not begin to control," Matthews wrote. "Ethiopia finished nothing, but it started a great deal."[47]

THE LADY FROM BALTIMORE

The *Times* of London published a seemingly routine 30-line item
without comment on October 28, 1936, under a small headline:

UNDEFENDED DIVORCE SUIT.

The account dealt with a case at Ipswich Assizes the previous day, in which Mrs. Wallis Warfield Simpson, of Baltimore, Md., had been granted a decree nisi from Ernest A. Simpson, an insurance agent, on the ground of his adultery. The decree was to become absolute on May 3, 1937.

The rest of the British press was similarly discreet in handling the story, which for the first time introduced the dark-haired lady from Baltimore to its readers. Such unanimity could not, of course, have been accidental. Because of the solicitude of Lord Beaverbrook and Esmond Harmsworth, later the second Viscount Rothermere, the London and provincial press had unanimously agreed at a meeting with them in Warwick House, St. James's, on October 16, 1936, to spare the King unpleasant publicity and give Mrs. Simpson's case the barest mention. It wasn't considered necessary to have the *Times,* the *Daily Telegraph,* and the *Morning Post* represented at the meeting, since their discretion, to use the *Times*'s own phrasing, was not in question.[48] The King himself later referred to this as a "gentlemen's agreement" to report the case without sensation. "The British press kept its word," he said, "and for that I shall always be grateful."[49]

The American press was something else again, for Mrs. Simpson already was a sensation in the United States. Gossip columnists had been printing items for weeks, referring to her association with the King. More serious journalists and their newspapers had been paying attention to the royal romance of late. Mrs. Simpson's divorce was considered such big news by the more sensational American papers that it crowded the latest war, Franco's Spanish uprising, off the front pages.

Nothing could have illustrated more dramatically the difference between the British and the American press. The Americans were determined to publish anything that was newsworthy, a kind of journalistic anarchy that had often pained their own government. The British were resolute in disapproving of the conduct of the American press and refusing to let it influence them. And yet, many a British editor and publisher had been uncomfortable about the Mrs. Simpson matter for some time, despite their confidence that they were doing the right thing. A few were beginning to express doubts that the royal romance could be kept a secret from the British public much longer. Others sharply criticized such Americans as Hugh Baillie, president of the UP, because his news agency already had carried several stories about the King and Mrs. Simpson.[50]

The sensitivity of the British press was such that Geoffrey Dawson, editor of the *Times,* sent directly to Buckingham Palace a letter from a

British subject in East Orange, N.J., who deplored the "poisonous publicity attending the King's friendship with Mrs. Simpson" and hinted that the King should abdicate. Dawson gave another copy of the letter to Stanley Baldwin, the Prime Minister, on the day before Mrs. Simpson's divorce.[51] Thus, five weeks before the crisis finally broke, the *Times* was already delicately raising the possibility of abdication. Nor was the *Times* alone. The Free Churches were becoming restive, Walter Runciman said.

Prime Minister Baldwin saw the King on November 16 and learned that he intended to marry Mrs. Simpson and, if necessary, to abdicate. At 10:30 that night, in response to a summons, Dawson met Baldwin at the House of Commons and discussed the problem with him. While Baldwin did not disclose specifically what the King had told him, Dawson nevertheless gained the impression that abdication was likely.[52] However, even then, it wasn't quite as certain as it may have seemed to the Prime Minister and the editor of the *Times,* for on November 26 the King asked Baldwin about the possibility of a morganatic marriage to Mrs. Simpson. The scheme, suggested by the first Viscount Rothermere, would have enabled the King to marry Mrs. Simpson, but she could not have been the queen, and their children could not have aspired to legal succession to the throne.[53] The cabinet met on this suggestion, and the Dominions were consulted, but the answer was negative.[54]

By this time, literally hundreds of persons were in the closest touch with what was going on in London. As could have been expected, since some of them undoubtedly wanted the matter out in the open, numerous versions of what was going on behind the scenes appeared in the American press. Moreover, any editor of experience could tell that this was no longer gossip but serious business. The very fact that the British press had been sitting on the story for three months was in itself a matter for comment, and not particularly admiring comment, at that.

It was neither a statesman nor a journalist, finally, who broke through the traditional British reticence about the members of the royal family. The Bishop of Bradford, at his diocesan conference on December 1, expressed hope that King Edward VIII would be aware of his need for God's grace at his coronation, scheduled for May 12, and a wish that the King would give "more positive signs of this awareness." The *Times* of December 2 ran the full text of the Bishop's remarks. It also ran a story on the visit of the Duke and Duchess of York to Edinburgh and referred to the Duke, the King's brother, as the heir presumptive to the throne. There was no editorial comment in London, but northern papers began expressing doubt over the strength of the King's character without, of course, giving their reason.[55]

That night, one of the most respected of American foreign correspondents, Ferdinand Kuhn, acting chief of the New York *Times* bureau in London, filed a story to his home office which began:

LONDON, Dec. 2 — The reign of King Edward VIII came perilously close to the breaking point tonight after a day of such fantastic happenings as the proud British monarchy has not had to experience for hundreds of years.

Upon the utterly astounded country there has burst a constitutional crisis involving the possible abdication of the King tomorrow and succession of the Duke of York to the throne. The crisis is no longer hidden; the conflict between the King and his Ministers has blazed up into an open flame.

The New York office was worried. Kuhn received the following:

THIS IS PRETTY STRONG STUFF. NONE OF THE AGENCIES CARRY IT. YOU SURE IT'S OKAY?[56]

It was, Kuhn insisted, okay. He had, as it was learned years later, checked with Dawson. The story ran for three full columns in the New York *Times* next day under a four-column headline on page 1. That same day, while the morning papers in London still were discussing "a marriage incompatible with the throne," and not mentioning the lady's name, the evening papers finally identified Mrs. Simpson. The King sent her out of the country to Cannes to await the outcome.

On December 4, at last, the *Times* of London stated its objections which, because of Dawson's closeness to Baldwin, was tantamount to a report on the position of the cabinet. It was irrelevant, the article said, that the lady was a commoner or an American; but the fact that she had two living husbands from whom she had in succession obtained divorces could not be overlooked. To this, Harold Laski pointed out in the *Daily Herald*, the cabinet would have to address itself, since the King was bound to accept the cabinet's advice in everything, including marriage. If he refused to do so, the only alternative was abdication.[57]

Now that the whole thing was finally in the open, the British press gave itself over almost entirely to the royal romance and its consequences. Despite the New York *Times*'s prediction that the King would abdicate, there was still so much uncertainty that the UP twice decided against sending similar accounts. One was from Frederick Kuh, a first-rate diplomatic reporter, and the other from the old reliable, Webb Miller. Finally, on December 8, the exiled Queen Victoria of Spain told the same story to still another UP man, Henry Tosti Russell, saying that the King's decision to marry Mrs. Simpson and abdicate was "irrevocable." That was the one the UP carried.[58] Its soul-searchings were no different from those of the other foreign services and foreign correspondents. Nobody could afford to be wrong on this story.

On Thursday, December 10, the Act of Abdication was signed and announced in the House of Commons. Prime Minister Baldwin, in an almost conversational manner, gave the essential parts of the story and its inevitable consequences. The New York *Times* broke out three eight-column headlines over the solemn account that was written by the spritely little Englishman, Frederick T. Birchall, who was now the chief of its foreign service:

> LONDON, Dec. 10 — Some time Saturday morning, perhaps even as soon as tomorrow night, Edward VIII will cease to be a King and Emperor. He has made his choice between a woman and a throne, and the woman has won.[59]

The next day, Edward spoke to the world by radio after laying down his responsibilities as King: "At long last I am able to say a few words. . . . You must believe me when I tell you that I have found it impossible to carry the heavy burden of responsibility . . . as King . . . without the help and support of the woman I love."[60]

George VI succeeded his brother on the throne. The former King, who had been created the Duke of Windsor, was married to Mrs. Simpson on June 3, 1937, at the Chateau de Cande, Monts, France, with only five correspondents in attendance as representatives of a huge press corps.[61] From these five, the world learned of the third marriage of the lady from Baltimore, who became a duchess, but not a queen. The role of the press in determining her fate was very great. As the *Times* of London put it with becoming modesty, "The royal abdication question preoccupied the minds of the government in London throughout the last three months of 1936, and the papers' influence on the December crisis is not undeserving of mention. . . . The abdication was of social importance but, as accomplished by Baldwin's adroitness, of no political significance, though he may have bequeathed a quasi-constitutional question to historians."[62]

THE SPANISH TRAGEDY

Lester Ziffren, of the UP Madrid bureau, sent a long and seemingly garbled message to London on July 17, 1936, which began:

MOTHERS EVERLASTINGLY LINGERING ILLNESS LIKELY LARYNGITIS. AUNT FLORA OUGHT RETURN EVEN IF GOES NORTH LATER.

It was a simple code, as London quickly realized, in which the first letter of each world formed a message:

MELILLA FOREIGN LEGION REVOLTED MARTIAL LAW DECLARED[63]

In this manner, Ziffren managed to inform his organization despite a tight military censorship that the Spanish Civil War had begun. That day, the army leaders in Spanish Morocco, Generals Francisco Franco, Emilio Mola, and José Sanjurjo, had rebelled against the Popular Front government of the Spanish Republic, which Manuel Azana had formed on February 19. The liberalism and anticlericalism of the government had raised many enemies against the Republic. There would be many more. But worse than any enemy would be the indifference of its professed friends.

The revolt, covertly backed by Nazi Germany and Fascist Italy from the outset, spread to the garrisons of Burgos, Saragossa, Seville, Cadiz, and elsewhere. The air force and the large Moorish army contingents were with the rebels. The Republic had little in the beginning except the people of Madrid and Barcelona, who defended it with fierceness and passion. Hopefully, the Republic looked to the democracies for aid. The answer from Britain was a nonintervention pact, a cruel diplomatic device that fooled no one, least of all Generalissimo Franco. Yet, France and the United States adhered to it, and even the Soviet Union joined for a few weeks early in the war. The unrealistic theory was that everybody would play fair and withhold arms from the combatants.

The illusion of nonintervention was quickly punctured not by the soft-voiced diplomats, but by a journalist. On August 11, less than a month after the beginning of the revolt, Frank Kluckhohn of the New York *Times* picked up telling evidence of Nazi-Fascist intervention in Seville and sent it by courier to Gibraltar. The next day, the *Times* published his account, which began:

SEVILLE, Aug. 11 — Twenty heavy German Junker bombing planes and five German pursuit planes manned by German military pilots arrived at rebel headquarters in Seville today. The airplanes had been landed from a ship at the rebel port of Cadiz and were then flown here.

With these and seven Italian Caproni bombers, which arrived during the past few days piloted by Italians, the rebels are in a position to sweep the Madrid Leftist government's planes from the air. . . .

The writer saw some of the new German planes. The German consul here privately admits they were flown by German military aviators. . . .

The The Italian and German aviators are living at the Hotel Cristina here. Neither group is in military uniforms.

Kluckhohn had to get out of Spain after his disclosure, but his paper backed him up. Arthur Hays Sulzberger, who had become president and publisher of the *Times* on May 7, 1935, called his work "an excellent example of where the sending of a single story is worth the expulsion that may follow it. It was not until the dispatch was published that the full extent of Fascist aid to rebel Spain was comprehended."[64]

The bombers were the first installment of the Nazi-Fascist dictators' aid to Franco, who on October 1 became Caudillo and chief of state. Mola by that time was his subordinate rather than his equal, and Sanjurjo was dead, having been killed in a plane crash at the opening of the revolt. Italy had more than 50,000 troops in Spain before the war was over, and Germany had at least 10,000 additional "volunteers," plus the necessary military supplies and hardware. On the side of the Republic, the Soviet Union broke with the noninterventionist nations on October 23, 1936, and began sending in aircraft, pilots, military advisers, and supplies, while many sympathizers flocked to the International Brigade. Yet, Sumner Welles called Soviet aid to the Republic "only a token compared to that obtained by Franco,"[65] and the Loyalists paid dearly for it, both in gold and in loss of support abroad.

This was more than civil war. It was an ideological war, fought with all the ferocity of which human beings are capable. From the outset, foreign correspondents saw that there was no romantic nonsense on either side. In September 1936, Henry T. Gorrell, a 26-year-old UP correspondent, was picked up by a Loyalist patrol in Madrid because he spoke Italian and clapped into prison as a spy. Had his office not located him in time, he would have been shot. In the following month, on October 25, he was outside Madrid in a small car when he ran into a Rebel ambush and a hail of bullets which he fortunately escaped. When he was brought before the Rebel commander and established his identity, he was told, "We have killed 300 Reds on that road today and you are the first man to come out alive."[66]

Some of the old-timers had no stomach for this kind of business. Floyd Gibbons, arriving for his ninth war, this one for INS again, left after about 30 days and a look at each side, saying: "It is the bloodiest and costliest war, in men and money, that I have ever seen. It is horrifying to see how inhumane . . . men can be to each other."[67] Karl H. von Wiegand, the old Hearst correspondent, proclaimed Spanish censors his worst enemy, particularly those "from pinkish left Republican to Communistic Red" in the Loyalist service in Madrid. He accused them of suppressing news, of the burning of churches and convents, among other things. The Hearst newspapers were, of course, for Franco, as were many others in the United States and Britain; with few exceptions, the best the Loyalists could hope for among the independent press was a judicious neutrality.

Yet, the reporting from the Loyalist side was effective and often brilliant. Herbert L. Matthews of the New York *Times,* who had been decorated by Marshal Badoglio with the Italian war cross for valor in the Ethiopian campaign, threw himself into the Spanish war with an almost selfless enthusiasm. On February 11, 1937, when the Rebels announced they had cut the highway to Valencia outside Madrid, he drove through machine gun and mortar fire to disprove it. Moreover, while others were filing Rebel victory claims at the Battle of Guadalajara in the following month, he correctly reported that the Loyalists had stemmed the advance on Madrid at that point and routed an Italian force while they were doing it.

Matthews was one of the correspondents in the much-battered Hotel Florida in Madrid during the spring of 1937, when the Germans were shelling the area so that meals had to be cooked in the rooms and just about the only light entertainment was a phonograph playing a scratchy Chopin record. Ernest Hemingway, back as a journalist in the service of North American Newspaper Alliance, memorialized the scene in a play, *The Fifth Column.* Among other correspondents in the hotel at the time were Martha Gellhorn of *Collier's,* whom Hemingway later married; Sefton Delmer of the London *Daily Express;* Henry Buckley of the London *Daily Telegraph,* and the novelist, John Dos Passos.[68]

Hemingway wrote that spring, in an NANA piece published in the New York *Times* and other papers:

MADRID, April 4 — The window of the hotel is open and, as you lie in bed, you hear the firing in the front line seventeen blocks away. There is rifle fire all night long. The rifles go "tacrong, carong, craang, tacrong," and then a machine gun opens up. It has a bigger caliber and is much louder — "rong, cararibg, rong, rong."

Then there is the incoming boom of a trench-mortar shell and a burst of machine-gun fire. You lie and listen to it, and it is a great thing to be in a bed with your feet stretched out gradually warming the cold foot of the bed and not out there in University City or Carabanchel. A man is singing hard-voiced in the street below and three drunks are arguing when you fall asleep.[69]

The correspondents came and went on both sides as the war continued, but few stuck it out. They were pulled off by their organizations for other assignments, or they were relieved in rotation from duty that was at times intensely dangerous. Nearly every major correspondent

then active was in Spain at one time or another during the fighting —
H. R. Knickerbocker for INS; Frank King, Richard G. Massock, and
Alexander Uhl for the AP; Reynolds Packard, his wife, Eleanor, and
others for the UP; and a host of Europeans and British.[70]

Matthews, for the New York *Times,* stayed with the Loyalists until
the end. He enjoyed one great moment in the life of a correspondent
when, through overeagerness, he and Hemingway and Sefton Delmer
entered Teruel just before Christmas, 1937, and found to their surprise
and joy that they had "captured" the embattled city. It was the climax
of a short-lived Loyalist counteroffensive to take Teruel from the
Rebels.

"We were almost mobbed, but not by desperate Fascists," Matthews
wrote. "These were men and women who wept for joy to see us. They
embraced us, shook our hands until they ached, patted and prodded
and slapped us and poured out a flood of incoherent but happy talk. It
took a long time to make them realize that we were not high staff officers, Russian or otherwise, and had nothing to do with the taking of
Teruel, but it did not make any difference. When I told a little girl that I
was an American she laughed hysterically and repeated, 'Norteameri-
cano!' many times as if it were the funniest thing she had ever heard."

Matthews's story was cut in half when it reached his office and, as he
himself put it, "buried inside the paper." There was a lot of other news
in the world that day, particularly in the renewed Japanese war on
China, as a cable from the managing editor reminded him.[71] But that,
too, was part of a correspondent's life.

On the Rebel side outside Teruel, preparations already were being
made to recapture the city, and the correspondents were alerted. One of
the most capable, who had been covering Franco almost from the beginning, was Edward J. Neil, Jr., the AP sports writer who had first
distinguished himself in the Ethiopian war. He was 37 at the time, prematurely gray, soft-spoken, and popular with his fellows. He had attended Bowdoin for three years and joined the AP in 1926. Like his
father, an AP telegrapher, he had never known another employer and
hadn't ever seemed in the mood to look for one. In the Spanish war, he
had had several close calls. Like Matthews, at Teruel, Neil had entered
Bilbao ahead of Franco's troops and filed an exclusive story. He had
been under fire repeatedly since that time; once, during the drive on
Santander, he had had a particularly narrow escape. But it hadn't made
him shy away.[72]

When he learned that the campaign to recapture Teruel from the
Loyalists was under way after Christmas, 1937, Neil eluded the press

officer at the base at Saragossa and made his way to the front. On December 29, he filed an eyewitness story of the fighting in the snow around the city. Two days later, Franco headquarters announced it would permit correspondents to move up. Once again, Neil was ready. He and a close friend, Richard Sheepshanks of Reuters, a graduate of Eton and Cambridge and a fellow-campaigner in the Ethiopian war, decided to drive up together. With them, they took Bradish Johnson of *Newsweek*, a 23-year-old Harvard graduate, and Harry Philby of the *Times* of London.

When they reached the village of Caudete, three miles behind the front, it was after noon on December 31, and snow had begun falling again. A Franco press officer told them that Rebel troops were in the outskirts of Teruel and expected to be inside the city by nightfall. He refused to let the correspondents go on, despite their pleas. "Too dangerous," he said.

The four correspondents decided to wait in their car, which was parked some distance away from several others. Heavy artillery fire nearby didn't seem to disconcert them. They sat in the car, talking and eating chocolate. All at once, shells began dropping all about them. Philby managed to get out of the car and ran to Karl Robson of the London *Daily Telegraph*, who had taken cover. "They're in there!" Philby yelled.

Robson found Johnson dead, Sheepshanks unconscious, and Neil riddled with shrapnel wounds. When Sheepshanks died, an effort was made to keep the news from Neil, but he learned about it anyway. William P. Carney of the New York *Times*, who had covered the war for many months from the Franco side, called on the AP correspondent on New Year's Day with Philby.

"They're burying poor Dick here tomorrow and I'm afraid I can't go to the funeral," Neil said. "They keep me here on my back and I'm getting so sick I soon may be unable to write a story or do anything, but old Philby has told everything there is to tell by now, haven't you? Tell my office I'm going to Paris as soon as I can and I will soon be all right again."

Gangrene developed in Neil's left leg and he died January 2. He had written to a friend: "One nice thing these wars do teach you—when your number comes up, you grin, shrug, and make the best of it. No one has time to listen to a bleat."[73]

Franco took Teruel. Then, Barcelona was singled out for punishing bombing raids such as few cities had ever experienced. The horror of Guernica, which the Germans destroyed in a pitiless air bombardment on April 26, 1937, was small compared to it. On March 17, 1938, Matthews wrote in a dispatch for the next day's *Times:* "Barcelona has lived through twelve air raids in less than twenty-four hours, and the city is shaken and terror-struck. Human beings have seldom had to suffer as these people are suffering under General Francisco Franco's determined effort to break their spirit and induce their government to yield. . . . The destruction is in one sense haphazard, for the bombs are dropped anywhere at all, without any attempt at specific objectives. However, there is an obvious plan, that every part of the city, from the richest to the poorest, shall get its full measure of tragedy."

Yet, for ten months more Barcelona held out. On January 23, 1939, Harold Peters, the UP manager in Barcelona, reported that a town 10 miles to the west had fallen to Franco's advancing armies. Next day, while he was on the telephone to London with 700 words of monotonous dictation of government communiqués, he dropped in a remark without changing tone or pace of delivery, "Big shots scrammed Franceward."[74] The Spanish censor missed it, but the London office of the UP did not. With word that the Republican government had fled, the fall of Barcelona was at hand. On January 26, Franco's insurgents and their Italian allies entered the city. Until February 13, the fighting kept up on the French border with the government maintaining a semblance of resistance while 200,000 refugees streamed out of Spain into internment.

Watching it all at Perpignan, Matthews wrote, "I was sick at heart . . . when I wrote my last dispatch on the Spanish Civil War but at least I, in a humble way, felt vindicated. . . . I, like the Spaniards, had fought my war and lost, but I could not be persuaded that I had set too bad an example."[75] He was, however, a far different correspondent than the one who had been inclined, at the end of the Ethiopian war, to believe Mussolini's statement that he wanted 25 years of peace to develop his latest conquest. After all, the most important influence on any correspondent has been the essence of the time in which he has lived and the extent to which he has observed it.

On March 28, 1939, with the surrender of Madrid and Valencia, the long agony of the Spanish Republic was over. The rest of the civilized world would be the next to be tested on the rack of a black and terrible age.

CHANGES IN MOSCOW

Russia lay stunned in her "time of troubles." Lenin was dying. Behind the ornate façade of the Kremlin, his colleagues already were grappling for his power in a deadly rivalry that some of them would not survive. Walter Duranty of the New York *Times,* carefully considering all the possibilities in Moscow, rejected the determined Leon Trotsky, and saw little hope for either Leo Kamenev or Gregory Zinoviev. On January 15, 1923, he cabled:

"There is the Georgian Stalin, little known abroad but one of the most remarkable men in Russia and perhaps the most influential figure here today. . . . During the year Stalin has shown judgment and analytical power not unworthy of Lenin."[76]

Lenin died January 21, 1924, with the Zinoviev-Kamenev-Stalin trio succeeding him. Three years later, Stalin triumphed over the so-called Left opposition and banished Trotsky and Zinoviev from the Communist Party. From the moment of Stalin's election in 1922 as General Secretary of the Party, Duranty had realized that the Georgian was in control. The correspondent had used the trait he had so admired in William Bolitho — insight, doping things out, "seeing through a brick wall." Whatever it was called, it was the indispensable ingredient for any foreign journalist in Moscow.

In the supercharged atmosphere of the Soviet capital, it was never easy to maintain a balanced, judicious attitude. Fact-gathering was a sparse occupation, since it hinged almost entirely on what was put out by *Pravda* or *Izvestia,* circulated by Tass or the Soviet radio. Analyses by correspondents were all-important when they were permitted through censorship. Yet, not every correspondent could do what was expected of him at the outset. William Henry Chamberlin, the distinguished *Christian Science Monitor* correspondent, wrote: "My first two trips to Russia [in 1922–23] left me, on balance, a Communist sympathizer although with a good many more doubts and reservations than I had felt before leaving America. I still remember a little shamefacedly some of my naive first messages to the *Monitor* from Moscow, especially one in which I rashly accepted the word of a walrus-moustached Commissar for Justice that there were only two hundred political prisoners in Russia, and that these were lodged pretty comfortably in places where the climate, in the euphemistic words of the Commissar, was 'clear although cold.' But continued residence in the Soviet Union was a good cure for credulity. Some time in 1924 the last traces of partisanship slipped away, and I no longer experienced even an unconscious desire to report developments from the standpoint of an apologist."[77]

The situation of the news agencies in those critical years was even more difficult. Through a friend of Karl Radek of *Izvestia,* Jacob Doletzky, who was the director of the Rosta agency, the Soviet regime made determined efforts to influence the kind of wire service news that went out of Russia. Doletzky in 1923 bucked the Reuters-Havas-Wolff-AP news cartel by entering into an exchange agreement with the United Press. But in the following year, when several British papers helped upset the Labour government by printing a forged "Zinoviev letter" calling for a Red uprising in England, the UP's account evidently didn't satisfy Moscow. Doletzky canceled the UP contract and signed up with the AP and the news cartel.[78] The UP's man in Moscow at the time was Frederick Kuh and the AP had Jim Mills, both tough competitors, who concentrated on news and left ideology to the specials.

The UP sent in a new man early in 1928, Eugene Lyons, who had been born in Russia but brought up and educated in New York, where he had been one of the first employees of Tass when it changed over from Rosta. At 30, Lyons, like Chamberlin, expected far more from Russia than he was to find, and he was even more disillusioned. But at the outset, he was indignant over criticism of Russia by the veteran British correspondent, Ellis Ashmead-Bartlett, and wrote: "It was through an emotional haze that I viewed the new Bolshevik world around me. My early dispatches out of Moscow were laudatory, though toned down to conceal my bias." He felt impatient with the calm and often critical dispatches of some of his colleagues — Chamberlin, "exact and scholarly and passionless"; Junius Wood of the Chicago *Daily News,* whose "indisputable detail . . . added up to ridicule"; Edward Deuss of INS, who ignored "the deeper meanings of the revolution"; and Duranty, who even in comparatively favorable dispatches "left a fuzzy margin of uncertainty."[79]

Then, perhaps most expert of all, there was Paul Scheffer of the *Berliner Tageblatt,* who saw that the Leninist thaw, the New Economic Policy, was over as soon as Stalin attained power. And with Stalin's bloody and remorseless conquest of the kulaks in 1929–30, Lyons's disillusion with the Soviet regime set in. He was soon a bitter opponent of the way of life he was reporting.[80]

While the handful of embattled regulars stayed on to try to understand what was happening in the Soviet Union and tell what they could of it through censorship, the parade of distinguished visiting journalists passed in and out of Moscow with regularity year after year. It was a status symbol to have gone to the Soviet Union, even briefly, and to have remarked on its progress or lack of it. In the years when Stalin was consolidating his position by methodically wiping out his political opposition — by exile, by stage-managed treason trials, or, as in the case of Trotsky, by murder — all semblance of good will toward the Soviet

Union vanished in the responsible world press. Even perfectly objective articles, such as those H. R. Knickerbocker wrote for the Philadelphia *Public Ledger* and New York *Evening Post* in 1930 had to have a heading such as "The Red Trade Menace."

Edwin L. James of the New York *Times* wrote a similar series in the same year, shortly before he became managing editor, and sent this explanatory note to his office: "What I saw of Russia was miserable. It was dirty and hungry and the people seemed to be strictly out of luck. But then, they always were. I do not believe anyone can say what is going to happen there. . . . I do not believe any people in the world expected the Russians would stand for what is being done, but they *have* been standing for it for some years and may keep on doing it. Who knows? I don't. I asked [Maxim] Litvinov if they could sit on the Russians for ten years or more. He answered: 'I don't know; do you?'"[81]

Dorothy Thompson, Vincent Sheean, Sinclair Lewis, Max Eastman, Theodore Dreiser and many more came and went during the early Stalin period, passing judgment as they did so. Specialists like Louis Fischer soberly studied what evidence they could find on the surface of the success or failure of the regime, but could only suspect the machinations in the background. Isaac F. Marcosson wrote a series of 12 articles for the *Saturday Evening Post* that so annoyed the Soviet regime that he was barred thereafter.[82] Paul Scheffer was expelled, too. But Maurice Hindus stayed on for a time.[83] And Anna Louise Strong, who had been transplanted from the radical Seattle *Daily Call* to Moscow because of the persuasive Lincoln Steffens, began putting out the Moscow *News* in 1929.[84] She would spend much of the rest of her life in the Soviet Union and Communist China.* Of them all, Eugene Lyons was selected for a rare interview with Stalin on November 23, 1930, the only previous one having been given to Japanese correspondents of the Osaka *Mainichi* in 1926.[85]

U.S. recognition of the Soviet Union in 1933 in itself produced no change in the flow of information between Moscow and the West. As Duranty explained it: "Both sides outsmarted the other, and so outsmarted themselves, because when some months later, after an exchange of ambassadors and the establishment of full diplomatic relations, an attempt was made to create a working business arrangement along the lines laid down in Washington, a serious deadlock occurred, in which each side seemed convinced, I believe with full sincerity, that it

*Miss Strong was ordered out of Russia after World War II but was still acceptable in Red China.

was right and honest and that the other was wrong and tricky."[86] After eighteen months, Ambassador William C. Bullitt and Foreign Minister Litvinov reached a far more modest agreement which in essence did nothing to improve relationships. The foreign correspondents learned that they were still subject to the same restrictions.* Their "time of troubles," like those of the Russian people, seemed to increase as the years went on.

After the struggle and the agony that had marked the collectivization of industry and agriculture, Stalin moved with ruthless and devastating energy against the chiefs of the Red Army and some of his own closest followers in the purge trials of 1937. To the foreign correspondents, it seemed madness for the dictator to tear apart his military high command at a time when Nazi Germany and Fascist Italy were demonstrating their might on the Spanish battlefields. But Stalin, in his single-minded devotion to the security of his state, was not to be dissuaded by shock from abroad. Marshal Mikhail Tukhachevsky and seven of his highest associates in the Red Army were executed, just as Zinoviev and Kamenev had been in the previous year. Radek, the faithful, got off with 10 years for testifying for the state, but was never heard from again.

In such an atmosphere of terror and conspiracy, the American correspondents, in particular, drew closer together. Ambassador Joseph E. Davies often consulted them during the period of the purges and thought of them as his unofficial advisers. The corps, of course, had changed; Lyons, for one, had been expelled after putting out a story through censorship of a Soviet-Japanese clash which he had obtained from Soviet sources.[87] Of those who were with him in 1937, Davies wrote: "Every evening after the trial, the American newspapermen would come up to the Embassy for a snack and beer after these late night sessions and we would hash over the day's proceedings. Among these were Walter Duranty and Harold Denny of the New York *Times*, Joe Barnes and Joe Phillips of the New York *Herald Tribune*, Charlie Nutter and Dick Massock of the Associated Press, Norman Deuel and Henry Shapiro of the United Press, and Jim Brown of International News. They were an exceptionally brilliant group of men. I came to rely on them. They were of inestimable value to me in the appraisal and estimate of men, situations and Soviet developments."[88]

The Americans and the rest of the foreign press corps well under-

---

*However, Max Eastman managed to publish in the New York *Times* Lenin's celebrated secret testament warning his associates not to trust Stalin.

stood the meaning of the purge trials. Stalin was now not only the master of the Soviet people but also of their armed forces; in the war which was approaching with such certainty, he had freedom of movement to do as he wished. But as to exactly what he would do and how he would do it, that remained a mystery locked inside the Kremlin. The foreign correspondents could only speculate and that was profitless, under the circumstances.

Their sources of information now were tightening up. They dealt with different Soviet officials. Jacob Doletzky, the founding director of Rosta and Tass, was gone, a victim of the Stalinist purges; Nikolai G. Palgunov, who had begun working for Tass in 1929, replaced him.[89] The old wire service cartel arrangements, of course, were dead. Tass was now exchanging news, under contract, with the AP, the UP, Reuters, and Havas, although the Tass file meant very little. Nor was there much in *Pravda* or *Izvestia* to provide guidance in the critical years when Soviet policy balanced on the edge of Hitler's knife. It was even more difficult now to see Soviet officials. The Soviet censors worked as diligently as ever over wire copy and carefully monitored the telephone transmissions. Correspondents who transgressed, even in a minor sense, faced expulsion; everybody was careful. The visiting journalists still came and went, making their solemn pronouncements on the state of the Soviet Union at a safe distance from its borders. The men inside Moscow who served the Western press had to contain their feelings.

In view of all the limitations, it is remarkable that the world knew as much as it did about the condition of the Russian people as they approached the darkest years in their history. As for the outlook from Moscow, it was clouded with doubt and suspicion. The betrayal of Munich, followed by the treachery of the Hitler-Stalin pact, lay just ahead.

THE COMING OF WORLD WAR II

Bud Ekins, who had seen the mutilated face of war in Asia and Ethiopia, flew from New York to reach embattled Shanghai in the early part of August 1937 as a UP war correspondent. The Asian mainland was aflame once more. On July 7, there had been a night clash at the Marco Polo Bridge outside Peking. Japan, seeing the Western democracies paralyzed by the aggressive designs of Hitler and Mussolini, had used the incident as an excuse to resume its conquest of China. Before the month was out, Peking and Tientsin had fallen.

Now it was Shanghai's turn again. The journalistic veterans of the battles of five years ago were returning to tell the world the same sorry story all over again, Ekins among them. His hair was silvered now, although he was only 36. Like so many of the journalists of his generation, he had seen much of war. In the previous year, as a change of pace, he had won an airplane race around the world from two colleagues, Dorothy Kilgallen of the Hearst service and Leo Kieran of the New York *Times.* That had been a lark

It was a lot different when he drove to the Palace Hotel on Saturday, August 14, in Shanghai with John R. Morris, the UP Far Eastern manager. Chinese warplanes were swooping over the Japanese fleet in the Whangpoo River in a surprise raid; but by a gross miscalculation, the bombs were dropping in the International Settlement. The car Morris and Ekins had just abandoned was hit by a bomb. Another cracked the Palace Hotel after they had entered it, killing 247 persons, but they escaped unscathed. Ekins hurried across the street to Sassoon House, where the UP's office was located, and found that the building had also been bombed. But, picking his way through jagged broken glass and debris, he reached his office and began doing his eyewitness story. That was his job.[90]

It was the job, too, of all the rest of the correspondents who had been pulled into Shanghai, some from other posts in China, some from the ends of the earth. This war, the Spanish war, and the tensions aroused in Europe by Germany and Italy had strained the century-old system of gathering foreign news by crisis priority. There were now far too many crises, too much to be told, too little time to do it, too few who really knew how, scant opportunity to try to explain why all this horror was piling on a frightened world.

The leading correspondents in Shanghai were seasoned men — Tillman Durdin and Hallett Abend of the New York *Times,* Arch Steele of the Chicago *Daily News,* Jim Mills, Morris Harris, and Yates McDaniel of the AP, Jack Belden of UP, Colin McDonald of the *Times* of London, and Leslie Smith of Reuters among them. But the work they had to do in Shanghai as the fighting progressed taxed the resources of both their organizations and themselves. Visiting newspapermen, even youngsters, were impressed into service. Few took precautions and, inevitably, there was tragedy.

At one point after the battle had been going for some weeks, Edgar Snow of the *Saturday Evening Post* and Pembroke Stephens of the London *Daily Telegraph* accompanied a husky captain in the U.S. Marines, Evans Carlson, to the Nantao section where the Japanese were attacking. The marine and the correspondents were inside the French concession, which was neutral territory, and had taken cover behind a brick wall. But Stephens, with the eagerness of one new to battle, wanted to see what was going on and climbed a ladder. Carlson brought him down; he had been shot to death in a fusillade.

That night, depressed over Stephens's death, Carlson remarked to Snow, "That's not only the end of Stephens. It's the end of Shanghai, and maybe the end of the war."

"So Japan has won?"

"I know what you're thinking and you may be right," Carlson said. "You're going to tell me Mao Tse-tung has the answer. Guerrilla war."

There was some more talk, mainly about the Chinese Communists in distant Yenan who were cautiously reentering into relations with Chiang Kai-shek to oppose the Japanese. Snow finally challenged, "Why don't you go see for yourself?"

Carlson did. The necessary clearances were obtained all around, and he spent a considerable time with Mao, Chou En-lai, and General Chu Teh. From that visit came confidential personal reports to the White House. It also resulted in the creation of Carlson's guerrillas, the Marine Raiders.[91]

There were two far more important consequences of the Japanese attack. President Franklin D. Roosevelt, without mentioning Japan specifically, called upon the world to quarantine aggressors on the night of October 5, 1937, in Chicago. "War," he said, "is a contagion, whether it be declared or undeclared. It can engulf states and people remote from the original scene of the hostilities. . . . It seems unfortunately true that the epidemic of world lawlessness is spreading. When an epidemic of physical disease starts to spread, the community approves and joins in a quarantine."

Relman Morin of the AP, newly returned to Tokyo, was at a Japanese Foreign Office dinner for correspondents the following night and saw that the regular Foreign Office spokesman, Tetsuo Kawaii, was agitated. They talked about the Roosevelt speech, and Kawaii said, "We are wondering what he means by a 'quarantine' and whether this is a way of announcing some change in American foreign policy."

"He didn't mention any governments by name," Morin said.

"No, but he spoke of wars 'declared or undeclared.' "

"So you think he had Japan specifically in mind?"

"What other interpretation could there be?"

But the President wasn't ready to elucidate. At a press conference in Washington soon afterward, he spoke with reporters and then put the whole thing off the record. What happened was that Ernest K. Lindley of *Newsweek* brought up the possibility that the US Neutrality Act would have to be revised in order to give aid to countries that were the victims of aggression.

"Not necessarily," the President said. "That's the interesting thing."

"You say there isn't any conflict between what you outline and the Neutrality Act?" Lindley asked. "They seem to be on opposite poles to me, and your assertion does not enlighten me."

"Put your thinking cap on, Ernest," the President said.[92]

Whether or not the President meant to affront the Japanese, relations deteriorated. On December 13, 1937, Japanese planes bombed and sank the U.S. gunboat *Panay* in the Yangtze River above Nanking. Sandro Sandri, correspondent for *La Stampa* of Turin, Italy, was killed. Jim Marshall of *Collier's* and Luigi Barzini, correspondent of the *Corriere Della Sera* of Milan, were wounded. Three other correspondents aboard the *Panay*, Weldon James, a 25-year-old newcomer to the UP, Norman Soong of the New York *Times,* and Colin McDonald of the *Times* of London escaped injury.[93]

The incident created a furor all over the world. The Japanese apologized and settled the *Panay* case to the satisfaction of the United States, but the damage was done. When the Japanese captured Nanking on December 15–18 with a senseless display of brutality that took tens of thousands of lives, Arch Steele called it "four days in hell" in his dispatch to the Chicago *Daily News*.

"The Japanese," he wrote, "could have completed the occupation of the remainder of the city almost without firing a shot, by offering mercy to the trapped Chinese soldiers, most of whom had discarded their arms and would surrender. However, they chose the course of systematic extermination. It was like killing sheep."[94]

Much as the American people resented Japanese aggression in China, it did not shake their dominant mood, which was to sympathize with the victims but stay out of war. In Berlin, Hitler was so little impressed with the possibility that the United States might go to war that he left the Americans entirely out of his calculations, which he announced in confidence to his closest associates on November 5, 1937. In planning for the annexation of Austria and Czechoslovakia that night, he argued that the Third Reich could expect a free hand—Japan would keep both Russia and Britain on the alert, India would be an additional British problem, France would be busy as always with internal troubles, and Italy would be a Nazi ally.[95]

The Kaiser, of course, had made the same mistake about the United States. Yet, everything that came out of Washington now testified to a renewed American drive for isolation, despite President Roosevelt's efforts. The wire services still carried the bulk of American news abroad, since specials in the American capital had always been few and numbered little more than a score in those crucial years. (There had been five foreign correspondents in Washington in 1910, 20 in 1916, 18 in 1930, principally British and Canadian, with Sir Willmott Lewis of the *Times* of London as dean of the corps.) Even if there had been many more foreign specials, they could scarcely have told a different story, although some, possibly more familiar with American temperament, might have cautioned against pushing the United States too far.

The news supported German calculations and diplomatic soundings in other areas, as well. Mohandas K. Gandhi, the aging Mahatma, had been one of Britain's major difficulties in world affairs for well-nigh two decades with his campaign for Indian freedom. It had been a mark of distinction for foreign correspondents to be received by him, to quote him, to depart with marks of his favor; Americans, in particular, had given him consistent notice in their press and, through it, the press of the world. France, as the Germans knew perfectly well through Otto Abetz and his agents, was so wracked with inner dissension that it could never be a threat in its present enfeebled state. The purge trials in Russia were sufficient evidence that Stalin was preoccupied with domestic considerations.

That left Britain as the major problem, and here, fortunately in the German view, a campaign of appeasement of the dictators was being waged with great vigor in an important section of the independent press. Despite the friendliness of the so-called Cliveden "set" of important British personalities* toward the Third Reich and the attitude of forbearance toward Hitler in much of the press, German diplomacy overreached itself. On August 5, 1937, the British government, for the first time since the end of World War I, ordered the expulsion of three German correspondents — little-known journalists working for the controlled Nazi press — because they had been doing espionage work. The Nazi regime immediately ordered the removal of Norman Ebbutt, who for more than 12 years had been the senior correspondent in Berlin of the *Times* of London and at one time had written dispatches so pleasing to the Nazis that they had been reproduced in Germany.[96]

William L. Shirer made this record in his *Berlin Diary* of August 16: "Norman Ebbutt of the London *Times*, by far the best correspondent

*Among them, Lord and Lady Astor, Dawson of the *Times*, Neville Chamberlain, and J. L. Garvin.

here, left this evening. He was expelled, following British action in kicking out three Nazi correspondents in London, the Nazis seizing the opportunity to get rid of a man they've hated and feared for years because of his exhaustive knowledge of this country, and of what was going on behind the scenes. The *Times,* which has played along with the pro-Nazi Cliveden set, never gave him much support and published only half of what he wrote. . . . We gave Norman a great sendoff at the Charlottenburger station, about fifty of the foreign correspondents of all nations being on the platform despite a tip from Nazi circles that our presence would be considered an unfriendly act to Germany! Amusing to note the correspondents who were afraid to show up, including two well-known Americans. The platform was full of Gestapo agents noting down our names and photographing us."[97]

The *Times*'s reputation for appeasing the dictators was based primarily on its support of the policies of the Prime Minister, Neville Chamberlain, and its "complete disinterest" in the Spanish Civil War, which made it a target of British Liberals. Said the *Times*'s historians of that period; "All The *Times* wanted Russia to do was to drop Comintern interference and Germany to 'settle down.' The way to get Germany to settle down was to be reasonably conciliatory. Fortunately, in the opinion of The *Times,* this was the policy of the Prime Minister and the Foreign Secretary."[98]

This policy of being "reasonably conciliatory" toward Nazi Germany and Fascist Italy was by no means confined to the *Times* and the like-minded conservative British press. In the United States, it was also favored, but for different reasons, by the isolationist press. There was no Cliveden "set" here, but a band of anti-Roosevelt supporters who sounded the call for "America First" at the cost of being accused of pro-Nazi sympathies, whether fairly or not. Among them were the Hearst newspapers, Colonel Robert R. McCormick's Chicago *Tribune,* and Captain Joseph Medill Patterson's New York *Daily News.* The New York *Times* was generally regarded as the leading supporter of Roosevelt's foreign policies and, therefore, the spearhead for intervention.

A third factor now entered into this journalistic war for public opinion—a band of talented former newspapermen who were recruited by Paul W. White and others for CBS. As much as anyone else, a lean and talented North Carolinian, Edward R. Murrow, made possible this brief but brilliant chapter in radio journalism. Turning from university student organization work, which he had pursued in the United States and Europe since his graduation from Washington State College in 1930, Murrow joined CBS in 1935 and two years later became its European director. With him, he had Elmer Davis, one of the stars of the New York *Times* staff from World War I on, whose commentary won a wide following in the crucial days ahead. When the Hearst service dropped Shirer after Universal Service was discontinued, Murrow hired him on the spot. Eric Sevareid was taken on later, and other strong and independent voices were added.[99] The whole added up to a potent and widely influential force in the United States, counterbalancing much of the isolationism in the press. NBC, an older service, expanded its news coverage but could not match the Murrow-directed commentary in the prewar period.

It was Shirer's change of jobs that made it possible for him to be in Vienna on the night of March 11–12, 1938, when Austria ceased to exist. As Chancellor Kurt von Schuschnigg bowed out before Hitler's threats and violence, and ill-prepared Nazi armies poured across the Austrian border to make the *Anschluss* complete, Shirer fought his way through singing Nazi crowds on the Kaertnerstrasse toward the old red-brick Haupttelegraphenamt, and the Cafe Louvre nearby, the unofficial headquarters for foreign correspondents. There, he encountered Robert H. Best of the UP, a fat and grinning South Carolinian who seemed mightily pleased that the Nazis had taken over the Ballhausplatz — the ancient foreign ministry. M. W. Fodor, the Manchester *Guardian* correspondent, who long since had become known as the "Duranty of the Danube," was out on the story. While he was away, his wife, Martha, was waiting in the Cafe Louvre for him, trying to keep from crying. Shirer saw Emil Maass, his former assistant, come strutting in. Maass had posed for a long time as an anti-Nazi, but now he exclaimed, "Well, meine Damen und Herren, it was about time." He turned over his lapel and showed a swastika emblem which he now pinned outside. Some women shrieked, "Shame!"

Nothing but controlled news would be sent out of Vienna, it was clear. Shirer telephoned Murrow, who was in Warsaw that night, and was told to go to London and prepare for a broadcast the following night. Before he left, he phoned Fodor, who was staying on the job — but only for a short time. Fodor knew he would have to get out before the Nazis came in; for years, he had been a marked man. "I'm all right, Bill," Fodor said. But he was sobbing. It was the end of an era for Austria.[100]

Maintaining his time schedule, Hitler did not wait long to begin his assault on Czechoslovakia. As the uproar of the Sudetenland and the Nazi blackmailing tactics against the Czechs surged toward a climax, the *Times* of London published an editorial on September 7, 1938, that created a sensation. As revised and approved by Geoffrey Dawson, the editor, the leader pointed out the indisputable fact that the Sudeten Germans "did not find themselves at ease" within the Czechoslovak republic. It continued:

> It might be worth while for the Czechoslovak Government to consider whether they should exclude altogether the project, which has found favour in some quarters, of making Czechoslovakia a more homogeneous State by the secession of that fringe of alien populations who are contiguous to the nation with which they are united by race. In any case the wishes of the population concerned would seem to be a decisively important element in any solution that can hope to be regarded as permanent, and the advantages to Czechoslovakia of becoming a homogeneous State might conceivably outweigh the obvious disadvantages of losing the Sudeten German districts of the borderland.[101]

The Foreign Office was widely believed to have inspired the scarcely veiled suggestion to the Czechs to yield, but the *Times* denied it. Nevertheless, an angry and determined Jan Masaryk, then Czech minister to London, demanded an explanation of the Foreign Office and was told in silky British tones that the editorial "in no way represented the views of His Majesty's Government." Dawson, the storm center, lunched with Lord Halifax, the Foreign Secretary, and the next day wrote indignantly, "It is really grotesque that so much righteous indignation should be expended on the mere suggestion . . . that a revision of boundaries should not be excluded entirely from the list of possible approaches to a settlement."[102]

Hitler drew his own conclusions. Obviously, Britain was the key to any prospect of successful Czech resistance; just as clearly, the British were not really too enraged over the *Times*'s indiscretion, whether it had been calculated or not. In any event, the Nazi leader pushed ahead, forced Britain and France into the showdown at Munich, and eventually walked off with Czechoslovakia. Eight hours before the agreement in Munich was announced, Louis Lochner, the AP's Berlin correspondent, predicted basically the terms on which a settlement would be reached.[103] It was the settlement with which Neville Chamberlain came home to a cheering, relieved London, flourishing his umbrella, and proclaiming he had found "peace in our time."

DeWitt Mackenzie, the AP's foreign analyst, was one of many correspondents who did not believe peace would last long. Hitler's appetite was great; and Poland, which had shared in the spoils of Czechoslovakia, was well-nigh defenseless before him. Mackenzie talked with Marshal Josef Pilsudski, the so-called strong man of Poland. "Hitler,"

Pilsudski said, "is the master of central Europe. Poland doesn't have much choice. It is prepared to play his game economically and in other ways as long as he makes no efforts to intrude on our sovereignty. . . . But if it ever becomes necessary to defend Polish sovereignty, be assured that the Poles will fight to defend themselves." Mackenzie returned, to Britain and at once detected a fundamental change in the government's attitude toward the Third Reich. When he asked a leading member of the Chamberlain cabinet what had happened, he was told, "We have come to the conclusion that the policy of appeasement is a failure. . . . Hitler is not susceptible to any moral influence. . . . We must smash him."[104] At that late date, Hitler would take a good deal of smashing.

On May 3, 1939, the foreign correspondents in Moscow found a story tucked away on the back page of Soviet newspapers: "M. Litvinov has been released from the Office of Foreign Commissar at his own request." It was the end of the roly-poly Russian with the British wife who had staked his career on collective security. Vyacheslav M. Molotov, the grim little undertaker with the rasping voice and the ice-cold eyes, came in as Stalin's Foreign Minister.

Now, the pressure on Poland mounted, and strange rumors began to appear about a rapprochement between Hitler and his sworn enemy, Stalin. Not even the old-line foreign correspondents, hardened to anything, could help but express surprise. Nobody of any consequence in the independent press of the West would believe it possible. But on the night of August 23, 1939, when Shirer went to Tempelhof in Berlin to greet H. V. Kaltenborn, the news was out. Kaltenborn was not permitted inside Germany, since he had made broadcasts critical of Hitler, and was hustled back to London on the next plane. Shirer went on to the Taverne in Berlin where, at 2 a.m., the terms of the Hitler-Stalin Pact became known to him. "It's a virtual alliance," Shirer noted sadly in his diary, "and Stalin, the supposed arch-enemy of Nazism and aggression, by its terms invites Germany to go in and clean up Poland. The friends of the Bolos are consternated."[105]

The special correspondent of the *Times* of London in Moscow (the staff man, by this time, had come and gone) thought the whole business was still a poker game and wrote: "If there is one thing the contracting parties can be sure of it is that no Pact that they sign will necessarily be binding."[106]

In London, Wallace Carroll of the UP took the crisis far more seriously. He stood outside No. 10 Downing Street and watched the members of the British cabinet file out, one by one, ducking the waiting press and refusing to answer questions. But Carroll noticed so great an air of decision and exuberance about Walter Elliott, the Minister of Health, that he trailed him to his car.

"What did the Cabinet decide?"

Elliott retorted firmly, "We decided that if Poland is invaded we will fight."[107]

At 5:11 a.m., on September 1, Hitler announced that his armies had invaded Poland. Jerzy Szapiro, the New York *Times* correspondent in Warsaw, opened his dispatch with the news of the bombing of Gdynia, Cracow, and Katowice. He closed it with these words: "While this dispatch was being telephoned, the air raid sirens sounded again in Warsaw."[108]

On the morning of September 3, in the AP headquarters in New York, the bells warned of a major news break over the cables. In a moment it came:

FLASH CHAMBERLAIN PROCLAIMED BRITAIN AT WAR WITH GERMANY[109]

It was the end of appeasement.

7 The Ordeal
of World War II

A balding, 39-year-old Memel-born correspondent wrote 10 days after the Nazis crossed the Polish border on September 1, 1939: "Poland is being crushed like a soft-boiled egg." The correspondent, Otto Tolischus of the New York *Times,* neither wept nor philosophized. He reported with utter candor that Polish defenses had been thin, weak, and archaic, that 4,000 German planes had control of the air, and that 70 Nazi divisions had moved in on wheels with devastating effectiveness. "God," he wrote, "has been with the bigger battalions."[1]

A new type of correspondent was reporting a different kind of war. The colorful, romantic figure exemplified by Richard Harding Davis had gone out of style. In his place had come calm, determined, professionally trained men such as Tolischus. Fresh out of Columbia, he had been disciplined in a Cleveland city room and given his first European assignment by International News Service.

Working under a dictatorship, this new breed had to take a lot of abuse. Correspondents like Louis Lochner of the Associated Press were accused unfairly of being apologists for the Nazis, on the one hand; on the other, correspondents like Emlyn Williams of the *Christian Science Monitor* were forced out of the country. Experienced men like Frederick Oechsner of the United Press, Pierre J. Huss of INS, and the radio correspondents, Max Jordan of NBC and William L. Shirer of CBS, were under constant pressure. The Nazis were determined to build up a good press in neutral America. Tolischus incurred their displeasure and was barred. It took skill, devotion, and sheer luck to stay in the country and still refuse to play the Nazi game, a feat that was accomplished by Joseph C. Harsch of the *Christian Science Monitor,* among others.[2]

In those first months of the Nazi blitz, correspondents worked under incredible conditions and performed with extraordinary skill. It was James Bowen, NBC correspondent in Montevideo, Uruguay, who first brought the sea war home to the American public. On Sunday, September 17, while he was waiting to broadcast the departure of the trapped Nazi warship *Graf Spee,* he suddenly yelled, "Give me the air!" The crew of the *Graf Spee* had blown her up rather than deliver her over to the British. Bowen poured out a memorable eyewitness account that thrilled all who heard it.[3] The land war, far less dramatic and far more difficult, endangered both Ed Beattie of the UP and Richard Mowrer of the Chicago *Daily News,* son of the old correspondent, Paul Scott Mowrer. They both got out of Warsaw just in time; Melvin Whiteleather of the AP, coming from the east with the Russians, was first into the ruined city after it surrendered September 27. On November 30, Norman Deuel of the UP heard the shriek of sirens and crump of Russian bombs in Helsinki. While the raid was still on, he dictated the first bulletins of the Finnish war to Copenhagen.[4]

Leland Stowe of the Chicago *Daily News* scored over all others as the Nazi blitz spread to Norway. On April 16, 1940, a week after escaping from Oslo, he reached Stockholm with the story of how the traitor Vidkun Quisling had helped the Nazis take Norway. With Edmund Stevens of the *Christian Science Monitor* and Warren Irvin of NBC, Stowe was an eyewitness — and got over the border first with the news.

Stowe's exploit was all the sweeter for him because the New York *Herald Tribune,* for which he had been a Pulitzer Prize-winning correspondent for 13 years, had declined to send him to war in 1939 on the dubious ground that he was too old at 40. He had promptly joined the Chicago *Daily News.*[5]

Yet, the fortunes of war did not smile on all veteran journalists. On the morning of May 5, 1940, the body of Webb Miller was found on the railroad tracks near his home in London. As Hugh Baillie explained, Miller had been on the way home the night before "when he stepped off or was flung from the train at the high curve near Clapham Junction."[6] Eleven wars had not harmed him. A blackout accident, however, proved fatal.

An even greater tragedy than Norway's was in the making then: the fall of France. It came with a tremendous shock because the world was so little prepared for it. Since the previous autumn, a generation reared on the legend of the bravery of the French *poilu* and the unbreakable

Maginot Line had waited confidently for the Nazi attack. A few correspondents — Geoffrey Cox of the London *Daily Express* and Eric Sevareid of CBS among them — had covered the debarkation of the first British troops at Cherbourg as if they had been the "Old Contemptibles" of glorious memory. People had been trying to recapture the spirit of "Tipperary," of "Madelon," and even of "Over There," but the best they had had was a ridiculous ditty called, "We'll Hang Out Our Washing on the Siegfried Line." The French and British had been stuffy about letting correspondents move about the quiet front, and they had been censoring a war in which there was no news. Tough, capable young correspondents like William McGaffin of the AP had taken in despair to writing about what French women were doing while their men were at the front, an always interesting subject.

The world could not really grasp the shocking swiftness of the Nazi attack in the West on May 10, 1940 until the correspondents' stories came in. M. W. Fodor of the Chicago *Daily News,* falling back with the Allied armies, told how Louvain once again had been mercilessly bombed by the Germans, how Brussels and Antwerp had shuddered under the attack. A trail of refugees 200 miles long, he reported, was pouring from Belgium into France.[7] Taylor Henry of the AP and British-born P. J. Philip of the New York *Times* tried to get through the mob of refugees by using bicycles. At one point, Philip was seized and nearly shot as a spy, but he and his fellows managed to get through to Paris. The Nazi propaganda machine, just to be certain that the West appreciated what was going on, transported Lochner, Oechsner, Huss, Shirer, and the rest from Berlin to the Western front.

The Nazis needn't have bothered. On May 15, Joseph Kessel, a war correspondent for *Ce Soir,* staggered into the office of his chief, Pierre Lazareff, and told him it was all over. It was the first word Lazareff had had that General André Georges Corap's army had been broken before Sedan, that the Germans this time would overwhelm Paris. There would be no heroic resistance on the Marne.[8] But there would be a Dunkerque.

For nine days, from May 28 to June 4, almost unbelieving correspondents saw the Royal Air Force battling the Luftwaffe over the Dunkerque beaches while a remnant of the French army held off the Germans, thus permitting 330,000 British troops to be saved. By June 1, Douglas Williams of the London *Daily Telegraph* was referring to the operation as a miracle.[9] On June 4, the *Times* of London proudly reported that a motley array of British rescue vessels had completed, in the words of the Admiralty, "the most extensive and difficult combined operation in naval history."[10]

Now Winston Churchill, the old war correspondent and historian, assuming his greatest role as the King's First Minister, rose on June 4 in the House of Commons and made the most celebrated speech of the war. Raymond Daniell, the slim and high-spirited chief of the New York *Times*'s London bureau, one of more than a hundred foreign correspondents who heard him, called it "moving and dramatic." He told how the sonorous Churchillian phrases rolled out in their majesty before a hushed Commons: "We shall go on to the end. We shall fight in France; we shall fight on the seas and oceans; we shall fight with the growing confidence of strength in the air; we shall fight on the beaches; we shall fight on landing grounds; we shall fight in fields, streets and hills. We shall never surrender."[11]

Unlike Lincoln's Gettysburg address, which was rescued from oblivion by his admirers rather than the correspondents who heard him, the greatness of Churchill's speech was recognized at once. But even had the correspondents been cold to his magnificent rallying cry, the tens of millions who heard him by radio would have been deeply moved. The time had passed when world leaders had to depend on the newspapers or their correspondents to communicate with their publics. There is no doubt whatever that radio magnified the influence of Churchill that day and helped him arouse the world's admiration for Britain at a time when she confronted the Nazi aggressor almost alone.

By June 12, the Nazis were in the suburbs of Paris. The Paris *Herald,* true to its tradition of being more French than the French themselves, came out for the last time with the banner:

GREAT BATTLE FOR PARIS AT CRUCIAL STAGE.[12]

At the *Ce Soir,* Lazareff turned the keys over to two neutral office boys who were staying. He said good-bye to an elevator operator, Joseph Schlesse, who remarked, "Don't worry about me. I'll be all right." He was. When the Nazis marched in next day and draped the swastika from the Eiffel Tower, the elevator operator, a German army officer in disguise, took over the new Nazi edition of Paris *Soir* as personnel director.[13]

The Nazis may have thought that all resistance to their will in Europe had been crushed when they forced the French to sign the papers of surrender in the old railroad car of 1918 in the Compiegne Forest on June 22. Correspondents like Shirer mourned. In his CBS broadcast that day, he cried, "What a turning back of the clock, what a reversing of history."[14] But all Europe did not despair. On the very border of the all-conquering Reich, Willi Bretscher, editor of the *Neue Zürcher Zeitung,* wrote: "We are not called upon to glorify the new masters of Europe, nor to praise their political ability and insight: in doing so we should implicitly approve in advance the most cruel measures which may be taken . . . in the conquered and occupied states and in yet others which may include our own."

That editorial was published on July 1, 1940. That same day, Reto Caratsch, the NZZ's able Berlin correspondent, reported that the Nazis were uneasy over Russian occupation of Bessarabia and northern Bukovina. Caratsch was accused of poisoning Soviet-German relations and ordered out of the Third Reich in 24 hours. There was at least one great newspaper in Europe that dared to print the news and speak its mind, whatever the cost.[15]

Such was the new role of the correspondent in a world of total war. In less than a hundred years, from the battlefields of the Crimea to the battlefields of France, his freedom of movement had been increased by the swift development of his communications, but his freedom of expression had been vastly curtailed. Moreover, if he did not go to the battlefield, it now came to him. It was so in France. It would be so again in Britain.

THE CONQUEROR FALTERS

For most of the summer and fall of 1940, Britain presented to the world an image of unmatched gallantry and courage while her enemies pressed for victory in the air. Of the correspondents who came and went in London during the Battle of Britain, none was more persevering or more influential than Edward R. Murrow of CBS. Night after night he began his broadcasts with a sepulchral. "This . . . is London." He would relate in calm and measured tones the extent of the bombings he had observed. Sometimes he would even kneel in a gutter and reach out his microphone so that people in the United States could hear the crump of the bombs as they whacked into the ancient streets. "If the purpose of the bombings was to strike terror into the hearts of the Britishers," he reported on the climactic night of September 15, 1940, "then the bombs have been wasted."[16]

Another who had wide influence in the United States was a large, 38-year-old Brooklyn Irishman, Quentin Reynolds, an editor for *Collier's*. In his magazine articles, radio talks, books, and a movie he brought back to the United States with him, he sounded the constant theme, "London can take it." And he was right. For that matter, so was the more experienced newscaster, Raymond Gram Swing.

Among those who carried the heaviest responsibility was the New

York *Times* bureau chief, Raymond Daniell, who from August 8, 1940, and for nearly five years thereafter, directed the London staff of this most influential of American newspapers. He was, as Meyer Berger often said, a man utterly without fear. On many a night, as he did on September 8, near the climax of the air war over London, he drove for miles through the bombed city to see for himself what damage the Nazis had done. Of the British, he wrote, "They are living through hell and behaving like angels."[17]

There were many, many more—Drew Middleton, William McGaffin, and Robert Bunnelle in the AP office; Wallace Carroll of the UP; Robert J. Casey, the great Chicago *Daily News* reporter, and his sardonic colleague, William H. Stoneman; the tall and gracious Helen Kirkpatrick, who came to the same bureau out of college and distinguished herself; Rebecca West, the Scottish-born novelist whose pieces in the *New Yorker* caused the more elegant American readers to shudder quite as much as the mass audience. To the *Times* office, joining Daniell, came a solemn-eyed, 31-year-old Scot, James B. Reston, who had been successively a sports writer, baseball publicity man, and AP correspondent in London, and a charming girl from the New York *Herald Tribune,* Tania Long, who became Mrs. Daniell.

The cumulative effect of the reporting of the Battle of Britain by such talented journalists was incalculable. It served to generate an atmosphere in which President Roosevelt could arrange with Churchill for the destroyers-for-bases deal, for lend-lease, and for the close cooperation that made continued British resistance stronger. As Churchill himself said, "The effects in Europe were profound."[18] All these things served as a counterweight to Japan's menacing move in joining the Berlin-Rome Axis with the conclusion of the tripartite pact.

The spearhead of the war on land, meanwhile, had turned to the Greek front. Mussolini, understandably upset over being reduced to a minor figure in the Axis, made a bid to restore Italian prestige by invading Greece on October 28 with an army that had no stomach for a fight While Herbert L. Matthews of the New York *Times,* John T. Whitaker of the Chicago *Daily News,* and Richard Massock of the AP vainly sought permission to go to the scene, Reynolds Packard of the UP suddenly turned up near the front lines and began filing. His wife and fellow-correspondent, Eleanor Packard, had doctored up an old pass with which he had fooled the Italians. Then, he had sent his dispatches back to Mrs. Packard in Rome through the kindness of an Italian correspondent. Thus, the UP had the first nonpropaganda dispatches from the front and the first intimation that the Italians would not easily defeat the tough Greek army. Ultimately, Packard was expelled from Albania and reprimanded, but he and Eleanor remained in Rome.[19]

One of the most active of the war correspondents was killed that winter of 1940–41 as the Italians faltered in the winter war. Ralph Barnes of the New York Herald *Tribune* died in a British bomber crash in Yugoslavia. As spring approached and the Nazis moved in the Balkans, Ray Brock of the New York *Times* reported a dramatic turn of events. He telephoned from Belgrade that the Yugoslav military had seized power, throwing out a pro-Axis cabinet. It didn't help Yugoslavia. On April 6, Brock phoned again (he worked through Berne) with a bulletin that the Nazis had invaded Yugoslavia. He escaped. Others weren't so lucky.

Robert St. John, a 41-year-old Chicagoan, fled from Belgrade to the Adriatic shore with Russell Hill of the New York *Herald Tribune* and Leigh White of CBS. In a 20-foot sardine boat without a compass and provisioned only with black bread, they started for Corfu. Dive bombers killed their pilot. In subsequent raids, both St. John and White were wounded, the latter critically. When the frail craft reached Greece, White wound up in a hospital there as a Nazi captive, but St. John and Hill kept going. Three weeks after the fall of Yugoslavia on April 18, St. John turned up in a Cairo hospital.

Some of those who escaped unscathed from Yugoslavia were caught soon afterward in the collapse of Greece under the Nazi pile-driver. Max Harrelson, a quiet young Arkansan who had narrowly avoided capture in the Nazi invasions of Denmark, the Netherlands, and Yugoslavia, where he had been an AP correspondent, was evacuated safely from Greece. Another AP correspondent, Dan DeLuce, a tall, 30-year-old Arizonan, and his wife fled in a fishing boat to Izmir, Turkey. Cyrus L. Sulzberger of the New York *Times,* then 28 years old and at the outset of his career, went with them. Sulzberger also had been in Belgrade and escaped just before the entry of the Nazi forces.

Many another British and American correspondent was trapped in the evacuation of the defeated British Expeditionary Force that had been sent in to bolster Greek resistance. Geoffrey Cox of the London *Daily Express* was caught when the Nazi parachutists took Crete, but managed to escape. Richard D. McMillan and Henry Gorrell, both of them seasoned UP war corespondents, underwent constant machine-gunning with the British forces as they plodded toward the Greek beaches. So did Brooklyn-born, 36-year-old Edward Kennedy of the AP, who wrote of plunging from his truck with the Tommies and lying flat in ditches many times while the Nazi dive bombers thundered past.[20]

Cecil Brown of CBS, who had been working previously for INS at
$65 a week, was captured by the Nazis in Belgrade. With Sam Brewer
of the Chicago *Tribune,* he was shipped out through Rumania to Istan-
bul, where they were catapulted into the Middle East war. Such British correspondents as Alan Moorehead of the London *Daily Express,*
David Woodward of the London *News Chronicle,* and Leonard Mosley
of the London Daily Sketch were already active there, and many more
were to come. Moreover, a newer generation of American war correspondents, typified by mild-looking Richard Mowrer, had begun work
under fire.[21]

There were hazards for correspondents outside the battlefield, of
course. Richard C. Hottelet, who was on the UP staff in Berlin, was
held by the Nazis all that spring on trumped-up espionage charges and
eventually expelled from the Third Reich. There was no peace for any
correspondent in Europe, either at the front or behind it.[22]

As for the major newsgathering organizations, all of them were under a strain that brought many changes. Havas, after more than a hundred years of European domination, had gone under with the fall of
France. In its place was an official Vichy agency, Office Français d' Information, an admitted propaganda organ. Reuters took over some of
Havas's staff and newspaper contracts, but also accepted help from the
British government — additional transmission facilities and a defraying
of some of the heavy cable costs — on the theory that it should spread
the British view throughout the world. The only trouble with this was
that the government soon began to insist on editing Reuters, objecting
to the inclusion of enemy communiqués in its service, among other
things. Sir Roderick Jones, the managing director, a wholehearted sponsor of government aid for Reuters, finally resigned on February 5, 1941,
at the climax of the struggle for a more independent agency. Reuters
then broadened its base to reduce the need for government assistance,
being reorganized as the Reuter Trust, jointly owned by both the London and the provincial newspapers, on October 17, 1941.[23]

At about the same period, the *Neue Zürcher Zeitung,* the leading
independent paper in neutral Switzerland, was undergoing trouble of a
different kind. Its London correspondence had aroused bitter Nazi criticism. In a dispatch to the NZZ dated November 28, 1940, reporting on
the Nazi terror raid at Coventry, the London representative, Egli, had
called it futile: "In Coventry, the determination of the people to stick it
out has been fortified." The response was an all-out drive in the Nazi
press against Switzerland. Editor Willi Bretscher was unmoved, however. There would, he wrote, be "no spiritual blackout upon Switzerland" to appease the Nazis.[24] It was the paper's finest hour.

The Nazi attempt to intimidate the neutral press was no accident. It was the NZZ which had first published reports of rising tension between the Third Reich and Russia. Throughout the spring of 1941, from Swiss, Turkish, and Finnish sources, the rumors kept building up. German troops were concentrating in eastern Poland. There were a million more in the Balkans. Yet, as late as April 13, 1941, Ambassador Friedrich Werner, Count von der Schulenberg, was wiring Berlin: "Stalin publicly asked for me . . . and threw his arm around my shoulders: 'We must remain friends and you must now do everything toward that end.' "[25] The Soviet dictator's private attitude of blind hope which was, of course, not known to the correspondents, seeped out to the world in strange and indirect ways. Tass on June 13 denied that Nazi and Soviet troop movements toward their common frontier were "of a hostile character." The Soviet propaganda apparatus screamed "warmonger" at all who differed. The Moscow correspondents, prisoners of censorship, were powerless to combat this monumental example of the Communist failing for self-deception.

On Sunday, June 22, when Hitler gave the signal for the grand assault, the first break in the story came not from Moscow but from Berlin. It was an announcement from the German propaganda ministry which was heard in New York shortly after midnight. The lead in the New York *Times,** locally written, was "Germany last night declared war on Soviet Russia, according to an official Berlin radio broadcast heard by short wave listening stations."[26]

It should not be imagined that this was a violation of Dr. Paul Joseph Goebels' declared policy: "News policy is a weapon of war. Its purpose is to wage war and not to give out information."[27] Rather, the prior announcement of such major developments, couched in a manner tending to support Nazi war aims, tended to build up credibility in German communiqués which conformed to Goebbels's policy. As long as the war swung in Hitler's favor, Goebbels could therefore count on propaganda successes. It could not work, however, in support of failures because with rare exceptions they cannot be kept secret. The hard-pressed Moscow foreign correspondents, thus, usually came trailing in with their dispatches after the Nazi victory announcements. It was by no means their fault, for there were excellent men on the job — among them Henry C. Cassidy and Robert Magidoff of the AP, Harold King of Reuters, and Henry Shapiro and M. S. Handler for the UP.

As the Nazi armies drove deeper into Russia, the Goebbels-created

---

*There were only three American correspondents in Moscow at the time. The New York *Times* was unrepresented.

legend of Nazi invincibility gained wide acceptance. In Cairo, where the British even then were wondering how they could stop Marshal Erwin Rommel and his Afrika Corps beyond Tobruk, Cecil Brown noted somberly that "the Russian show will be over in anywhere from five to six weeks."[28] That was on June 29, a week after the invasion. The world press faithfully mirrored that opinion. Even in a Moscow air raid shelter Ilya Ehrenburg reported on July 24 that he had talked with Alexander Werth, Erskine Caldwell, and others who were in a "skeptical mood" and feared a "lightning denouement."[29]

Ehrenburg, Vassily Grossman, Konstantin Simonov, Mikhail Sholokhov — journalists, poets, novelists — joined with many less famous to report on the rising Russian resistance in *Pravda, Izvestia, Red Star,* and the rest of the Soviet-controlled press. The foreign correspondents had to get their information from that source until September 14, when Nikolai G. Palgunov, director of Tass, took a party to a point near Vyazma. Major General Vassily Sokolovsky was one of the Red Army briefing officers whose estimates impressed the correspondents — among them Werth, a Reuters special correspondent at the time; Cyrus L. Sulzberger of the New York *Times;* Arch Steele of the Chicago *Daily News;* Philip Jordan of the London *News Chronicle;* Mrs. J. B. S. Haldane, wife of the British scientist and correspondent of the London *Daily Sketch;* A. T. Cholerton of the London *Daily Telegraph;* Henry C. Cassidy of the AP; Wallace Carroll of the UP; Vernon Bartlett, a member of Parliament and the BBC representative; and Erskine Caldwell and his wife, the *Life* photographer, Margaret Bourke-White.

It was an influential group. Persuaded by what they saw and by the eloquence of Sokolovsky's briefing, they began reporting things differently. Carroll, for one, vigorously disputed the view, prevalent at the time, that the Russians would be finished by Christmas. He wrote for the UP that the Russians by the spring of 1942 would still be resisting and gathering strength. The whole tone of the world press began to change. Even though the Battle of Moscow was joined shortly afterward, even though Leningrad was besieged for many terrible months, even though the diplomatic staffs and foreign correspondents were moved to Kuibyshev, no one of importance again would write that the Russians were licked. It was, as Cassidy reported, "a frightful, all-devastating struggle between two giants, fighting savagely to the death."[30]

As the winter of 1941–42 approached, the Germans had enough power left to fling themselves savagely at the British in Africa. The most prominent correspondent in the area was Harold Denny of the New York *Times,* who then was 52 years old and had been a World War I sergeant. He was a correspondent who had covered six foreign wars and spent nearly ten years in Russia. He had been in Ethiopia, in Finland, and at Dunkerque. Now, attached to the British Eighth Army, he looked for action; and on the morning of November 22, 1941, he ran into it. The British were attacked by forty-five German Stukas and, next day, by Rommel's tanks. Denny was captured with Edward Ward, a BBC correspondent, and several others.

Rommel's depleted reserves, which had been drawn off to the Russian front, frustrated his offensive, but Denny wasn't around to report it. "We correspondents," he wrote. "had all accepted the possibility of being killed or wounded, though the mathematical chance of being hit was small. But we hardly thought of being captured."[31] The attitude was typical of correspondents. They didn't really think the war could go on without them. In one sense, they were right. For these relatively few men and women were the ones on whom the world depended for the truth at the high tide of Hitler's conquests.

THE TURNING POINT

Cecil Brown, a brisk, aggressive American in his 30s, landed at Singapore's Kalang Airport on August 3, 1941, prepared for a new CBS assignment. A British official said: "It sounds bad when all you journalist vultures start flocking here."[32]

Brown was not alone. All over the Pacific, and elsewhere, correspondents were getting into place. In Indo-China that hot and menacing summer, Relman Morin of the AP was on a bus between Pnom Penh and Saigon when he saw a column of tough little men in baggy uniforms slogging through the beautiful countryside. They were the vanguard of 50,000 Japanese troops who had taken over Indo-China under a phony "protective occupation" which the Nazis had forced on the Vichy French. Morin realized at once that Malaya was outflanked, that Singapore could be attacked from the rear, that war could come at any time.[33]

In Tokyo, Otto Tolischus noted that Rear Admiral Tanetsugu Sosa, a naval commentator, on August 4 demanded strong measures against Britain and the United States, warning that East Asia was on the verge of war by reason of an economic blockade against Japan. Moreover, in his careful way, Tolischus suggested in the New York *Times* that the Japanese march across Indo-China to the borders of Thailand might have still graver consequences. Having seen Germany at war, Tolischus knew all the signs, and they were present in Japan. The Japanese press fairly bristled at the warning by the United States and Britain of "grave consequences" if Thailand were invaded.[34] The correspondent was not taken in when the Japanese military appeared temporarily to have backed down. But it was difficult to specify exactly what Japan would do.

The atmosphere in Tokyo was not reassuring to any correspondent from the West except, of course, the Germans and Italians. On the previous July, in 1940, Melville James Cox of Reuters had been seized by the secret police during a spy scare and found dead under mysterious circumstances. The Japanese had contended that Cox had jumped out of a fifth floor window while he was being questioned, but nobody who knew the correspondent believed them. Moreover, Relman Morin had been taken from the AP office and questioned sharply because he had sent a story advancing the theory of murder as well as suicide. The Japanese from then on redoubled their surveillance of correspondents. Somehow, they still overlooked Dr. Richard Sorge, who had now become the correspondent of the *Frankfurter Zeitung* and a functionary in the German embassy as well. In his double role, he learned of the Japanese plan to attack Pearl Harbor, and sent his information to Moscow.[35]

In Washington, D. C., during the summer of 1941, Masuo Kato was working as a special correspondent for Domei, the Japanese news agency, reporting on the negotiations for the settlement of the crisis. He had been sent over from Tokyo shortly after Admiral Kichisaburo Nomura, the new ambassador to the United States. Joseph C. Harsch, the *Christian Science Monitor* correspondent, newly returned from Berlin, had told him, "It will be the biggest diplomatic juggling trick of all time if Japan can come to an understanding with the United States while having an alliance with Germany." The antagonistic atmosphere was thick, Kato observed. Like other Japanese, he resented the increasing American trade restrictions on Japan and the freezing of Japanese assets in the United States. By September, he was beginning to hear some of the Japanese embassy staff predict war.[36] Not even the arrival of Saburo Kurusu, the special "peace envoy" from Tokyo, could change that feeling, for by November, when he arrived, the whole world knew the hour was late.

On November 28, Tokyo set up its "winds code" by notifying its operatives in Washington secretly that notice of an emergency would be inserted in the middle of the daily Japanese language short-wave news broadcast as follows:

1. In case of Japan-U.S. relations in danger, HIGASHI NO KASEAME (east wind rain).
2. Japan-U.S.S.R. relations, KITANOKAZE KUMORI (north wind cloudy).
3. Japan-British relations, NISHI NO KAZE HARE (west wind clear).[37]

The bitterly neutralist Chicago *Tribune* was to disclose later the extent to which the United States had been able to break the Japanese code, but for the present the secret was safe. The American intelligence officers began listening for the "winds code execute" message. Meanwhile, Secretary of State Cordell Hull and the Nomura-Kurusu team kept up their interminable and futile talks in Washington, which reassured nobody.

Most correspondents were certain that the Japanese intended to strike, but neither they nor the War Council in the United States were prepared for the daring and brilliance of the enemy's concept. The consensus in the War Council late in November was that a Japanese attack was most likely in Thailand, Malaya, or the Dutch East Indies. Hawaii wasn't mentioned in this estimate,[38] although as early as January 1941, the Peruvian embassy had accurately forecast it to Ambassador Joseph C. Grew in Japan. It was then that Admiral Isoroku Yamamoto had begun serious staff work on a Pearl Harbor attack, but the Peruvian rumor had been dismissed by both Grew and American intelligence as fantastic.[39] Grew, however, had later given the sternest warnings that Japan was planning a major military adventure and in mid-November had told Washington that he was in no position to forecast the timing of any surprise attack. Yet, even then Consul General Nagao Kita in Honolulu was sending itemized news to Japan of movements at Pearl Harbor, which was intercepted and faithfully decoded by American specialists for the edification of Washington.

On November 26, the 32 warships bearing the Japanese Pearl Harbor striking force sailed from Tankan Bay in the Kuriles. At dawn on Sunday, December 7, Commander Mitsuo Fuchida, leader of the attacking force, approached Vice Admiral Chichi Nagumo on his flagship, *Akagi*.

"I am ready for the mission," Commander Fuchida said.

"I have every confidence in you," was the quiet reply of the Japanese leader.

The fleet was then 230 miles north and slightly east of Oahu. The final signal for the attack had been flashed in code from Tokyo on December 2, so the airmen had known for five days that they were going in, and they were prepared. The small midget submarine force had been on its way to Pearl Harbor for some hours then. Up on the *Akagi*'s mast fluttered the flag Admiral Togo had flown at Tsushima Straits in 1905. At 6 a.m., the 353 attack aircraft began taking off in two great waves—the torpedo and dive bombers first, with their cover of fighter aircraft, and the high-level bombers, more dive bombers, and more fighters afterward. An hour and forty-five minutes later, Commander Fuchida was over Oahu and fired his signal pistol for the beginning of the attack. Nobody except Private Joseph Lockard had noticed the flight of enemy aircraft coming in on Hawaii that peaceful Sunday morning in December, and he had been told to forget about it. The commanders at Pearl Harbor couldn't have their sleep disturbed.[40] When the Japanese swooped over the Aloha Tower in Honolulu, the great clock registered 7:55 a.m.

At 8 a.m., Frank Tremaine, the UP manager in Honolulu, woke up with a start when he heard antiaircraft guns. From his living room, which overlooked Pearl Harbor, he saw a sky full of hostile aircraft and the pride of America's Pacific bastion exploding. To his wife, who was still in bed, Tremaine yelled, "It's an attack by Jap planes. . . . I'll put in a call for San Francisco. If it comes through, you tell them everything you can see."

In a half-hour San Francisco was on the line, and Mrs. Tremaine, standing at her living room window, told how the second wave of Japanese planes was coming in over the wreckage in Pearl Harbor. Her story, the first eyewitness account, went out as she gave it until drastic censorship cut off Hawaii, and all communications were closed down.[41]

Not all correspondents were in Tremaine's position and did not realize what was going on. As experienced and able a man as Joseph C. Harsch of the *Christian Science Monitor,* who had just arrived in Hawaii, woke up his wife and told her the noise was a "good imitation" of an air raid in Europe.[42] He thought it was practice and went for a swim, only to find out by radio that he had missed the big story.

In Washington that day, the UP was so unprepared for big news that Arthur F. DeGreve, upon receiving word from the White House during a conference call with the AP and INS also on the line, found he couldn't flash New York by teletype. He telephoned Phil Newsom on the news desk in New York, yelling:

"This is DeGreve in Washington–FLASH–White House announces Japanese bombing Wahoo."

"Bombing what?"

"Wahoo, dammit, Wahoo."

"Spell it, for pete's sake."

"O-A-H-U — Wahoo! We've got a war on our hands."[43]

The AP flash went out at 2:22 p.m., Eastern Standard Time. An NBC correspondent broke into the account of a New York Giants football ball game with the thundering news, told his stunned listeners that it was no drill, and was cut off. Masuo Kato of Domei, on his way to attend a friend's funeral in Washington, heard the report in a taxicab by radio and obtained an immediate reaction from his driver: "God damn Japan. We'll lick hell out of those bastards now."[44] The FBI soon took him and other Japanese officials and correspondents into custody, but treated them with courtesy and consideration.

It was not so in Tokyo. There, patriotic hysteria had taken hold. All foreign correspondents were regarded as spies, and Otto Tolischus of the New York *Times* was one of the first to suffer. Marched off to prison, mercilessly questioned, forced to sit on his heels for hours, given little to eat, he felt his days were numbered. Nor was he alone. Max Hill of the AP and other American correspondents were reduced to mere shadows of themselves by the police treatment.[45] In Saigon, Relman Morin was seized by Japanese soldiers and imprisoned with seven other correspondents. The AP correspondent was told he was being "protected."[46] Robert P. Martin and William H. McDougall of the UP bureau in Shanghai had better luck. They feigned drunkenness and managed to get through the Japanese lines, turning up later at the Chinese wartime capital, Chungking. They were able to warn their colleague, Frank Hewlett, at the UP office in Manila, just before the Japanese bombs began to fall on Luzon.[47]

In Singapore, Cecil Brown knew the war was on when the bombs began dropping around him while he was in a rickshaw on his way to a British press conference. It was the British way to call a press conference to announce that a war was on. The bombs made it unnecessary. It wasn't very long before Brown, O'Dowd Gallagher of the London *Daily Express,* and Tom Fairholl of the Sydney *Telegraph* were being asked by a British officer if they wanted to go on a four-day assignment, nature unspecified. Fairholl refused, saying Singapore was the story. But Gallagher, after a brief reconnaisance, came panting to Brown: "Cec, it's the *Prince of Wales.* . . . They're just asking one American and one Britisher to go. . . . We've got to pull out right away."

The *Prince of Wales* and the *Repulse,* the pride of the British fleet, were lying in the harbor, awaiting action. When they steamed into the Straits of Johore at twilight on December 8, Brown and Gallagher were on the *Repulse.* It was there that they heard President Roosevelt make his "Day of Infamy" speech before Congress, committing the United States to war. It was on the *Repulse,* too, beginning at 11:15 a.m. on December 10, that they witnessed the beginning of the Japanese torpedo bomber attack that destroyed both the great warships. Admiral Tom Phillips had run his powerful fleet, with accompanying destroyers, headlong into disaster 150 miles north of Singapore and 50 miles from the Malayan coast in the South China Sea.

Without air cover, without sufficient antiaircraft weapons, the *Prince of Wales* and the *Repulse* were sunk in a little more than an hour. Fished out of the water by doughty seamen, Brown was dumped half-dead on the deck of the destroyer *Electra*. Gallagher also was saved. But it was Brown, somehow, who revived sufficiently to get on the air when he reached Singapore next day and make one of the most dramatic broadcasts of the war for CBS:

"I was aboard the *Repulse* with hundreds of others and escaped. Then, swimming in thick oil, I saw the *Prince of Wales* lay over on her side like a tired war horse and slide beneath the waters. . . . I jumped twenty feet to the water from the up end of the side of the *Repulse* and smashed my stopwatch at 12:35. The sinking of the *Repulse* and the *Prince of Wales* was carried out by a combination of high-level bombing and torpedo attacks with consummate skill and the greatest daring."[48]

The action now centered on the Philippines where the Japanese invaders soon seized Manila and penned General Douglas MacArthur and his little American army into Bataan Peninsula and Corregidor. Hong Kong fell, and Singapore, too. The Japanese swarmed into Burma and Thailand and the Dutch East Indies. But on Bataan and Corregidor, to the wonder of the world, the Americans tenaciously held out in a stubborn exhibition of gallantry as remarkable in its way as that of the city of London. The few correspondents remaining in the Philippines told the story of that tragedy with heroism worthy of the deeds they recorded. Big Clark Lee remained in bombed, fire-swept Manila until the last moment, as did Frank Hewlett of the UP and Melville and Annalee Jacoby of *Time*, a brave young couple who had been married only a month. On New Year's Eve, Hewlett left his wife in the care of the American High Commissioner in Manila and, accompanied by Richard Wilson and Julio Carpio, drove to Bataan just before the bridges were blown up. Lee and the Jacobys got out of the wrecked Filipino capital on New Year's Day, 1942, on a small freighter and safely landed in Bataan. Franz Weissblatt of the UP wasn't so fortunate. He was wounded and captured by a Japanese patrol.[49]

Once on Corregidor, they found Brigadier General Carlos P. Romulo, then a colonel on General MacArthur's staff, who as editor and publisher of the Philippines *Herald* had won a Pulitzer Prize for his foreign correspondence. Romulo had warned often enough in print of Japanese ambitions, of the mistakes of the British and the United States in the Far East. He had not been heeded. As he walked into the Malinta Tunnel on Corregidor that New Year's Day, he recalled:

"The smell of the place hit me like a blow in the face. There was the stench of sweat and dirty clothes, the coppery smell of blood and disinfectant coming from the lateral where the hospital was situated. . . . I stood there gaping, bewildered and alarmed by the bedlam going on about me. This was the final refuge of a fortress we had all assumed had been prepared and impregnable for years. Now that disaster was upon us, soldiers were rushing about belatedly installing beds and desks and sewage drains and electric lights."[50]

The correspondents covered the war, day by day, and lived through the Japanese assaults by air and land. On March 11, when General MacArthur roared away from Corregidor in a PT boat on direct orders from President Roosevelt, it was the signal that the end was near. His departure, leaving General Jonathan M. Wainwright in command, was disclosed seven days later after he had succeeded in reaching Australia. In the Chicago *Sun* on March 19, H. R. Knickerbocker radioed from Melbourne, called the exploit "harrowing," and told how MacArthur saved himself, his wife, his four-year-old son, and his staff by "speeding through enemy-infested waters by night and hiding in jungles by day."

It was a true index of the extent to which the Japanese dominated the Pacific. The correspondents slipped away from Corregidor from then on by whatever means were available — PT boats, fighter aircraft, even trainers. Clark Lee and the Jacobys were among those who made it safely to Australia but, only a short time later, Melville Jacoby was killed in an air crash. Finally, only Frank Hewlett of the UP and Dean Schedler of the AP were left. After the fall of Bataan on April 9 and the beginning of the terrible "death march" of the prisoners taken by the Japanese, everybody knew it was only a question of time before Corregidor would have to surrender.

Only two trainer aircraft were in flying condition when General Wainwright quietly advised the correspondents that they had better go. Schedler departed on April 12, Hewlett the following day. The last man off Corregidor was the indomitable Romulo, who followed the rest on the long and arduous trip to Australia where he once more joined MacArthur's staff. On May 6, 1942, Corregidor fell. An epic of resistance against overwhelming odds had been written into American history by the correspondents who had remained almost until the last.[51] MacArthur wrote: "Corregidor has sounded its own story at the mouth of its guns. It has scrolled its own epitaph on enemy tablets. But through the bloody haze on its last reverberating shot, I shall always seem to see a vision of grim, gaunt, ghostly men, still unafraid."[52]

The nightmare of defeat glowered over the Pacific. Just before the surrender of Singapore on February 15, the last correspondents left.

Yates McDaniel of the AP caught a ship bound for Java with 55 other men and a Chinese girl. "In my seven and one-half day journey," he wrote, "I abandoned a bombed ship, was cast up on an uninhabited island, made my way through a storm in a small launch to Sumatra, crossed the island's mountain wilds by truck, rail, and pony cart, and completed 1,200 roundabout miles safely through the Indian Ocean aboard a destroyer."

There was a more tragic outcome to the Java defeat for some of the veteran correspondents. McDaniel, Harold Guard of the UP, and others who had fled from Singapore were taken off the Dutch island by bombers flying to Australia. Only Bill McDougall of the UP, DeWitt Hancock of the AP, and Kenneth Selby-Walker of Reuters chose to stay to the end. When the enemy was very near, McDougall and Hancock boarded a ship for Ceylon March 4, but it was sunk by Japanese bombers. Hancock was killed. McDougall was rescued but dumped into a Japanese prison camp. Selby-Walker's last dispatch on March 6 ended: "I'm afraid it is too late now. Good luck!"[53]

It seemed as if the Japanese would sweep everything before them until, on April 18, an electrifying announcement came over the Japanese home radio. Tokyo had been bombed that day. So had Yokohama, Nagoya, and Kobe. Washington grimly withheld the details until, days later, President Roosevelt at the White House publicly awarded the Congressional Medal of Honor to the leader of the raid, Brigadier General James H. Doolittle. Even then, instead of telling the story of how the planes had taken off from carriers, the President reported they had left from a base, Shangri-La, the mythical Asian land invented by novelist James Hilton. The Berlin radio took him seriously. With that, the United States had to be satisfied until newsmen interned in Japan came home. Then, Joe Dynan of the AP and others told how the raiders gave them "the thrill of a lifetime" as they swooped low over their prison camp.[54]

Early in May, the first great American victory, the battle of the Coral Sea off Australia, also produced one of the most dramatic narratives of the war and made a hero for a few weeks out of Stanley Johnston of the Chicago *Tribune*. He was a plucky, 42-year-old Australian who had fought in World War I, become an American citizen, and turned himself into a war correspondent almost by accident during the Nazi invasion of the Low Countries in World War II. As a Press Wireless official caught in the war, he had begun filing for the Chicago *Tribune* and after Pearl Harbor had been transferred to the Pacific. He was the only American correspondent with the fleet at the battle of the Coral Sea and was saved when the aircraft carrier *Lexington* went down.

The battle disclosed, Johnston later wrote for an appreciative American audience, "how completely the carrier has displaced the battleship in importance in modern war." The two fleets never saw each other but struck all their blows with their air arms. Two Japanese aircraft carriers, a number of other ships, and 80 aircraft were lost. The American losses were heavy, although not as great. Of the *Lexington,* Johnston wrote the magnificent epitaph: "She never wavered. She kept her head up and went down like the lady she was."[55]

That was on May 8 at the end of an epic five-day running battle. In a little more than a month, after the American victory at Midway on June 3–6, both Johnston and his paper were in deep trouble. The correspondent was accused of publishing information concerning the Japanese strength at Midway that could have tipped the enemy that the United States had broken the Japanese code. A federal grand jury investigated, but nothing ever happened either to Johnston or the Chicago *Tribune.* Subsequently, it was shown that the Japanese had not realized at that time that the United States had the secret of their code. Yet, the issue haunted the *Tribune* for the rest of the war and thereafter.[56] It was one factor that led to more tolerance for the government's own news coverage in the field, the Office of War Information, headed by Elmer Davis.

The road back in the Pacific was long and wearisome for the United States. For the troops who began the bloody campaign of island-hopping, as well as for the correspondents assigned to tell their story, it was an arduous, often tragic, and seldom rewarding struggle. On the day of the first landing by American forces at Guadalcanal in the Solomons on August 7, Vern Haugland of the AP had to bail out of a plane over New Guinea and for a month wandered in the jungle, living on grass and roots until he was rescued. Soon afterward, aboard the heavy cruiser *Astoria* off Guadalcanal, Joe James Custer of the UP lost his left eye in a Japanese dive bomber attack. Jack Singer, a 27-year-old INS correspondent, was killed when the aircraft carrier *Wasp,* to which he was assigned, took a torpedo amidships during a battle in the Solomons September 15. His shipmates forwarded his last story. In the thick of the Guadalcanal battle, meanwhile, another INS man, Richard Tregaskis, escaped without a scratch only to be wounded later in the war in Italy. An even more ironic fate befell Byron Darnton of the New York *Times,* who volunteered for war duty at 45 years of age. He was killed in action on October 18, when American warplanes mistakenly shot up a small landing craft laden with American soldiers bound for an attack on nearby Buna. One of the few fortunate ones was Ira Wolfert, a 32-year-old New Yorker who in mid-November witnessed the decisive fifth battle of the Solomons from a Guadalcanal beach and wrote a Pulitzer Prize-winning story for North American Newspaper Alliance.[57] Such experiences as these set the pattern for the correspondents in the Pacific war—a crazy-quilt patchwork of heroism, tragedy, and good fortune. Theirs was the toughest profession. Unlike the fighting men whose deeds they recorded day by day, they had to keep slogging along without even the satisfaction of being able to strike back at the enemy.

The exchange of interned diplomats and correspondents that spring and summer told the Allies something of the plight of their enemies. Twenty-two Americans came home on the *Drottningholm,* a Swedish liner, after internment at Bad Nauheim. Lochner, Oechsner, Huss, and others reported rising difficulties on the home front in the Reich. Their colleague, Richard Massock of the AP, called Italy a "hungry land with no love for her war partners, rife with defeatism and disillusion." Harold Denny of the New York *Times,* greatly cheered by the first bomber raids over Germany, returned with such colleagues as Herbert L. Matthews. The only American of this group to stay behind was a South Carolinian who had worked for the UP in Vienna, Robert H. Best. He was to die in a Boston prison after the war. One other who stayed behind was Sisley Huddleston, who had broken his connection with the *Christian Science Monitor* and chose to stay in Vichy France. The rest of the Americans came out of Bad Nauheim with only one thought—to get back to their dangerous trade.

From the 26 who were interned in Japan came tales of great personal hardship, torture, beatings, and worse. John B. Powell, the Chicago *Tribune* correspondent, came back crippled from his confinement in freezing prisons, injuries that were to prove fatal. Otto Tolischus of the New York *Times* was another who suffered brutal mistreatment. Max Hill of the AP, who had been seized at the same time as Robert Bellaire of the UP and placed in solitary confinement, told of being tortured and starved in an icy cell. At Lourenco Marques, where the Japanese repatriates were waiting, Hill heard from Masuo Kato how the Japanese had been maintained in the greatest luxury at the fashionable Greenbriar Hotel, White Sulphur Springs. The emaciated Hill said quietly, "I am proud of my country."[58]

Unlike the desperation of the Pacific war, the Allied fortunes changed dramatically as 1942 progressed; yet, it was no easier on the correspondents. Larry Allen, a 33-year-old AP man, went down with the British cruiser *Galatea* on December 16, 1941, in the Mediterranean but survived, even though he could not swim, when he was picked up by a rescue party. His colleague, Alexander Massey Anderson, of Reuters, was killed.[59] Larry Meier of INS, covering his first big battle at

Dieppe during the Allied raid of August 19, 1942, took a burst of shrapnel in the face and chest, wounds from which he never recovered. A. B. Austin of the London *Daily Herald,* covering at Dieppe for the combined British press, sent back his messages hour after hour and, in an older tradition of war correspondence, passed mortar shells in his spare moments. He was to lose his life later in the Italian fighting.[60]

The correspondents never knew precisely what to expect, although the best of them kept looking for action. On the night of October 23, 1942, outside El Alamein, three of them showed up at a brigade headquarters of one of the key outfits commanded by General Bernard Law Montgomery, the 51st Highland Division. They were Richard D. McMillan of the UP, Christopher Buckley of the London *Daily Telegraph,* and an Australian correspondent, Jack Hetherington. Shortly after their arrival, under cover of an earth-shaking barrage, the British surged over the desert. It was the opening of Montgomery's offensive.

"The biggest battle of Egypt is under way," McMillan wrote. "The British have attacked violently and have penetrated the enemy position at many points. . . . I walked five and a half hours and covered nearly five miles, two of which were into the German lines."[61]

On November 8, when Rommel had fallen back to the Libyan frontier with no more than 25,000 of his original army, the Americans struck their first massive land blow at Africa to catch the Axis forces in a pincers. Under the command of General Dwight David Eisenhower, an Anglo-American army stormed ashore on the North African beaches of Morocco and Algeria before dawn. By radio and loudspeaker, they trumpeted messages to the Vichy French, held captive by Marshal Pétain and Hitler: "Cease firing. We are your friends." But in some sections, French warships and armed forces blindly followed orders and resisted.

Nowhere was the action hotter than in the harbor of Oran in Algeria. Leo Disher, a UP correspondent on the former American Coast Guard cutter *Walney,* found himself in the thick of the battle and at an extreme disadvantage. On the way from England, he had slipped on deck and broken his ankle, which was put in a cast. Now, on the bridge of the *Walney,* he was under fire from both French warships and harbor guns. The cutter shuddered under repeated hits. Disher fell, wounded in both legs. Everybody else on the bridge was killed. As the cutter sank, the correspondent drifted clear. Although he was hit by many more bullets, he managed to swim to a pier, kept afloat by his life belts, and eventually was hauled in by a French patrol. In an Oran hospital, a doctor found 26 wounds but, somehow, Disher managed to survive.[62]

The smooth leads out of headquarters at Algiers, of course, gave no hint of such experiences that first night. Everything was neatly laid out so that the main points could be quickly absorbed by editors, writers of headlines, and the public. Wes Gallagher of the AP, one of the best, and a correspondent who had undergone his own share of frontline activity, wrote:

ALLIED HEADQUARTERS IN NORTH AFRICA, SUNDAY, NOV. 8 — AMERI-CAN SOLDIERS, MARINES AND SAILORS FROM ONE OF THE GREATEST ARMADAS EVER PUT INTO A SINGLE MILITARY OPERATION SWARMED ASHORE TODAY ON THE VICHY-CONTROLLED NORTH AFRICA SHORE BEFORE DAWN, STRIKING TO BREAK HITLER'S HOLD ON THE MEDITER-RANEAN.[63]

Such was the way things looked from headquarters. Of course, it wasn't the way Disher saw the war. Nor was it the way a wizened, gnome-like little man saw it when he staggered from a British transport two weeks later at Mers-el-Kebir in Algeria, suffering from "one of the Ten Best Colds of 1942." Ernie Pyle, then just another writer for Scripps-Howard newspapers, poked around outside General Eisenhower's headquarters and soon cabled:

WE HAVE LEFT IN OFFICE MOST OF THE SMALL-FRY OFFICIALS PUT THERE BY THE GERMANS BEFORE WE CAME. WE ARE PERMITTING FAS-CIST SOCIETIES TO CONTINUE TO EXIST. ACTUAL SNIPING HAS BEEN STOPPED BUT THERE IS STILL SABOTAGE. THE LOYAL FRENCH SEE THIS AND WONDER WHAT MANNER OF PEOPLE WE ARE. . . . OUR ENEMIES SEE IT, LAUGH, AND CALL US SOFT. . . . OUR FUNDAMENTAL POLICY STILL IS ONE OF SOFT-GLOVING SNAKES IN OUR MIDST.

It kicked up a sensation. Nobody knew how the story ever got through censorship. But then, the censors didn't know Ernie Pyle at that time, which explains a lot of things. Soon, as the invasion of North Africa gathered headway and Ernie went out and lived with the "God-damned infantry," all America began reading him and admiring him. Al Jolson, who had come to North Africa to entertain the troops, said enviously: "Everywhere I went the soldiers told me how wonderful Ernie Pyle was. Heck, he doesn't sing or dance and I couldn't figure out what he did to entertain them, but they acted like he was Mr. God." A new force had been found to bring the war home to the American people, a force weighing a mere 110 pounds who sometimes wrote his stuff in the field with a pencil while under fire. And yet, A. J. Liebling truly wrote of him: "War for him meant not adventure, as for Bob Casey; a crusade, as for Bill Stoneman; an enthrallment, as it did for Hemingway; or a chance to be a prima donna or get away from the sports department, as for a number of other fellows. He treated it as an unalleviated misfortune."[64]

The American public, having discovered Ernie Pyle, eagerly followed the progress of the war in North Africa — and scarcely realized until it was over that one of the decisive battles of history was being fought at Stalingrad. Nor was the world much better informed, although Allied leaders, of course, were well aware of the significance of the struggle. The Russians, cautious in the extreme, kept foreign correspondents away from the city and, at the most critical stage, held up even the work of inspired Soviet correspondents. The foreign press kept in touch with developments through communiqués issued in Moscow and the Stalingrad dispatches of such writers as Ehrenburg, Grossman, Simonov, and a score or more of less prominent *Red Star* combat reporters.[65]

The crucial hour came between 6 and 7 a.m. on November 19, 1942, when the defenders of Stalingrad at last heard intensive gunfire on their own side north and south of the city — the signal, as they later learned, for the opening of the Soviet counteroffensive that was to destroy the German Sixth Army. However, there was no announcement of the Russian action for three days. On November 27, when the Soviets broke through the German salient north of Stalingrad and joined forces, there was a special communiqué. But not until December 1 was there a correspondent's article in *Red Star* — Grossman's — and not until December 12 was a foreign correspondent able to write directly from Stalingrad. Henry Shapiro of the UP was the first to visit the Volga battleground after the encirclement of the Nazi forces. "I found among the officers and soldiers an air of confidence the like of which I had never seen in the Red Army before," he recalled. "When I returned to Moscow, I wrote, 'The Germans are doomed.'"[66]

Alexander Werth, writing for the London *Sunday Times,* went to Stalingrad afterward and wrote: "Walking over the frozen, tortured earth of Stalingrad, you felt that you were treading on human flesh and bones. And sometimes it was literally true."[67] The end came on February 2, 1943. Only 91,000 Germans remained of the 330,000 in the Sixth Army, and they were prisoners.

On February 3, there was a roll of muffled drums over the German radio, followed by the second movement of Beethoven's *Fifth Symphony.* Then the High Command broke the news to the German people with this bulletin: "The battle of Stalingrad has ended. True to their oath to fight to the last breath, the Sixth Army under the exemplary leadership of Field Marshal [Friedrich] von Paulus has been overcome by the superiority of the enemy and by the unfavorable circumstances confronting our forces."

Thus, after three years and five months of war under Hitler's demoniac leadership, the German people faced their moment of truth. Beaten at El Alamein, beaten at Stalingrad, reeling back under the Anglo-American invasion of North Africa, facing the invasion of Hitler's Fortress Europa itself, the Germans could have little hope for the future.[68] In this manner, the turning point of the war was reached; and in this manner, it was made known to a suffering world.

VICTORY IN EUROPE

The work of Ernie Pyle was inextricably bound up with the reporting of the victory of the United Nations coalition in Europe. Among the professional correspondents, there were many whose work was outstanding, some who achieved fame, and a few who became truly distinguished. But there was only one Ernie Pyle. Not even Ernest Hemingway and John Steinbeck, who descended from the lofty heights of literature to come to grips with the blood and sweat of wartime journalism, were able to attract so large and ardent a newspaper audience. Nor were their dispatches preserved in book form with the same reverence, and even love, that was bestowed by many millions of Americans upon the little man from Indiana who hated war and yet gave up his life to it. William Howard Russell, the great Britisher, proudly called himself the first war correspondent. The mild and self-effacing Ernie Pyle wanted to be the last.

Pyle was one of those kindly and modest men who regard fame as a curious kind of insect when it alights by chance upon their chest and gently try to brush it off. He was born Ernest Taylor Pyle, although nobody in later life ever called him that, on August 3, 1900, in the village of Dana, Indiana. He acquired an education in fits and starts, attending journalism classes and editing the *Daily Student* at Indiana University for four years, leaving before graduation in 1923 to become a reporter on the LaPorte *Herald*. Soon, he was able to move on to the Washington *Daily News,* a new Scripps-Howard newspaper, where he wound up on the copy desk, editing reporters' copy, and scribbling headlines. With the exception of a brief stint in New York on the *Evening World* and the *Evening Post* in 1926, he remained with the *Daily News* until 1935, rising unhappily to the estate of managing editor and quitting as soon as he was decently able to do so.

Nothing in those early years marked Ernie Pyle as a man who could move a great mass audience with his simple, kindly, and unaffected prose. But in 1935, when he set out on a career as a wandering columnist with his deeply troubled wife, Jerry, whom he had married in 1925, people began to notice him and read him. In five years as a wanderer who crisscrossed America in an old jalopy and wrote about the plain people he met and the things he saw, he attracted a modest public in two-score newspapers that carried his column. Briefly, in 1940, he was in London covering the Blitz, but personal troubles and his wife's mental state brought him home. He was divorced in 1942. On November 9 of that year, when he was desolated over his shattered marriage, he sought release on the war front. That was the day the UP in London cabled the home office informatively, "Pyle Frontwarded."

The wizened little man in the ill-fitting, sloppy correspondent's uniform was just one of 70 American war reporters in North Africa at the beginning. At 42, he was the oldest of them all, save the ancient Gault MacGowan of the New York *Sun*. The younger correspondents somehow thought of Pyle as fragile and slightly elderly, although he was tougher than any of them, and tried to take care of him. Hal Boyle of the AP, one of his major rivals, saw him first sprawled in bed in a drafty Oran hotel, "mopping his nose and gently cursing the people who had reported that Africa was a warm country." He went to Biskra and did some pieces about the bomber crews, but his heart wasn't really in his work. Then, suddenly and quite astonishingly, he met GI Joe fighting his heart out in the mud on the Tunisian front during the last gasp of the Nazi legions there — the beginning of a historic mutual admiration society.

"Now to the infantry," he wrote, "the God-damned infantry as they like to call themselves. . . . I love the infantry because they are the underdogs. They are the mud-rain-frost-and-wind boys. They have no comforts, and they even learn to live without the necessities. And in the end they are the guys that wars can't be won without."[69]

From then on, Pyle made common cause with the infantryman and became his hero. In the thick of the fighting in Tunisia, on desolate night marches, in retreat, and in sudden and daring offensive actions that finally crushed Rommel's forces, GI Joe from then on was seldom without his Boswell. Across America, newspapers began running his column, many on page 1, under massive human-interest headlines, and millions who had never before heard of Ernie Pyle took him nightly into their homes and their hearts. Somewhere, in this new career, he found the courage to remarry his Jerry by proxy in a cable ceremony and think of renewing life with her after the war.

The difference between Ernie Pyle and his colleagues was that he never bothered to whip up a newsy first paragraph on which an editor could slap a sensational headline. He didn't pay much attention to the formal communiqués out of headquarters, out of which almost any competent news mechanic could manufacture what is known to the trade as a lead story. Instead, he looked for the story of the individual swallowed up on the massive battlefront, and he took his time about gathering the material for his work. He was respectful of deadlines, but never enslaved by them.

There were others like Pyle who, by the nature of their assignment, had to follow the news closely and didn't have his comparative freedom of action. There was John O'Reilly of the New York *Herald Tribune,* known as Tex, who had begun as an itinerant printer and was also over 40 now. He followed the Tunisian war from start to finish, the surrender of 25,000 Germans of the Afrika Korps on the Cape Bon peninsula on May 9, 1943. With the other reporters a month later, he heard General Eisenhower at headquarters tell them in confidence that the overture to the invasion of Europe, an offensive against Sicily, would begin in a month. O'Reilly called home for reinforcements and soon was joined by a big, slow-moving, 36-year-old reporter with a mild manner and a controlled stutter—the introduction of Homer Bigart to frontline reporting. At first, O'Reilly was at the front, going ashore four times on the night of the Sicilian landings, July 9–10, with Bigart backing up the *Herald Tribune* from headquarters in Algiers. But later, they switched and Bigart, born in Hawley, Pa., and introduced to newspaper work as a *Herald Tribune* copy boy, began his own career under fire as a great war correspondent.[70] This was the method, too, for Milton Bracker and Herbert L. Matthews of the New York *Times,* who both saw action as the Italian campaign progressed.

Pyle and Hal Boyle and O'Reilly and the rest of their celebrated company did the GI proud, but the interpreters among the war correspondents were important, too. Soon after the landing in Sicily, Matthews warned that "one ought to ask not whether Italy is going to collapse but whether she can collapse." The point was that Matthews expected the Germans to take over Italy and the Italians and force the continuation of the fighting. The only trouble was that he made it two days after the aged Marshal Pietro Badoglio seized power in Rome and forced Benito Mussolini to resign on July 25 while the Allies were still fighting in Italy. It was clear that Matthews had not anticipated so sudden an Italian overturn, which to the casual reader, at least, made him look a little foolish. Yet, very soon, his fear of a continued Italian campaign by the Germans proved correct.

There was another aspect to the war that drew the attention of many a war correspondent other than Ernie Pyle and the rest who preferred to slog along with the foot soldier. That was the steadily rising fury of the Allied bombing raids over Germany and, to a lesser extent, other Axis centers. Walter Cronkite of the UP, flying on a raid over Wilhelmshaven on February 26 of that year, had written that it was "an assignment to hell — a hell 26,000 feet above the earth, a hell of burning tracer bullets and bursting gunfire, of crippled Fortresses and burning German fighter planes, of parachuting men and others not so lucky."[71] Among the unlucky ones on that raid was Robert P. Post, a former Washington correspondent of the New York *Times* who had briefly attracted attention when he had had the temerity to ask President Roosevelt his intentions about a third term and had been told to "go over in the corner and put on your dunce cap." Bob Post was killed in action over Wilhelmshaven.[72]

Matthews flew on the first raid over Rome on July 19 with six other correspondents. "The irony of fate and journalism," he wrote, "brought me back, watching with no satisfaction . . . a triumphant Allied force landing something more than 1,000 tons of bombs in the heart of Italy's capital." All the correspondents came back from that raid, but three of them — Raymond Clapper of Scripps-Howard service, Joseph Morton of the AP, and Tom Treanor of the Los Angeles *Times* — lost their lives before the war ended.[73] That's the way it was for the correspondents. They never knew whether they would get it in some major battle or fall prey to a sniper on a sunny day when little or nothing was going on. Nevertheless, they accepted one mean assignment after another.

With the crossing of the Straits of Messina by American and British forces on September 2, the way was open for the long-awaited Italian surrender, which was announced on September 8. The joy was premature. Tex O'Reilly, going into Salerno next day to cover the 36th Division's amphibious landing, reported terrific German resistance in his New York *Herald Tribune* story. After a bloody 10-day battle, O'Reilly entered Naples with the first patrol and was appalled at the destruction. Matthews, who followed him, found that the Germans had destroyed the University of Naples with its priceless heritage of art and literature.[74]

Ernie Pyle, returning from a brief rest in the United States, joined the 36th Division in its mountain fighting against the Germans. It was during the bitter winter campaign that he wrote one of his most famous stories — the death of Captain Henry T. Waskow of Belton, Texas.[75] It helped win him a Pulitzer Prize.[76] On the beachhead at Anzio not long afterward, he had a narrow escape in a place he called "Shell Alley." Outside Naples, artillery fire killed Stewart Sale of the London *Daily Herald,* A. B. Austin, then of Reuters, and William Mundy, of the Australian AP. Pyle wrote to Jerry: "I really was tremendously lucky to come out alive."[77]

Of the almost 500 American correspondents who gathered in England in the spring of 1944 for the cross-Channel invasion, 28 were picked to go in by sea and land. Ernie Pyle was one. With the other old hands, he figured his chances. Bill Stoneman of the Chicago *Daily News,* who had been wounded, was ready to go. So were Don Whitehead of the AP, Henry Gorrell of the UP, winner of the American Air Medal for bravery, Clark Lee of INS, Tex O'Reilly of the New York *Herald Tribune,* and Jack Thompson of the Chicago *Tribune.* All had seen a great deal of action. Pyle wrote: "We felt our chances were not very good. . . . I was the worst of the lot and continued to be."[78]

It didn't help much when the correspondents learned on June 4 that the AP London office had let loose a flash by mistake:

EISENHOWER HQ ANNOUNCES ALLIED LANDINGS IN FRANCE

However, the German Fifteenth Army had been fed so many phony messages that the AP's slip was discounted, particularly when a check showed all quiet along the Channel coast. Thus, when General Eisenhower moved, he managed to surprise the defenders.[79] Walter Cronkite, at 28 a UP veteran, flew in over the invasion coast at dawn, one of several reporters in a B-17 bomber group.[80] Leonard Mosley of the London *Daily Telegraph,* a veteran of some of the great battles of the war, jumped with the paratroops.[81] Collie Small of the UP flew with the Ninth Air Force. Don Whitehead hit the beach on D-Day with the troops, going in under heavy enemy fire. Jack Thompson of the Chicago *Tribune* was in soon afterward. Roelif Loveland of the Cleveland *Plain Dealer* wrote: "We saw the curtain go up this morning on the greatest drama in the history of the world, the invasion of Hitler's Europe."[82] And George Hicks of ABC stood on the U.S.S. *Ancon* as a network pool reporter and gave a superb description of the panorama of D-Day on the Normandy shore.[83]

Knowing that these and many others had ably covered the first shock of the invasion, Ernie Pyle spent most of the time walking up and down the beach when he went in on the morning after D-Day. The action, by that time, had moved inland. As always, he wrote about GI Joe. But in a letter home, after 10 days under fire, he wrote of himself: "I haven't had too bad a time, and yet the thing is about to get me down. . . . I'm so sick of living in misery and fright."[84] But he went on.

The nature of the correspondent in the Western world is such that he will take incredible chances, at times, to get a story. Every one in

France, from the greenest youngster to 57-year-old Mark Watson of the Baltimore *Sun*, wanted to be in on the capture of Paris. In fact, after the American breakout in that summer of 1944, all the correspondents watched each other to make certain that nobody took off alone for Paris. On August 15, there was a diversion when Eric Sevareid, Chester Morrison, and Vaughn Thomas led with radio reports, in colorful detail, of the Allied landings in the south of France.[85] The race for Paris was stepped up. When the First Army was a hundred miles west of Paris, Pyle, Thompson, Gorrell, and Clark Lee asked for permission to move ahead but were refused. Nevertheless, some correspondents got into the City of Light as early as August 23–24, among them Ernest Hemingway. Larry Lesueur, a CBS war correspondent with extensive service in Russia and the Middle East, broadcast from Radio Paris before the French troops entered the city. So did Jim McGlincy of the UP and three Britishers. The bold vanguard of the corps of correspondents was set down with light penalties, a temporary suspension of credentials, for failing to submit their copy to censorship.[86]

But that did not lessen the enthusiasm of the main groups who came in with the French forces, leading the Americans and the British, on August 25, one of the great days of the war. Ernie Pyle, riding in with Hank Gorrell of the UP in a jeep, wrote of the hysterically joyful Parisian crowds: "We all got kissed until we were literally red in the face, and I must say we enjoyed it. . . . The fact that I hadn't shaved for days and was gray-bearded as well as bald-headed, made no difference."[87] But it was just about all he could take. He had been overseas for 29 months, nearly a year of that in the front lines, and had written 700,000 words. "The hurt," he concluded, "has finally become too great. All of a sudden it seemed to me that if I heard one more shot or saw one more dead man I would go off my nut. And if I had to write one more column I'd collapse. So I'm on my way."[88]

Among many others, he left durable Mark Watson of the Baltimore *Sun* behind him to report the entry of General Charles de Gaulle into Paris on August 26 amid sniper fire at the Hotel deVille, one of the fine and colorful stories of the war. Watson won a Pulitzer Prize for that, and the bulk of his war correspondence, in the following year. And there were many, many others now, seasoned and reliable, to tell the story of the American dash across France, the stubborn British action at Arnhem, the Battle of the Bulge, the spanning of the Rhine at the Remagen bridgehead, and the final thrust into a shattered and bombed-out Germany to meet the Russians.

Some of the finest correspondence in these latter stages of the war in

Europe came from the relatively small staff of the *Christian Science Monitor,* whose instructions were to play down adventure and the "home town boy" angle and concentrate on the significance of the war. Under the supervision of Charles E. Gratke, foreign news editor, and the veteran European editorial manager, Walter Mallory-Browne, who worked for six years in bomb-wracked London, the *Monitor*'s men ranged over the European battlefields. Probably the most active was Ronald Maillard Stead, who observed the fighting in North Africa, at the Anzio beachhead, and went into Germany with the U.S. Ninth Army, finally being rowed across the Elbe by two Russians in a racing shell. Emlyn Williams, the veteran correspondent in Germany, was among the earliest to return to destroyed Berlin. Joseph Harrison, who escaped from Greece after the Nazi takeover, and Dan DeLuce of the AP were among the first to go back to Europe, making their way into Yugoslavia and reporting on the resistance of the Communist partisans headed by the enigmatic Tito. Edmund Stevens, a youthful Columbia graduate at the outset of the war, followed up his frustrating experience during the Nazi conquest of Norway by covering the war in Russia, the Middle East, and Africa. Their business, as the *Monitor* stated it, was "to keep the long-range meaning in view and to write about it."[89]

These things were not easy to do, either for the *Monitor* men or anybody else. One of the Reuters correspondents with the U.S. First Army, William Stringer, was killed in action during the dash across France. In Moscow, Harrison E. Salisbury, who had been sent there by the UP late in the war to relieve Henry Shapiro, was threatened with expulsion. A UP man in London had filed a tale, current at the time, that Stalin had hit Marshal Semyon Y. Timoshenko over the head with a bottle to silence him during a party for Winston Churchill. In vain, Salisbury pleaded that he knew nothing of the story and presented UP's apologies. The Russians would have turned him out but for the agency's own apology. Still another hazard for correspondents was illustrated by the plight of John Wilhelm of the Baltimore *Sun,* caught with the American army in the Bulge, who told of soldiers "fighting even when surrounded beyond hope," and seemed to have little hope left himself.

Thus, even in victory there was turmoil and heartache and grief. On April 12, 1945, when President Roosevelt died at Warm Springs, Ga., there was such a universal outpouring of sadness that even the German radio for a short time stilled its venom and its lies. The first word to the United States was an INS flash, read over CBS by John Daly. Then in rapid succession came the BBC, in London, and in Paris. Charles Collingwood of CBS truly said in his Paris broadcast, "It is as though a light went out."

Six days later, on tiny Ie Shima in the Pacific, Ernie Pyle was killed by a Japanese sniper. He had been in the Pacific for four months and had gone into Ie Shima with the 77th Division. When the sniper opened up, Pyle hit the ditch beside the road, then raised his head to see if everybody else was all right. The bullet hit him in the right temple.

Again, the United States mourned, this time for a gnome-like little man who had been almost as well-loved as his commander-in-chief. There were formal statements of grief from President Truman and all the other great ones. But none missed him more than his own kind. For when Hal Boyle cried out to his sleeping colleagues in ruined Leipzig, "Ernie got it!" they got up and drank themselves into a stupor.[90]

Now, the European war surged toward its climax. In mid-April, the Allied armies began overrunning the Hitler concentration camps. Shocked correspondents, seeing the terrible evidence of Nazi mass murders and listening to the numbing tales of atrocities that were told by emaciated survivors, poured out the truth. From the beginning of the war, the world had heard such stories from time to time. William Shirer, while he was still in Berlin, had noted them in his diary. Almost from the outset of the German attack on Russia in 1941, Ilya Ehrenburg had been reporting instances of the mass extermination of Jews by Nazi murder squads. In 1942, following a joint statement by the Allied governments on the persecution of the Jews in Europe, the Soviet foreign office had charged the Nazis with seeking the systematic extermination of the entire Jewish population of Europe. But, as Alexander Werth wrote, "It was all so monstrous that even in Russia many felt that these things had first to be seen to be believed."[91]

Now they were seen. One of the first accounts, and among the most searing, was a CBS broadcast on April 15, 1945, from Buchenwald by Edward R. Murrow. Three days later, Gene Currivan piled up still more horror in a dispatch to the New York *Times* from the same spot. As more and more correspondents entered the death camps, it became all too tragically certain that Hitler's *Einsatzgruppen* under the domination of Adolf Eichmann had killed 6,000,000 Jews and millions of other helpless people, chiefly Slavs, in the murder factories of Buchenwald, Auschwitz, Maidanek, and all the rest.[92] This was to be the "final solution" of the Jewish problem for the Nazis. Yet, no government opened up this story. It was the correspondents who did it, and it was the correspondents, too, who did not let the world forget what had happened.

The meeting of the Americans and Russians at the Elbe River broke in a curious way toward the end of April as the murder-camp story was developing. A UP woman correspondent, Ann Stringer, was in a small U.S. Army plane with two officers when it landed at the town of

Torgau, Germany, on the Elbe. There, she saw a Russian soldier running through the streets and, later, she noticed Russians swimming in
the Elbe. That was on April 25, when it was not definitely known the
Russians had reached the river.[93] Within a short time, Don Whitehead
and Hal Boyle were in Torgau, too. On April 26, they described the
meeting of American and Soviet troops there, an outburst of good will
between GI Joe and his Russian counterpart that lasted for only a day
or two.[94]

Three days later, on April 29 in Milan, Benito Mussolini and his
mistress, Clara Petacci, were strung up by the ankles from the girder of
a gasoline station in Milan by infuriated partisans. Milton Bracker of
the New York *Times* was there to see it and wrote in next day's paper:
"Benito Mussolini came back last night to the city where his Fascism
was born. He came back on the floor of a closed moving van, his dead
body flung on the bodies of his mistress and twelve men shot with
him." The *Times* also published exclusively the pictures of Mussolini's
end, taken by an Italian photographer and radioed across the Atlantic.
Then, in a grand gesture, despite offers as high as $5,000 for republica-
tion, Arthur Hays Sulzberger released the pictures free for the use of
any newspapers that wanted them.[95] In the splash made by the *Times*'s
exploit, a first-rate reporting job by James E. Roper of the UP received
less attention than it deserved, for he, too, had trailed Mussolini to
Milan and sent the story of the end of the Sawdust Caesar in pitiless
detail.[96] Fittingly enough, the German armies in Italy surrendered unconditionally on the day that Mussolini's body was flaunted in disgrace
before the Milanese who had witnessed his rise to power.

In the *Fuehrerbunker* in Berlin, Hitler learned of Mussolini's igno-
minious end and made elaborate preparations for his own demise. On
April 30, he shot and killed himself, and his mistress, Eva Braun, whom
he had married the day before, took poison. The Hamburg radio made
the announcement next day, which the Russians soon confirmed when
they took over the chancellery. Pierre J. Huss of INS, who came in as an
American war correspondent, learned the story of Hitler's last days up
to April 22 from his secretary, Gerhardt Herrgesell. Another who
pieced together the factual account of Hitler's end was Jack Fleischer of
the UP. But not until official American, British, and Russian accounts
were made available, based on sworn testimony taken from many survivors, did the full story become known.[97]

Once again, as in World War I, there was trouble over the announcement of the end of the war in Europe. The German surrender came at
2:41 a.m. Monday, May 7, 1945, in General Eisenhower's Reims head-

quarters. At 2 p.m. the same day, the Germans used the Flensburg, Denmark, radio to broadcast a cease-fire order to their troops. At 3:24 p.m., Edward Kennedy, the chief AP correspondent at Eisenhower's headquarters, phoned this bulletin from Paris to London over regular military lines:

REIMS, FRANCE, MAY 7 — GERMANY SURRENDERED UNCONDITIONALLY TO THE WESTERN ALLIES AND THE SOVIET UNION AT 2:41 A.M. TODAY.

The British cleared it. The AP in New York, after eight minutes' delay, flashed it around the world. It was a monumental beat for Kennedy, but it cost him his job. Fifty-three correspondents in Paris charged him with a violation of confidence. The New York *Times,* after using his story, denounced him for a "grave disservice" to his profession. Robert McLean, president of the AP, expressed his regret that the news broke "in advance of authorization" by SHAEF.

Like Roy Howard's experience with the UP false armistice report at the end of World War I, Ed Kennedy's premature disclosure of the Nazi surrender made journalistic history of a sort and led to years of argument. His experience began on Sunday, May 6, when he was selected by Supreme Allied Headquarters as one of 17 representatives of the world press to be flown to Reims for an "important announcement." Once aboard an Army Air Force C-47, he and the rest were told they were to cover the German surrender. But the SHAEF public relations director, Brigadier General Frank Allen, pledged them not to make public the story until 3 p.m. on Tuesday, May 8. This was done by agreement between President Truman and Prime Minister Churchill.

The press delegation duly covered the story at the big red schoolhouse in Reims, then was flown back to Paris. Boyd Lewis of the UP and Jim Kilgallen of INS filed their material in the communications center at the Scribe Hotel in Paris ahead of Kennedy on all five outgoing routes and at five times normal cost. But Kennedy didn't seem particularly worried. Lewis and Kennedy repeatedly protested the embargo, particularly after the BBC used the Flensburg announcement. Finally, Kennedy told the SHAEF censor, Lieutenant Colonel Richard Merrick, that he intended to file by any means that he could. "I give you warning now that I am going to send the story," he said.

Supposedly, all outgoing lines from Paris were strictly controlled. But Kennedy had a member of his staff, Morton Gudebrod, put through a call to the London AP bureau, and it was handled routinely through the military switchboard. Kennedy himself then told London to clear his story. The worst of the imbroglio that followed was due to the refusal of the military for all the rest of May 7 to permit correspondents to explain to their home offices what was going on and why. The home offices, meanwhile, sent furious "rockets" to their correspondents, demanding confirmation or denial of the AP story. The correspondents, including Ed Beattie (who had just been freed from a German prison camp), Ray Daniell, Mark Watson, and Charles Collingwood of CBS wrote to General Eisenhower: "We have respected the confidence placed in us by SHAEF and as a result have suffered the most disgraceful, deliberate, and unethical double cross in the history of journalism."

The rest was anticlimactic. The first AP flash reached New York at 9:35 a.m. (3:35 p.m., Paris time) on Monday, May 7. At 11:15 a.m., the AP was told its story was "unauthorized," but by then newspapers all over the world were carrying the news. All the AP could do was to report that SHAEF had neither authorized nor denied the story. Four hours after the first flash was sent, the British Information Ministry announced that Prime Minister Churchill would proclaim V-E Day at 3 p.m., May 8, and shortly afterward an announcement by President Truman was scheduled for the same hour, which was 9 a.m., Washington time. Premier Stalin's announcement was then synchronized with those of the other leaders. But, the New York *Times* observed, "Washington . . . was confused."

The AP was denied filing facilities from Europe for six hours and twenty minutes. When that ban was lifted, however, a specific exception was made for Kennedy, whose suspension lasted until July 1946. The defiant correspondent, who became managing editor of the Santa Barbara (Calif.) *News-Press* after leaving the AP, insisted for the remainder of his career that he'd have done the same thing again, given the chance. He maintained that the Flensburg announcement had been authorized by SHAEF, that the censorship was political, and that he had given fair warning that he no longer felt bound by it.[98] But if statesmen, generals, and journalists were disturbed and upset, the people were not. In bomb-ravaged London, Paris, Washington, Moscow, and hundreds of other cities that had felt the war in greater or less degree, there was rejoicing and thanksgiving that was exceeded only in the ranks of the frontline soldiers who had borne the brunt of the fighting.

Ernie Pyle had begun a column for that day: "My heart is still in Europe, and that's why I'm writing this column. It is to the boys who were my friends for so long. My one great regret of the war is that I am not with them when it has ended. For the companionship of two and a half years of death and misery is a spouse that tolerates no divorce."[99]

The piece was never finished. It was found in his pocket the day they picked him up and buried him on Ie Shima.

PACIFIC FINALE

The war in the Pacific — "the war of magnificent distances," as Ernie Pyle called it — was being reported with gallantry and devotion by a small army of correspondents. From the New York *Times* alone went Foster Hailey, who was on Guadalcanal; Tillman Durdin, one of the wisest and most experienced of correspondents in Asia; Robert Trumbull, who had an excellent knowledge of the Pacific area; Frank Kluckhohn, a veteran Washington correspondent who had covered the Spanish Civil War; George Horn, the Commodore, from ship news; Lindesay Parrott, a first-rate rewrite man; Warren Moscow, from City Hall; William H. (Political Bill) Lawrence, from Washington; and even Brooks Atkinson, the drama critic.[100]

There were the heroics of Jack Belden, the reporter from Time, Inc., who retreated from Burma with General Joseph W. (Vinegar Joe) Stilwell in May 1942, and with others faithfully reported his words: "I claim we got a hell of a beating. We got run out of Burma, and it is humiliating as hell. I think we should find out what caused it and go back and re-take it." After Guadalcanal, there were more heartening experiences, such as that of Gordon Walker of the *Christian Science Monitor,* who went into New Georgia in the Solomons with the Marines in June 1943, then hired a native war canoe which conveyed him and his copy to a base at Rendova after a 10-hour night journey.[101]

Moreover, there were human interest stories in the Pacific that cried for a master's touch. One of the best broke on August 19, 1943 — the heroism of Lieutenant (j.g.) John F. Kennedy, the 26-year-old son of Joseph P. Kennedy, the former American ambassador to the Court of St. James's. As the AP reported the story, Kennedy's PT boat No. 109 was rammed and cut in two on August 2 in Blackett Strait west of New Georgia. Two of the crew of 12 were killed. Kennedy himself saved another, who had been badly burned, by clenching his teeth about the strap of the victim's life preserver and swimming with him for five hours to an island three miles away. From island to island, the party slowly made its way for four days until, eventually, all were rescued. Ten months later, John Hersey, one of a brilliant group of *New Yorker* war correspondents that also included Janet Flanner, Mollie Panter-Downes, and A. J. Liebling, did a full-dress job on the Kennedy story. It was called "Survival," and it became the basis for innumerable accounts of the exploit after John F. Kennedy was elected President of the United States.[102]

Perhaps it was inevitable, but the most violent of all the political disagreements within the Allied coalition developed in the Pacific, which added spice to the correspondence. The center of the action was Chungking, the wartime Chinese Nationalist capital; the actors, for the most part, were quartered in the Press Hostel which was made available by Hollington K. Tong, in charge of press relations. It was a distinguished group — Arch T. Steele of the Chicago *Daily News,* a correspondent in China for many years; Theodore H. White (summa cum laude, Harvard, 1938), correspondent for *Time-Life-Fortune;* Brooks Atkinson and Tillman Durdin of the New York *Times;* Spencer Moosa of the AP, Walter Rundle of the UP, Jack Belden, who had shifted to INS, Tommy Chao (Chao Ming-heng) of Reuters, and many others.

The touchiest story with which these correspondents had to deal was the relationship between General Stilwell, the commander of the CBI theatre, and Chiang Kai-shek. The story which was subject to the heaviest censorship was anything that impinged on relationships with Mao Tse-tung's Communist regime in Yenan. The fight between Chiang and Stilwell reached such a point that the crusty general finally told his story to Brooks Atkinson. And it was Atkinson, the drama critic, who made his way out of wartime China and broke the detailed account of how Chiang had forced Stilwell's recall.[103] Going on to Moscow, Atkinson was later to win a Pulitzer Prize for his war correspondence.

It was the Stilwell story, however, that blew the lid off the unsavory situation in Chungking. Hanson Baldwin, Tillman Durdin, and others of the New York *Times,* Teddy White, Belden, and Edgar Snow of the *Saturday Evening Post* and New York *Herald Tribune,* Harrison Forman of the *Times* of London, and many others participated in the searching criticism of Chiang's regime. The Chinese Nationalists responded with bitter attacks on the press for its supposed bias against the government to which it was accredited. Hollington Tong complained of a "flood of pro-Yenan publicity from Chungking correspondents in 1944," which didn't help matters. Neither did the killing of dispatches written by Atkinson and White, among others. Finally, capping the argument over Stilwell, correspondents like Harrison Forman and Edgar Snow traveled to Yenan and pointed up the sharp differences between the Nationalists and the Communists. Nor did Mao, Chou En-lai, and Chu Teh fail to take advantage of their opportunity to present their case in the world press, to the disadvantage of Chiang's unhappy regime in Chungking. The uproar became so great that the Nationalists late in the war barred Harold Isaacs of *Newsweek* and Darrell Berrigan, a former UP man who later worked for the New York *Post,* from returning to their territory. Isaacs's major offense was that he had written: "The Americans will at best find themselves backing a government with no real basis of power except American support." The correspondents did not create the difficult situation in which Chiang found himself toward the end of the war, but they used every bit of influence they could exert to explore the reasons for it. Yet, for all that, the world was ill-prepared for the startling rise of the Communists and their transformation of China into a great power.[104]

While the China argument was raging, American forces in the Pacific were engaged in their long and difficult campaign of island-hopping. The public at home could understand this—desperate landings, resistance to the death by the defending Japanese, tales of great heroism and, above all, a steady and measurable progress that could be shown on maps with arrows in the Pacific. Beside the glowing superlatives of the correspondents who covered these events and lived through them, the quarrel over China seemed a pale matter, indeed. Battles won, battles lost, that was the news! Nothing else seemed to matter on page 1, or in the broadcasts that dinned in the ears of the American public.

At Tarawa in the Gilberts, Richard W. Johnston of the AP went in with the Marines in this situation: "I landed at the center beach . . . and like the Marines I had to walk 500 yards shoreward through a machine gun crossfire. . . . Throughout the last sixty hours, and probably through the next sixty, Japanese snipers have been taking, and will take, a heavy toll." That was on November 23, 1943, when the American drive was beginning to make headway. On the morning of October 20, 1944, William B. Dickinson of the UP waded ashore with General MacArthur on the island of Leyte in the Philippines and recorded the General's first dramatic words: "I have returned." During the succeeding days, George E. (First Wave) Jones of the UP waited aboard the carrier *Lexington* for the outcome of the second battle of the Philippine Sea, then wrote:

ABOARD ADMIRAL MITSCHER'S FLAGSHIP, OCTOBER 25 (UP) TODAY THE JAPANESE FLEET SUBMITTED ITSELF TO THE DESTINIES OF WAR AND LOST. FOUR ENEMY CARRIERS HAVE BEEN SUNK, EIGHT BATTLESHIPS HAVE BEEN DAMAGED.

It was, as Jones later learned, a far greater victory than that. Forty Japanese ships had been sunk, 46 others damaged, 405 planes destroyed. Moreover, Jones had a lucky break. He was able to get the news out by giving his story to a fighting politician, Commander Harold E. Stassen, who flew it to Guam and filed it at the radio station there.

Kwajalein, Eniwetok, Saipan—one by one the Japanese island strongholds fell, and the American bombers moved their bases ever closer to the Japanese home islands. But as eagerly as the American public read of these victories, the greatest boost to home front morale was yet to come. In the fighting for the then little-known island of Iwo Jima on February 23, 1945, an AP photographer, Joe Rosenthal of San Francisco, went in on a landing craft to get pictures of the Marines in action during the early days of March.

"See that spot of red on the mountainside?" shouted the bos'n. "A group of Marines is climbing up to plant our flag up there. I heard it from the radioman."

It was all the encouragement Rosenthal needed. He toiled up Mount Suribachi, paying little attention to the fighting, and reached the top just as five Marines were propping a long flagpole into place. He shot three pictures blindly, fearing he would miss. A Marine near him was killed. Until sometime afterward, he didn't know that he had taken the greatest picture of the war—the flag-raising on Mount Suribachi—which thrilled the nation. It won him a Pulitzer Prize.[105]

THE BOMB

In all of World War II, the least probable candidate at the outset for distinction as a war correspondent was a fiercely intense, graying science writer for the New York *Times,* William Leonard Laurence. By 1939, at the age of 51, much of his career was behind him, fine as it had been. As a native of Lithuania who had emigrated to the United States in 1905, Bill Laurence had picked his family name from a street sign in Boston and proceeded to make it famous in the annals of journalism. He had taken his LL.B. at Harvard in 1921, worked on the New York *World,* then joined the New York *Times* in 1930. In 1937, with four others, he had won a Pulitzer Prize for his coverage of science. Yet, nobody was quite prepared for the story that Bill Laurence would tell at the climax of the Pacific war, least of all Laurence himself.

Edwin L. James, the old World War I correspondent who had become managing editor of the *Times,* obviously couldn't grasp the significance of Laurence's inquiries when the reporter came to him in the spring of 1940 with a detailed memorandum about atomic energy.

"Go ahead and write it," James said, the invariable answer of an editor to something he doesn't understand.

Laurence warned, "I'll need a good deal of space to tell it properly."

"You may have a column and a half."

"I'll need more than that."

"Then make it two columns. There's a war on."

To the credit of Jimmy James and the *Times,* Laurence's story ran nearly seven columns on May 5, 1940. It disclosed for the first time that German and American physicists were working to develop atomic energy from an isotope of uranium. However, the reaction to the story was zero. Like Laurence's piece in the *Times* of January 31, 1939, reporting a Columbia University announcement that an atom of uranium had been split with an enormous release of energy, nobody seemed to care. Subsequently, Laurence submitted a detailed article on the subject to the *Saturday Evening Post,* which published it on September 7, 1940, after much checking with scientists, under the title, "The Atom Gives Up." But it seemed to Laurence, at least, that Washington couldn't have cared less.

From August 2, 1939, when Albert Einstein had written to President Roosevelt that it had become possible to construct an atomic bomb and that the Germans were working at it, the United States had proceeded on the great experiment with dismaying slowness. Until December 2, 1942, when Enrico Fermi had demonstrated the first nuclear chain reaction on a squash court under Stagg Field in Chicago, there had been intense doubt, even among scientists close to the project. But soon afterward, the genius and wealth of America were mobilized in secret to do what man had never done before — to unlock the power of a thousand suns on earth in one blinding release of energy that would wipe out a city and perhaps win the war.

Neither Bill Laurence nor any other journalist knew what was going on at that time, although the editors of the *Saturday Evening Post* should have been suspicious at the very least. Late in 1942, the *Post* was told to remove the September 7, 1940, issue from circulation and to notify the FBI if anyone so much as asked for a copy of the magazine. As for Laurence himself, he was subjected to a thorough check by the FBI because he already had demonstrated an astonishing amount of knowledge of the theory behind the atomic bomb. However, if he thought of being deeply involved in the biggest story of the war and one of the most significant of all time, it was only a dream. All he knew was that any story he wrote speculating on the atomic bomb was promptly returned from Byron Price's voluntary press censorship office with a request not to publish. It seemed that he was doomed to fight the war in Times Square.[106] The Pacific and Japan were far removed from his thoughts. As for Hiroshima, he knew only that there was such a city in Japan. Was there a place for a science writer? It seemed not.

The stories of the war correspondents and the tremendous impact of Joe Rosenthal's great picture of the flag-raising on Mount Suribachi left their mark on Bill Laurence, who by the spring of 1945 had passed his 57th birthday. It had never occurred to him that his own contribution might be as great until Jimmy James stopped him one day in the *Times*'s city room and said that a General Leslie R. Groves wanted to see him.

"What do you suppose he wants of me?" Laurence asked.

"Don't know," was the reply. "Better be here. He's coming tomorrow."

General Groves gave James and Laurence no inkling of his mission in their discussion next day, but asked for and received permission to borrow the reporter for work on a top-secret job. Laurence shrewdly suspected what was up and couldn't help needling the general. "If you want me to do any writing," he said, "I must be given access to first-hand sources. I hope you'll permit me to go to Tennessee, Washington, and New Mexico."

So it happened that a tense little man with the eyes of a scholar, the pressed-in nose of an unsuccessful prize-fighter, and the keen brain of a first-rate scientist vanished from his usual haunts in New York. Not even his wife knew where he was. In order to allay her alarm, it was arranged to plant a story in the *Times* under his by-line, dated London. But in reality, Laurence never saw London. He had been whisked inside the secret atomic empire headed by General Groves, the Manhattan Engineer District. Here, he worked in the cities that had been built to develop the $2 billion project — Oak Ridge, Tenn., Richland, Wash., and Los Alamos, N.M. And he associated with the world-renowned scientists who had been brought together to construct an atomic bomb that would bring about Japan's ruin.

Laurence was, in effect, the official historian of the project. More than that, he was the only journalist permitted to have an inside view of all its ramifications. Consequently, he was entrusted by General Groves and his associates with the responsibility of preparing all the public announcements and descriptions that were to be released once the first bomb was used as a weapon against the enemy. The trickiest part of the assignment was to develop cover stories to explain away the tests that might come to public attention and to account for the possibility of failure. The security on the story was the tightest of the war.

On July 12, 1945, after Laurence had been at work for two months and knew the climax was near, he wrote to James in a confidential letter: "The story is much bigger than I could imagine, fantastic, bizarre, fascinating and terrifying. . . . The world will not be the same after the day of the big event. A new era in civilization will have started. . . . After the story breaks I will be the only one with firsthand knowledge of it, which should give the *Times* a considerable edge. Much of it, however, will be kept on ice for some time." James sent the letter to Arthur Hays Sulzberger, the publisher, who scrawled across the top of it: "This looks like IT."

Near Alamagordo, N.M., in the great southwestern desert, all preparations for the first atomic test were completed on July 16. At dawn Laurence waited in a control tower five miles from Ground Zero, where the bomb was to be set off in its steel cage. "From the east," he wrote, "came the first faint signs of dawn. And just at that instant there rose as if from the bowels of the earth a light not of this world, the light of many suns in one. It was a sunrise such as the world had never seen. . . . On that moment hung eternity. Time stood still. Space contracted to a pin point. It was as though the earth had opened and the skies had split. One felt as though he had been privileged to witness the Birth of the World."

The announcement that went out to the press, however, was maddeningly prosaic, and it was sent in this form by the AP from Albuquerque, N.M.:

> An ammunition magazine exploded early today in a remote area of the Alamagordo Air Base reservation, producing a brilliant flash and blast, which were reported to have been observed as far away as Gallup, 235 miles northwest.

The native curiosity of American editors was not piqued in the slightest by the kind of ammunition that could produce so catastrophic an explosion. The cover story was published. Except for the disturbed citizenry of New Mexico, nobody wondered very much. The arrangements proceeded for the use of the bomb against Japan, including a vaguely phrased warning by President Truman during the Potsdam conference. As for Laurence, he was given sealed orders, put on an airplane, and headed for the Pacific, thinking that he would be the reporter on that first atomic flight. When he finally arrived at Tinian island after being delayed three days en route, he was crushed to discover that he was too late. The fist atomic bomber was scheduled to go next morning, August 6, 1945.

That was how it came about that Laurence, with the rest of the military spectators, watched the *Enola Gay* and two other B-29s take off that day from parallel runways at 2:45 a.m., Marianas time, on their 3,000-mile round-trip flight. The target, depending on the weather, was to be either Hiroshima, Kokura, or Nagasaki. As he watched the big bombers disappear into the night, Laurence was in the unenviable position of a man who had provided the world with the raw materials of history and expected to receive scant notice for it. Many another unsuspecting reporter would inherit the responsibility of telling the story, not he. Or so he thought.

The first reporter on the job was Bin Nakamura, sub-chief of the Domei bureau in Hiroshima. In a suburb of the city that morning of August 6, he had seen three enemy planes on what he guessed was a reconaissance mission. The air raid alarm had been sounded, then the all-clear. Nakamura had gone on with breakfast, seated on a mat inside his house, after coming in from his garden. At 9:15 a.m. (8:15, Hiroshima time) an earth-shaking blast flung him sprawling, and a wave of intense heat singed his face. Disregarding splintered window glass, he rushed outside and saw an orange ball of fire and smoke shooting up from the center of Hiroshima, two miles away. He got out his bicycle and raced furiously toward the Domei office. When he got there, he found only rubble. In common with the rest of the center of the city, the office had been vaporized and only the outer walls of the concrete building still stood. Of the Domei staff, some of whom were away on volunteer work, seven out of 20 were killed, two were injured seriously, and two were slightly burned. Tokuho Koyabashi, the chief, was fatally injured. Appalled by the death and destruction he had seen, Nakamura gathered as many details as he could. Twelve hours later, he arrived at a radio station in suburban Haramura and dictated a story to the only point he could reach, Okayama. It was the first story of what had happened to Hiroshima.*

While Nakamura didn't know what had hit the stricken city, the Japanese soon found out. The first word came in early on the morning of August 7, when a Domei monitorin¥ station outside Tokyo picked up President Truman's announcement that an atomic bomb had been

---

*In the spring of 1964, Nakamura retired from the Kyodo News Agency in Tokyo, successor to Domei, after many years of faithful service. He was still in excellent health at that time.

dropped on Hiroshima. Saiji Hasegawa, Domei's foreign news editor, was awakened and told the news, but he couldn't put it out immediately. The Japanese army tried to keep the destruction of Hiroshima a secret, issuing the following announcement at 6 a.m. on August 7:

> A small number of B-29s penetrated into Hiroshima city a little after 8 yesterday morning and dropped a small number of bombs. As a result, a considerable number of homes were reduced to ashes and fires broke out in various parts of the city. To this new type of bomb are attached parachutes and it appears as if these new bombs exploded in the air. Investigations are now being made with regard to the effectiveness of this bomb, which should not be regarded as slight.

But by that time the United States Office of War Information, under the direction of Edward W. Barrett, the overseas chief, was beaming its broadcasts of the story to all Japan. Millions of leaflets were being loaded at Tinian to be dropped from planes over the home islands. The Japanese were not in doubt for very long over what had hit them. Long afterward, the dread totals were issued: 78,150 dead, 13,983 missing, 9,428 seriously injured, and a city destroyed.

Curiously, the United States was extremely reticent at the outset to claim great damage. At the hour the bomb was dropped over Hiroshima, it was 6:15 a.m., August 5, in Washington. General Groves had not scheduled a presidential news release at the White House until 11 a.m. on August 6, Washington time. He knew that Colonel Paul W. Tibbets Jr., the pilot of the *Enola Gay,* had radioed Tinian fifteen minutes after the atomic strike, "Mission successful!" After the *Enola Gay* had landed at Tinian safely five and one-half hours later, there had been a great deal of awesome eyewitness detail. But the pall of smoke that billowed over Hiroshima had made it impossible for photographic reconaissance planes to get a decent picture. Therefore, General Groves decided to go with the dropping of the atomic bomb and announce the details of the destruction later.

At the White House, the reporters were told on the morning of August 6 that there would be an "important announcement" from the President at 11 a.m. It didn't arouse much interest. Some correspondents sent their assistants. Even so, the White House moved up the time to 10:45 a.m. and provided piles of publicity releases, including all the material over which Bill Laurence had labored during his secret mission. First, the President's announcement was read. The reporters grew tense. At the words that the new bomb had released the force of "more than 20,000 tons of TNT," there was a great surge toward the press handouts. The race for the telephones was on—and soon the bulletins were out.

The New York *Times,* of course, had many hours to prepare its paper next morning. Despite Laurence's service, it did not receive a break on the news, only an intimation. Well in advance, General Groves was thoughtful enough to alert Turner Catledge, the acting managing editor, and suggest the assignment of Sidney Shalett, the *Times*'s man at the War Department. On the weekend before the bomb was dropped, Catledge made all the necessary arrangements to cover a major story. When he received the first bulletin from Washington, he phoned Arthur Hays Sulzberger: "They dropped it—on Hiroshima."

On August 7, 1945, the *Times* ran the atomic story across 10 of its 38 pages, with this page 1 headline of eight columns:

FIRST ATOM BOMB DROPPED ON JAPAN;

MISSILE IS EQUAL TO 20,000 TONS OF TNT;

TRUMAN WARNS FOE OF A 'RAIN OF RUIN'

Even then, the White House and the War Department made no claims of major destruction, saying that "an impenetrable cloud of dust and smoke" hung over the target area. There was a UP story, quoting an Osaka radio announcement that all train service to Hiroshima and adjacent areas had been suspended. The Osaka radio by that time had also given the bare news of President Truman's statement, but nothing more. The awesome tale of Hiroshima developed in succeeding days, bit by bit, as the Japanese government anxiously debated whether to surrender.

Now, at last, Bill Laurence's moment came. The *Times* had disclosed in its August 7 issue (on page 5) that he had been the sole reportorial witness and chronicler of the story of the atomic bomb. On the next evening in Tinian, August 8, while he was having a beer at the Officers' Club, a messenger summoned him to duty. He was to fly with the second atomic bombing mission next morning as the official reporter. At 3:50 a.m., August 9, when the B-29 *The Great Artiste* took off from Tinian, the 57-year-old correspondent could see for himself how an atomic bomber looked on its way to wipe out a city. He rode in one of the two B-29s that accompanied *The Great Artiste,* with the second atomic bomb in its bomb bay. This, he wrote, is what happened when the plane arrived over Nagasaki at 12:01 p.m.:

> We heard the prearranged signal on our radio, put on our arc welder's glasses, and watched tensely the maneuverings of the strike ship about a half mile in front of us.

'There she goes,' someone said.

Out of the belly of *The Great Artiste* what looked like a black object went downward. . . . A giant flash broke through the dark barrier of our arc welder's lenses and flooded our cabin with intense light.

A tremendous blast wave struck our ship and made it tremble from nose to tail. This was followed by four more blasts in rapid succession, each resounding like the boom of cannon fire hitting our plane from all directions.

Observers in the tail of our ship saw a giant ball of fire rise as though from the bowels of the earth, belching forth enormous white smoke rings. Next, they saw a giant pillar of purple fire, ten thousand feet high, shooting skyward with enormous speed. . . .

Only about forty-five seconds had passed. Awestruck, we watched it shoot upward like a meteor coming from the earth instead of from outer space, becoming ever more alive as it climbed skyward through the white clouds. . . .

Then, just as it appeared as though the thing had settled down into a state of permanence, there came shooting out of the top a giant mushroom that increased the height of the pillar to a total of 45,000 feet. . . .

We landed in Okinawa in the afternoon, our tanks nearly empty, and there, to our great relief, was No. 77 [*The Great Artiste*]. . . . While we were refueling we learned that the Soviet Union had entered the war against Japan.

That account, and his preparatory work for the government, earned Bill Laurence his second Pulitzer Prize. It also made him the first, and for at least the succeeding generation, the only correspondent to witness an atomic strike in wartime. A plane-load of correspondents, chaperoned by Lieutenant Colonel J. F. Reagan McCrary, had flown from Washington through Europe and India on the supposition that they were to cover a "big story," but on August 6 they had only been able to read about the dropping of the atomic bomb in the newspapers of Calcutta. That was the closest anybody came to rivaling the work of one of the oldest — and most effective — war correspondents of all time.

Nagasaki meant the end for Japan. Casualties later were estimated by the US Strategic Bombing Survey at 35,000 killed and 60,000 injured, with 44 percent of the city destroyed. On August 10, Japan announced acceptance of the terms of the Potsdam Declaration with a reservation that ensured the continued reign of the emperor. Domei was permitted to broadcast the news outside Japan to stave off more attacks, if possible, but the Japanese people were told by the Japanese Board of Information to continue their resistance. On August 12, at 9:33 p.m., the New York office of the UP flashed a false report of the Japanese surrender, but killed it three minutes later. Subsequently, the UP offered a reward for the conviction of the author of the hoax, but nobody ever collected. Finally, after an attempted insurrection in Tokyo had failed, Emperor Hirohito on August 15 broadcast his cabinet's acceptance without qualification of the Potsdam Declaration. That meant unconditional surrender. At 7 p.m. on August 14, Washington time, President Truman called a special press conference at the White House, signified his satisfaction, named General MacArthur to receive the formal surrender, and told the Japanese to order their forces to stop fighting.

The news crowded the wires, the cables, and the air waves. Jubilant crowds cut loose with victory celebrations, the wildest of all by people who jammed into New York City's Times Square.[107] Yet, in the Pacific, the killing and the destruction went on. There was no cease-fire order on either side.

Bill Laurence's work as a war correspondent was over. But for the rest, there was still much to do. Of them all, the correspondent who had won the most respect, and even in a way taken the place of Ernie Pyle, was Homer Bigart of the New York *Herald Tribune.* That night when all America was celebrating peace, he was riding toward Japan with a cluster of B-29s for a raid on the small industrial city of Kumagaya. Aboard the bomber *City of Saco,* Bigart and the crew heard a San Francisco announcer say, "I hope all you boys out there are as happy as we are at this moment. People are yelling and screaming and whistles are blowing." To which a crewman sourly replied, "Yeah, they're screaming and we're flying." The B-29s unloaded their bombs and returned to Guam despite determined Japanese antiaircraft fire. It was the last raid of the war.

In subsequent dispatches, Bigart described the ruins of Japan. Joining Col. Tex McCrary's group of delayed newsmen, direct from the Pentagon, the big *Herald Tribune* correspondent ventured into Hiroshima. On the outskirts, he saw destruction that resembled the ruins of Europe's bombed cities. But in the city, he reported, "there was only flat appalling desolation, the starkness accentuated by bare, blackened tree trunks and the occasional shell of a reinforced concrete building." A month after the atomic blast, he found that survivors were "still dying at the rate of about one hundred daily." The descriptions he and his associates filed of Hiroshima touched off a shocked reaction in the United States. Few stories about the consequences of atomic bombing had such an impact, the only one that exceeded it being John Hersey's exhaustive and lengthy study of Hiroshima long afterward.

General MacArthur and his staff went to Japan in his private plane on August 30. Both Allied and Japanese reporters clustered about him at Atsugi Airport, a strange fraternity bent on covering the same story. MacArthur held a casual and impromptu press conference, just as if he had been talking with old friends, which impressed the Japanese. After that, despite the most earnest warnings of the Japanese newsmen, some of the Americans took off for Tokyo. They wanted to describe the ruins, of course; but, even more, they wanted to find the woman who had been broadcasting over the Japanese radio for so long as Tokyo Rose. Bigart and Arch Steele, who now was on the New York *Herald Tribune* staff, were among those who made that first expedition. With them went Gordon Walker and Frank Robertson of the *Christian Science Monitor,* Frank Kluckhohn of the New York *Times,* Clark Lee of INS, Robert Reubens of Reuters, and a number of others. Thus, the occupation of Japan began.

On September 2, aboard the USS *Missouri* in Tokyo Bay, more than 200 Allied correspondents and four Japanese covered the formal surrender by the Japanese. It was an anticlimax. Bigart, in a plain and straightforward report, began his story: "Japan, paying for her desperate throw of the dice at Pearl Harbor, passed from the ranks of the major powers at 9:05 a.m. today when Foreign Minister Mamoru Shigemitsu signed the document of unconditional surrender." Masuo Kato, covering for Domei, had far different thoughts than the mere formal beginning of a news story calculated to take a page 1 headline. As he watched General MacArthur and reflected on the weakness of General Wainwright, the hero of Bataan and Corregidor, the Japanese journalist couldn't help wondering. "When Perry's ships came, the people of Japan did not welcome them, but they had no choice except to yield," he wrote. "Now that the Americans had come again, there was, perhaps, much of the same feeling. How long would they stay? How many would come? What would happen to Japan? Those questions were foremost in the minds of Japan that day. There were few who recognized the occupation forces as benefactors any more than Perry had been regarded as a benefactor. I was wondering how many years Japan had been set back."

Having returned to the United States to work among the scientists and in the laboratories in which he had found so much world-shaking news, Bill Laurence was not as discouraged. He dared to hope that the atomic bomb — and the refinements that were certain to follow — would make peace inevitable. "These earth-destroying weapons, now being constantly reduced in size and increased in power," he wrote, "thus make it certain that no nation, no matter how powerful, could dare risk a thermonuclear war."

Out of the 70,000,000 who fought in World War II, with an estimated death toll of 17,000,000 who died in battle and 18,000,000 civilians who were killed in other ways, the total number of war correspondents on all sides could not have amounted to much more than a brigade. The United States, by all odds, had the largest number of working journalists at the war fronts, with 1,646 accredited correspondents in service, of whom 37 were killed and 112 wounded. This did not take into account the combat correspondents who worked for *Stars and Stripes,* the soldier's newspaper, and *Yank,* the GI magazine, but their numbers were never great. Moreover, with the exception of the British, no other belligerent power sent independent war correspondents to the front in any significant number, although the Germans and the Russians, in particular, organized efficient groups of propagandists for their newspapers and radio and used soldier correspondents freely. As for the Japanese correspondents, many underwent great hardship at the front. Yet, whether these observers worked for a free or a controlled press, they did not exceed a few thousand in total numbers at any time during the war.[108]

It may be taken for granted that the world tended to see the war most frequently in the terms presented by the wire services—the AP, UP, INS, Reuters, and Tass and, to a lesser extent, DNB and Domei. As for the newspaper correspondents, those who worked for powerful individual newspapers, newspaper groups, or radio organizations exerted a greater effect on public opinion than their fellows. Finally, there were a few journalists of outstanding talent who stood far above the rank and file—Ernie Pyle, Homer Bigart, William L. Laurence, Alan Moorehead, Edward R. Murrow, Ilya Ehrenburg. Each in his own way was more important to his own country than an army when home front morale was sagging and all seemed lost.

With the end of the war in Japan, the demobilization of the correspondents in the Allied nations was even swifter than that of their victorious armies. A hard-core group remained to cover the war crimes trials and the execution of the culprits. But after that, the slow and painful news of reconstruction and reconciliation persuaded only the leading news organizations to leave correspondents in Japan and Germany. The bitter division of the wartime coalition, which left Russia glowering at the West, caught the journalists of the United States, Britain, and France ill-prepared; few, unhappily, knew much about the Soviet Union, and even fewer could speak the language. Despite the possession of the atomic bomb, the United States soon found itself at a disadvantage with the well-prepared Russians in a propaganda struggle for world opinion. Thus, while the guns of World War II had fallen silent and the bombs no longer dropped, there was no peace. The most durable of all war correspondents, Herbert Bayard Swope, was the first to call it the Cold War.

8 The Peace That Failed

THE PEACE CORRESPONDENTS

During the sultry summer of 1944, James Reston began publishing the secret papers of the Dumbarton Oaks conference in the New York *Times*. Through his enterprise, the initial planning for the United Nations was spread before the world. It was his special virtue as a journalist that he made the reporting of peace as exciting as that of war.

Reston did not act alone in disclosing the Dumbarton Oaks proceedings. When Under Secretary of State Edward R. Stettinius protested to the *Times*, Arthur Hays Sulzberger coolly replied: "I think, Mr. Stettinius, that the *Times* will feel compelled to continue Reston's series. The documents are authentic, and the people have a right to know what they contain. It is their interests that are at stake in this meeting."

The frustrated government officials then turned loose the FBI on Reston and the *Times* to try to find his sources, an unpleasant maneuver that ill became the United States, but finally gave up.[1] Despite Reston's supposed interference, the delegates of the United States, the United Kingdom, and the Soviet Union successfully completed their talks at the lavish Dumbarton Oaks estate in Georgetown, on the fringes of Washington, D.C.

Reston's example of independence as a diplomatic correspondent soon encouraged others. In the waning days of the war in Europe, Bert Andrews of the New York *Herald Tribune* broke the story of the secret UN voting agreement at Yalta. Under it, the Soviet Union was to receive three votes in the General Assembly, its own and the captive ballots of the Ukraine and Byelo-Russia. While the decision was one of the least important at the controversial Yalta conference, its disclosure served once again to underline the futility of a policy of secrecy in areas where

248

it didn't apply. As Sulzberger had said, "The people have a right to know."

At the UN Conference on International Organization at San Francisco, beginning April 25, 1945, the New York *Times* demonstrated its leadership again by publishing a daily four-page wirephoto edition in San Francisco. Once more, Reston and his colleagues demonstrated that it was possible to cover the news of closed as well as open meetings without doing violence to world concord. The result was that the new world organization won a favorable press at the outset, for most of the correspondents followed Reston's lead.[2] Few since Blowitz's time had established such prestige in the diplomatic field.

Thus, the United Nations at birth was a wonder child. And if Reston could take a fair share of the credit for the favor with which it was regarded in the United States, he also had to accept part of the blame for overselling it. Reinforcing the glowing promises of world leaders, who should have known better, the press as a whole helped raise public expectations for the United Nations out of all proportion to its powers. Inevitably, disappointments were to follow.

No doubt the United Nations would have been buffeted by every political storm whatever its location in those tense postwar years. But by being set down in New York City,[3] center of a great engine of publicity, it could not hope to escape being turned into what Sir Winston Churchill inelegantly called a "brawling cockpit." For it became that, too.

If the world's diplomats had any lingering notion of working in private at their leisure in 1946, as they had at Geneva in the days of the League, they were quickly disabused. The opening salvo of publicity in the Iranian case, when Andrei A. Gromyko of the Soviet Union became a world figure by walking out on the Security Council at Hunter College in the Bronx, stirred attention in the United Nations to fever pitch. More than 1,000 correspondents from all parts of the world had seen him and understood that Russia would be difficult to deal with in the peace making. It scarcely mattered that Russian troops eventually were withdrawn from Iran, despite Gromyko's protest over the UN's decision to hear the case. The pattern had been set.[4]

THE COLD WAR BEGINS

When Stalin had to withdraw the Red Army from northern Iran after the United States and the Western allies took public positions against the Soviet Union's land grab in the first major case before the UN Security Council, he turned his attention to Greece and Turkey.[5] This should have been no surprise. In what amounted to a "hate America" campaign, the Soviet dictator's aims in opposing the West had been stated in his speech of February 9, 1946, before he had tried the Iranian approach.[6]

To quote Dean Acheson, the Under Secretary of State at the time and later President Truman's Secretary of State:

> The [Stalin] offensive was mounted on territory thought most favorable to the interior lines of the Soviets, where their military power was superior, and on political issues in international discussion, where stubborn and skillful opposition to American proposals could be successful with little cost.
>
> Geographically, therefore, the attack was concentrated along Russia's borders in Eastern Europe and the Middle East, where Soviet physical position was strongest and that of the United States weakest. Politically it centered against efforts to create a United Nations military force and the United States plan to put atomic energy under effective international control.[7]

Poland became the first victim of Soviet aggression in the postwar era, and the Balkans followed. Pressures mounted on Greece through Yugoslavia and Bulgaria to detach the Greek northern provinces. And in Turkey, the Soviets demanded participation in defense of the Turkish Straits leading to the Black Sea, tantamount to the occupation of Turkey.

At the UN's temporary headquarters at Lake Success, there was a sense of despair when it became clear that the Soviet veto would render the Security Council powerless and make the General Assembly in its temporary site at a former skating rink in Flushing Meadow nothing more than a debating society. As one of the members of the first permanent press corps at the world organization, I expected to be recalled at almost any time by my newspaper and either returned to my old political assignment or sent abroad.[8]

Secretary General Trygve Lie, a big, cheerful Norwegian, had been forewarned by the violence of an initial UN debate over the Greek problem in London and wrote long afterward: "Here was another chilly forewarning of the 'Cold War' to come — the (Soviet) clumsiness, the rigidity of position, the refusal to participate, even in non-essentials, in the give-and-take and the hammering out of acceptable positions that are the very life blood of politics and diplomacy in the Western democracies."[9]

As for the effect on the UN itself, Lie's fears were aroused at the outset by the Soviet diplomatic attack. "It was a bad omen," he wrote "and a dull chill descended on my optimism. . . . I was deeply shocked by the bitterness of the debate, and alarmed at what the public reaction might be. I did not want popular good will for the UN to be dissipated at the very beginning."[10]

But that is what happened. The huge corps of correspondents at the opening of the UN sessions in New York dwindled rapidly as soon as it became clear that nothing could be expected of the UN in cases involving disputes with the Soviet Union. Only the AP and the New York *Times* and one or two others maintained more than a single correspondent after the opening salvos in the Iranian case.

Among those who remained, Thomas J. Hamilton of the New York *Times* had the largest staff with four people, and the New York *Post* kept on three. The AP, with Max Harrelson in charge, usually had one or two others on call. So did Reuters, with Michael Frye. Agence France-Presse, the postwar successor to Havas, was represented by Jean Lagrange and INS by Pierre J. Huss. Robert Manning was the UP's first correspondent.

The earliest British correspondents included Alex Faulkner and Barbara Fischer-Williams of the London *Daily Telegraph* and Henry Brandon of the London *Sunday Times*. Sven Ahman, whose father had been a correspondent in Berlin for the *Dagens Nyheter,* represented the same paper at the UN. Peter Freuchen, the old Arctic explorer, turned correspondent for the *Politiken* of Copenhagen and Max Beer served the *Neue Zürcher Zeitung* of Switzerland. With William R. Frye of the *Christian Science Monitor* and an occasional correspondent from the New York *Herald Tribune,* that just about made up the regular corps of UN correspondents that hung on through the early years of the Cold War at New York headquarters.[11]

But the major American initiatives in international affairs took place elsewhere. On March 12, 1947, President Truman sent a message to Congress demanding immediate action to forestall Soviet pressures on Greece and Turkey and obtained passage in a little more than two months on May 15.[12] And on June 5, Secretary of State George Marshall called for American aid for beleaguered Western Europe in his historic commencement address at Harvard, with the result that Congress appropriated $12 billion in European aid for the next four years.[13]

Now the struggle was joined. The adoption of the Truman Doctrine for Greece and Turkey and the Marshall Plan for the support of Western Europe were the twin blows of the United States that opened the

Western phase of the Cold War that was to last for 45 years. The watchword thereafter was *containment* of the Soviet Union as it was first enunciated by the head of General Marshall's policy planning staff, George F. Kennan.[14] But sooner rather than later, it would lead inevitably to war, as the nation learned to its shock and surprise when a Soviet ally in the Far East, North Korea, opened fire on an American ally, South Korea, within three years.

STALEMATE IN KOREA

As the summer of 1950 approached, the UN was at the nadir of its influence. The handful of American and foreign correspondents who remained at headquarters gloomily concluded that the war everybody seemed to expect would be a curtain-raiser to World War III. Nor was there much cheer in the radio broadcasts from time to time of the regular UN commentators, Pauline Frederick of NBC, Larry Lesueur of CBS and John MacVane of ABC.

From the time of the Truman Doctrine and the Marshall Plan, the struggle with the Soviet Union had deepened. On April 1, 1948, the Soviet Union had clamped a land blockade on the allied part of Berlin, after which the United States supplied 2,000,000 Berliners by air until Moscow lifted the blockade on September 30, 1949, after 2,343,315 tons of food and coal had been flown into the beleaguered German city.[15]

In the previous week, on September 23, President Truman had announced that the Russians had exploded an atomic bomb of their own, and early in 1950 he had ordered the US Atomic Energy Commission to "continue with the development of the so-called hydrogen bomb, the ultimate nuclear weapon.[16]

Then, on a beautiful summer morning, Sunday, June 25, 1950, North Korea's Communist armies swarmed south of the 38th parallel to invade South Korea. At the request of the United States, the UN Security Council went into emergency session at Lake Success. When Russia's Jacob Malik as Gromyko's replacement boycotted the session on orders from Moscow, his fellow-members of the Council voted for intervention against the Communist invaders.

By that time, the Americans already were in the war and fighting for their lives against the North Koreans. The difference the UN made was that General MacArthur became not only the American commander but also the UN military chief, with 15 nations providing about 60,000 foreign troops to assist the small initial American force and the wavering South Korean army. With the UN reinforcements came foreign correspondents from all parts of the world.[17]

Yet, nobody inside or outside the UN went into the Korean War with any enthusiasm. In the thick of the fighting, a GI once said, "It's a war we can't win, we can't lose, we can't quit." The correspondents spread the remark widely in their dispatches because they concurred. It also was an expression of mingled frustration and resentment in the United States. To a large extent, it explained why the hard and hazardous work of the correspondents, 17 of whom were killed in action, including 10 Americans, failed to arouse the nation.

Peter Kalischer of the UP watched the first American infantrymen go into action in Korea on July 5, saw them break and run before Communist tanks and himself narrowly escaped capture. When he walked into a makeshift pressroom at Taejon nearly three days later, he had a tragic story to tell. But neither he nor any of the other 70 correspondents who were in Korea at the time (only five had been around at the beginning) could get much out unless they flew back to Japan. Censorship was tight.

In 24th Division headquarters in Taejon, there was only one military line to Tokyo over which the correspondents could phone their copy. They had to stand in line, rationed to a few minutes each, and dictate bulletins — and sometimes a little detail.

The bad news came in small doses. Moreover, General MacArthur made things worse by decreeing a policy of self-censorship (he couldn't spare enough people who were qualified censors.) As a result, the correspondents never knew when they would be accused of giving aid and comfort to the enemy, and some of them suffered unjustly. The policy did not last long, giving way to a more conventional system when MacArthur had the time and personnel to set it up; but while it existed, it complicated an already difficult situation.[18]

There was no place to hide in Korea. If you were in the field, you were under continual attack, and there was no way of explaining that a war correspondent was protected by international conventions. Ray Richards of INS, who wrote his first story of the war on June 28, was killed in action July 9. Five other American newsmen and photographers were also killed that month. Maurice Chanteloup, an Agence France-Presse correspondent, was captured. Burton Crane of the New York *Times* and Frank Gibney of Time, Inc., were injured in the blowup of the Han River bridges outside Seoul on the first day of the retreat. Yet, correspondents kept coming. By September, 238 were accredited to Korea, and eventually there were 270; but less than a quarter of that number, by the best estimates, ever were at the front at any one time. As for the hard day-to-day coverage, no more than a score stuck it out through the war.

Marguerite Higgins of the New York *Herald Tribune* became the most discussed correspondent of the war and one of the most daring. Early on, she was ordered back to Japan because, as General Walton H. Walker put it, "There are no facilities at the front for ladies." Miss Higgins, who had been viewing the front from foxholes, violently objected. With the support of her newspaper, she appealed to General MacArthur, who permitted her to remain.

She was in the fifth wave of Marines at Inchon on September 15 when MacArthur made his first offensive move, halting the retreat.[19] It was her Trib colleague, Homer Bigart, who carried off the honors by double-filing his story of the Inchon landing from Korea and Tokyo, hoping one would get through the censors. The Tokyo copy was cleared, and Bigart had a beat.[20]

The correspondents, including Miss Higgins, were among the first into recaptured Seoul and crossed the 38th parallel with the troops when MacArthur gave the order.[21] Although the United States was privately warned on October 3 by K. M. Panikkar, India's Ambassador to China, that the Communists would enter the war if the UN forces crossed the 38th parallel, nobody on the UN side believed it at top level. MacArthur's fast-moving forces took the North Korean capital of Pyongyang on October 19, and about 135,000 North Korean troops surrendered.

It scarcely seemed a matter of concern when Glenn Stackhouse of the UP learned on October 25 that a Chinese prisoner had been taken by an American unit. But a few nights later, when Joe Quinn of the UP had to swim across the Kuryong River to escape a Chinese attack, there was no longer any doubt that Mao's forces had entered the war.* Even MacArthur agreed after Chinese air and cavalry strikes, informing the UN Security Council on November 5 that he was "in contact" with the Chinese military forces.[22]

Still, MacArthur remained sufficiently unconcerned to spend Thanksgiving Day, November 23, in Tokyo, and promised his American troops they'd have Christmas dinner at home if they reached the Yalu River at the North Korean–Chinese border. They did, but found out quickly enough that MacArthur had made an empty promise.[23] On November

---

*Albert Ravenholt of the Chicago *Daily News* warned of a Chinese attack as early as August 1950.

25, the Chinese began probing attacks. Next day, amid bugle calls, whistles, and the clash of cymbals, 250,000 Chinese regulars attacked before dawn, and the UN forces weren't prepared for it.

To resist the combined Chinese–North Korean offensive, MacArthur had 205,000 men at the time, mostly Americans and South Koreans, but also including two British brigades, one Turkish, and a battalion each from Canada, the Philippines, the Netherlands, and Thailand. What the Chinese did was to strike at a gap in the X Corps of Mac-Arthur's American forces that were strung out along 78 miles of a slender road between Hungnam and the Chosin reservoir.[24]

Keyes Beech of the Chicago *Daily News,* who stayed three days with the 1st Marine Division, which bore the brunt of the assault, called it a "trial by blood and ice." The mercury was 15 below zero in a hostile land. The correspondent wrote of the Marine breakthrough after being almost surrounded by the attacking Chinese: "Whatever this campaign was—retreat, withdrawal or defeat—one thing can be said with certainty. Not in the Marine Corps' long and bloody history has there been anything like it. And if you'll pardon a personal recollection, not at Tarawa or Iwo Jima, where casualties were much greater, did I see men suffer so much. The wonder isn't they fought their way out against overwhelming odds but that they were able to survive the cold and fight at all."[25]

After the Marines were able to bridge a river at Koto-ri under heavy fire, they reached safety, and the Chinese were at last beaten off. As Major General Oliver Smith said at the time, "Gentlemen, we are not retreating. We are merely attacking in another direction."[26]

From that time on, the war seesawed across the 38th parallel, the boundary between the two Koreas, throughout the winter. Then suddenly, on March 24, 1951, General MacArthur in effect defied President Truman's orders not to make any declaration on foreign policy and issued the sternest warning of a broadened war to the Chinese Communists. This time, the crisis wasn't in the field, it was in Washington.

After midnight on April 11, 1951, calls went out from the White House that the President would have an important statement at 1 a.m. William H. (Political Bill) Lawrence of the New York *Times,* who had covered the Korean fighting, was one of the first to arrive. He warned his office, then put a photographer on an open telephone line to the *Times*'s newsroom. At 1:04 a.m., he rushed from the White House with the news that President Truman had removed MacArthur. For 28 minutes, he dictated his story for the post-midnight edition, and at 1:46 a.m. the *Times* was on the street, ahead of the competition.

The radio, of course, had had the first break on the news, but the hour was so late in the populous centers of the eastern United States that its impact was not as great as that of the press later in the morning.[27] When the nation learned what had happened, the public's perplexity over the Korean War deepened. It was as if Alexander the Great had been removed from command of his triumphant legions.

Lieutenant General Matthew Ridgway, MacArthur's successor, took over for the rest of the war with 150,000 Americans, the larger South Korean army, and 60,000 foreign combatants. The contrast between Ridgway, the soldier-diplomat, and MacArthur was striking in its effect on the eventual outcome of the conflict. By June 13, 1951, the new Supreme Commander had forced the North Korean-Chinese armies back across the 38th parallel; and in the UN Security Council, upon orders from Moscow, Jacob A. Malik of the Soviet Union proposed a truce.[28]

The talks began at Kaesong on July 10 in the stalemated war, but it would be many weary months before a cease-fire agreement was signed. The fighting men on the UN side never really understood, as a group, why they were in Korea, and the correspondents, even the best ones, never were able to explain it cogently to the nation.

There was an epilogue to the conflict after General Eisenhower was elected President in 1952. In fulfillment of a pledge he had made in his campaign against President Truman, Ike traveled to the Korean battlefields for six days but his whereabouts remained secret from the public at the time to ensure his safety until December 5, 1952, when he was on his way back to Washington. Then Don Whitehead of the AP, one of three pool reporters, wrote a masterful account of what he called "The Great Deception." It won him the second of his two Pulitzer Prizes that were awarded to him during the war.[29]

Despite the President-elect's trip, the peace making was not easily accomplished. The new Secretary of State, John Foster Dulles, who always fancied himself as a manipulator of press and public opinion, fell into a dispute with some of the correspondents with whom he had dined in April 1953 about the outcome of the peace making. Afterwards, the result was a series of articles in the New York *Times* and other papers that suggested the United States was about to accept a partitioned Korea. However, since the identity of the informant was kept secret under the Lindley Rule,* the confusion was twice compounded.

---

*The rule, named after its originator, Ernest Lindley of *Newsweek,* specifies that the reporter will not identify the source but will use the source's information. It is also called "reporting on background."

Those who were left out of the Dulles briefing took pleasure in identifying him as the source of the "split Korea" story, but the White House issued a denial. James Reston wound things up neatly in the *Times* as follows: "The art of denying the truth without actually lying is as old as government itself. . . . In announcing that the reported policy on Korea . . . was 'without foundation of fact' the White House denied what was essentially true about Korean policy."[30]

A little more than three months later, Reston's plaint was shown to have been justified. The "foundation of fact" was supplied on July 27, 1953, when the cease-fire finally was agreed upon, and the war ended. Korea was partitioned at the 38th parallel, and the weight of Communist pressure shifted toward more promising Western weak spots in Asia.

THE THAW

The Moscow radio announced at 4 a.m. on March 6, 1953, that Joseph Stalin had died at 9:50 the previous night. In this manner, the world learned that nearly three decades of a reign of Byzantine intrigue and unexampled ferocity in Russia had come to an end.

Harrison E. Salisbury, the lean, sandy-haired New York *Times* correspondent, had to wait until 9 a.m. for his story to be cleared through censorship and transmitted. When he left the telegraph office at last, he was astonished to find the troops of the Ministry of Internal Affairs, the MVD, had moved into the central part of the city with tanks. As Salisbury quickly concluded, that meant the boss of the MVD, Lavrenti Pavlovich Beria, could make himself the master of Russia at once if he chose to do so. Why he did not, nobody outside the Kremlin ever knew; the MVD kept its grip on Moscow until March 9, then unaccountably retreated.

The follow up to the Beria mystery became public knowledge months later as Georgi Malenkov sought to consolidate his rule as Stalin's successor. The luckless Beria was arrested within three months and executed in December 1953. Although the correspondents were permitted in their stories to infer that the deed had been done in the blood-stained cellar of Lubianka Prison, tales went around that Beria had been surprised, shot, and killed in his own office. Nor was this the only rumor of foul play in the Kremlin. Another was that the 73-year-old Stalin was stricken when he excitedly tried to call for help to quell a revolt in the party presidium. Another, even more widely circulated, was that, while he lay ill, he had been poisoned.

None of this, obviously, could go through censorship. As long as the correspondents remained in the Soviet Union, they were sealed up and permitted to send only the approved developments of the party line.[31] Truly, as Winston Churchill had said at Fulton, Mo., on March 5, 1946, "From Stettin in the Baltic to Trieste in the Adriatic, an iron curtain has descended across the continent."[32] And so it remained, for the influence of Stalin, even in death, could not easily be exorcised.

Stalin's removal brought about no immediate release to Russia, nor were the correspondents aware of any major changes under Malenkov. They knew that a great power struggle was under way in the Kremlin, and they were already aware that Nikita S. Khrushchev was likely to ascend to the dictatorship in place of Malenkov eventually. But by the beginning of 1954, nine months after Stalin's death, the entire regular corps of Western correspondents in Moscow consisted of five men — Richard R. Kasischke, AP; Kenneth Brodney, UP; Sidney Wieland, Reuters; Jean Nau, Agence France-Presse; and Salisbury of the New York *Times*, who was then on leave in the United States.

William L. Ryan, the AP's foreign news analyst, who visited Moscow at the time, wrote that the correspondents' position was impossible. They were unable to drive their own cars, but had to be chauffeured. Their telephones were bugged. Red tape and bucreaucracy frustrated any attempt at independence. The five men worked 14–16 hours a day, seven days a week because they had no relief in their offices. "And," Ryan concluded grimly, "there is the ever-present censor."[33]

For any who were inclined to rebel against such pressures, the fate of Bill Oatis and George Polk was a powerful deterrent. Oatis of the AP had been thrown into a Czech prison after a trumped-up trial in Prague. And Polk of CBS had been found slain on a Greek beach while looking for the Greek Communist leader, Marcos Vafiades.

Early in February 1955, there was a break in the Kremlin intrigues when a visiting Hearst team went to Moscow for interviews with Khrushchev, Marshal Nikolai Bulganin, Marshal Georgi Zhukov, and the crusty old diplomatic undertaker, Foreign Minister Vyacheslav M. Molotov. The US Navy at the time was evacuating 15,000 Chinese Nationalist troops from the Tachen Islands, and Khrushchev was voluble in his assurances that the Chinese Communists wouldn't interfere.

That made an immediate impression on the visitors, William Randolph Hearst Jr., Kingsbury Smith, and Frank Conniff. And before they left, they had another story; for on February 8, Khrushchev brought about the downfall of Premier Malenkov with Bulganin as his temporary successor. However, the Hearst team returned convinced that Khrushchev was the real boss in the Kremlin as the First Secretary of the Communist Party. They were right, and they won a Pulitzer Prize for their perceptive reporting.[34]

A period of "de-Stalinization" set in under Khrushchev, even though he did not formally assume the Soviet premiership until March 27, 1958, and he lasted only six years after that. He began with a "secret speech" before the 20th Communist Party Congress in Moscow on February 14, 1956, in which he denounced Stalin and ushered in a period called "the thaw" in which he professed to seek relaxed relations with the West in general and the United States in particular. That had been the title of an Ilya Ehrenburg book.[35]

It didn't amount to much of a thaw, although Khrushchev did make several gestures in the beginning—signature of an Austrian State Treaty, an armistice in the Indochina War during a Far Eastern conference in Geneva, and a 12-member Russian visit to Iowa in response to an invitation from Lauren K. Soth of the Des Moines *Register* to study "the greatest feed livestock area in the world."[36]

But there were riots in Poland which weakened the position of Wladyslaw Gomulka, the Polish Communist leader. And in Hungary, when there were demonstrations in Budapest in favor of the Poles, the police opened fire; but Russian troops had to be called in to put down what turned into a full-scale revolution in 1956.[37]

Nor did the Russian actions in the Suez War do anything to restore the Kremlin's damaged position. It was the United States, acting on President Eisenhower's initiative, that forced a cease-fire on the British, French, and Israelis on November 7, 1956, thus sparing the defeated Egyptians from further damage. The Russians were put in the position of supporting the American initiative, although the Kremlin's propaganda machine might have taken greater advantage of the rift in the ranks of the West.[38]

However, if there was any Western complacency over the seeming weakness of the Khrushchev regime, it was severely jolted on October 5, 1957, by a Tass announcement that the first *Sputnik* had been put into global orbit, inaugurating the space race in a blaze of electronic reporting and old-fashioned print headlines. Although the British and French rather calmly accepted the Soviet lead in space, the American press fairly howled that it presaged a national disaster—an exhibition of the American habit of self-criticism at its worst. Nor was there much satisfaction in the United States when a 30-pound satellite was shot into orbit the following year. It was too small.[39]

Thereafter, a few more correspondents were admitted into the Soviet Union, but one of the best, A. M. Rosenthal of the New York *Times,* a future executive editor of the paper, was unceremoniously ordered out of Warsaw. His fault was that he had "written very deeply and in detail about the internal situation, party matters and leadership matters," according to an official at the Polish Foreign Ministry, who added that "the Polish government cannot tolerate such reporting."

As Rosenthal, his wife, and three sons moved out to Vienna on their way to their next assignment, Japan, the small band of Western correspondents behind the Iron Curtain absorbed the lesson. Thaw or not, everybody was on trial who did not conform to the peculiar Soviet concept of journalism.[40]

Khrushchev's thaw also resulted in an interchange of visits in which Anastas Mikoyan, his First Deputy Foreign Minister, went to the United States briefly in the winter of 1959 and Vice President Richard Nixon turned up in the Soviet Union from July 23 to August 5.[41] These were a preliminary to Khrushchev's own tour of the United States from September 15 to 28, with 39 Soviet correspondents accompanying him. With the support of the Premier's son-in-law, Alexei I. Adzhubei, the editor of *Izvestia,* the Soviet journalists for the first time tried to cover the news as it happened. If Khrushchev praised the US economy or found broad support among the American people for the policies of its government, that was the way it went into *Pravda* and *Izvestia* for once. There was even an air reminiscent of an American political campaign with Soviet photographers delightedly taking shots of their burly premier in a butcher's apron in Iowa.[42]

Of course, Khrushchev had his troubles. Wherever he went, he was asked to explain his celebrated threat to the United States, "We will bury you." At the National Press Club in Washington, he retorted that he meant it in its historical sense, not in any physical sense. In Los Angeles, when Mayor Morris Poulson was critical of the proposed interment, the visitor angrily threatened to go home. He was also upset because he wasn't permitted to go to Disneyland.

The Khrushchev tour was a natural for TV—a Hollywood can-can dance that the Russian viewed as immoral, a mob scene on an Iowa farm, a formal luncheon at the Waldorf Astoria in New York City, where the visitor was serenaded with "The Star-Spangled Banner," a disarmament speech at the UN, and, finally, a private meeting with President Eisenhower at Camp David during which the President let himself be persuaded to consider a summit meeting the following year.

From the work of 375 touring correspondents and much local and national TV photo ops, Khrushchev emerged as an international curiosity. The impression he made on America was somewhere between a traveling salesman and a clown, but over Soviet TV, the kinescopes of his best moments portrayed him as a conquering hero.[43]

However, if the Soviet leader had hoped to stimulate good will for the Soviet Union in his American travels, subsequent events must have jarred his complacency, for on May 1, 1960, Francis Gary Powers and his U-2 spy plane were shot down by Soviet aircraft over Sverdlovsk. The State Department, not knowing that both plane and pilot were in Soviet hands, blandly announced that "there was no deliberate attempt to violate Soviet airspace and there never has been." Khrushchev brushed aside the American cover story that Powers might have strayed off course. On May 7, the Soviet Premier waved pictures of the wrecked plane and announced Powers would be brought to trial after having confessed. It was a moment of confusion in the twisted history of the CIA and embarrassment for American espionage.

However, Khrushchev lost his favorable world press overnight when he wrecked the Paris summit conference on May 16 by demanding apologies from President Eisenhower, and later at a two-and-one-half hour press conference, heating up the Cold War.[44] Still, it did not make the American position in the U-2 case look any less foolish to the world at large. When Powers was tried and sentenced to prison in Moscow during August, all contact with the defendant's attorneys and witnesses was refused and the number of reporters in the courtroom was limited.[45]

Still in a bellicose mood, Khrushchev came to New York again to attend the UN General Assembly that fall, beginning September 20. Before a distinguished audience three days later, the Soviet dictator demanded the removal of the UN from the United States; the ouster of Secretary General Dag Hammarskjold in favor of a *troika,* or committee of three; the abolition of all American bases abroad; and complete and total disarmament of the United States and other Western powers on Soviet terms.

Later, he heckled British Prime Minister Harold Macmillan, was gaveled down by the Chairman and proceeded to beat his desk with his fists as a sign of disapproval. When Lorenzo Sumulong of the Philippines referred on October 12 in unflattering terms to the Soviet domination of Eastern Europe, Khrushchev shouted in Russian that the Filipino was an "imperialist lackey" and a "jerk." Then, with TV cameras trained on him, he took off his shoe and again pounded his desk with it.

Throughout the General Assembly until his departure for Moscow on October 13, he gave interviews from the balcony of the Soviet mission at 68th Street and Park Avenue, frequently tying up Park Avenue traffic when crowds gathered to watch the visitor's histrionics. There was even a traveling road show when he also granted interviews at the gates of the Soviet mission at Glen Cove on Long Island and elsewhere.[46]

What motivated Khrushchev's extraordinary behavior? Without doubt, it was a response to Stalinist criticism at home that the soft line he had taken toward the West during the thaw had shown lamentable Soviet weakness, as was evidenced by the U-2 incident. What he seemed to be trying to do at the UN and in Paris earlier was to attack the "Western imperialists" in their own domain, mainly to defuse his enemies within the Communist Party.

It didn't seem to matter to him that the General Assembly rejected his UN reform program and gave Secretary General Hammarskjold an ovation. There was still control over what Tass could say on the home front and what *Pravda* and *Izvestia* could print. However, Khrushchev seemed to have been under the illusion on his return to Moscow that he had learned how to handle the Western press to his advantage, for he ended formal censorship of foreign copy in March 1961 and permitted a score of Western correspondents (including 17 Americans) the rare luxury of travel and editorial discretion to a limited degree. But the recipients of this dubious favor were well aware that whatever they did and wrote or broadcast was carefully scrutinized and that expulsion was still the penalty for incurring the Kremlin's disapproval. As Editor Earl J. Johnson of UPI put the position, "Moscow is no post for the hip-shooting cowboys of journalism." His judgment was based on the expulsion of two West Germans and a Frenchman who thought they could do as they pleased.[47]

When the iron curtain descended once again, the party for the correspondents ended in silence. After the thaw, the deep freeze set in once again between the Moscow censors and the Western press.

THE CUBAN STORY

At a time when Fidel Castro was just a beleaguered rebel who was believed to have been killed in the wilds of Cuba's Sierra Maestra, Herbert L. Matthews of the New York *Times* eluded President Fulgencio Batista's troops to reach the fugitive, interview him, and make him an international figure.

Long afterward, Matthews wrote, "It was an accident that my interview with Fidel Castro in the Sierrra Maestra on February 17, 1957 should have proved so important. There was a story to be got, a censorship to be broken. I got it and I did it—and it so happens that neither Cuba nor the United States is going to be the same again."[48]

At the time of the Matthews interview, Castro had only 18 men under arms with him. He was almost surrounded by Batista's soldiers and in momentary danger of extinction. His only previous revolutionary experience had been his unsuccessful attack on the Moncida Barracks in Santiago de Cuba on July 26, 1953, from which his movement had taken its name. "He was not well armed and had very slender funds. His resources were an idea, a cause, a talent for guerrilla warfare and a lot of stupid opponents," Matthews wrote.[49]

His story was built almost entirely on the theme of adventure — Castro's guerrilla battle against overwhelming odds and the 57-year-old Matthews's hazardous journey to find him. As time went on, Castro's originally favorable press in the United States turned against him when all doubt was removed of his identification as a Communist. A few had already concluded that he had been supplied from Russia, among them Joseph Martin and Philip Santora of the New York *Daily News,* who also correctly predicted his eventual rise to power.

However, there were serious miscalculations about Castro. On April 9, 1958, when the rebel leader against Batista called for a general strike and it failed, all but a handful of correspondents forecast his failure. And even on the night Batista fled from Cuba, December 31, 1958, the AP circulated a dispatch reporting that the dictator had won a decisive battle at Santa Clara, which he lost. Next day, the reinforced and reinvigorated Castro took Havana and Batista was in exile.

All in all, there had been ample reason for confusion about Castro's politics not only in the United States but in the world press as well, mainly because Batista had lost the confidence of the Cuban people. The Soviets alone seemed sure. They took the relatively elementary line that whatever embarrassed the United States could not be too bad for their side.

Two years later, when refugee Cuban groups in New York and Florida were already talking openly about an invasion of Cuba to overthrow Castro, it was too late for anything but a full-scale military operation. Once in power and with Soviet help, Castro had assembled a well-equipped army of 250,000 — a powerful force that could not have been overcome by a handful of poorly armed refugees. Yet, on April 9, 1961, in New York City, José Miró Cardona, President of the Cuban National Revolutionary Council, appealed to all Cubans to participate in "an inevitable and just war" to remove Castro. So many reports were published thereafter of an imminent invasion from the United States that President Kennedy, who had been in office a little more than three months, announced on April 12 that United States armed forces would not "under any conditions" attempt to invade Cuba.[50]

They didn't. But on April 15, three old B-26 bombers made ineffectual raids on three Cuban air fields. Two days later, 1,400 Cuban exiles and a few sympathizers left Guatemala and landed at the Bay of Pigs in Cuba's Las Villas Province. Dozens of correspondents, some tipped by the CIA, which had expected a popular uprising in Cuba, were on hand to cover D-Day at the Bay of Pigs but Castro's regulars were there, too. By April 20, most of the invaders were either killed, wounded, or captured; and the ragtag remainder fled to safety.[51]

The AP informed its subscribers after the failure at the Bay of Pigs: "The process of 'agonizing reappraisal' of the Cuban invasion has produced one of the greatest information foulups in Washington history. . . . The contradictions over the CIA's role characterized the mix-up. One source said faulty intelligence from the CIA had caused the invasion's defeat. Later, another said the CIA did just fine but some other branch of government fell down."[52]

Although a subsequent Senate inquiry found no excuse for the CIA's role in the Bay of Pigs imbroglio, President Kennedy, on April 27, in effect put much of the blame on the press for its coverage and appealed for some form of voluntary self-censorship in the future for sensitive military operations. The New York *Times,* in an indignant editorial on May 10, summed up the press's attitude:

> A democracy . . . our democracy . . . cannot be lied to. This is one of the factors that makes it more precious, more delicate, more difficult, and yet essentially stronger than any other form of government in the world.
>
> The basic principle involved is that of confidence. A dictatorship can get along without an informed public opinion. A democracy cannot. Not only is it unethical to deceive one's own public as part of a system of deceiving an adversary government; it is also foolish. Our executive officers and our national legislators are elected on stated days, but actually they must be re-elected day by day by popular understanding and support. This is what is signified by a government by consent.[53]

The next time around, the Cuba story would come dangerously close to touching off a thermonuclear war between the United States and the Soviet Union.

The rumors of a Soviet armed intervention in Cuba had been circulating for much of the summer of 1962. Cuban visits to the Soviet Union, supposedly to arrange for greater exports of Cuban sugar, had been viewed in the West with suspicion. Reports of Soviet support for Cuban military buildups, too, had been current.[54]

Premier Khrushchev's position, meanwhile, had been weakened not only by the criticisms of his performance in the United States and at the UN but also by the opposition he had aroused among the Chinese Communists who attacked his "adventurism." What he badly needed, as any well-informed foreign correspondent realized, was a show of strength against the West that would dispose of the enemies he had made in his attack on Stalin, particularly in the "secret speech" that no longer remained secret abroad when the US State Department circulated a credible series of extracts.

By early October, U-2 overflights in Cuba had produced photographic evidence of the preparation of missile sites there at about the same time that Soviet vessels were delivering military supplies in quantity to Castro, the nature unspecified. Next came reports, such as one that Hal Hendrix published in the Miami *News,* that Russian military experts were building rocket bases in Cuba. But the Pentagon would not confirm.

The American public remained relatively calm while the Cuban buildup was proceeding mainly because the Kennedy administration had been stressing that it had no objection to purely defensive measures taken by the Castro regime. But soon, the government's mood changed. And on October 21, as a result of a dinner party leak the previous night, the Washington *Post* reported an air of crisis had gripped the capital. The New York *Times* also had information that grave events were in the making but published nothing following a direct appeal from President Kennedy.

The Washington press corps, however, had been alerted. It would have been a dull reporter, indeed, who could not see that there was extraordinary activity in the White House, the State Department, and the Defense Department. The agencies were carrying reports of Army and Air Force movements toward Florida.

Then, on October 22, in a nationwide TV address, President Kennedy disclosed that the Soviet Union was building offensive missile bases in Cuba capable of flinging thermonuclear warheads to major points in the United States. The President demanded dismantling of the bases, ordered the imposition of an air and naval blockade, and the disarming and return of all missiles to the Soviet Union. He called upon Khrushchev "to halt and eliminate this clandestine, reckless threat to world peace and to stable relations between our two nations."[55]

At the same time, Secretary General U Thant called the UN Security Council into session to support the American demand.[56] And afterward, both the American people and the nation's allies in the Western world rallied to stand by the President. The confrontation between the two superpowers for the first time put hundreds of millions of people across half the earth at risk of thermonuclear annihilation by missiles flying from American, Cuban, and Soviet bases.

Within 24 hours, signs accumulated that the Soviets were wavering.

The Washington *Post* reported that Premier Khrushchev had sent President Kennedy a letter proposing to withdraw the Soviet missiles from Cuba. Endre Marton of the AP disclosed that U Thant had conferred with Castro on dismantling the bases a little more than two hours after a top-secret report had been given to the State Department. But in addition, literally scores of reports on the tension between the superpowers also came from the broadcasters, from the major newspapers, and from the news agencies.

On October 24, the Defense Department announced that some Soviet ships en route for Cuba had headed back toward their bases. The crisis was near an end. And within a few hours, Khrushchev announced the bases would be dismantled, the missiles disarmed and returned to the Soviet Union. It was in this manner that the missile crisis ended.[57]

With Castro's connivance, Khrushchev had taken a colossal gamble to maintain himself in power in Moscow, and both had lost. At home, he had managed so badly that the Soviets had to purchase grain from abroad, and his attempts to destroy the Stalinist cult had backfired against him. In Hungary, in Poland, and in Czechoslovakia, he had compromised Soviet credibility and aroused hatred among Communist Party authorities by his attempts toward a rappropchement with West Germany. Probably his worst time after his failure in the Cuban missile crisis had been caused by Communist Chinese charges of "adventurism" and his capitulation to American demands to destroy the Cuban bases and disarm and remove the missiles.

After the celebration of Khrushchev's 70th birthday in 1964, during which he was awarded the Order of Hero of the Soviet Union and given other honors, his effectiveness in high office ended. On October 14, the Kremlin carried an announcement for the foreign press that he had "resigned due to advanced age and poor health."

Leonid I. Brezhnev, as First Secretary of the Communist Party, and Alexei Kosygin, as Premier, replaced him and almost at once discarded the cover story that he had left because of ill health and advanced age. Instead, the fallen leader was attacked for "hare-brained schemes," "half-baked ideas," and "hasty decisions." But without doubt, as Soviet archives will show one day when the Russian republic gets around to releasing pertinent documents, the Cuban missile crisis had a great deal to do with the destruction both of Khrushchev and of the thaw that turned into a hurricane.[58]

9 Surviving the Cold War

THE VIEW FROM THE WHITE HOUSE

After President Eisenhower's disheartening experiences in settling the drawn Korean War, he was understandably reluctant, as was the great majority of the American people, to be drawn into another land war in Asia. It was on this basis that he upheld his Joint Chiefs of Staff when they rejected French appeals for American armed intervention in Indochina to save their last stronghold from the encircling Communist hordes at Dien Bien Phu in 1954.

As he wrote at a later date: "If the United States were unilaterally to permit its forces to be drawn into conflict in Indochina and in a succession of Asian wars, the end result would be to drain off our resources and weaken our over-all defense positions."[1]

Eisenhower's views were not altogether pleasing to his ferociously anti-Communist Vice President, Richard Milhous Nixon, who on April 16 that year had suggested in a speech that there was a qualified possibility for the use of American ground forces in Indochina.[2]

Ike thereupon had the unpleasant duty of facing the issue squarely at a news conference on April 27, when a reporter asked him whether the beleaguered French could expect American combat forces to raise the siege of Dien Bien Phu. Without referring to Nixon's position, the President replied that there was "no plausible reason" for American military intervention in Indochina and that he also doubted the Vietnamese population "would want us to do so." The most he had previously agreed to was economic and humanitarian assistance for the French as a valued ally — and that was still as far as he would go.[3]

On May 7, when the fortress at Dien Bien Phu fell, signifying France's loss of all of Indochina (Vietnam, Laos, and Cambodia) after eight years of war with Ho Chi Minh's Vietminh combat veterans and their Vietcong guerrilla allies in South Vietnam, there was no perceptible reaction in the United States. The event seemed to have made little impression on the public at large, then or later.

As for the French, who had resumed possession of their Indochinese colony after the Japanese occupation during World War II, what they had to settle for at the Geneva peace conference was an enlarged independent North Vietnam under Ho Chi Minh's rule and, mainly through American pressure, an anti-Communist buffer area in South Vietnam presided over by the former French-supported Emperor of Annam, Bao Dai. The United States had paid 80 percent of the war costs.[4]

However, Bao Dai didn't last long, being swept aside by a ruthless new American-supported pro-consul, Ngo Dinh Diem, who took over in South Vietnam with the help of its reorganized army, a police force schooled in brutality, and an undercover plainclothes unit of intelligence operatives known as the Sûreté. However, Diem's revived South Vietnam defense forces still were no match for Ho's probing guerrillas, who regularly crossed the 17th parallel dividing line between the two Vietnams in a continuing small-scale action that was apparently intended to keep Diem on the defensive.[5]

This was the situation when Senator John F. Kennedy defeated Vice President Nixon in the presidential election of 1960 and came to power in the White House the following year, determined to do something to crush Ho's guerrilla forces and stabilize South Vietnam as an anti-Communist bastion in Southeast Asia. As the new President's military adviser, he selected the former chairman of the Joint Chiefs of Staff, General Maxwell Taylor, whose doctrine of "limited war" against Communism seemed a promising way to contest Ho's guerrilla warriors in the vast Indochinese jungles.

With Taylor's first visit to Diem's capital of Saigon in South Vietnam in 1961, the General's strategy of a "flexible response" to Ho's guerrilla tactics became the order of the day. What he wanted to test with the help of the South Vietnamese government was an effective method of counterinsurgency to defeat Ho's initial probing tactics. Only, the northern guerrillas and their southern allies regrettably wouldn't stand and fight the South Vietnamese regulars with their glistening American military equipment. Instead of obliging Taylor by flinging themselves against his counterinsurgency forces in the testing he advocated, the guerrillas simply melted away into the jungle — a most frustrating procedure for the dean of Western military tacticians and the author of a much-admired work, *The Uncertain Trumpet*.[6]

On his return to Washington, Taylor advocated the introduction in South Vietnam of a limited number of American advisers to help train Diem's South Vietnamese cohorts in this destabilizing kind of war that Ho was fighting. Accordingly, without consulting Congress, much less asking for a declaration of war, President Kennedy began sending the first detachment of American soldiers to Vietnam as "advisers," their official description. In that first year, there were only 1,364 of them, and the American public neither took particular notice of the commitment nor even seemed in the slightest concerned about it.[7]

But in Moscow at about the same time, Nikita Khrushchev announced to a Communist Party gathering from sympathetic nations that he was supporting all national wars of liberation, one of the relatively few positions he took that agreed with those of his Communist Chinese critics. It wasn't really news. Along the Asian Pacific rim, it was common knowledge that Ho's regulars and his guerrilla detachments all had had training under either Communist Chinese or Soviet auspices, sometimes both, and both also had supported him in his war against the French. Assuredly, they also would do so now against the new American initiative that was being prepared for President Kennedy's approval by General Taylor.

The first detachment of "advisers" didn't make much difference in the situation but when the total reached 9,865 in 1962, some in combat against the guerrillas from the north, a handful of war correspondents — not all of them Americans — took notice of what was going on in a way that profoundly disturbed both President Kennedy and the South Vietnamese dictator, Ngo Dinh Diem.

One of them, the redoubtable veteran, Homer Bigart of the New York *Times* (and formerly the *Herald Tribune*), wrote as follows about the new order in South Vietnam: "Saigon is a nice place to spend a few days in. The food and wine are good, the city is attractive, most hotels and restaurants are air-conditioned. But to work here is peculiarly depressing. Too often correspondents seem to be regarded by the American mission as tools of our foreign policy. Those who balk are apt to find it a bit lonely, for they are likely to be distrusted and shunned by American and Vietnamese officials."

Bigart, having covered other American wars around the globe, both open and covert, perhaps had some personal feelings about the matter because of a ditty he had composed on the spur of a mischievous moment that portrayed American policy in South Vietnam in this manner:

Sink or Swim,
With Ngo Dinh Diem.[8]

At the Kennedy White House, nobody believed that was the way a distinguished foreign correspondent should react to an American counterinsurgency offensive against the Communist threat to South Vietnam. Government people thought the press was not very helpful.[9]

THE VIEW OF THE CORRESPONDENTS

The mighty and the powerful went to Saigon in a continual processional in 1962 as a four-star general, Paul D. Harkins, arrived to take charge of the Military Assistance Command, Vietnam (MACV).[10] It was as if both the Kennedy administration and its military arm in the Pentagon needed continual reassurance over the course the war was taking. The cloak about the nature of the American "advisers" by this time had long since been discarded. For with the arrival of American helicopter gunships to escalate the warfare against the elusive Vietcong and their comrades from the north, American officers had begun leading the fighting more often than not in these numerous small but invariably vicious encounters with the enemy.

On an average day or night, this was a war that was difficult to describe and tricky to report because the size of the clashing units was generally small, and the casualties, accordingly, tended to be fewer than those in an ordinary shoot-out between police and gangsters in New York City or Chicago. Still, an experienced correspondent like Homer Bigart or a foreign specialist like François Sully of *Newsweek* had little difficulty in concluding that the Americans simply weren't very good at this kind of war and their instruction didn't seem to be making their South Vietnamese charges any more effective in combating the enemy.

Very little could be done about Bigart because he was tough, knowledgeable, an American citizen, and he worked for the New York *Times*. But Sully, being a French national and working for a weekly publication that was not as well known in Vietnam, became a favorite target of the Diem family within a relatively short time. The Sûreté plainclothesmen followed him around, pried into his office procedures, and generally made a nuisance of themselves. Because he did a critical piece on a member of the Diem family, he also became persona non grata at the palace, as Diem's headquarters was known.

Matters between the American government's representatives and Sully came to a head with his coverage of a new twist in the American-led offensive against the Communist foe, the Strategic Hamlet Program, which opened with an attack called Operation Sunrise. The objective was to force the Vietcong or their sympathizers in South Vietnam or both to disperse by burning their rude homes in peasant villages. After Sully wrote of such events with photos of flaming huts that he took for *Newsweek,* the American Ambassador, Frederick Nolting, Jr., furiously rebuked the reporter.

At one point, he demanded, "Why do you always see the hole in the doughnut?"

The Frenchman replied gravely, "Because there *is* a hole in the doughnut, M'sieu l'Ambassador."

It wasn't long before Sully was expelled from Vietnam by President Diem.[11] That coincided by accident with the arrival of a new correspondent for the New York *Times,* David Halberstam, a Harvard graduate still in his 20s who had worked previously for the Nashville *Tennessean* and had been selected for training by James Reston, then the Washington bureau chief of the *Times.* Halberstam would become by all odds the most difficult of correspondents to persuade that the war in Vietnam was being won.[12]

Another correspondent who had been singled out for special treatment by the American brass early on was Malcolm Browne, then the chief of the AP bureau in Saigon. The story was told to all newcomers to the coverage of the Vietnam conflict that Admiral Harry Felt, the Commander of the U.S. Pacific Fleet, was so offended by the apparently skeptical tone of a question Browne had asked him that he snapped: "Browne, why don't you get on the team?"[13] Like his fellow-correspondent in the AP office, Peter Arnett, a cheerful and hard-working New Zealander, Browne never did make it to the team.

More correspondents, some veterans of the Korean War like Peter Kalischer and younger ones like his UP associate, Neil Sheehan, were also inclined to take an unfavorable view of the war as early as 1962. Then and well into 1963, the accounts of the conflict that appeared in the American news media were so uniformly negative that Admiral Felt's team would have had difficulty fielding a set of a dozen regulars.

In my knowledge of the field from the time I became the administrator of the Pulitzer Prizes in 1954, others who also did much of the reporting early on were seasoned journalists of excellent reputation, such as Stanley Karnow of *Time* and the *Saturday Evening Post,* Charles Mohr who then reported for *Time,* Pepper Martin of *U.S. News and World Report,* Nick Turner of Reuters, James Robinson of NBC, and Bernard Kalb of CBS. (Robinson, incidentally, followed Sully in expulsion for some imagined fault of electronic reportage that offended the Diems.)[14]

After an engagement with Ho's guerrillas on January 2, 1963, that was forever after known as the Battle of Ap Bac, the problems of the Diem regime and the American establishment in South Vietnam intensified. The correspondents who either saw a part or all of the encounter or toured the area after the battle was over concluded with searing unanimity that the fight had been a clear victory for the Communists. For the first time, they reported, several hundred of Ho's regulars and some Vietcong had stood and fought the well-armed South Vietnamese and their American advisers instead of fading away into the jungle. And when they did go, it was no rout by any means but an orderly breaking off of an engagement in which they had given a good account of themselves.

What bothered the correspondents, the UP's Sheehan and Halberstam of the New York *Times* among them, was that the American commander, General Harkins, coolly insisted when the fighting ended that the Communists had been caught in a trap and were about to be extinguished apparently at the pleasure of the South Vietnamese. However, when the correspondents hurried to the scene of the supposed trap, all they were told by a despairing American officer who had witnessed the fight was that the Vietminh and Vietcong were nowhere to be found. Asked what happened, he was quoted:

What the hell do you think happened? They got away.[15]

Up to the time of Ap Bac, the clashes between north and south had been relatively small, groups of a few dozen on each side. But after that, Ho's command began putting a few hundred guerrillas at a time into the field, most of whom proved to be more than a match for anything the American command was able to produce from the South Vietnamese side. Among the correspondents, nearly all of whom agreed that the war was not going well for the American side, Halberstam was the most outspoken in his criticism of General Harkins and in his dispatches to the New York *Times* that documented the way the war was being lost. But the American wire service reporters — Browne, Arnett and Sheehan — also became targets of the Diem regime and its Sûreté plainclothesmen.

At one time, Sheehan was told by one of his cameramen that a Diem official had threatened to kill him and make it look as if the Vietcong had been responsible. In another incident, a group of the Diem Sûreté plainclothesmen had grabbed Arnett and were about to punch and kick him once they'd wrestled him to the ground; but Halberstam, who was a pretty fair brawler, rescued him with a single-handed attack on Diem's people.[16]

The offensive against the correspondents reached a peak of intensity in the early summer of 1963. Then Marguerite Higgins and Joseph Alsop, both of the New York *Herald Tribune,* went to Saigon and openly accused a few of the younger correspondents of falsely reporting that the war was being lost. Miss Higgins, having won a Pulitzer Prize for her reporting in the Korean War, and Alsop, a columnist who had a faithful readership among conservatives, were not alone in making such charges. *Time* magazine and Hearst's New York *Journal-American,* among others, also had been editorially critical of the negative reports out of Saigon.

However, most of the resident correspondents who had been reporting the war stood by the chief defendants, Malcolm Browne and Peter Arnett of the AP, Neil Sheehan of UP, and David Halberstam of the New York *Times,* all of whom later became Pulitzer Prize winners themselves. In fact, Charles Mohr of *Time* resigned in protest over his magazine's role in the affair, switched to the staff of the New York *Times,* and asked Sheehan to join him there in covering the war at a later date — a bid that the UP correspondent accepted.

Nobody accused the correspondents point blank of lying during this dispute except, of course, the embattled Diem regime. Even Alsop conceded at one point that what the correspondents had written and broadcast was "true or part true." What Alsop objected to was what he termed a "high-minded crusade" against President Diem. Miss Higgins, however, was unqualified in her attack on the correspondents' credibility: "Reporters here," she wrote angrily, "would like to see us lose the war to prove they were right."

As for *Time* magazine, it complained of distorted and exaggerated reporting as follows: "The reporters have tended to reach unanimous agreement on almost everything they have seen. But such agreement is suspect because it is obviously inbred. The newsmen have themselves become a part of South Vietnam's confusion; they have covered a complex situation from only one angle, as if their own conclusions offered all the necessary illumination."

To that, Halberstam replied with no less vigor and forthrightness: "What's been exaggerated? The intrigues? The hostility? It's all been proven. We've been accused of being a bunch of liberals but even that's not true."[17]

Events in Vietnam were now moving toward a climax for the Ngo Dinh Diem family and their closest associates. Through their cruelty and arrogance toward their own people, they had lost the respect of the devoutly Buddhist section of the populace in South Vietnam. That, of course, was known to the Kennedy administration in Washington. And while General Harkins was still confident that he was presiding over a war that the South Vietnamese were winning with more than 15,000 American "advisers" now in the field, some of the major figures in the administration in Washington were receiving contrary reports from their own sources in Saigon.

In the spring of 1963, President Diem and his brother, Ngo Dinh Nhu, had taken the fatal step of antagonizing their Buddhist people in the southern city of Hue by refusing to let them fly the Buddhist flag on the 2,587th birthday of Buddha, May 8. When a crowd protested, some of President Nhu's civil police opened fire with at least 14 fatalities and many more wounded. To make the situation much worse, the Catholic Diems authorized further assaults on the Buddhist monks themselves.

In a protest that shocked millions of people in both South Vietnam and the United States, an elderly monk, Quang Duc, let himself be doused with gasoline at a busy street corner in Saigon, then calmly touched a match to the gasoline, turning himself into a flaming torch. Malcolm Browne of the AP was present and took the picture that hor-rified all who saw it.[18] Both President Kennedy and Ambassador Nolt-ing appealed to President Diem to drop his persecution of the monks but he refused. Apparently, he was determined to tear down the monks' pagodas and hem them in with barbed wire rather than admit he was wrong. He was far more vigorous in putting down the Buddhists than in fighting the Vietcong.

That was about all President Kennedy could stand. He authorized an exchange of ambassadors with Henry Cabot Lodge, Jr., scheduled to replace Ambassador Nolting later in the year. Just before Lodge's ar-rival, more than 15,000 Buddhists massed before the main pagoda in Saigon for hours of peaceful protests. Two nights later, President Diem unleashed thousands of soldiers and police in an attack on every pagoda housing monks in Saigon, Hue, and other cities, in which 1,400 monks were arrested and an unspecified number were killed, wounded, or re-ported missing. Martial law and a 9 p.m. curfew were imposed while Diem's forces continued to seize other opponents of the regime. When university students in Saigon rioted in protest, Diem shut down the uni-versity and began carting students to jail by the score.[19]

Ambassador Lodge arrived on August 22 to take charge of a thor-oughly demoralized American command and deal with the problem of what to do about the Diems, who by now seemed to be obsessed with the notion of making war on their own people rather than the Commu-nist foe from the north. If ever there had been a sign that this war was being lost, the evidence was now all too devastatingly clear. And yet, in Washington, there were still conflicting signals about who was at fault.

While Lodge was going about the grim business of disposing of the Diems and bringing on an as yet unidentified new government in Saigon, President Kennedy received a courtesy call in October from Arthur Ochs Sulzberger, who had just become the new publisher of the New York *Times*. During the course of polite conversation, the President suddenly asked whether the *Times* thought well of Halberstam as its correspondent in Saigon. Sulzberger said he was doing well. And, in response to another question from the President, the publisher replied that he had no plans to transfer the reporter (who, during the Buddhist crisis, had been obliged to spend his nights with a friendly American official who safeguarded him).[20]

And so it turned out that Halberstam was still around, with Browne, Arnett, Sheehan, and the rest of the beleaguered American reporters when the roof fell in on the Diem family. Two of the President's top generals, Duong Van Minh and Tran Van Don, headed a junta of other generals who staged a successful coup on November 1 in which both Ngo Dinh Diem and Ngo Dinh Nhu were shot to death during an armed uprising staged by the plotters. The rest of the family was either scattered or otherwise disposed of, except for Madame Nhu, who had been in the United States at the time trying to drum up support for a losing war.[21]

The greatest tragedy of all occurred on November 22, when President Kennedy was assassinated in Dallas. With the advent of President Lyndon Baines Johnson, who had been Kennedy's Vice President, there was at least a chance that the United States now would heed Eisenhower's advice against the pursuit of a land war on Asia fought by American troops against a Communist enemy. LBJ, however, wasn't about to quit. He wanted to win the war.[22]

THE VIEW FROM SAIGON

While President Johnson was preoccupied with plans for his 1964 election campaign against Barry Goldwater, the eventual Republican nominee, the lines were forming in Saigon for a new phase of the war. Ambassador Lodge, having set in motion the coup that disposed of the Diem family, now realized that Duong Van Minh's junta was unable to govern amid the continuing Buddhist riots and boosted another small war lord, a French-trained paratroop general, Nguyen Kanh, into the South Vietnamese leadership. With only 17,000 Americans in the country to oppose the rapidly growing Vietcong guerrilla force, Lodge saw that this would have to continue for the time being as a South Vietnamese, not an American, war.

However, when Lodge came home in July and was replaced by General Maxwell Taylor as a kind of proconsul, serving as ambassador and also as the superior of General Westmoreland, General Harkins's replacement, the Pentagon brain trust approved a new program of American-directed guerrilla operations against the master of that military art, Ho Chi Minh. This was Taylor's concept, essentially, a policy of harassment and interdiction of the enemy.

By land, sea, and air, the American-trained South Vietnamese guerrillas, often under American leadership, began raiding the north, wrecking any installation that they believed to be helpful to the enemy. At sea, the new offensive used PT boats to try to institute a semiblockade that would hamper fishing and water-borne military actions. There also was a bid for help from the mountain people in the central highlands on the theory that they might be valuable allies.

Like everything else General Taylor tried, it looked good on paper but it didn't work out. The raids weren't very well organized and didn't do the kind of damage that the Vietcong were able to exact from the disorganized South Vietnamese. And as for winning the loyalty of the mountain people, quite the opposite resulted. The *montagnards,* as they were known from the era of French occupation, were fearful of Saigon's domination and were better able to get along with the Vietcong.

The one important development that arose from Taylor's hit-and-run strategy was the success of a Johnson-approved plan to lure the North Vietnamese into an attack on two American destroyers in the Gulf of Tonkin on August 2, 1964. Regardless of the antiwar protests that were already erupting all over the United States over this unpopular war, LBJ now managed to maneuver Congress into approving the punitive Tonkin Gulf resolution that was tantamount to a declaration of war on August 7. When the President easily defeated Goldwater in November, the way was cleared for the Americanization of the war—a tragedy in itself, although Generals Taylor and Westmoreland in Saigon looked upon it as the beginning of the end of their time of troubles.

And at the Pentagon, General Curtis LeMay, the champion of air power, boasted that the North Vietnamese would be bombed to hell. Even the Secretary of Defense, Robert McNamara, who had become fearful after so many disappointments in the field, found new hope that at last—to use a Dean Acheson slogan—he might see light at the end of the tunnel.[23] As a footnote to the era in which the journalists had been blamed for causing the public to believe that the war was being lost, Messrs. Browne and Halberstam were jointly honored with a Pulitzer Prize for international reporting.

Reinforced by his electoral victory in November 1964, President Johnson authorized the massive bombing of North Vietnam below the 20th parallel beginning in February 1965. In Saigon, Generals Taylor and Westmoreland were confident this was to be the death blow to the intruders from the north. Although American ground forces weren't then to be used because of Washington's nervousness over the growing disorders caused by the antiwar movement, at least 125,000 American troops were scheduled for transfer to Vietnam during that year.

To make sure that the South Vietnamese understood that the United States now was running the war, there was another shakeup in their command under American auspices. The French-trained paratrooper, Nguyen Kanh, was replaced by a younger group of generals headed by Marshal Nguyen Cao Ky with General Nguyen Van Thieu as his second in command, theoretically operating a South Vietnamese army variously estimated at between 400,000 and 600,000 effectives.[24] The problem with determining how many really were fighting on the South Vietnamese side, as always, was to gauge the extent of the widely-known corruption in the military under which conscripts paid off district and other commanders to be listed on the rolls without undergoing the inconvenient obligation of being shot at.

There was no such trouble in the north so far as it could be determined from Saigon. There, the myth was that the Ho Chi Minh Trail that supplied the Vietcong battalions was a small, narrow dirt strip through the jungle which would be wiped out by mass bombing. Actually, the supply route from the north was developing into an enormous network of roads, many paved with crushed rock, that penetrated the mountain fastnesses and could be interdicted but never entirely cut off.

Nevertheless, the Johnson-approved air strikes — an operation called Rolling Thunder — kept hammering away at every kind of military facility in the north[25] in so heartless a manner that the liberal Americans for Democratic Action was moved to protest directly to the President. A delegation from ADA's Washington convention in April 1965, stiffly reminded LBJ that the antiwar movement in the country was by no means confined to draft-conscious young men on or off college campuses. (At the time, there were deferments for college students, but upon graduation their status changed, a policy that ended in 1967 when the colleges no longer became a refuge from the draft.)

The ADA spokesmen argued, as well, that the unrestricted bombing of civilian peoples was contrary to everything America stood for and should be stopped at once. In reply, LBJ argued that he intended to try to give the Vietnamese people the same opportunity for self-development that he was advocating for all Americans, but he convinced nobody. For during that confrontation, perceptive Washington correspondents were informing the nation that the bombing campaign, after six weeks, was showing no indication of forcing the North Vietnamese to sue for peace and that the Pentagon now was intent on forcing a decision on the White House to favor General Westmoreland's subsequent demand for a ground-troop war.

The President was already wavering. Vice President Hubert Humphrey, for one, was against a wider war with ground troops by the hundreds of thousands — someone from the Pentagon already had shocked him by suggesting as many as 300,000 soldiers might be needed. And Humphrey was not alone. Influential senators like William Fulbright and Mike Mansfield were also opposed and let LBJ know it. However, Westmoreland, backed by General Taylor, saw no other way to go when it had become abundantly clear that the air war wouldn't stop the Communists.

LBJ had another jolt soon after his bout with the ADA when he was reviled as a bomber-President at the annual Festival of the Arts at the nation's capital. Some of the more prominent literary and artistic figures were boycotting the festival as a form of protest against LBJ's conduct of the Vietnam War, which moved him to comment at one point that he'd been insulted by the half that stayed away as well as the other half that attended. Nevertheless, he didn't back down.

On July 28, 1965, the President admitted that 125,000 combat troops were being sent to Vietnam but in the same news conference denied the obvious — that he was Americanizing the war.

"We did not choose to be the guardians at the gate but there is no one else," he said. "Nor would surrender in Vietnam bring peace . . . as we have learned from the lessons of history."[26]

At the end of 1965, 184,000 American soldiers were in combat in Vietnam. At the end of the following year, there were 385,000, more than had been sent to Korea, and half a million tons of bombs had been unloaded on North Vietnam from the air war without in any way changing the course of the war. By that time, the protests in the United States had become violent on college campuses throughout the land. Whatever public support there had been for the war in the United States was overwhelmed by the continual outcry:

Hey, hey, LBJ,
How many kids have you killed today?

The chant was heard in volume at the Pentagon itself when 50,000 demonstrators marched there on October 21, 1967, a year when the number of American troops in Vietnam reached 475,000 amid continued bombing of all North Vietnam.[27] But still, the Vietcong's disruptions in the south were reaching epic proportions, and, watching anxiously in Saigon, General Taylor still saw no light at the end of the tunnel.

General Westmoreland remained confident, having spent a part of 1967 on the lecture circuit in the United States as a morale booster. He also had addressed both houses of Congress, gone on TV with NBC's *Meet the Press,* and even told a meeting at the National Press Club in Washington, D.C., that "the end was coming into view."[28]

It was, but not in the way that the General had supposed. For the traditional Tet holiday in Vietnam at the end of January 1968, he had ordered a 36-hour cease-fire to oblige the South Vietnamese, but he had also been sufficiently cautious to strengthen his defenses around the Bien Hoa Air Base, which with Tan Son Nhut, outside Saigon, was a major base for the air war. Having heard rumors of a coming Tet offensive from the north, he had no intention of being caught napping. He reacted as the enemy had expected.

Otherwise, Saigon was relaxed as the holiday began on the evening of Tet, January 29, 1968. There was a lively party on the lawn of the American Embassy presided over by a new ambassador, Ellsworth Bunker, who had replaced General Taylor once his doctrine of "limited war" had been discarded in the rush of combat ground operations and continual air strikes at the north. In the palace that once had belonged to the Diems, General Nguyen Van Thieu now was in residence as the newly-elected President of South Vietnam with Marshal Ky as his Vice President.

Everybody expected enemy action, but nobody was quite sure where and how the offensive would begin. Before dawn, after the revels in Saigon ushering in the new year, the first scattered reports of enemy attacks came from a number of cities and strong points in the south; but General Westmoreland was now convinced that Bien Hoa was the ultimate objective and concentrated on defending it. No cease-fire was in effect there.

Then, when the Vietcong struck in force with the main body of its assault troops, the first to feel the effects was Ambassador Bunker. His Marine guards awakened him at 3 a.m. on January 31 to tell him that Saigon itself was being attacked and that he had to leave at once to a safer place than his own residence. In his night clothes, the Ambassador scuttled to safety while the Marines were burning his private official papers to prevent them from falling into enemy hands.

The Vietcong had achieved complete surprise. While the Ambassador took refuge, the enemy blasted a big hole in the side of the American Embassy only a short distance away. The city of 4,000,000, including at least 1,000,000 refugees, would have been at the mercy of the invaders had it not been for a misdirected order that never arrived which would have put a sizable American force elsewhere. As it was, the defenders had to fight for their lives against the thousands of Vietcong in their midst, variously estimated long afterward as anywhere from 6,000 to 15,000 guerrilla fighters.

More than a score of provincial capitals were attacked as well as Saigon that early dawn. And worse even than General Westmoreland's monumental miscalculation was the sight of the invading forces fighting within Saigon, the American-occupied capital of South Vietnam, being shown to outraged American audiences in color on TV in millions of homes. Nothing could have been more devastating to the bitter-enders than that, for it was the final proof, if any had been needed, that this hapless war was now lost beyond recall.[29]

It was, in fact, more than three weeks before the defenders were able to haul down the enemy flag that had been hoisted in triumph with the beginning of the attack on Saigon's City Hall and replace it with the South Vietnam colors. The toll nationwide by official figures was 14,300 civilians killed, 24,000 wounded, 72,000 houses destroyed, 627,000 people rendered homeless. In Saigon alone, more than 6,000 civilians were killed, and twice that many were called seriously wounded, with almost 20,000 homes destroyed.[30]

That was all for Westmoreland. On March 22, President Johnson ordered him home to be Chief of Staff of the Army, a promotion to cover the national disgrace that fooled nobody. Eventually, after a certain amount of hesitation at the White House, Westmoreland's second in command, General Creighton Abrams, replaced him. McNamara disappeared as Secretary of Defense and became head of the World Bank, another Johnson move to bring on a more hawkish replacement, Clark Clifford.[31]

Once the 1968 election year began developing a riotous political peace offensive of its own on the home front, however, President Johnson apparently realized how precarious his situation would be if he sought re-election. And at about the same time, the faithful Dean Rusk, who as Secretary of State had closely followed his President's war policies, now began to suggest negotiations with the enemy for a truce in the fighting — a position that had led to the change at the head of the Defense Department.

It had been called to Rusk's attention belatedly that a North Vietnamese radio broadcast just before the Tet offensive had suggested negotiations to end the war if President Johnson would order a halt in the bombing of North Vietnam. But neither he nor any others in the President's confidence could tell whether this was a genuine feeler for an armistice or just another propaganda ploy. However, LBJ decided to test the enemy's position after only one of his senior advisers, at a strategy meeting on March 26, 1968, believed the war should be continued.

In a TV address to the nation on March 31, the President announced he was limiting the bombing of the north and proposed to halt the air war on October 31, meanwhile renouncing his candidacy for re-election.[32] He had to wait only three days for the North Vietnamese response, in which the foe agreed by radio to participate in a formal negotiation for peace but without any suggestion for a truce in the fighting.

LBJ gave up. As a result, on May 10, the delegates of the United States, North Vietnam, South Vietnam, and the Vietcong began discussing the possibilities in Paris for an end to the fighting and the development of a peace program that would be acceptable to all four parties.[33] It would take another four years before a settlement was reached; and even then, none of the participants would be satisfied.

THE VIEW FROM THE UNITED STATES

All President Johnson was willing to offer the North Vietnamese and the Vietcong in that dismal election year was an orderly withdrawal by all parties and a bombing halt that actually did take place on October 31. Vice President Humphrey, the front runner for the Democratic presidential nomination, would have wanted more and Richard Nixon, who eventually won the Republican nomination, would make it known upon his election that he was determined not to be the first President of the United States to lose a war.[34]

The hesitation of both great political parties to sponsor an all-out peace platform for their respective presidential candidates drove the antiwar protestors into a frantic series of demonstrations that spring and summer. By mid-June, the conflict in Vietnam had become the longest war in American history, with a toll of more than 30,000 dead on the American side alone.

At Columbia University in New York City, rioting undergraduates at Columbia College succeeded in closing most of the classes at the institution. Demonstrators at many of the other Ivy League campuses, both before and after the Columbia riots, followed suit, as did many another large university across the land.[35] During Nixon's nomination at the Republican National Convention in Miami, there was an outburst of black rioting that temporarily disrupted the proceedings.[36]

But in Chicago, where the Democrats convened with Vice President Humphrey virtually certain of the presidential nomination, scores of people were injured in street fights in Lincoln and Grant Parks. A Vietcong flag was draped around General Grant's statue, and there were outbursts of fisticuffs on the convention floor in successive arguments over a peace resolution and even a report of the Platform Committee to re-shape the party machinery for 1972.[37]

Mayor Richard Daley complicated the Democrats' problem by sending 70 police armed with rifles into Grant and Lincoln Parks to restore order with permission to shoot if resisted. On the night that Humphrey expected to be nominated, so much tear gas had been released by nervous police that it drifted out on the floor, causing sneezing and snuffling among the delegates. It also spread to nearby hotels, where Democratic delegates were affected before and after the riotous convention proceedings.

The disorderly scenes, displayed relentlessly before the nation by hard-working TV crews, put Humphrey at a tremendous disadvantage against Nixon to begin with — something that hampered his campaign and led to more disorder in his travels. Nixon, too, was affected but not to as great an extent, although once, at a demonstration outside the University of Tennessee at Knoxville, he was lucky to have the Reverend Dr. Billy Graham nearby to pacify the crowd.[38]

The presidential candidates, by their mere presence, also seemed to spread the war demonstrations to unsuspecting innocents whose connection with the Vietnam War was at best illustory. One such victim was James Reston, the chief Washington correspondent of the New York *Times* shortly after he had been promoted to Executive Editor and was discussing Nixon's problems as a candidate by invitation of New York University at a large campus auditorium. During the proceedings, a crowd of antiwar protestors began rushing up and down the aisles shouting "Ho-Ho-Ho Chi Minh!"

"He isn't here," Reston announced over the microphone, but the demonstrators were in no mood for mild humor. Reston and his audience had to give up.[39]

President Nixon defeated Humphrey by only half a million votes, or 8/10 of 1 percent of the total of 63.6 million cast—a measure of the damage that antiwar rioting had inflicted on the Democratic nominee. But Nixon's proposed program for "Vietnamizing" the war—that is, de-emphasizing the American role—didn't quiet the antiwar tumult in 1969 as the American armed forces in Vietnam peaked at 543,000—more than the American total in the Korean War.[40]

What Nixon tried to do through General Abrams and Ambassador Bunker was to induce the South Vietnamese to quit issuing "ghost figures" of the number of Vietnamese fighting units and personnel in uniform and making their draft of their own people more realistic. Once that program showed results, what the President proposed to do was to institute a gradual withdrawal of American forces to try to pacify the home front but, at the same time, to launch a new offensive through Cambodia to try to attack the foe in a different way. Just how he hoped to win the war through such a strategy never was made convincingly clear. However, given the power the Vietcong had shown in the Tet offensive and the almost complete disillusion of the South Vietnamese people with their American partnership, no strategy would have worked.

The largest antiwar demonstration of all took place during Nixon's first year in office, when 250,000 people marched in Washington in a demand for peace that echoed and re-echoed across the country in televised commentary. "Vietnamizing" the war wasn't much of a policy, and it was rejected by the public almost from the outset.[41]

During the fall of 1969, a disillusioned former Pentagon official, who was thoroughly out of sympathy with a war in which he had been a high policy adviser, decided to try to shock public opinion into greater efforts to end the conflict. The official, Dr. Daniel Ellsberg, having one of the highest security clearances of any top-level adviser, began secretly photo-copying each of the 7,000 pages of a top-secret report dealing with the development and operation of the war. The 47 book-length volumes, a total of 2,500,000 words, had been commissioned in mid-1967 by Defense Secretary McNamara so that his successors would have a detailed top-secret record of the American involvement in Vietnam, Laos, and Cambodia from the end of World War II, in supporting the French failure in Indochina, until May 1968, in the wake of the disastrous Tet offensive.[42]

Through Neil Sheehan, the former UPI correspondent in Vietnam who was now a New York *Times* reporter at the Pentagon and one of Dr. Ellsberg's acquaintances, the Pentagon Papers were made available to the *Times*. As the paper's Executive Editor, Reston recalled that the issue of publishing the gist of this explosive study turned into a bitter controversy between the editorial side and one of the *Times*'s lawyers. The publisher, Arthur Ochs Sulzberger, sided with Reston and the other editors who were in favor of publishing this classified, top-secret account of the nation's involvement in the Vietnam War after being assured by another member of the newapaper's counsel that the editors' position was legally defensible.[43]

The publication of the first three articles based on the Pentagon Papers created a nationwide sensation. But with the appearance of the third article on June 15, 1971, the federal court in New York City granted the government a temporary order restraining further publication. In this manner, the fundamental issue of press vs. government — the people's right to know what their government was doing — became a direct issue before the highest court in the land.[44]

The government contended that further publication would do "irreparable harm" to national security, a severe allegation against as responsible and outstanding a newspaper as the *Times*. However, the Supreme Court by a vote of 6–3 rejected the government's position and granted permission to continue publication to the *Times* and to the Washington *Post,* which had also started publishing its own Pentagon Papers series on June 19.[45]

As the first to publish and take the risk of being struck down through government action, the *Times* and Neil Sheehan were recommended for Pulitzer Prizes by journalism juries in 1972, but the Pulitzer Board, in consolidating the awards, voted only the newspaper the gold medal for public service. By custom, news organizations alone had been recognized with the gold medal — a bad break for one of the outstanding correspondents during the war, Sheehan.

Still another controversy ensued when the Columbia Trustees met to give the final judgment on the awards, as was the practice at the time. After hours of debate over the right of a newspaper to make public top-secret government information, the Trustees agreed to the prize for the *Times* but issued a statement that they would not have done so had the award been left to them alone.[46] Sheehan eventually received a well-deserved Pulitzer award in 1989 for his book about the war, *A Bright and Shining Lie.*[47]

Harrison Salisbury of the New York *Times* also created a sensation with a series of articles about the North Vietnamese side of the war, written from Hanoi from the time he landed there at dusk on December 23, 1966, until he left on January 17, 1967. The 58-year-old correspondent, the winner of a 1955 Pulitzer Prize for his reporting from Moscow, once again was nominated for a Pulitzer by his newspaper. An international reporting jury in 1967 voted for him 4–1, the one vote being in favor of an equally deserving feat by John Hughes of the *Christian Science Monitor* for his account of a purge in Indonesia following an abortive Communist coup. This time, however, the Pulitzer Board voted 6–5 in favor of Hughes, and the Trustees ratified the decision.

There is no doubt that government protests about "giving aid and comfort to the enemy" had something to do with the decision but both Salisbury and the *Times* did not let that bother them.[48] The point was that the reporter, for the first time, had been able to assess the damage American bombing raids had done to the North Vietnamese capital, certainly something the American public had a right to know about.

A 33-year-old free-lance reporter, Seymour M. Hersh, formerly a Pentagon correspondent for the Associated Press, gave the military a tremendous shock when he uncovered the My Lai tragedy in Vietnam. It led to the conviction of an American officer, Lieutenant William L. Calley, Jr., for his part in the senseless slaughter of villagers at My Lai in South Vietnam. The exposé was carried by a small news agency, the Dispatch News Service, which placed it in 36 American newspapers headed by the St. Louis *Post-Dispatch* that used it on page 1 on November 13, 1969. With the Pentagon Papers disclosure, the My Lai tragedy also was accounted to have swung American public opinion sharply against continuation of the war. Hersh won his Pulitzer Prize in 1970.[49]

At 74, a leading critic of the Vietnam War, John S. Knight, head of the chain of newspapers bearing his name, also was rewarded for his editorial criticism of the conduct of the war with a Pulitzer Prize in 1968.[50] In covering the killing of four antiwar student demonstrators at Kent State University in Ohio on May 4, 1970, by National Guardsmen who fired into a crowd of demonstrators, the Akron (Ohio) *Beacon-Journal* received a Pulitzer award. So did a 21-year-old photographer for the *Valley Daily News & Daily Dispatch* of Tarentum, Pa., John Paul Filo, who snapped a picture of a weeping girl kneeling beside the body of another student demonstrator who had been shot to death. These were the kinds of outrageous events that caused many an American to want the war to be done with, and quickly.[51]

Other awards based on battlefield reports and distinguished reporting on the home front were of a piece with the more publicized prizes that eventually made it impossible for President Nixon to continue the war any longer. One that was outstanding went to Peter Arnett of the Associated Press, whom David Halberstam once called the best reporter who covered the war.[52]

Nixon quickly reduced he number of Americans in the fighting from the peak of 543,000 in 1969 to 270,000 within two years; and by 1972, only about 70,000 were left, most of them advisers and supervisory officers. However, in his thrusts into Cambodia, a strategy that had little effect on the Vietcong or the North Vietnamese despite their continued heavy casualties, 21,000 Americans were killed in the fighting during the Nixon years and 53,000 were wounded.[53]

With the President facing re-election in 1972 and the weight of the Watergate misadventure about to break both his service in the White House and his career, the Cambodian offensive was called off with the deaths of tens of thousands of Cambodians. All but the final details of a settlement were worked out in Paris before election day; and in January 1973, the peace pact was signed that removed the last American military from South Vietnam. On April 29, 1975, Saigon fell to the Vietcong after the last American civilians fled and all of Vietnam was unified under the Communist government in Hanoi.[54]

The end was little noticed in the United States, nor was it referred to by President Gerald R. Ford, who as Vice President had succeeded Nixon when he was forced to resign or face impeachment for his part in the Watergate scandal. The former President was spared further humiliation with a blanket pardon from his successor for any crimes he may have committed while in the White House.

It was in this manner that the devastating effect of the Vietnam War on American public life was at last ended. More than 20 years passed before another President, Bill Clinton, resumed diplomatic relations with Vietnam. Ho Chi Minh, who had devoted his life to the creation of the united Communist state, did not live to enjoy his victory, but his grateful followers changed the name of Saigon to Ho Chi Minh City in his honor.[55]

THE VIEW FROM MOSCOW

There was scant comfort for the Soviet Union in the American defeat in Vietnam. The Red Army, too, became involved in a 10-year losing guerrilla war in Afghanistan after setting up a pro-Soviet puppet government in Kabul in 1979. A dedicated army of Muslim rebels began fighting the occupation of their country by Soviet forces in that year toward the end of the long regime of Leonid I. Brezhnev.

When Mikhail Gorbachev came to power in 1985 after the relatively brief governments of Yuri Andropov and Konstantin Chernenko, both of whom died while in office, the Afghan war was draining Soviet resources and decisively weakening the Red Army at a time when President Reagan was spending more than $2,000,000,000 to rearm the United States for what seemed like a coming showdown in the Cold War.

It was Gorbachev's first business to try to settle the Afghan war, and in 1988, through United Nations mediation, he thought he had succeeded; but the rebel guerrillas, now confident that they could drive the Russians from their country, refused to accept Gorbachev's terms. The Afghan war rumbled on, although neither the United States nor the rest of the Western world fully realized how desperate the Soviet position had become.[56]

The first crack in the Kremlin wall occurred on a stormy winter's night, December 3, 1989, when the international press had been summoned to meet President Gorbachev and his guest, President George Bush, aboard the Soviet liner *Maxim Gorki* off the island of Malta in the Mediterranean. The Soviet and American leaders, however, didn't seem to have agreed on much of anything; either that. or neither was in a communicative mood. In any event, the reporters were about to wash out the news conference and return to shore when Gorbachev hesitantly volunteered the following: "The characteristics of the Cold War should be abandoned. The arms race, mistrust, psychological and ideological struggle, all these should be things of the past."

For the dubious world press, all that seemed like a very large order, given the Soviet record for keeping its pledges and the indefinite nature of Gorbachev's remarks. Questions rushed at him from all parts of the ship's lounge as the correspondents tried for clarification of his remarks. When would this newest addition to the Golden Rule take place? What would happen to the armed forces and armaments on both sides, including the many thousands of nuclear weapons in the arsenals of the superpowers?

President Bush, mild-mannered and smiling, also offered no specifics when he was asked to comment on his host's pronouncement. He said merely: "With reform under way in the Soviet Union, we stand on the threshhold of a brand new era in Soviet-American relations. It is within our grasp to contribute, each in our own way, to overcoming the division of Europe and ending the military confrontation there."

Now the correspondents clamored for specifics. What, for example, would happen to partitioned Germany? To Communist-ruled Poland and Czechoslovakia? The rebellious Baltic states of Finland, Latvia, and Estonia? The Balkans that even then were on the verge of a merciless Serb campaign of "ethnic cleansing" against the helpless Muslim minority in Bosnia-Herzegovina as Yugoslavia appeared to be on the point of dissolution? What of NATO and the Warsaw Pact countries? And all the chemical and bacteriological weapons of mass destruction that were nearly as horrible as the nuclear-tipped missiles each superpower was aiming at the other?

Neither President did more than smile diplomatically. Through the marvels of hindsight, it is possible to understand Gorbachev's reticence in view of the deplorable state of the Red Army, bogged down as the Americans had been in a hopeless guerrilla war. And while President Bush may not have then known that the Soviets were also arming Iraq in what was later to develop into an Iraqi attack on American oil resources in the Persian Gulf area, he knew enough not to be trustful of Soviet designs. So much for the realities behind the Cold War announcement.

However, regardless of the correspondents' doubts, the deliberately fuzzed up remarks of the principals about the prospective end of the Cold War had to be the story to spread to the world that stormy December night. But in all truth, it was the press, and not the Soviet Union nor the United States, that was signing off on the Cold War, as the unfolding nature of events made clear at a later date.[57]

The principals, having made their comments, discreetly uttered no protests later over the broad interpretation of the termination of the Cold War that had been placed on their statements after the Malta summit. It would take awhile longer before that happened.

What the correspondents saw of events in Moscow after the Malta exhibition may best be described as utter confusion. The Soviets, despite efforts to realize a large profit from the sale of their arms to all comers, had a virtually bankrupt economy. Gorbachev did his best to bargain for more massive American and European aid for his people. But the West was in no hurry to oblige him.

The breakup of the Soviet Union had already begun. Of the 15 constituent republics, some had voted to depart, but none had actually done so. During the difficult winter of 1990–91, while Saddam Hussein's Iraq was gobbling up Kuwait and the Americans were counterattacking and defeating him in Operation Desert Storm, it strained the Gorbachev regime merely to keep Yeltsin's Russia from breaking away.

The empty shelves in the food shops in the cities, towns, and villages; the shortages of the essentials of life in the countryside; and the continuing strikes in the coal mines and elsewhere all had created a no-win situation for the Kremlin. And that, in turn had served to increase the challenges from the Right in Yeltsin's Russia as well as from the old Bolsheviks on the Left.

Taking advantage of the perceptible weakness in Moscow, the fiercely nationalistic Poles, Czechs, and Hungarians disposed of their own Communist regimes. The revolutionary mode spread quickly after that. The Berlin Wall was leveled. The captive East Germans rushed into reunion with the West German economic powerhouse. In Bulgaria and Romania, there were less than complete breaks with their Communist past, but enough to give them recognition from the Western powers. And in what had once been a Communist state that resisted Soviet domination, Yugoslavia split wide open when the Serbs pressed their bloodthirsty campaign to exterminate their Muslim neighbors. The undoing of Communism in eastern Europe was complete.[58]

The call for the final breakup of the Soviet Union became louder. The most prestigious foe of the Soviet system, the Nobel Prize-winning novelist Aleksandr I. Solzhenitsyn, in exile in the United States at the time, proposed to create a new Slavic state in an article published September 18, 1990, in *Komsomolskaya Pravda,* which no longer was a parrot for the Communist party line. It was an immediate sensation.

In his proposed Slavic state, the novelist projected a composite likeness. Together with the Russian republic, he linked the Ukraine as the granary of the land and Byelo- (white) Russia, which had been renamed Belarus. For the revitalization of this portion of his native land, he argued, "What has *perestroika* [change] brought us but a half-hearted reshuffling of the Communist Party Central Committee and an ugly, fake election system with only one goal: for the Communist Party [of the Soviet Union] not to lose power."

He stressed the need for an end to the union as it then existed as an essential to progress, continuing: "Everyone can see that we cannot live together and only by separating will we have a clear view of the future. . . . By this seeming sacrifice, Russia, on the contrary, will liberate itself for precious inner development. At last, it will be attentive and industrious in itself. . . . Is there any hope to preserve and develop Russian culture? Less and less. Everything is wasted."

The essay demonstrated first of all that there was no basis for a merger of views between Gorbachev and his distinguished critic. Even more important, the Solzhenitsyn argument provided support for Boris

Yeltsin's mounting threat to separate the vast Russian republic from the Soviet and bring about the almost immediate collapse of the union.[59]

Perhaps by coincidence, perhaps not, Yeltsin soon moved in that direction. His opportunity came when Gorbachev called for a national referendum to test the extent of public support of his policies. Once the results were shown to be inconclusive, Yeltsin staged the largest rally against the government in the history of the Communist state on March 28, 1991. The editors of the government newspaper *Izvestia* were so shocked that they put out a special edition with the banner headline:

STOP THIS MADNESS[60]

The demonstration continued, however, until an informal truce was arranged at a meeting of the leaders of nine of the 15 Soviet republics with Gorbachev on April 24. The price the Soviet President had to pay was to share power with the nine republics' representatives, to cut prices on necessities for the public, and to speed reforms to bolster the economy.

All this was widely reported by Tass, the government news service, and Reuters, Agence France-Presse, and the American agencies and networks. Nevertheless, conditions did not improve.

It was a heady time for the long-suppressed Moscow citizenry. As more antigovernment rallies ensued, riot police and the Red Army exercised the greatest restraint in avoiding clashes with the protestors. In one instance, an American telecast of a riot focused on a demonstrator who was apparently challenging a riot cop until the latter pulled back pleading (in a translation from the Russian), "Please be careful. We do not want to hurt anybody."

Yeltsin still held back in carrying through Russia's threatened break with the Soviet Union, but smaller states were already conducting plebiscites for independence. Even so, Gorbachev temporized in the summer of 1991 while the outside world watched the scene with morbid fascination. What he seemed to hope for was a massive infusion of American and European funds; but the Soviet Union was such a poor investment just then that, even if political considerations were put aside, so large a foreign bailout was out of the question.

Bluntly put, what the United States wanted was a less-threatening Soviet Union militarily, but there was no way in which Gorbachev could undercut the Red Army in his isolated position as chief of state. To add to the concern of the Bush administration in midsummer, the CIA was predicting that a coup in Moscow was imminent. As if he'd been acting on cue, a leading Communist, Aleksandr Yakovlev, resigned from Parliament and forecast an attempt to overthrow the Gorbachev regime within days.

When it came in late August, the Soviet President was in the Crimea on vacation and was seized there. At the same time, Tass announced the President had been "taken ill" and was being replaced by a group headed by Defense Minister Dmitri Yazov. After that, tanks began rolling into Moscow, and the Red Army was on the march. There was only one problem. Nobody had consulted the Russian President, Yeltsin, who didn't like what was going on, refused to join the plotters, received the backing by telephone of President Bush and Prime Minister John Major in London, and called for the immediate return of President Gorbachev.[61]

The coup failed. But by the time Gorbachev returned from the Crimea, it had become apparent that Yeltsin was pursuing an independent course. He had persuaded his own Russian Parliament to grant him emergency powers to initiate radical reforms to salvage the economy of the largest of the republics with a population of 150,000,000 and a huge land base that extended from the fringes of eastern Europe to the far Pacific.

The first thing Yeltsin did in November to make the Russian republic a going independent concern was to refuse further contributions to what he considered to be a defunct Soviet Union, its ministries, and its foreign debts and subsidies. The Ukraine and Belarus soon joined him in a loose association, and some of the other republics seemed to like the idea of a non-authoritarian commonwealth of independent states, Yeltsin's idea.

Before President Gorbachev quite realized what was going on, he was presiding over a ghost Soviet Union. On Christmas Eve, 1991 (Dec. 25 for the Western world, but for Orthodox Christians it wouldn't be observed until January 7), the chief of a nonexistent state formally broadcast his resignation a few minutes after 7 p.m. with these words: "I hereby discontinue my activities at the post of President of the Union of Soviet Socialist Republics. We are now living in a new world."

It marked the end of the Soviet Union. The new world to which Gorbachev had referred was the emergence of the Commonwealth of Independent States, mainly Yeltsin's creation, which consisted of Russia and the 10 other surviving republics of the former Soviet Union. Sounding very much like a beaten man, the 60-year-old Gorbachev mechanically checked off a few of his accomplishments—the end of the arms race, the "mad militarization" that had crippled the nation's economy, and the removal of the threat of nuclear war. He avoided mention of the Afghan guerrillas, who in their 14 years of resistance to the Red Army, had restored their country's independence.*

As his last official act, Gorbachev signed over the launching codes for the new Russian nation's huge stock of nuclear-tipped missiles to Yeltsin, turned off the lights, and went home. If he had looked up while passing through lonely and lit Red Square, he might have noticed that the old Czarist flag of an earlier Russia had replaced the hammer and sickle red flag that had waved over the Soviet Union for 73 years. It was in this manner, almost unnoticed, that the Cold War ended after 45 years, and the Union of Soviet Socialist Republics crept into history.[62]

THE GLOBAL VIEW

During the 1992 presidential campaign, President Bush was fond of talking of the emergence of a "new world order" that would follow the collapse of the Soviet Union. It was a pleasant distraction, but the American public paid little attention to it, being far more concerned with the nation's mounting problems at home — the theme of Governor Bill Clinton's ultimately successful drive as the President's Democratic challenger. No matter how desirable a better world might be, even a dull school child knew it couldn't come about automatically.

After the nation's sacrifices in two World Wars as well as the conflicts in Korea and Vietnam and other aspects of the long struggle against the power of Soviet-style Communism, there could be no immediate return to peace and prosperity. The national debt had reached a record $4,500,000,000 in a sinking economy. More than 10,000,000 people were without jobs, and 30,000,000 others were so poor that they qualified for federal food stamps. Moreover, in a turbulent world where outlaw nations were trying to acquire atomic arms and others were already fighting their neighbors, it would be impossible to make a sudden reduction in the armed forces to peacetime levels when peace remained so tragically elusive.

The United Nations, which had been designed to keep the peace after World War II, still did not have the means to do so. Nor could the United States, as the sole remaining superpower, afford to contribute peacekeeping troops wherever the UN needed them. It followed, once

---

*The fighting continued in Afghanistan until April 28, 1992, when the anti-Communist rebels seized Kabul and installed their own president four months after the collapse of the Soviet Union. In the struggle for Afghan independence, it was estimated that at least 2,000,000 Afghan freedom fighters died.

President Clinton assumed office in 1993, that he suffered immoderately from criticism by the globally minded that he was doing too little and by the remnants of American isolationism for doing too much.

For the United States, all too often, George Bush's view of a "new world order" developed either into a delusion or a bog of contradictions. From Haiti to Somalia and from Bosnia to Rwanda, the clamor for American assistance became a nightmare for the White House.[63]

The complicated tribal warfare in Somalia, which had caused widespread famine among the unfortunate peoples on the horn of Africa, partially fronting on the Red Sea, was a case in point. One of the first military decisions President Clinton had made on assuming office was to recall all but a small part of the 25,000 American ground troops that had been dispatched there during George Bush's presidency in response to the pleas of the UN. However, other foreign troop replacements suffered casualties when one Somali war lord, General Mohammed Farrah Aidid, reacted to massive humanitarian assistance by opening fire on American and other peacekeepers.

General Aidid's first victims were 24 Pakistani soldiers among the UN's peacekeepers who were killed in an ambush. Next came assaults on the 4,000 remaining Americans and 18,000 troops from other UN members that led to open warfare in 1993. The climax came when Somalis dragged the body of an American airman through the streets of Mogadishu — a picture and report forwarded by a correspondent who risked his life to do it.

The result was so disillusioning to both the Clinton administration and the public that Congress voted an end to the American mission with all American ground forces being withdrawn in the spring of 1994.[64] As President Clinton conceded to more than a hundred television people from abroad at a conference in Atlanta, the problem for the United States was to determine when humanitarian aid in such situations should end and American supply forces should be withdrawn.

The much larger war in the Balkans, in which Serbian aggressors had been conducting a campaign of "ethnic cleansing" against Muslims in Bosnia-Herzegovina, also led to repeated calls for American intervention in 1993–94 after more than 200,000 people had been killed in a ruthless display of genocide. The most President Clinton would do this time was to permit American aircraft to keep Serb aircraft out of the skies over Bosnia, consistently refusing to provide ground troops after the Somalian experience.

Since 1991, the UN had reported that more than 50 correspondents had been killed including some Americans — more than sufficient warning of the frenzy with which the Serb attackers regarded any form of seeming intervention in their affairs. Although President Clinton had appealed to the nation's European allies to lift an arms embargo to permit the Bosian Muslims to defend themselves, the response within the UN was that to do so would only widen the war.

What the President and the Joint Chiefs of Staff finally decided to do in Bosnia, in keeping with the American policy of nonintervention except for humanitarian assistance, was to dump tons of food and other supplies on a series of UN-approved "safe havens," where refugees supposedly could gather; but the ferocious Serbs responded by shelling hospitals and churches in some such places. A minimal display of American bombing from the air as a threat caused the Serbs to accede to temporary withdrawals in the long war, but inevitably the problem of restoring a durable peace became immensely difficult. It was another lesson in how greatly the creation of a "new world order" differed from the brutal reality of the era toward century's end.[65]

Such circumstances greatly complicated the UN's problem of halting still another outbreak of genocide, this one in an African country, Rwanda, after its President Juvenal Habyarimana and President Cyprien Ntaryamina of neighboring Burundi were killed when an aircraft in which they were traveling was shot down in 1994. In the previous year, a cease-fire between two tribal opponents in Rwanda had been agreed upon after a savage outbreak of fighting, but the majority Hutu tribe now began slaughtering the minority Tutsis by the tens of thousands, including women and children. More than a quarter of a million Rwandan refugees streamed into neighboring Tanzania until the border was closed, and almost as many waited in terror, without shelter of food or even drinkable water, beside the river that marked the boundary. It was a pathetic sight that was exposed to the world by television people who risked their lives to film it.

Secretary General Boutros Boutros-Ghali of the UN could no longer obtain agreement from either Europeans, Americans, or Asians to serve as peacekeepers in force to respond to such an emergency. Instead, he asked neighboring African nations to mediate a halt in the murderous preoccupation of the Rwandan majority amid appeals for more humanitarian aid from the United States and other leading nations.[66]

By stark contrast at the time, the Republic of South Africa was celebrating the end of almost 300 years of apartheid with the election of Nelson Mandela as its first black President at the head of a multiracial government that included his white predecessor, F. W. de Klerk. Despite the efforts of a bitter-end white minority that had killed several score blacks in an effort to frighten them away from the polls in the nation's first free election of a government and legislature, quite the opposite was the result — a heartening sign for the future.

The friendly participation of the largest peacetime complement of global press and TV people, including representatives of most major American news sources, made the South African election one of the great events of the post-Cold War world. Regardless of future problems, what Mandela had achieved after spending 27½ years in jail was bound to have a positive effect eventually on the outlook for a more stable South Africa.[67]

Closer to home, the United States had a difficult problem all its own in the repeated refusal of a military government in the island nation of Haiti to permit the return from exile of the Reverend Jean-Bertrand Aristide, the duly elected President of Haiti who had been forced out of office in 1991 and had taken refuge in the United States. Despite the signed agreement of the leader of the ruling military junta, Lt. Gen. Raoul Cedras, the Haitan army commander, he refused to permit Father Aristide's return to power in 1993, and the junta still clung to power. It took an American task force of 20,000, supported by air and naval strength, to return Father Aristide to his Presidency on October 15, 1994, after three years of exile. Three days before his return, Gen. Cedras and other members of his junta fled the country, Cedras going to Panama in the face of the massed support of tens of thousands of Aristide's Haitian supporters.

President Clinton made possible Father Aristide's return by issuing an executive order that took American forces to Haiti. It was the second time in a little more than a decade that an American President had employed troops against a government in the hemisphere. In 1983, to oust a pro-Castro government in the island republic of Grenada in the Caribbean, President Reagan sent in Marines to dispose of a mercenary regime that had been set up by Cuban forces on the orders of Fidel Castro.[68]

Peace had been elusive, too, in the Middle East, from which a steady flow of oil from Saudi Arabia and neighboring emirates was so necessary to sustain American industry. Again, TV first told the story.

Here, there was no question that American interests were vitally concerned, the factor that had caused so many conservatives to complain of American involvement in the area that had led to President Bush's attack on Saddam Hussein's Iraq after he had seized Kuwait in 1991. A parallel issue in the Middle East, the pledges of the United States since President Truman's era to support the State of Israel as a Jewish homeland, had led successive American presidents for 40 years to seek an Arab-Israeli peace accord without avail.

After a secretly negotiated agreement, Israel's Premier Yitzhak Shamir and the Palestine Liberation Organization's Yasir Arafat shook hands on the White House lawn September 13, 1993, with a nudge from President Clinton while their representatives at long last signed a peace accord. It guaranteed an exchange of territory Israel had seized from warring Arabs, for PLO recognition of Israel, and cooperation toward a peaceful Palestine.

Despite fatal gunplay and rioting by extremists in both Israel and the ceded territory in the Gaza Strip and the West Bank of the Jordan River, successive phases of the peace accord were completed amid continuing uproar in Gaza and Israel itself. And although the position remained risky for both sides, amid agonized predictions among conservatives that the much-sought peace would fail, the five-year schedule giving the Palestinians their own land under their own control continued haltingly. Like black rule in South Africa, this had been called an impossibility, but correspondents reported the reality.

Egypt, largest of the Arab states that had made a separate peace with Israel in 1970, was no longer alone in recognizing the Jewish state's right to exist. Along with PLO recognition, Jordan followed suit in 1994 and Syria was impelled to negotiate amid all the familiar cries that peace never would be possible in the Middle East under such terms. And yet, somehow, hope persisted.

Barring a successful fundamentalist Muslim attack on Egypt from Iran, the American government still hoped for the establishment of a stable Middle East. Russia and other Soviet successor states could no longer afford to encourage a state of war among Middle East countries, once an unadmitted policy in Moscow. Iran, the source of most fundamentalist Muslim attacks, had effectively isolated itself from the pro-American Arab countries in the area and was suffering the consequences in a trade boycott. And the old American enemy, Saddam Hussein's Iraq, was under continual surveillance after another threat to Kuwait in 1994.

The position seemed to be remarkably improved over May 14, 1948, when Israel declared itself to be a nation and at once had to resist being strangled by five invading Arab armies that eventually were repulsed. That night at the UN, after the General Assembly had failed to adopt a resolution dividing Palestine between Jews and Arabs, a group of correspondents gathered about Israel's first Foreign Minister, Moshe Sharett, and asked him whether his country could be expected to last 200 years — the time span of the Judean state of the Maccabees of 2,000 years ago.

Without a moment's hesitation, Sharett replied: "I'll settle for 200 years."

Through continued American support and the participation of the PLO and additional Arab states in the accord, the feeling grew toward century's end that Israel just might make it; but the road toward peace would be hard, and there would be many a detour past the wreckage of the highest hopes.[69]

The greatest threat to world peace with the approaching 21st century remained the estimated 100,000 atomic warheads that were now in existance among the nuclear powers, admitted and unadmitted. Of the total, about half belonged to the United States and the Soviet successor states — Russia, Kazakhstan, and the Ukraine — all of them pledged to reduce their arsenals by two-thirds over a period of years. Except for Britain, the other nuclear powers were slower to undertake any phased reduction of their atomic arsenals. And the Chinese, toward the end of 1993, resumed atomic testing in a remote desert area — a move that sent a shiver of horror through the civilized world. In self-defense, the United States also announced a limited return to testing but did not do so immediately, as correspondents soon reported.

Instead, there were complicated negotiations with China to try to reduce the atomic threat. These eventually took the shape of persuading Beijing to try to curb the atomic experiments of its neighbor and ally, North Korea. The Koreans had been defying both the international community and the United States to continue their efforts to make a crude atomic explosive out of a nuclear plant for reprocessing nuclear fuel and producing plutonium, a key element in one method of making atomic explosives.

After prolonged negotiations, the United States announced North Korea's agreement in Paris October 17, 1994, to end its effort to make a plutonium-type bomb in exchange for a U.S. supply of two light water nuclear reactors for the peaceful uses of atomic energy — a deal estimated to be worth $4,000,000,000.[70]

South Africa was still the only country that actually produced an atomic bomb, then voluntarily gave it up.

When Bernard M. Baruch told the UN Atomic Energy Commission in 1946 that its members must elect world peace or world destruction by regulating and disposing of the ultimate weapon through peaceful means, he pointed to the course the world's peoples will have to follow in the next century and beyond. There is no other way to go if civilization as we know it is to survive.[71] That, to date, has been the only conclusion that could be drawn from a half century of nuclear reporting.

10 Tomorrow's Foreign Correspondents

WORDS AND IMAGES

During the Persian Gulf War, Peter Arnett received permission from Saddam Hussein's beleaguered Iraqi forces to report from Baghdad, the enemy's capital. It was a first for TV news when the veteran war correspondent broadcast from behind enemy lines for CNN as the only journalist who was brave enough to take such chances in the midst of a conflict in which American aircraft were repeatedly bombing Baghdad and the surrounding countryside.

Arnett remained in Baghdad for most of the American attack — the air war from January 17 to February 22, 1991, and the 100-day ground war from February 23–27, until President Bush ordered a cease-fire. However, the correspondent won no Pulitzer Prize this time to go with the one he had earned in Vietnam in 1966 as an AP reporter. Nor was he praised for his courage and professional skill.[1]

Like Harrison Salisbury of the New York *Times* who reported from the North Vietnamese capital of Hanoi in the earlier war from December 23, 1966, to January 7, 1967, Arnett was also unfairly accused of providing little useful information from Baghdad at best and, at worst, being an enemy sympathizer. It made no difference what medium Salisbury and Arnett served, as reporters they had to take a lot of flak.

A little more than two months after the Persian War ended, Arnett replied in an opinion piece in the Washington *Post:* "The reason I stayed . . . is quite simple. Reporting is what I do for a living. I made a full commitment to journalism years ago. If you ask, are some stories worth the risk of dying for, my answer is yes — and many of my journalistic friends have died believing that."

In Salisbury's case, he responded in his book, *Behind the Lines —
Hanoi*, in this manner:

> When I began to send back my reports some U.S. officials, notably
> civilians in the Pentagon, felt called upon to turn loose a barrage of invec-
> tive which diverted some attention from the essence of what I was able to
> garner. They made much of the fact that I had not always specifically
> attributed casualty figures to the local Communist officials, although
> what other source one might have in a Communist country I really don't
> know.
>
> But perhaps they wanted to twist attention away from what I was
> reporting. If so they did themselves and the country a disservice. My im-
> pressions centered not only on what we had done and what we apparently
> had tried to do. They also centered on what we had not done and not
> tried to do.

What Salisbury was able to confirm through his observations from
Hanoi was the failure of America's bombing offensive to knock the
North Vietnamese out of the war. It lasted for six more years.[2]

In Arnett's case, both he and CNN continued to take abuse as late as
1994, when an academic critic, in reviewing his memoir as a battlefield
reporter, wrote:

> Television correspondent Peter Arnett's memoir devotes barely 80
> pages to his experiences covering Baghdad. Most of the discussion deals
> not so much with the war as with himself and CNN, the television net-
> work that employed him. CNN's self-absorption is mirrored by Arnett's.
> The Gulf War was good for CNN, which reveled in having a correspon-
> dent in Baghdad on the air, even if he could not see all that much of
> interest or cover the Iraqis in a serious way. The network was delighted
> by the inadvertent commercials offered by air war planners, who con-
> firmed the success of their attacks on the Iraqi electric grid by watching
> the lights go out in Baghdad on cable television.[3]

The New York *Times* had done better for the veteran with a favorable front page commentary on the same Arnett memoir in its Sunday
book review section. All of which would seem to indicate that whether
foreign correspondents work with words or images or both, the fundamental problems of gathering and transmitting news from abroad remain what they were 200 years ago when dispatches had to be mailed.
The armchair critic at home, disdainful of the wretch in the field who
takes the needless risk of reporting from the enemy's capital, still bela-
bors him and his news organization at leisure for not producing some
thundering disclosure of enemy treachery.

Despite that, as Messrs. Salisbury and Arnett demonstrated respectively in Hanoi during the Vietnam War and Baghdad during the Gulf War, correspondents are bound to venture into unfriendly territory as Jared Ingersoll did first in 1765 in London with his report for the New London *Gazette* — a spark that flared a decade later into the Revolutionary War.

It is therefore worth emphasizing Max Frankel's observation[4] of the "difficulties, and often even danger, of trying to reach, understand, report on and explain other peoples, often at times when they are undergoing extraordinary trials and stress." In the century yet to come, the only certainty is that the correspondents' risks are bound to increase with the growth of the information superhighway in which they operate — reason enough for the redoubled support they require at home and abroad.

From time to time, anxious officials have revived old devices to try to maintain the work of correspondents within bounds. The pool reporting system, for example, was attempted several times during the Vietnam War but with lamentable results. And yet, newcomers to the Pentagon tried the pool device again in the 1983 American invasion of the island state of Grenada in the Caribbean during the Reagan administration.

As usual, the theory was that the correspondents selected to follow the fighting up front were supposed to share their material with everybody else, including the military censors. But in the Grenada incident, the correspondents omitted from the pool complained that they had received nothing of use to them for TV, radio, or print. Nevertheless, this is what General H. Norman Schwarzkopf and his superiors at home still insisted upon when the Gulf War began.

Although a conference of editors at home opposed the pool system before the firing started in the Gulf area, they couldn't agree on an alternative plan, and so the Pentagon had its way almost unopposed. The military argument was that it couldn't accommodate an expected 1,600 reporters, broadcasters, photographers, and magazine people who all wanted very much to follow the fighting.

This, in brief, is a summation of what happened after the four-day ground war began.

Several different press pools had a total of 132 reporters and photographers with Army and Marine units, and 27 others were scattered among ship and air bases. However, the delivery of pool reports to all members of the correspondents' corps who had to sit out the war weren't always timely. As one disappointed wire service editor said after it was all over, he received a pool report dated February 25 on March 5, long after President Bush had ordered a cease-fire.

At home, other editors contended that there never were anywhere near 1,600 reporters in the field; by one estimate during the ground war, no more than 300 correspondents actually applied for membership in the pool operation, and a few disregarded military regulations to try to follow the action and report without military escorts.

After it was all over, Burl Osborne of the Dallas *Morning News,* the outgoing president of the American Society of Newspaper Editors, blamed the correspondents' troubles on the failure of the editors to agree in advance on what they wanted from the military.[5] In any event, TV had the last word on the confusion in a critical PBS report prepared by Bill Moyers.

In his production, *After the War,* he supported Arnett's reports from Baghdad that could not confirm Pentagon claims of "pin-point accuracy" in bombing enemy targets. It was, Moyers said, somewhat less than the glorious victory President Bush had proclaimed in ordering his early cease-fire.[6]

What the war did do was to free Kuwait quickly from Iraqi domination and break the invading army that Saddam Hussein had used in the previous year for his conquest. It also demonstrated the usefulness of TV reporting under fire through words and images.

TV AND DIPLOMACY

Clare Boothe Luce, a magazine editor who became a member of Congress, once observed that TV had replaced diplomacy.[7] Well, hardly. But the impact of the medium, in reality, can make itself felt in other ways that differ from newspaper and news periodical journalism. Of that, there is no doubt. This is one experience that is worth preserving for the record.

In an examination of China's observance of human rights in the 1990s, a continuing argument at the time between Washington and Beijing, CBS-TV's *60 Minutes* went underground by using hidden cameras to document how the products of five Chinese prison labor camps were entering the American market in violation of Chinese pledges to the contrary.

Under the direction of Ed Bradley as the correspondent in charge, and with the help of a former Chinese labor camp inmate, the CBS cameras recorded the pictorial evidence in the camps and the businesses of Hong Kong merchants at the sales end.[8] One of the results coincided with a demand by President Clinton for an end to the linkage as part of an agreement to renew China's controversial most-favored-nation, low-tariff trading status.

It was after this that the President also announced the end of the annual practice, instituted under a law approved during the Cold War, that linked China's human rights performance with its continued most-favored-nation trading status.[9] The argument over that diplomatic move had nothing to do with CBS's exploit in revealing how the aged mandarins of Beijing operated in word and deed. What it did establish was the way film and camera can be used to influence foreign policy. It may not happen very often, but the Chinese labor camp story on *60 Minutes* demonstrated that TV can have an impact on diplomacy even if it cannot replace the ancient art of dissembling in the national interest.

The inquiry received a broadcast award from the Du Pont/Columbia University jurors in the distribution of their annual honors.

In another TV exploit that verged on diplomacy, Hedrick Smith, a former Moscow bureau chief of the New York *Times,* produced four one-hour broadcasts for WGBH, Boston, entitled *Inside Gorbachev's USSR,* that were similarly honored. What made these PBS documentaries memorable was that the Soviet Union even then was on the verge of collapse, although few in the outside world realized it.

What Smith's cameras showed, in hindsight, should have been a clear indication that time was running out for Gorbachev and his attempted reforms after more than 70 years of rigid Communist rule. The evidence was all there, including the many different views of a people in transition and how they conducted themselves toward a government that no longer could be of any use to them or to their families.

The American viewer, seeing such scenes on the home screen, was given the opportunity of understanding the kind of judgments of a foreign people that previously had been restricted to career diplomats in the foreign service and correspondents who had lived among the people of Russia long enough to appreciate their plight and the changing nature of their country.

This, too, was the task assigned to Peter Jennings of ABC News in Cambodia when he took his cameras directly into the killing fields of Indochina to record the activities of the Khmer Rouge guerrillas as well as the new-found ally of the United States in Cambodia, Prince Norodom Sihanouk. The result was a one-hour investigative report that illustrated the extent of the continuing impact of defeat in Vietnam on American policy in the Asian Pacific.[10]

There were several other TV ventures into foreign reporting that yielded extraordinary results, not all of them outside the regular 22-minute news segments of the 30-minute network evening news programs. Among them were the following:

For Dan Rather's feature segment in the *CBS Evening News,* he produced some striking reports from eastern Europe that helped explain the doubt and torment of millions of people who lived in the shadow of a new Russia without knowing whether the Soviet Union's largest successor state would be a friend or foe.

In connection with broadcast coverage of China, Mike Chinoy produced a special for CNN that dealt with the uprising of dissidents, and Ted Koppel reported for ABC on what he called the untold story behind the slaughter of some 5,000 dissidents in the 1989 attack in Tienanmen Square in Beijing.[11]

One of the most important series of regular news broadcasts for the American TV networks was the reporting on the problems besetting Israel's peace initiative with the PLO from the time of the White House Rose Garden ceremony, at which the effort was first made known. More than all the words that have been written, the risks in that undertaking were emphasized by TV reports of the slaughter of Muslim worshippers at a Hebron mosque by an American Jewish settler and the Arab revenge that was taken against young Jewish students in New York. Cameras can be more eloquent than words.

Earlier in the century, in the era of Edward R. Murrow, Eric Sevareid, and Walter Cronkite, TV and radio had an important voice in debating and influencing American policies abroad. The enterprise and talent that went into the production of the various TV inquiries in foreign fields toward century's end indicates that the medium's potential for public service is still enormous.

STATE OF THE ART

The American people still receive most of their foreign news through a combination of initial TV, radio, and agency reporting that is amplified by newspaper and periodical coverage, but the system is changing.

Some of the nation's larger and wealthier news organizations are offering skeletonized newspaper reports in electronic form as a monthly service for a relatively modest fee.[12] For the present, this combination of print and electronic services is restricted to those with home computers — a feed-in to the long-anticipated information superhighway of the next century.

For those electronic enthusiasts who predict the ultimate death of newspapers as we know them, however, the obsequies over print are likely to be indefinitely delayed. Even though the total of the number of newspapers has been cut in half with the outreach of the electronic media, most of the survivors show no immediate sign of disappearing from the communities and areas they serve.

On the contrary, the earnings of most of the major corporations that own both newspaper and electronic properties seem to have satisfied their stockholders, with few exceptions. What has happened in the process of change is that the necessities of corporate ownership have imposed a largely conservative cast on the entire field of public information, both print and electronic. The once robust liberal section of the press is dead, with the exception of a few scrawny dailies and weeklies that appear to have an uncertain hold on a relatively small audience. The result, with few exceptions in the field of foreign affairs, is an almost monotonous uniformity of editorial opinion.

Given the mercurial nature of the American people as a whole, it is difficult to predict how long this conservative trend will last. The condition of the marketplace, undoubtedly, will help determine that along with the changes in the media field. There never has been anything neat or predetermined about that pattern, even when the government tried to intervene, as occurred with the attempted censorship of the Pentagon Papers. Mainly, this has been due to the disclosure of exclusive information, sometimes by the leaders in print or TV, at other times by units as small as the Dispatch News Service that broke the story of the My Lai tragedy.

Serving the entire field as the largest of the world's news agencies, the Associated Press usually has been the main source of foreign news for the bulk of the news media, with important exceptions.[13] These are the limited number of news organizations that are still able to maintain permanent staffs abroad, shifting them from one assignment to another every few years. Some of these syndicate their daily reports to clients in the same manner as the AP, Reuters, and smaller agencies.

The weakness of the broadcast media in the daily coverage of foreign affairs is that they post relatively few permanent correspondents abroad, with key exceptions such as London or a central point from which to cover the small wars of the latter part of the century. As Tom Brokaw of NBC put the position for his TV colleagues: "Nobody ever will have permanent correspondents in Paris, Rome and Johannesburg again."[14] He also conceded that the system of TV foreign coverage could be improved.

In consequence, what TV has to do to handle the breaking news quickly is to depend in most instances on local correspondents, either part-time stringers or agents for several different noncompeting services, plus larger foreign organizations like the BBC, ITN, and others. Since the audience for foreign news is relatively small when there's no war in which Americans participate, TV makes no apologies about economizing on day-to-day coverage.

That leaves the basics of daily foreign reporting to the AP, its competing agencies, a relatively few major newspapers with permanent staffs abroad and the local and national news media in the country involved.

The system is admittedly patchwork at best; but that is the way foreign news has been gathered, processed, distributed and presented in the United States for more than 200 years. Nor will the institutional changes now under way make much difference in the process unless government traffic cops make unduly strenuous efforts to police the eventual information superhighway.

To illustrate the way the essentials of foreign news are presented in other than the daily fare of TV bulletin services, I have used the records of the Pulitzer Prizes for international reporting that are awarded annually to newspapers, wire services, and their correspondents.[15]

During the 30 years since Congress voted for war in Vietnam in 1964, 15 American news organizations have won Pulitzer awards in foreign correspondence for themselves or their people. And while a much larger number, more than a hundred, usually send a few correspondents on foreign assignments for this country, not as many have either the money, the staff, or the audience that make possible a wide range of coverage of foreign affairs for daily use.

Those that can't afford such services, even temporarily, generally use either the AP or the syndicated services of the larger newspapers.

During the 30-year period under examination, the New York *Times*'s staff correspondents won nine prizes for foreign correspondence and shared in three others among the 29 Pulitzers issued in this category. The Washington *Post* followed with three prizes and three that were shared. Then came two each for the Los Angeles *Times* and its associate, *Newsday* of Long Island; two for the *Wall Street Journal,* and the AP had one prize and one that was shared.

Other winners with single international awards in the same period were the Chicago *Tribune, Christian Science Monitor,* Dallas *Morning News,* Dispatch News Service of Washington, D.C., Louisville *Courier-Journal,* Miami *Herald,* Philadelphia *Bulletin,* Philadelphia *Inquirer,* and the San Jose (Calif.) *Mercury-News.*

The Vietnam War was the subject in which most of the foreign prizes were won during the period studied, eight in all, with Israel and the Middle East next with six prizes. Two awards each were granted in reporting from China, the Soviet Union, Eastern Europe generally, the Persian Gulf War, South Africa, and Africa generally.

As for the rest, single prizes were given for reporting from Central America, Bosnia, German reunification, one of the Indo-Pakistan wars, the Philippines, Indonesia, and finally, the epidemic of violence against women in many nations that was investigated by the Dallas *Morning News*.

Vivid as the exploits of the TV correspondents have been in this examination of the quality of American foreign correspondence, the Pulitzer Prize summary would seem to indicate that there can be no substitute for the assignment of correspondents to specific areas of importance to American audiences. Most of the Pulitzer Prizes were won by such specialists, whose background and knowledge in their areas gave their dispatches an authenticity no "drop-in" or "parachute" correspondent could hope to achieve. (The broadcast media are ineligible for Pulitzers, but have their own award system.)

It is this kind of reporting that only a few leading newspapers and news agencies are now able to afford to a considerable degree — the quality that distinguishes much of the work of the great reporters of the past as well as the present. And it is this kind of reporting, too, that the free press of the United States cannot ignore for the future, regardless of what combination of the media emerges from the changes now under way.

Aside from the case histories of correspondents already detailed in these pages, the following citations should establish once again the necessity for permanent correspondents abroad for any news organizations that aspire to important national or regional stature:

The China reporting prize awarded to Nicholas D. Kristof and Sheryl WuDunn of the New York *Times* for their work in covering the punishment of leaders of the democratic movement in that country beginning with the Tienanmen Square massacre in Beijing in 1989. A "drop-in" correspondent without knowledge either of the country, the people, or their language would have been hopelessly at odds in trying to cover so important a story over a long period.[16]

The same is true of the reports of Glenn Frankel of the Washington *Post* and the two prizes won by Thomas Friedman of the New York *Times*.[17] Both correspondents were cited for their reporting of Israel's long struggle for survival and its consequences for the Middle

East, in which American interests are so vitally concerned. Aside from China, no area in the world can be more confusing to a correspondent who knows neither the languages or even the histories of the peoples involved.

Other areas where prior knowledge of places and people are essential include the Americas, the subject of Shirley Christian's prize for the Miami *Herald,* and African affairs for which six correspondents won honors for three newspapers — Michael Parks of the Los Angeles *Times,* three members of the staff of Long Island's *Newsday* and two members of the staff of the Chicago *Tribune.* Parks in particular broke new ground in 1987 when he received the first Pulitzer for covering the South African crusade against apartheid.[18]

It is for such reporting in particular that the international award of the Pulitzer Prizes has retained its usefulness. But it is also this type of foreign correspondence that may be sharply reduced if new techniques and new methods make it too costly for the media to support the few specialists who still work from knowledge of their subject.

I do not mean to imply that the foreign correspondent is about to go the way of the knight in armor or Robin Hood. That isn't likely to happen, regardless of future developments. However, there are already almost as many foreign correspondents covering the United States as those the United States news media send abroad with any degree of regularity. There is also no sign that the trend can be reversed in either direction in the forseeable future in all but a wartime situation.

To the American news media today, that is one of their most urgent problems, and it can't be solved merely by saying, as so many editors do under pressure, that foreign news doesn't count for much because the audience is too small. The billions of dollars that the United States earns annually in foreign trade and the millions of jobs that depend on such activity affect every part of the land, as does much of the annual tourist trade from abroad.

It is for such reasons as these, if no others, that closer public attention to the way the information system works should be a prime necessity for the future. The news media as a whole have operated for too long near the bottom of public opinion polls of basic American institutions. Both the public and its media interests might be better served, as an opening to new times, if greater attention were paid to Hispanics as the dominant minority in this country for the next century and to Asians as the fastest-growing group of American immigrants.

In the first instance, after all, foreign news is basically about relationships between peoples. And that can never be ignored.

A NEW JOURNALIST

The grimness with which some foreign correspondents go about their assignments can be matched only by the wariness of sensitive government officials. Neither side trusts the other, but neither can do without the other. This is a condition that has caused a veteran journalist like Henry Anatole Grunwald, for many years the editor-in-chief of *Time* magazine, to write in near despair of the journalistic dispensation in which television and radio compete with newspapers, news weeklies, and monthlies for public attention: "Amid this bewildering welter of communications, who will pay attention, to what and how carefully? The sifting of truth from falsehood, fact from propaganda, sentiment from argument will be even more difficult — and necessary — than before. It will not be the end of journalism, but in many ways the beginning of a new one."[19]

On the government side, there is an even greater feeling of uncertainty about what, if anything, can be done to maintain adequate foreign communications through a free press. A leading example may be considered in the writings of David Gergen, a communications adviser to Presidents Nixon, Ford, Reagan, and Clinton, and a former editor-at-large for *U.S. News and World Report*:

> For a President, the degree to which the modern media — print as well as television — can shape the public's foreign policy agenda is a mixed blessing, indeed.
>
> In some cases, the fact that the media ignore a problem of serious interest to the government makes it more difficult to generate support for action there; more often, the media may goad a President to action, even when no large U.S. interest is at stake.
>
> And as many Presidents have found, the press can be notoriously fickle, helping to build public attention in a potential conflict and then on the eve of potential military action, as in Kuwait and Bosnia, nearly frightening the public out of a military response because of the horrible consequences that may flow. Every contemporary White House thus finds the modern media both unpredictable and difficult to master as it tries to marshal public support for its international initiatives.[20]

In such extremities as these, as Gergen has good reason to know, successive administrations have handled this familiar pattern of democracy in action by matching the compelling images of television against the slower but more rounded reports provided by foreign correspondents for the wire services and leading newspapers and magazines.

Within broadcast and print, of course, there are divergent interests as well that cause most of them to favor some presidential actions and oppose others. And on the side of the Chief Executive, the same situation exists as happened in the Vietnam War and later in Watergate with a notable, if unexpected contribution, from the government side by the fabulous inside source "Deep Throat."

There isn't anything particularly new in all of this any more than there is in the constitutional concept of the separation of powers in which the executive, legislative, and judicial branches of government are expected to contend with each other. What makes the position more difficult toward century's end is the heightened antigovernment feeling among the public that appears to have given the news media a little more influence than usual in the fashioning of public policy, particularly in foreign affairs.

Coming at a time when the collapse of the Soviet Union has deprived the American government of a convenient bogeyman to blame for the always complex conduct of foreign policy when it goes wrong, it follows that the usual confrontations between the media and government have become a matter of greater public concern than usual as new situations arise in the post-Cold War world.

In Somalia, for example, TV has been credited with arousing American sympathies with its shocking images of starving children and causing President Bush to order humanitarian aid guarded by 25,000 American troops. Then, when TV also showed tribal natives attacking American troops, the mighty tube was supposed to have forced Congress to bring the troops home.

The script is neat and persuasive but not very convincing. Undoubtedly, the images of starving children did stimulate American sympathies, but it took an executive order from President Bush to release the food and order the troops into Somalia. And once the mission was over and the native troops attacked, it was incumbent upon either Congress or the President to act quickly to end the American intervention. Congress acted first.

For the future, if the information superhighway comes into being, there's little doubt that even greater claims will be made for the effect of computer-driven TV on public opinion. But such instruments in themselves, effective as they may be in arousing emotion, cannot produce the facts on which a government's foreign policies must be based.

What usually happens in emergencies is that foreign correspondents' reports inform the public while American embassies and consulates abroad communicate with the White House through the State Department. In cases where the government must act quickly, the President then gets TV time automatically to inform the nation and Congress of the event and any necessary decisions.

Through the press and radio, and now TV, that is how the United States proceeded in war and peace through most of this century. No matter how powerful communications may be, there is no reason to believe that it will change the fundamentals of government. On the contrary, it is TV that is in the midst of change in the struggle of the network system to survive against the pressures for the opening of hundreds of channels in the next century. The Federal Communications Commission, too, will have a certain amount of influence, along with the marketplace, in deciding how the public interest can best be served.

Still another player in this complicated operation, Rupert Murdoch, the Australian entrepreneur who only recently became a naturalized American citizen, is likely to make a difference in these proceedings. Having set up the Fox network as a rival to ABC, CBS, and NBC, he seems intent on continually expanding it by buying station affiliates from his rivals, as happened in the case of CBS; but the FCC in the final analysis will also have something to say about whether such raids can continue.[21]

Whatever happens, TV won't be quite the same some years hence.

MORE POWER TO WOMEN

From the time of Margaret Fuller and Jessie White, relatively few women have attained prominence among foreign correspondents, but that position, too, is changing. For the United States alone toward century's end, about a quarter of the permanent staffs abroad are women.

One of the most prominent of the new breed, Christiane Amanpour of CNN, earned distinction for having reported the war in Bosnia longer than any other American network correspondent. In accepting a Du Pont/Columbia University award for a CNN reporting team in Sarajevo that included her colleagues, Jackie Shymanski, Jim Clancy and Brent Sadler, she made it clear that all were part of the team citation: "They have focused the world's eye on the former Yugoslavia, particularly on the plight of Sarajevo's children and elderly, soldiers and victims of war."[22]

Ms. Amanpour also won the praise of President Clinton for her work a few months later in the middle of a long-distance question-and-answer session conducted through satellite transmission while she was in Sarajevo and he was in Atlanta. Although she had annoyed the President at first by asking him why he had "flip-flopped" on aid for Bosnia, something he denied, he later got over his temper tantrum when he talked about the length and quality of her service and self-sacrifice.*

In the Pulitzer Prize competition during 1991, Caryle Murphy of the Washington *Post* also distinguished herself by winning an award for her dispatches from occupied Kuwait during the opening stages of the Persian Gulf War. Despite the occupation of the country by Saddam Hussein's Iraqi army at the time, Ms. Murphy continued to file her dispatches to her paper, even though she sometimes had to do it while hiding from the enemy.

Other recent Pulitzers were won by Karen Elliott House of the *Wall Street Journal* for a series of significant interviews with Jordan's King Hussein in the always troubled and dangerous Middle East, Katherine Ellison of the San Jose (Calif.) *Mercury-News* team that tracked the hidden wealth abroad of President Marcos of the Philippines and Sheryl WuDunn of the New York *Times* and Shirley Christian of the Miami *Herald* respectively for their reporting from China and Latin America.[23]

The latter two were honored mainly for the extraordinary duration of their reporting, Ms. WuDunn's in association with Nicholas Kristof, and for their knowledge and understanding of the areas in which they served.

The remarkable part of the rise in the number of women correspondents abroad for American news media is that it occurred at a time when the small military actions involving the American armed forces had very little about them that was worth remembering. Here were no massive war panoramas like the American assaults on Hitler's Europe, the triumphant entry of American forces in Rome and Paris, or the raising of the flag on Iwo Jima's Mount Suribachi in World War II.

What many women reporters had to observe and describe instead from far-removed areas of UN peacekeeping, with or without American protection, were the sight of scores of victims' bodies, weeping mothers, starving children, the weariness of survivors of nameless battles, the blood and dirt and ineffable tragedy that accompanied desperate tribal and civil wars among native peoples. And occasionally, too, there came the revolting sight, as occurred in Somalia, of an American body being dragged in the filth of a foreign land.

Few women correspondents enjoyed the plaudits earned by Christiane Amanpour, Caryle Murphy or Shirley Christian. Many worked

---

*The incident occurred during a CNN-sponsored visit of several score foreign TV representatives in Atlanta before whom the President appeared the last week of April 1994.

long hours for a few paragraphs on the wire, a blip on TV in a brief scene from a tribal war, a long trip to nowhere on the Gaza Strip, a riot in a native village in a South African election.

As has already been shown, the Spanish-American War correspondents of the last century had a far different tale to tell of supposed male chivalry under fire. There was the example of Richard Harding Davis who was stirred to admiration when he wrote for the New York *Herald* after watching a young Theodore Roosevelt as he led his Rough Riders in that historic charge up San Juan Hill: "Roosevelt, mounted high on horseback, and charging the rifle pits at a gallop and quite alone, made you want to feel you would like to cheer." And also remember how William Randolph Hearst, in a rare moment of exaltation, knelt beside one of his wounded reporters and exclaimed, "I'm sorry you're hurt, but wasn't it a splendid fight?"

Judged by these idyllic outbursts of another day, such attitudes toward war were akin to those of a dozen centuries past, when knighthood was in flower and all wars were regarded as great and noble enterprises. Yet, it had only been a little less than a century between the fantasies of Richard Harding Davis and William Randolph Hearst in a romantic fog in Cuba and the horrible realities that Christiane Amanpour had to describe nightly during the year-long siege of the Bosnian Serbs against the beleaguered people of Sarajevo.

With an estimated 200,000 dead in that city alone, it would have been a rare correspondent by today's standards who would have proclaimed such dirty little wars to be anything other than the horror they actually were — conflicts that the international community had not yet learned to deal with and provide relief for suffering humanity.

After World War II, when some of those accused of the worst crimes against innocent people in that conflict were tried, convicted, and put to death, it was hoped that such punishments would deter similar outrages. That, unfortunately, did not happen. As all correspondents at the fighting fronts in Bosnia, Somalia, and Rwanda reported in horrifying detail, the atrocities witnessed in these areas fully deserved the same punishment upon trial that was given the reckless criminals of World War II. It remains to be seen what the Hague tribunal will do to summon and convict the Bosnian Serb criminals accused in a UN Commission's long-awaited report of crimes against humanity, systematic rape, and genocide in Bosnia-Herzegovina.[24]

The correspondents, particularly the women who often seemed more sensitive than the men, have done their part by calling the world's attention to the crimes confirmed in the UN report. It now becomes the duty of the international community to see that the victims of Serb "ethnic cleansing" are properly avenged.

THE MULTITUDES

Despite all the opinion polls and crowd psychology forecasts, the American public seldom follows a predictable course. Its usual interests are frequently subject to change. And its emotions can often be engaged in support of aid for the needy or another generous cause. Sometimes, under the impact of events, the supposed indifference of many a citizen to affairs outside the nation's borders can change overnight. When that happens, the usually modest numbers of foreign correspondents at home and abroad can swell suddenly to crisis proportions.

The TV screens in close to 100,000,000 homes then become a world stage and its inhabitants a fascinated audience.

That was particularly true when President Clinton paid the nation's homage to its war dead in Italy, in Britain, and on the plains of Normandy 50 years after D-Day in 1994.[25] And in the previous year, when Pope John Paul II visited the United States, the American news media also behaved better than could have been expected, except for crowding about the Pontiff's comings and goings that was due as much to competitive professional rivalry as it was to the public's awareness of the importance of the occasion.[26]

It is not difficult to understand, therefore, why the public believes that so much of our foreign reporting today resembles an unrehearsed mob scene in a Grade B movie. The impression is not confined to the United States by any means. The unfavorable image of the mass correspondent exists, too, in Britain and Western Europe, in Japan and China and India, and doubtlessly in a number of other places.

The public's notion is, of course, grievously unfair to the serious and permanently assigned professionals of all nations who provide the world with the bulk of its international news. But it is not based on fantasy. Let there be a summit meeting, a Cape Kennedy space shot of a new type of rocket, a grand tour of another president, pope, or uninhibited movie queen, an emergency session of the UN about some small-time dictator who is trying to produce an atomic bomb and the correspondents pour in from all directions with cameras, probes, and listening devices.

The issue of herd journalism, which is very definitely a part of the problem of foreign correspondence in general, was muted during World

War II and in the Korean and Vietnam wars. There was more than enough work in all three engagements to keep the correspondents busy, and the public then wanted all the news from abroad that it could get.

But during and after that period, the press's foreign legion again stirred angry debate on more than one occasion. One of the worst outbreaks of reportorial eagerness to cover an event occurred during Soviet Premier Khrushchev's 1959 tour of the United States, when an unrestrained mob of correspondents, photographers, and technicians disgraced themselves and their profession. As James Reston wrote at the time: "We didn't cover the Khrushchev story, we smothered it. We created the atmosphere of hysteria. We were not the observers of history, we were the creators of history."[27]

The AP sounded out its members at the time on whether some limitation should be placed on correspondents, but the returns were inconclusive then — and later as well.[28] The debate flared again after President Eisenhower's 22,000-mile good-will tour of Asia. Robert W. Richards, of the Copley Press, commented sourly: "Our part of the trip was herd journalism at its worst. . . . It's stupid, ridiculous and isn't worth it. The job should be left to the wire services."[29]

There was also criticism of the role of the press as well as praise in the aftermath of the assassination of President Kennedy in Dallas in 1963. Although the correspondents then conducted themselves with both gravity and responsibility, the killing of Lee Harvey Oswald as the assassin before the TV cameras loosed an avalanche of abuse.

The New York *Times* wrote: "The Dallas authorities, abetted and encouraged by the newspapers, TV and radio press, trampled on every principle of justice in their handling of Lee H. Oswald." To which the Dallas *Times-Herald* added that the authorities had made the Oswald murder possible by trying to accommodate the press. Nevertheless, when the accused killer, Jack Ruby, was convicted and sentenced to death, the proceedings were on TV.[30]

The United States wasn't the only place where mob journalism added to the complications of foreign correspondence. An earlier Pope, Paul VI, was trapped in a screeching mob in the Old City of Jerusalem in 1964 partly because the Jordanian authorities had failed to provide security, partly because there were too many journalists, real or fancied, who tried to follow the Pope's visit. However, the Pontiff made no protest at the time, nor did any move to limit correspondents gain headway.[31]

Under the circumstances, therefore, the comparative calm that accompanied John Paul II's visit to the United States in 1993 and the solemnity with which much of President Clinton's ceremonial visit in 1994 to the World War II battlefields was reported came as a welcome change from the circus atmosphere of the past. The hope for the future is that it will continue to prevail.

The nature of the problem of mass coverage may be graphically illustrated by examining the foreign correspondents' listing of those permanently assigned at UN headquarters in New York City for more than three months as of the end of 1993. In some cases, more nationals of a particular country use UN facilities in the event of major news breaks there than are accredited in Washington, D.C., and vice versa. So far as is known, that particular situation exists nowhere else, except in wartime. That is why it is worth study.

To obtain permanent UN accreditation, correspondents from abroad must submit relevant identification such as a passport, two copies of a CV with additional identifying photo, a letter from a top executive of a responsible news organization, and if necessary, an interview with an experienced professional among those who run the UN press center.

In normal periods when there is no crisis atmosphere at the green glass house in mid-Manhattan, about 200 foreign correspondents occupy their own offices at the UN and are served there with transcripts of all available information. Another 400 are likely to attend daily news conferences held by one of the UN's briefing officers, even when the Security Council and the General Assembly are not in session. Americans are in both groups.

During March 1994, a slow month at the time as UN operations go, one official gave a total of 1,147 correspondents who occupied offices, attended briefings, or otherwise figured in the news operation. But over all, as of the last month of 1993, the total official accreditation of non-United States correspondents at the UN in New York City came to 1,028 from 76 countries.

That broke down to 426 TV, 428 press, 68 radio, 44 TV/radio, and 62 photographers.

In the permanent listing, these were the figures for the most representative nations: the UK, 189; Japan, 158; Italy, 68; France, 66; Germany, 51; China, Brazil, and Spain, 30; Republic of Korea, 28; Sweden, 24; Turkey, 23; Russian federation, 19; India and Israel, 12 each; and Pakistan, 11.

Necessarily, whenever there is a Security Council crisis directly involving a proposed action by the United States, there is an immediate demand by all those permanently accredited who seldom attend briefings or meetings to cover the entire proceedings. That, of course, would make an orderly procedure impossible in the limited press space available.

What the UN does under such conditions, especially when many of the 984 accredited U.S. personnel also turn up, is to create a system of priorities, with precedence given to the wire services and major dailies, TV, and radio. For its greatest emergencies, the UN had to screen out correspondents in accordance with the circulation of their newspapers, the lowest receiving the least attention.

However, since the Security Council, General Assembly, and special briefings are all available electronically anywhere in the building, all of those shut out of direct participation in the proceedings are able to follow them elsewhere and obtain a running account of the record as it is compiled and made available in transcript.

At fixed spots elsewhere in the United States, such as Washington, D.C., and Los Angeles, where there are substantial numbers of foreign correspondents in addition to those at the UN, similar procedures are routine by U.S. government agencies when membership or attendance must be limited for any reason. This is especially true of sensitive operations under Secret Service observation, such as presidential news conferences.

However, where no control is possible, the very size of the corps of foreign correspondents in the United States, plus the United States media that also require priority consideration, can make for complete chaos if the authorities directly concerned cannot maintain an orderly procedure.

What can happen sometimes boggles the imagination. At the UN Conference on Environment and Development in Rio de Janeiro in June 1992, for example, more than 6,000 journalists had to be accredited and given access to the proceedings.[32] Scant wonder, then, that the Department of Defense, in arranging for coverage of the Persian Gulf War, tried to create a pool coverage system only to learn that it had pleased very few of the supposed beneficiaries who complained bitterly for months thereafter.

However, it should be noted on behalf of the Pentagon that no correspondent was either injured or killed in action so far as is known during the relatively brief conflict. Among others elsewhere that involved UN peacekeeping efforts among much smaller forces in the early 1990s, a

Foreign Correspondence

318 *Foreign Correspondence*

respected UN source estimated that 75 correspondents, including some Americans, had lost their lives "while covering recent events related to international peace and security."*

PROBLEMS OF REPORTING ABROAD

A dozen of my Columbia graduate students once were asked where they would want to be assigned if they became foreign correspondents for the New York *Times*. With one exception, the newcomers chose London or Paris. The nonconformist, a trenchcoat type, bravely chose a supposedly wild outpost of civilization, Hong Kong.

At the time, the Vietnam War was already well under way with a large commitment of American troops, but the *Times* needed no recruits there. What the students were advised to do, if they seriously intended to devote their young lives to foreign reporting, was to consider sub-Sahara Africa and East Africa as prime news sources for the future, together with Latin America, China, and the Indian subcontinent.

I remember the consternation of my charges when the *Times*'s foreign editor at the time, Emanuel R. Freedman, wasn't greatly impressed with their knowledge of and facility in Spanish, French, and German. As he explained:

"Some Russian will be more useful. And to young people who want to be foreign correspondents, I'd say that it was important to learn such languages as Chinese, Japanese, Hindi, Udu and Swahili. We can't cover the world from Washington, London, Paris and Hong Kong and our correspondents can't go on not knowing languages that are spoken by far more people than there are in any country in Europe except Russia."[33]

It might be added that foreign desks for TV networks and great newspapers today wouldn't be likely to station correspondents anywhere east of the Nile unless they knew Arabic. And a basic knowledge of Hebrew would be helpful, as well, for as long as it takes the Muslim

* The source was Behzat Baris, the former president of the UN Correspondents' Association. He was quoted by François Giuliani, Director of the Media Division, UN Department of Public Information. Ms. Sonia Lecca, Chief of the DPI's Media Accreditation and Liaison Unit, provided the detailed study of correspondents' accreditation and added a few details in a telephone interview.

For those who seek a complete list of all foreign correspondents in the United States, see the International Yearbook issued by Editor and Publisher Magazine. In the 1994 edition, the list is on pp. 16–31 in Part VII, "Foreign Press and Radio-TV Correspondents in the United States."

world to adjust to the reality of 6,000,000 or more Israelis living within its bounds. The time has passed when a reporter could cover Africa from Cairo to Cape Town and Asia from New Delhi to Tokyo as if he were Hildy Johnson racing to a four-alarm fire.

With ever-rising costs being what they are and journalistic efficiency still in short supply, the proposed extension of areas of American correspondence abroad is likely to depend more on the Associated Press than any other news organization.

Of the great American news agency's 233 news bureaus, 91 are established in foreign countries with a staff of 746 that includes editors, correspondents, and communications/technology employees. Among its 15,000 newspaper and broadcast outlets, there are 8,500 foreign subscribers in 112 countries. The AP translates its own service abroad into five languages, with many others being translated by foreign subscribers.

As a cooperative service, its membership of 1,786 American newspapers is the basis for its successful operation, with an annual budget in excess of $38,000,000 toward century's end. However, its 6,000 total broadcast/TV outlets also have become increasingly important for its domestic staff of 2,411 because its progress toward faster distribution of news and pictures for all its outlets has long since made its ancient 60-word-a-minute teletypes little more than museum pieces.[34]

In an annual report circulated by Louis D. Boccardi, the President and CEO, and Frank A. Daniels, Jr., the Chairman, the establishment of a software newsroom was announced in this manner:

> AP's television members in 1993 were introduced to AP NewsCenter, a full-featured newsroom softwear system that provides a tightly integrated approach to managing news production.
>
> Designed and developed by AP's Broadcast division, AP NewsCenter gives everyone in a newsroom shared access to key functions — including news wires, scripting, show rundowns, assignment planning, contact management, archives, prompting and closed captioning — through software that runs under Microsoft Windows on 386 and 486 personal computers linked via a local area network. . . . The news wire capture engine indexes up to eight incoming news feeds and has the most powerful full-text searching capabilities available.

As for the general service at home and abroad, another AP advance in recent years has been the filmless camera, called the PhotoLynx, that stores images on small, inexpensive hard drives, which can be removed more easily than film from a conventional camera. The disks, to quote the engineering description, "slide quickly into a slot on the side of the transmitter and images are immediately available for editing and transmission."[35]

This kind of expanded service and the financial investment that is necessary to remain competitive in the foreign news field would be impossible for all but the greatest of individual American news organizations plus the relatively few remaining competitive agencies, TV operations, and news organizations abroad. It is the principal reason for the widespread belief that the future is likely to be linked to the growth of news agencies more than any other element in the field.

The situation is painfully familiar to old hands in the foreign news business who believed, quite mistakenly, that the expenses of world coverage had reached unexampled heights 30 years ago. Then, American managers were paying as high as $50,000 a year to maintain a single correspondent abroad without regard to transmission expenses and other basic costs.

Toward century's end, that top figure has risen to $200,000, and the relatively few news organizations with more than two or three regulars abroad have sometimes had to go beyond that in crisis situations. As for the cost of maintaining a foreign correspondent in the United States, that has also increased astronomically, so that relatively few from abroad can operate without some kind of subsidy, real or thinly disguised, except for the most prosperous foreign news organizations.[36]

————

It was to be expected, outside the agency field, that there would be a decline in the number of American correspondents abroad once the Cold War ended and there was at least a temporary lull in warlike moves directly after the Persian Gulf War. However, experience has shown that even the most well-meant attempt at a census of foreign correspondents is usually viewed with qualifications, a judgment that cannot easily be set aside.

Having accepted these parameters, I would cite as a basis for comparison a survey of overseas correspondents for U.S. news media — including agencies — that was conducted in 1963 in 84 countries by McGraw-Hill World News. This gave a total of 1,233 correspondents, of whom 310 were listed as stringers. That left a total of 923 correspondents for newspapers and news agencies, most of them in Europe and Asia, with a scattering elsewhere. Presumably, this count did not include the communications/technology specialists who have since become so important a supporting staff.

In a 1992 survey of American correspondents abroad, which apparently was similarly limited, the E. W. Scripps School of Journalism at Ohio University came up with a figure of 1,735 journalists abroad who worked for the American news media, of whom at least 54 percent or 937 were described as full-time correspondents. Of the rest, 234 were called stringers, and the status of the remainder was not known.[37]

Two years into the post-Cold War period at the end of 1994, however, an estimate by Max Frankel placed the total number of full-time American correspondents abroad at only 400 "plus a few hundred foreign nationals who assisted them." Having been the Executive Editor of the New York *Times* and a Pulitzer Prize-winning foreign correspondent himself, Frankel's conclusions deserve consideration. These were his figures for the leaders in all media: *Wall Street Journal,* 24, "plus 60 more on the roster of its European and Asian editions"; New York *Times,* 36; Los Angeles *Times,* "almost as many"; Washington *Post,* 24; *Christian Science Monitor* and Chicago *Tribune,* 12 each; ABC, CBS, and NBC, "seven or eight each."

He wrote, "A great shroud has been drawn across the mind of America to make it forget that there is a world beyond its borders. Except when showing 'Star Trek' or some imitation, the three main television networks focus their cameras obsessively on domestic tales and dramas, as if the end of the Cold War rendered the rest of the planet irrelevant."

Nor was Frankel at all satisfied with the performance of the printed press as a whole in covering the world. As he put the case: "Are newspapers any better? Not many." With reference to *USA Today,* the Gannett paper that ranks in circulation (more than a million copies a day) with the *Wall Street Journal* and the New York *Times,* he added, "[It] normally devotes more space to the U.S. weather map than to all foreign news," then continued, "That leaves too many people depending on the eyes of too few. And what journalism neglects, politics will inevitably ignore. A shallow understanding of the world will damage the nation's sense of itself, its commerce and its standard of living and may blind it to even greater threats. Will America end this century more isolationist than when it began?"[38]

Whatever one may think of television's performance in the foreign field, especially the practice of network stars who occasionally fly to the scene of action abroad for a quick one-night newscast, there can be no doubt that the American public toward century's end gets more of its news from TV and radio than anywhere else. As to numbers, amid all the usual shifting of posts that is inevitable in any daily news operation, whether American or foreign nationals are involved and whether the totals are in the neighborhood of 400 or 900, the only conclusion that can be independently reached is that the United States as a world power is inadequately served by the bulk of its free press in world affairs.

It doesn't help any to blame the public as isolationist or war-weary or too preoccupied with its own affairs. It is only necessary to recall that Britain, at the end of World War II, tossed Winston Churchill out of office at the peak of his career as a great statesman and victorious wartime leader. This is how a free people sometimes reacts at the end of a deadly trial by arms, even in victory. Surely, that can't be attributed to the news media.

SUMMATION

With all the troubles that lie ahead of tomorrow's foreign correspondents, they will do very well, indeed, if they are able to maintain the right to present an independent point of view in international affairs to a sufficiently large American audience. Unless circumstances change drastically, however, the odds may be against them more often than not in their quest for news in such authoritarian states as China and others under Chinese influence as well as the military regimes that still dominate so many nations in Africa and other developing countries.

The fate of the news media in Russia and the associated federated states in the former Soviet Union, too, remains an open question with the coming of the next century. The old Bolsheviks of the Communist era still have power to create trouble, as do the reckless nationalists in the Duma. What happens there, especially in the continued performance of treaty obligations to dismantle the second largest stock of the world's nuclear weaponry, remains a matter of the first importance to the peoples of the next century and the correspondents who serve the outside world.

The handicap of heavier costs will be another constricting factor in tomorrow's foreign correspondence. If the communications superhighway is to be used effectively for the benefit of the public in the dissemination of foreign news, film, and still pictures, it is probable that some more equitable way of sharing costs will have to be devised. With still more newspapers in decline, it is clear that many of today's operations in American journalism are economically unrealistic.

The programs that offer specialized area and language training for journalists interested in foreign correspondence make more sense. Among these are a number of programs offered by the Council on Foreign Relations, the Nieman Fellowships at Harvard, and advanced international studies at the major universities.

The basic difference between the operations for the benefit of working journalists and others that are less practical is that the best ones, like the Niemans at Harvard, insist in the first instance that the student should show professional achievement as a journalist. Too often, foreign affairs specialists, their Ph.D. work behind them, assume that they can bestow their special talents on some palpitating news organization, electronic or print, merely by making themselves available. It doesn't work that way as a rule. Experience has shown that it is more practical to try to make an area specialist out of a capable journalist than to turn a scholar loose in a profession for which he generally has little capacity, scant sympathy, and no understanding. There have, of course been exceptions, but they have been rare.

The drawback to specialized training, however, is more serious. Some of the best prospects, having completed their course work, are too often attracted to opportunities in government or institutional public relations. The remedy, of course, is apparent. If prospective foreign correspondents are to be asked to undergo a longer and therefore more expensive preparation, then their rewards should be adjusted accordingly. Otherwise, we return to the point at which we started with specialized training — the increased use of "parachute correspondents" to cover the breaking news quickly with little understanding of either its importance or its consequences.

It may well be asked: "Why bother?" In the atomic age, when national survival may demand decisions that must be reached within minutes, there is little time for debate. That was made tragically clear in the Cuban missile crisis of 1962. The argument has been advanced, therefore, that it is sufficient to inform an elite group of foreign developments through the government's own information resources and leave the immediate action up to the Pentagon and its experts.

The argument misses the point. While no one can say that the efforts of popular government and an informed public will be able to preserve the spirit as well as the form of democratic self-rule in years to come, an ignorant and a craven public assuredly will kill it through indifference and neglect.

The hard and often unrewarding work of maintaining an informed public in a democratic society, therefore, must go on regardless of all the difficulties involved. Although the news media cannot and should not assume the burden of a whole free people, their influence continues to be vital in persuading large sections of the public in the United States to follow the conduct of the nation's affairs with closer attention to daily and weekly developments.

A case in point is the diddling process through which the international community permitted North Korea to continue its nuclear experiments for years, when it was clear from the outset that this small and well-nigh impoverished nation was embarked on a dangerous course and had powerful protectors. It is no excuse to argue that the objective was to settle the question through diplomacy without alarming Western publics. In the end, the matter had to be faced squarely, courageously, and honestly.

It is most encouraging that impressive and influential forces are attempting to stimulate wider interest in foreign intelligence that directly affects the United States. Chief among these special-interest groups are some of the nation's leading research foundations, the vital new programs and special publications made possible by the Council on Foreign Relations and other foreign-policy discussion groups, and the various international societies of a more general nature.

Probably the greatest stimulus toward the broadening of public interest in international affairs, however, comes from the American colleges and universities as their enrollments increase toward the coming of the next century. The preparation of effective survey courses in international relations at the undergraduate and pre-professional levels offer an increasingly large proportion of students the kind of background that is necessary if they are to understand the role of popular government in foreign policy. Eventually, such studies should help create a much larger audience that is is knowledgeable in foreign affairs.

But whether their publics are great or small, tomorrow's foreign correspondents will have to persevere to a greater extent than did their forebears. In the next century they will face their greatest challenge. Whatever their influence may be, they will have need of it and of wider public support for their activities abroad. For in every gathering crisis of the nuclear era, it will be their highest duty to make themselves heard and understood in a world that still is far too divided for its own good in the post-Cold War era.

In the next century, when the leaders of government will exercise frightening power in defense of national interests, it will be the role of foreign correspondents to seek to create a greater understanding between peoples by bringing them more meaningful news of each other. In so doing, the correspondents may one day become a decisive element in the solution of a crisis between nations. For it may fall to them in the future, as it has in the past, to provide the basic information that represents the difference between war and peace.

Notes
Bibliography
Index

Notes

THE STRANGEST OF HEROES

1. My trip to Vietnam was undertaken for the Council on Foreign Relations in connection with a book about Asian-American relations, *Between Two Worlds* (New York, 1967).
2. The general was William Westmoreland.
3. The bombed hotel was the Caravelle in what is now Ho Chi Minh City.

THE FIRST FOREIGN CORRESPONDENTS

1. Bernhard Knollenberg, *Origin of the American Revolution, 1759–1766* (New York, 1960), XX, p. 221 et seq.; L. H. Gipson, *The Triumphant Empire: Thunder Clouds Gather in the West, 1763–1766* (New York, 1961), pp. 272–73; L. H. Gipson, *Jared Ingersoll* (New Haven, 1920), pp. 140–41.
2. Wilbur C. Abbott, *New York in the American Revolution* (New York, 1929), attributes the founding of the Sons of Liberty to the Ingersoll dispatch. See also Gipson, *The Triumphant Empire*, X, p. 300.
3. Gipson, *Jared Ingersoll*, pp. 140–41.
4. Snyder and Morris, p. 34. See also Arthur Young, *Travels During the Years 1787–1794*, ed. C. E. Maxwell (London, 1929).
5. J. Mathews, p. 43.
6. *Ibid.*, pp. 127, 137–70 passim.
7. Bullard, pp. 6–8. See also J. Mathews, pp. 44–45.
8. J. Hall Richardson, *From the City to Fleet Street* (London, 1927), pp. 169–71.
9. UNESCO, pp. 146–53.
10. Bullard, pp. 6, 216–26.
11. Storey, pp. 1–31. Cooper, *Barriers Down*, pp. 27–28.
12. UNESCO, pp. 18–19; Storey, pp. 32–34, 37.
13. Gramling, *AP*, pp. 13–15; Hudson, pp. 365–67; Rosewater, pp. 57–60; O'Brien, pp. 166–67.
14. Stone, pp. 204–7; Gramling, *AP*, pp. 19–21; Rosewater, pp. 32–33.
15. Rosewater, pp. 100–37; Gramling, AP, p. 42, UNESCO, p. 18; Storey, pp. 52–53; Cooper, *Barriers Down*, p. 43.

16. Louis Untermeyer, *Heinrich Heine, Paradox and Poet.* (New York, 1937), gives the essentials of Heine as a journalist. Marx's journalism is in a number of works, the standard being Franz Mehring's biography (translated, 1935). Mazzini founded a propaganda sheet, *Pensiero ed azione* (Thought and action.) in 1858.

17. See Wiskemann for the NZZ story and Goethe; also Ebel's report on the storming of the Bastille.

18. Carlson, pp. 1–60 passim; Seitz, *Bennetts,* pp. 1–81; Pray, pp. 1–46 passim.

19. Essential material for this section has been based on such accounts as Fayette Copeland, *Kendall of the* Picayune (Norman, Okla., 1943); Bullard, pp. 351–74; J. Mathews, pp. 54–56; and Mott, pp. 248–49. The New Orleans *Picayune* for Oct. 14, 1847 is quoted.

20. Copeland, describes Kendall's Paris experience and return home.

21. Mott, pp. 267–78, 340–43.

22. Ross, pp. 400–3.

23. Bayard Taylor, *A Visit to India, China and Japan in the Year 1853.* (New York, 1855), p. 354; Marie Hanson Taylor and Horace Scudder, *The Life and Letters of Bayard Taylor* (Boston, 1884) I, 414; Taylor, *The Poetical Works of Bayard Taylor* for his "Bedouin Love Song," p. 69.

24. Elmer Davis, pp. 42–46; Salmon, p. 164.

25. *Un Souvenir de Solferino* (trans., "The Origins of the Red Cross") appeared in 1911. See a biography by Josephine Rich, *Jean Henri Dunant, Founder of the International Red Cross.* (1956).

2. THE MASTER CORRESPONDENTS

1. Russell, *Diary,* I, 57.

2. Times, the, *History,* II, 359–61.

3. *Ibid.,* p. 364; Russell, *Diary,* I, 7–8.

4. Ibid.

5. Furneaux, 7–20.

6. Russell, *Crimea.* Also Atkins and A. W. Kinglake, *The Invasion of the Crimea* (London, 1863–67), 8 vols.

7. Furneaux, 127–32.

8. Russell, *Diary,* 7–8.

9. J. Cutler Andrews, *The North Reports the Civil War* (Pittsburgh, 1955) pp. 1–5.

10. Furneaux, pp. 131–32.

11. Starr, pp. 48–50; New York *Herald,* July 23, 1861.

12. London *Times,* Aug. 6, 1861.

13. Starr, pp. 56–57; Bullard, pp. 57–58; Atkins, II, 69.

14. Times, the, *History,* II, 368–69; *ibid.,* pp. 372–73.

15. Furneaux, pp. 155, 159.

16. Times, the, *History,* II, 364, 384.

17. George Adam. *The Tiger* (New York, 1930), pp. 27–28.

18. Andrews, op. cit., estimated reporters from the northern side at about 300; and in a companion volume, *The South Reports the Civil War* (Princeton, 1970), identified 94 reporters who consistently followed the conflict.

19. Andrews, *North,* pp. 641, 650–51.

20. *Ibid.,* 640.

21. Reporters and papers are identified in the two Andrews books: *North,* pp. 751–59, and *South,* pp. 548–51.

22. DAB article on Smalley.

23. Smalley, pp. 129–56.

24. Baehr, p. 32.

25. Smalley, pp. 220–23.

26. Bullard, pp. 15–16; Smalley, pp. 235–36; Baehr, pp. 77–78.

27. Forbes, quoting White, *Memories*, p. 79, on White's journey, *ibid.*, 220–21; Smalley on White, pp. 236–42. See also Forbes, *Experiences*.

28. Smalley on Mueller, pp. 245–46; Bullard, pp. 21–22; Times, the, *History*, II, 434; Forbes, *Memories*, pp. 223–25; Smalley's conclusions, p. 228.

29. Bullard, p. 83.

30. Forbes, *Memories*, pp. 120–26, 228–30.

31. Furneaux, p. 198.

32. London *Daily News*, Feb. 4, 1871.

33. Stanley, *Livingstone*, Introduction, xv–xx; *Autobiography*, chaps. I–XI.

34. Seitz, *Bennett*, pp. 214–50 passim.

35. New York *Herald*, Aug. 10, 1873; Stanley, *Livingstone*, is the best account. See Stanley, *Autobiography*, chap. XIII.

36. *Ibid.*, pp. 264–66, 268, 278–84.

37. *Ibid.*, pp. 295, 512–16, 616–19. See also Stanley, *Dark Continent*.

38. Times, the, *History*, III, 23–39, 125–27. DeBlowitz, pp. 79–115 passim.

39. J. A. MacGahan, *The Turkish Atrocities in Bulgaria*. (London, 1876).

40. Mario, *The Birth of Modern Italy: The Posthumous Papers of Jessie White Mario* (New York, 1909). Carducci's estimate of Ms. Mario was in *Confessioni Battaglie*.

41. Josef Patai, *Star Over Jordan: The Life and Calling of Theodore Herzl*, trans. from Hungarian by Frances Magyar (New York, 1946), pp. 13–67, 351–52. See also Chaim Weizmann, *Trial and Error*. (New York, 1949), pp. 43–87.

42. Nicholas Halasz, *Captain Dreyfus: The Story of Mass Hysteria*. (New York, 1955), pp. 1–14 passim, 64–67, 119–20, 130–35, 159, 250–52, 265–66. Times, the, *History*, III, 795–98. Steed, I, 56–60, 149–50.

43. Seitz, *Pulitzer*, pp. 95–96, 356. For Pulitzer's life, see also Barrett.

44. Stone, pp. 108, 118, 127–28; Barrett, pp. 156–62; Seitz, *Pulitzer*, 352–85, 414–15; Ferrell, pp. 244–50; E. E.Morison, pp. 112–18.

45. Richard T. Baker, *A History of the Graduate School of Journalism, Columbia University*, p. 47.

3. REPORTS FROM A CHANGING WORLD

1. Coblentz, p. 59. See also Gramling, *AP*, p. 137.

2. James Creelman, *Pearson's Magazine* (Sept. 1906).

3. Abbot, p. 217.

4. Creelman, pp. 181–86; Mott, pp. 529–30; Swanberg, p. 120.

5. New York *Journal*, Feb. 9, 1898.

6. Swanberg, p. 138.

7. *Ibid.*, p.144.

8. Leech, pp. 203–5.

9. Barrett, p.178.

10. Seitz, *Pulitzer*, p. 241; Leech, pp. 304–5; Swanberg, pp.159–60; R. H. Davis, *Harper's* (May 1899), pp.941–42; Arthur Brisbane, *Cosmopolitan* (Sept. 1898), pp. 556–57.

11. Brisbane, *Cosmopolitan*, pp. 552–56.

12. Creelman, pp. 177–78.

13. *Ibid.,* pp. 1–119 passim; Seitz, *Pulitzer,* p. 197; Bullard, pp. 343–44.

14. Langford, pp. 166, 179, 192–93.

15. *Ibid.,* p. 201.

16. Creelman, pp. 196–210 passim.

17. R. H. Davis, *Notes,* pp. 95–97.

18. Gramling, *AP,* pp. 143–47. See also Brisbane, *Cosmopolitan;* R. H. Davis, *Harper's;* John R. Spears, *Scribner's* (Oct. 1898).

19. Essary, p. 38.

20. Seitz, *Pulitzer,* p. 241; Leech, pp. 304–5; Swanberg, pp. 159–60; R. H. Davis, *Harper's,* pp. 941–42.

21. Leech, p. 230, 270–71.

22. Brisbane, *Cosmopolitan,* p. 553.

23. Churchill, *Ian Hamilton,* p. 279.

24. Lucas, p. 385.

25. Churchill, *Frontiers,* p 70.

26. *Ibid.,* pp. 65, 87.

27. Lucas, p. 368.

28. Churchill, *River War,* I, 95–110 passim.

29. Bullard, p. 220; Burleigh, *Khartoum,* pp. 204–5.

30. Churchill, *London to Ladysmith,* pp. 24–25. See also Churchill, *Early Life;* Nevinson, pp. 94–95.

31. Churchill, *London to Ladysmith,* pp. 74–95, 102.

32. New York *World,* Nov. 25, 1890.

33. Churchill, *London to Ladysmith,* pp. 177–204 passim. War poster description is from Bullard, p. 320. Snyder and Morris, pp. 250–51, reprints original account of escape as sent.

34. Churchill, *London to Ladysmith,* p. 386.

35. R.H. Davis, *Notes,* pp. 176–77; Storey, pp. 134–37.

36. Langford, p. 220; Churchill, *Ian Hamilton,* pp. 270, 296.

37. Downey, p. 207, quotes Willard Straight.

38. *Ibid.,* p. 217.

39. Gramling, *AP,* pp. 177–78; Lionel James, "The Times and Wireless-War Correspondence," London *Times,* Aug. 27, 1904, p. 6. Times, the, *History,* III, 429–30.

40. R. H. Davis, *Allies,* pp. 232–33.

41. *Ibid.,* 233; "Correspondent Escapes from Port Arthur," New York *Times,* May 14, 1905; Gramling, *AP,* p. 184.

42. Richard Hough, *The Fleet That Had to Die* (New York, 1958), p. 187; Times, the, *History,* III, p. 424.

43. Gramling, *AP,* pp. 185–86; Nevinson, pp. 189–90; *Times,* the, *History,* III, 822, "Russia Expels Correspondent," Philadelphia *Bulletin,* Sept. 21, 1904.

44. Nevinson, pp. 6, 189–90. (Nevinson's complete record is in 3 vols. The vol. *Fire of Life* is a condensation of all 3 vols. It was written by Ellis Roberts, with an introduction by John Masefield.

45. Shub, pp. 176, 178.

46. Cooper, *Barriers Down,* p. 100; Gramling, *AP,* pp. 122–23; Storey, p. 117; Stone, pp. 50–116 passim.

47. Dennis, pp. 1–110 passim, 186–98; Rosewater, p. 219.

48. Gramling, *AP,* 121; Rosewater, p. 219.

49. Rosewater, 220–22, 225, 266–67; Gramling, *AP*, p. 155.

50. Rosewater, pp. 268–69, 270–77 passim; Dennis, pp. 296–298; Gramling, *AP*, pp. 154–57.

51. Stone, p. 244.

52. *Ibid.*, pp. 243–78 passim. Gramling, *AP*, pp. 164–74; Rosewater has technical material on rates, costs, methods of transmission, etc., 268–77 passim.

53. UNESCO, pp. 125–27, 148, 151–55; Storey, pp. 47–48, 88, 104; Gramling, *AP*, pp. 83, 95, 104.

54. Storey, pp. 92–93, 97, 109–11, 123–25.

55. *Ibid.*, 148–50; Cooper, *Barriers Down*, pp. 21–22. UNESCO, pp. 118–19.

56. Lazareff, p. 32. Lewis S. Gannett, "The Secret Corruption of the French Press," *The Nation* 118 (Feb. 6, 1924), 136–37.

57. Morris, pp. 17–24, 26–27. See also Gilson Gardner, *Lusty Scripps* (New York, 1937), pp. 152–63.

58. Morris, pp. 27, 32–52.

59. Cooper, *Barriers Down*, pp. 100–1.

60. Cooper. *Associated Press*, pp. 197–98; Swanberg, pp. 82, 245; Gramling, *AP*, pp. 284–86; Emery and Smith, pp. 557–59.

61. Berger, pp. 99–106; Elmer Davis, pp. 173–90.

62. Elmer Davis, pp.191–238 passim; Berger, 119–30 passim.

63. Berger, 129–30, 133, 151; Elmer Davis, 239–40; Mott, p. 580.

64. Times, the, *History,* III, 580.

65. Pound and Harmsworth, pp. 306–8; *Times,* the, History, III, 431–59. The lives of Northcliffe and Pearson are summarized in *Times,* the, History, III, and in Pound and Harmsworth.

66. Pound and Harmsworth, pp. 322, 440–43; *Times,* the, History, 734.

67. Berger, pp. 181–82.

68. Pound and Harmsworth, pp. 271–72, 324; Gramling, *AP*, p. 206.

69. Berger, pp.187–88; Pound and Harmsworth, pp. 375, 420.

70. New York *Times,* Sept. 7, 1909.

71. Gibbs, *Adventures,* pp. 36–45.

72. Gramling, *AP*, p. 209.

73. Berger, p. 176.

74. Gibbs, *Adventures,* p. 51.

75. Gramling, *AP*, p. 228.

76. Berger, p. 194.

77. Elmer Davis, p. 284; Berger, p. 166.

78. Gramling, *AP*, pp. 228–29; New York *Times,* April 28, 1912, published Bride's story.

4. THE CHALLENGE OF WORLD WAR I

1. New York *Times,* June 29, 1914.

2. Gramling, *AP*, p. 235.

3. Wile, pp. 245–48; London *Daily Mail,* June 29, 1914.

4. Williams, pp. 41–47 passim.

5. Steed, I, 393.

6. New York *Times,* June 29, 1914.

7. Times, the, *History,* IV, 186.

8. Steed, I, 404.

9. Times, the, *History,* IV, 187–88.

10. Steed, I, 407–8.

11. Times, the, *History,* IV, 189.

12. Wile, pp. 253–54.

13. *Ibid.,* p. 256.

14. *Ibid.,* pp. 257–61.

15. Crozier, p. 8, quotes Donohue's dispatch.

16. Times, the, *History,* IV, 203.

17. Pound and Harmsworth, pp. 462–63; Steed, II, 7–10.

18. Times, the, *History,* IV, 208.

19. Pound and Harmsworth, p. 463.

20. Steed, II, 16–25. An interview Ballin gave to Karl H. von Wiegand for the New York *World* in 1915 caused publication of the original letter in the *Times,* which Ballin disavowed. Later, the *Times* insisted the letter was accurate.

21. Tuchman, pp. 107–8.

22. *Ibid.,* pp. 84, 109.

23. Steed, II, 26–27.

24. *Ibid.,* p. 30.

25. Fermi, p. 103.

26. Tuchman, p. 128.

27. Wile, p. 288.

28. *Ibid.,* p. 289.

29. Pound and Harmsworth, p. 464.

30. Williams, pp. 50–51.

31. Viscount Grey of Falloden, *Twenty-Five Years* (London, 1935), II, 20.

32. London *Chronicle,* Aug. 23, 1914; New York *Tribune,* Aug. 24, 1914. See also R. H. Davis, *Allies.*

33. Langford, p. 290.

34. *Ibid.,* p. 293.

35. New York *Tribune,* Aug. 31, 1914.

36. Times, the, *History,* IV, 222–26.

37. Williams, pp. 54–55.

38. Forrest, pp. 106–12.

39. Palmer, p. 300.

40. *Ibid.,* pp. 307, 319–20.

41. Pound and Harmsworth, pp.476–80.

42. Huddleston, pp. 59–60.

43. Williams, p. 56; Palmer, p. 330.

44. New York *Tribune,* April 25, 27, 1915.

45. Herbert Bayard Swope, *Inside the German Empire* (New York, 1916), pp. 195–208.

46. Mowrer, pp. 229–52 passim.

47. Forrest, pp. 25–45; Gramling, *AP,* pp. 238–39.

48. Gramling, *AP,* pp. 239–40.

49. Downey, pp. 292–93.

50. London *Daily Telegraph,* Oct. 19, 23, 26, 31, 1916.

51. Gibbs, *Now Told,* pp. 384–85; H. G. Wells in London *Chronicle,* Dec. 18, 1916.

52. Williams, p. 68; Mowrer, pp. 271–72; Gibbs, *Now Told*, pp. 248–54.

53. Nevinson, p. 318. See also Ellis Ashmead-Bartlett, *The Uncensored Dardanelles* (London, 1928).

54. Williams, pp. 88–96; Berger, pp. 216–18.

55. Times, the, *History*, IV, 292, 304.

56. Gramling, *AP*, pp. 257–61.

57. Forrest, p. 82; Times, the, *History*, IV, 437.

58. Times, the, *History*, IV, 242–43.

59. Sala, I, 251 et seq.

60. Thomas F. O'Donnell and Hoyt C. Franchere, *Harold Frederic* (New York, 1961), pp. 56–60.

61. Times, the, *History*, III, 382–86, 406, 489–91.

62. *Ibid.*, p. 244.

63. *Ibid.*, p. 244.

64. Shub, p. 176.

65. *Ibid.*, p. 178.

66. *Ibid.*, pp. 181–82.

67. *Ibid.*, p. 184.

68. Wiskemann, p. 46.

69. Shub, pp. 186–87.

70. Times, the, *History*, IV, 249.

71. Isaac Don Levine, *The Russian Revolution* (New York, 1917), pp. 275–80.

72. Gramling, *AP*, p. 262.

73. Hicks, pp. 1–248, gives Reed's early career. Gelb, pp. 301–2, 309–10, 323–24, 330–31, has details on relations between Louise Bryant, O'Neill, and Reed.

74. Hicks, p. 260.

75. *Ibid.*, pp. 266–67.

76. *Ibid.*, pp. 276–77.

77. Details in Reed.

78. Times, the, *History*, IV, 256.

79. *Ibid.*, p. 257.

80. Gramling, *AP*, pp. 269–70.

81. Storey, pp.165–66.

82. Hicks, p. 282.

83. Shub, pp. 318–19.

84. Hicks, pp. 400–1. Louise Bryant later married William C. Bullitt in 1923 and was divorced in 1930. She died in Paris at 41. See Gelb, *O'Neill*, pp. 801–2. For commentators on Russia, see George F. Kennan, *The Decision to Intervene* (Princeton, 1958), pp. 331–34.

85. Forrest, p. 87.

86. Gibbons, p. 74.

87. Palmer, Parts I–VI, gives his career. Crozier lists all accredited American correspondents in World War I.

88. Palmer, p. 338.

89. Crozier, pp. 132–33.

90. Palmer, p. 359.

91. Palmer, p. 362; Crozier, pp. 138–39.

92. Gibbons, pp. 76–77.

93. Palmer, p. 364.

94. *Ibid.,* p. 366.
95. Williams, pp. 113–16.
96. Berger, p. 220.
97. Gibbons, pp. 85–93.
98. Fenton, p. 65.
99. Morris, pp. 90–92.
100. INS report, Oct. 19, 1917.
101. Berger, pp. 221–24.
102. Swanberg, pp. 307–8, 316; Huddleston, pp. 65–69.
103. Morris, pp. 94–101; Gramling, *AP,* pp. 277–83.

5. NOT SO BRAVE . . . NOT SO NEW

1. Barrett, pp. 360–61.
2. Steed, II, 267; Huddleston, pp. 127–30; Mowrer, pp. 333–34.
3. Bonsal, *Business,* pp. 1–2.
4. *Ibid.,* p. 28.
5. Morris, p. 116.
6. Bonsal, *Business,* p. 48.
7. Steed, II, 296, 317; Huddleston, p. 152.
8. Barrett, p. 361.
9. Snyder and Morris, p. 311.
10. *Ibid.,* p. 311; Barrett, p. 362.
11. Mowrer, p. 345.
12. Berger, p. 233.
13. *Ibid.,* p. 233.
14. Huddleston, p. 169.
15. Baillie, pp. 60–64.
16. Bonsal, *Business,* pp. 249–50, 259.
17. *Ibid.,* pp. 275–76.
18. Times, the, *History,* IV, 512–13; Barrett, pp. 327–28.
19. Times, the, *History,* IV, 624.
20. *Ibid.,* p. 584.
21. *Ibid.,* pp. 611–12, 669–77 passim; Steed, II, 365–69.
22. Times, the, *History,* IV, 678–98; Steed, II, 384–85; Pound and Harmsworth, pp. 859–81 passim. These three versions of Northcliffe's last days differ markedly in their conclusions.
23. Pound and Harmsworth, pp. 872, 877–78; Times, the, *History,* IV, 699.
24. Times, the, *History,* IV, 765–66.
25. Steed, II, 385.
26. Times, the, *History,* IV, 815.
27. O'Connor, p. 291.
28. Laney, p. 52.
29. *Ibid.,* pp. 53–54.
30. *Ibid.,* p. 31.
31. *Ibid.,* p. 59.
32. Emery and Smith, p. 527; Laney, pp. 60–61; Mott, pp. 554–57.
33. Heywood Broun, *It Seems To Me* (New York, 1941), pp. 201–4.
34. Mott, p. 643.

35. Fermi, pp. 209–10.
36. Shirer, *Third Reich,* pp. 46–48.
37. Jones, pp. 108–19 passim.
38. Storey, pp. 148–51 passim.
39. *Ibid.,* pp. 170–71.
40. *Ibid.,* pp. 170–74; Jones, pp. 137–62.
41. Cooper, *Barriers Down,* p. 100.
42. *Ibid.,* p. 101.
43. Cooper, *Associated Press,* pp. 41–42.
44. Cooper, *Barriers Down,* pp. 15–16, 34, 44.
45. *Ibid.,* pp. 50–51.
46. *Ibid.,* p. 79.
47. Morris, p. 106; Cooper, *Barriers Down,* pp. 81–84; Jones, pp. 371–74.
48. Cooper, *Barriers Down,* pp. 92–93.
49. *Ibid.,* p. 53.
50. Storey, p. 192; Morris, pp. 101, 119.
51. Cooper, *Barriers Down,* pp. 146–48.
52. Jones, pp. 340–41.
53. Cooper, *Barriers Down,* pp. 182–299 passim; Storey, pp. 193–94; Jones, pp. 386–90.
54. Berger, p. 249.
55. *Ibid.,* p. 240.
56. *Ibid.,* pp. 251–52, 254–55.
57. *Ibid.,* pp. 257, 270.
58. *Ibid.,* pp. 239, 270.
59. Ross, pp. 360, 366–68; Berger, p. 327.
60. Webb Miller, pp. 132–33.
61. Berger, p. 326.
62. *Ibid.,* pp. 327–28.
63. Duranty, pp. 95–96.
64. *Ibid.,* p. 122; see Gibbons, pp. 150–59.
65. Duranty, pp. 129–34 passim.
66. *Ibid.,* p. 329.
67. Mowrer, p. 400.
68. Huddleston, pp. 312–14.
69. Clarence Streit, *Union Now* (New York, 1939), pp. 1–11, 300–1.
70. Berger, pp. 280–90.
71. Markham, pp. 135–36.
72. Berger, pp. 292–93.
73. Edwin L. James in New York *Times,* May 27, 1927; Berger, pp. 294–305; Laney, pp. 218–30. See also Charles A. Lindbergh, *The Spirit of St. Louis* (New York, 1953), p. 501.
74. Russell Owen in New York *Times,* Nov. 30, 1929.
75. New York *Times,* Oct. 30, 1929.
76. Gibbons, pp. 160–77 passim.
77. Sheean, pp. 95, 127–28. His exploit is on pp. 91–124.
78. *Ibid.,* pp. 174–75.
79. Shirer, *Berlin Diary,* p. 4.
80. Williams, pp. 208–9; Ross, pp. 360–66.

81. Schorer, pp. 488, 494, 502–3.
82. Mowrer, pp. 532–33. See also *Time* (April 14, 1958), pp. 44–52.
83. Canham, pp. 159, 175, 183, 216, 240, 242.
84. Johnson, p. 414.
85. Laney, pp. 129–31.
86. Ross, 372–73.
87. Laney presents a delightful account of the English language press in Paris.
88. I was in Paris during this period, and summation is based on my observations.
89. Fenton, pp. 137–38.
90. *Ibid.,* pp. 65–66.
91. *Ibid.,* p. 136.
92. *Ibid.,* p. 140.
93. *Ibid.,* p. 142.
94. *Ibid.,* pp. 255–56.

6. THE DARKENING HORIZON

1. Morris, pp. 169–70; Snow, pp. 204–5.
2. Morris, pp. 172–73.
3. Gibbons, p. 278.
4. Snow, pp. 96–97.
5. Storey, pp. 204–5.
6. Willoughby, pp. 30–33.
7. Morin, pp. 183–94.
8. Snow, pp. 100–1, 157–83; see also Snow's *Red Star Over China* (New York, 1936).
9. Mowrer, p. 616; Shirer, *Third Reich,* pp. 191–200.
10. Tolischus, *They Wanted War,* pp. 97–108, Shirer; *Third Reich,* pp. 244–48.
11. Mowrer, pp. 616–17.
12. Lochner, pp. 225–27.
13. Shirer, *Berlin Diary,* p. 14.
14. Shirer, *Third Reich,* pp. 280–81.
15. Shirer, *Berlin Diary,* elaborates on this, entry of March 16, 1935.
16. Mowrer, p. 618.
17. Lazareff, p. 199.
18. *Ibid.,* p. 198.
19. *Ibid.,* pp. 196–97.
20. *Ibid.,* pp. 200–1.
21. Robert Dell, "The Corruption of the French Press," *Current History,* 35 (Nov. 1931), 194.
22. Laney, p. 74.
23. *Ibid.,* p. 75.
24. Desmond, p. 57*n.*
25. Lazareff, p. 33.
26. Desmond, pp. 199–200.
27. Leland Stowe, "Propaganda Over Europe," *Scribner's* (Aug. 1934), pp. 99–101.
28. Lazareff, pp. 101–3.
29. Sevareid, p. 125.
30. Webb Miller, p. 242.

31. Fermi, pp. 311–13.
32. *Ibid.,* p. 314.
33. *Ibid.,* p. 316.
34. Gramling, *AP,* pp. 407–13.
35. Gibbons, p. 315.
36. Webb Miller, pp. 243–47.
37. Gibbons, pp. 315–16.
38. Webb Miller, pp. 255–62; Gibbons, p. 315.
39. Morris, pp. 207–8; Webb Miller, pp. 264–71.
40. Hohenberg, pp. 138–42.
41. Gibbons, pp. 317–18.
42. Webb Miller, pp. 294–98.
43. Gramling, *AP,* pp. 414–15.
44. Matthews, *Education,* p. 44.
45. Berger, p. 420.
46. Matthews, *Education,* pp. 44–63 passim.
47. *Ibid.,* p. 63.
48. Times, the, *History,* IV, 1027–28.
49. Duke of Windsor, *A King's Story* (New York, 1947), p. 317.
50. Morris, p. 213.
51. Times, the, *History,* IV, 1028.
52. *Ibid.,* p. 1031.
53. Windsor, *King's Story,* pp. 340–42.
54. Times, the, *History,* IV, 1038.
55. *Ibid.,* pp. 1034–35.
56. Berger, p. 428.
57. Times, the, *History,* IV, 1038.
58. Morris, pp. 214, 215.
59. Berger, p. 428.
60. *Ibid.,* p. 428.
61. Gramling, *AP,* p. 444.
62. Times, the, *History,* IV, 905.
63. Morris, p. 209.
64. Berger, pp. 424–26.
65. Matthews, *Education,* p. 93.
66. H. T. Gorrell, "War Reporter's Own Story," *E&P* (Sept. 25, 1937).
67. Gibbons, pp. 321–22.
68. Matthews, *Education,* pp. 95–96.
69. New York *Times,* April 25, 1937.
70. "Spain's Revolt Draws Newsmen," *E&P* (July 25, 1936), p. 6.
71. Matthews, *Education,* p. 105.
72. Gramling, *AP,* pp. 444–52.
73. *Ibid.,* pp. 452–57; "3 War Correspondents Die," *E&P* (Jan. 8, 1938).
74. Morris, p. 211.
75. Matthews, *Education,* p. 192.
76. Duranty, pp. 199–200.
77. Canham, p. 242.
78. Morris, pp. 137–38.
79. Lyons, p. 96.

80. *Ibid.,* pp. 82, 291, 465–66.
81. Berger, p. 364.
82. Isaac F. Marcosson, *Before I Forget* (New York, 1959), p. 340.
83. Lyons, pp. 336–37.
84. Ross, p. 378.
85. Lyons, pp. 381–92; Desmond, p. 267n.
86. Duranty, p. 326.
87. Lyons, pp. 600–9.
88. Joseph E. Davies, *Mission to Moscow* (London, 1943), pp. 180–81.
89. Kruglak, pp. 35–38.
90. "U.S. Newsmen Dodge Death in Shanghai War," *E&P* (Aug. 21, 1937), p. 12; "China War Toughest News Job in Years," E&P (Jan. 1, 1938), p. 5. Morris, pp. 173–75.
91. Snow, pp. 195–97.
92. Morin, pp. 315–19.
93. "Writer Dies, 2 Others Hurt in Bombing of Panay," *E&P* (Dec. 18, 1937), p. 6.
94. A. T. Steele, Chicago *Daily News,* Dec. 15–18, 1937.
95. Shirer, *Third Reich,* pp. 305–8.
96. New York *Times,* Aug. 10 and 14, 1937.
97. Shirer, *Berlin Diary,* p. 78.
98. Times, the, *History,* IV, 911.
99. Shirer, *Berlin Diary,* pp. 80–87; Sevareid, pp. 106–8.
100. Shirer, *Berlin Diary,* pp. 96–103.
101. Times, the, *History,* IV, 929–30.
102. *Ibid.,* p. 934.
103. Gramling, *AP,* p. 483.
104. *Ibid.,* p. 485.
105. Shirer, *Berlin Diary,* entry August 23, 1939, pp. 178–81.
106. Times, the, *History,* IV, 977.
107. Morris, p. 221.
108. Berger, pp. 433–34.
109. Gramling, *AP,* p. 491.

7. THE ORDEAL OF WORLD WAR II

1. Tolischus, New York *Times,* Sept. 11, 1939. Shirer, *Third Reich,* p. 625.
2. Canham, pp. 292–97; Lochner, pp. 285–87.
3. Louis L. Snyder and Richard B. Morris, *They Saw It Happen* (Harrisburg, Pa., 1951), pp. 398–401.
4. Morris, p. 226.
5. Chicago *Daily News,* April 16, 1940.
6. Baillie, p. 143; Storey, p. 223.
7. M. W. Fodor, Chicago *Daily News,* May 17, 1940.
8. Lazareff, p. 288.
9. Douglas Williams, London *Daily Telegraph,* June 1, 1940.
10. London *Times,* June 4, 1940.
11. Berger, pp. 437–38.
12. Laney, pp. 317–18.
13. Lazareff, pp. 11–23 passim.

14. Shirer broadcast, CBS, June 21, 1940.

15. Wiskemann, pp. 72–73.

16. CBS, Sept. 15, 1940.

17. New York *Times,* Sept. 8, 1940.

18. Churchill, *Finest Hour,* p. 416.

19. Morris, pp. 229–30.

20. Berger, pp. 446–47; Gramling, *Free Men,* pp. 176–92 passim; Morris, pp. 234–35; Brown, p. 13; Max Harrelson to author, 1963.

21. Brown, pp. 1–52 passim.

22. Morris, pp. 235–36.

23. Jones, pp. 455–90 passim; Storey, pp. 212–18.

24. Wiskemann, pp. 74–76.

25. Shirer, *Third Reich,* p. 839.

26. Berger, p. 448; Cassidy, pp. 38–42; Morris, pp. 238–39.

27. Louis Lochner, ed., *The Goebbels Diaries* (New York, 1948), p. 210.

28. Brown, p. 73.

29. Ehrenburg, pp. 9, 15–16.

30. Morris, pp. 239–40; Cassidy, pp. 109–23 passim.

31. Berger, pp. 449–51.

32. Brown, p. 126.

33. Morin, p. 352.

34. Tolischus, *Tokyo,* pp. 222–24.

35. Morin, pp. 304–14, 334–40 passim.

36. Kato, pp. 18–32 passim.

37. Wohlstetter, p. 51.

38. *Ibid.,* p. 241.

39. *Ibid.,* p. 368.

40. Lord, pp. 12–51 passim.

41. Morris, pp. 241–42.

42. *Time* (Dec. 15, 1941).

43. Morris, p. 244.

44. Kato, p. 58; Gramling, *Free Men,* pp. 271–73.

45. Tolischus, *Tokyo,* pp. 322–26.

46. Morin, pp. 357–59.

47. Morris, pp. 247–48.

48. Brown, pp. 311–30 passim; CBS, Dec. 11, 1941.

49. Morris, pp. 248–49; Gramling, *Free Men,* pp. 312–15; Mott, p. 753.

50. Carlos P. Romulo, *I Saw the Fall of the Philippines* (New York, 1942).

51. Morris, p. 250; Mott, p. 753; Chicago *Sun,* March 19, 1942; Gramling, *Free Men,* pp. 344–46.

52. Snyder, p. 138.

53. Morris, pp. 251–53; Storey, p. 224; Gramling, *Free Men,* pp. 329–32.

54. Gramling, *Free Men,* pp. 351–53, 419–20.

55. *Ibid.,* pp. 368–80 passim.

56. "Stanley Johnston Is Dead at 62," New York *Times,* Sept. 14, 1962; see also J. Russell Wiggins, Proceedings of ASNE Convention, 1957, for his defense of the Chicago *Tribune.*

57. Morris, pp. 254–55; Mott, pp. 753–54; Bob Considine, On The Line column, May 30, 1958, distributed by INS; Berger, pp. 460–62; Hohenberg, 148–52.

58. Gramling, *Free Men,* pp. 389–94, 402–3, 419–26; Berger, pp. 451–52; Lochner, pp. 275–76; Baillie, pp. 127–28; Kato, pp. 77–81; Mott, p. 742.

59. Hohenberg, pp. 152–57.

60. Snyder and Morris, pp. 609–13.

61. Morris, p. 258; Shirer, *Third Reich,* pp. 919–21; Richard McMillan, UP file, Oct. 26, 1942.

62. Morris, pp. 258–68 passim.

63. Wes Gallagher, AP file, Nov. 8, 1942.

64. Lee Miller, pp. 218–19, 220–21, 293.

65. Werth, pp. 208–312 passim.

66. *Ibid.,* pp. 353, 357.

67. *Ibid.,* pp. 438–60.

68. *Ibid.,* p. 435; Shirer, *Third Reich,* pp. 932–33.

69. Lee Miller, p. 252.

70. McNamara, pp. 147–63 passim.

71. Walter Cronkite, UP file, Feb. 27, 1943.

72. Berger, p. 463.

73. Matthews, *Education,* pp. 408–10.

74. McNamara, pp. 156–60; H. L. Matthews in New York *Times,* Oct. 12, 1943.

75. Lee Miller, pp. 297, 299–301.

76. *Ibid.,* pp. 320–21.

77. *Ibid.,* pp. 239, 316–17; Matthews, *Education,* p. 436.

78. Lee Miller, p. 328.

79. Cornelius Ryan, *The Longest Day* (New York, 1959), p. 31.

80. Morris, p. 272.

81. London *Daily Telegraph,* June 9, 1944.

82. Cleveland *Plain Dealer,* June 7, 1944.

83. Berger, pp. 481–82; files of *AP,* Reuters, ABC for June 6, 1944.

84. Lee Miller, pp. 330–36.

85. Sevareid, pp. 431–32.

86. Morris, p. 274.

87. Lee Miller, p. 361.

88. *Ibid.,* p. 363.

89. Canham, pp. 311–22 passim.

90. Lee Miller, pp. 424–27.

91. Werth, p. 370.

92. CBS, April 15, 1945; New York *Times,* April 18, 1945; Shirer, *Third Reich,* pp. 937–79 passim.

93. Morris, pp. 284–85.

94. AP file, April 26, 1945.

95. Berger, pp. 486–87.

96. Morris, pp. 285–86.

97. Primary sources are H. R. Trevor-Roper, *The Last Days of Hitler* (New York, 1947); Shirer, *Third Reich.* See also Pierre J. Huss, INS file, May 15, 1945, and Morris, pp. 286–87.

98. Mott, pp. 757–58; Morris, pp. 287–90; Ed Kennedy, in *Atlantic Monthly* (Aug. 1948); AP file, May 7–8, 1945; New York *Times,* May 8, 1945, Snyder and Morris, pp. 688–93.

99. Lee Miller, p. 421.

100. Berger, p. 488.

101. *Time* (May 4, 1942); Canham, pp. 307–8.

102. AP file, Aug. 19, 1943; Burns, pp. 48–52; John Hersey, *The New Yorker,* June 17, 1944, pp. 31–43.

103. Berger, pp. 49–92; Hollington K. Tong, *Dateline: China* (New York, 1950), pp. 226–28; Snow, pp. 218–19.

104. Tong, *China,* pp. 241–57 passim.

105. AP file, Nov. 23, 1943; Morris, pp. 279–82; Hohenberg, pp. 302–4. See also Vincent S. Jones, "The True Story of a Famous Picture," Rochester (N. Y.) *Times-Union,* April 7, 1960, p. 28.

106. Laurence, pp. 1–94 passim.

107. Berger, pp, 510–15, 524; Laurence, pp. 42–43, 95–97, 112–14, 115–18, 153–60; Leslie R. Groves, *Now It Can Be Told* (New York, 1962), pp. 325–32, 364; Fletcher Knebel and Charles W. Bailey II, *No High Ground* (New York, 1960), pp. 114–15; Kato, pp. 196–98, 236–44; Japanese home service broadcast, 6 a.m., Aug. 7, 1945, included as Knebel and Bailey, *No High Ground* frontispiece; New York *Times,* Aug. 7, 1945; Dickson Hartwell and Andrew A. Rooney, eds., *Off The Record* (Garden City, 1952), pp. 224–28; Hohenberg, pp. 251–55; Mott, p. 759.

108. New York *Herald Tribune,* Aug. 16, 31, Sept. 1, 2, 3, 1945; Kato, pp. 261–62; Canham, pp. 306–8. Casualty figures from L. L. Snyder, *The War, A Concise History, 1939–1945* (New York, 1960), pp. 501–2.

8. THE PEACE THAT FAILED

1. Berger, pp. 498–99.

2. *Ibid.,* pp. 505–6.

3. Lie, p. 64.

4. New York *Post,* March 25, 26, 27, April 4, 5; May 6, 1946; New York *Times,* March 26, 27, 28, 1946.

5. Lie, pp. 74–79. See also Dean Acheson, "Present at the Creation (New York, 1969) p. 198 in section headed "Then to Greece and Turkey."

6. Acheson, p. 150 for Stalin speech and Kennan's comment on it.

7. *Ibid.,* p. 194.

8. I was the New York *Post*'s correspondent at the United Nations, 1946–50, between foreign and Washington assignments. Much of my impressions of those critical early years of the Cold War are reflected in my comments on the issues before the US government at the time.

9. Lie, p. 34.

10. *Ibid.,* 32.

11. These are my recollections.

12. Acheson, pp. 220–25.

13. *Ibid.,* pp. 325–53.

14. Kennan was a key figure in the policy making of both. His *Memoirs* (Boston, 1967) is recommended reading, especially his authorship of the "X" article in Foreign Affairs, the first elaboration of the "containment" policy.

15. On the Berlin blockade, see Acheson, pp. 261–75 passim.

16. Truman, II, pp. 307–8. See also Kennan, *Memoirs,* pp. 471–72.

17. Lie, pp. 327–40 passim.

18. Beech, p. 150; Higgins, pp. 15–34 passim; Morris, pp. 321–22; Mott, pp. 848–53.

19. New York *Herald Tribune,* Sept. 18, 1950; Higgins, pp. 95–109. See also James Michener's estimate of correspondents in Beech, pp. 7–15.

20. Mott, p. 853.

21. Higgins, pp. 130–31.

22. Truman, II, 362–65; Morris, pp. 325–26; Lie, pp. 349–50; Leckie, pp. 176–82.

23. Leckie, pp. 193–209 passim. Relman Morin, "Home by Christmas," *E&P* (Feb. 22, 1960), p. 56.

24. Chicago *Daily News,* Dec. 11, 1950.

25. *Ibid.,* See also, Higgins, pp. 195–96; MacArthur, *Reminiscences,* p. 339.

26. Leckie, pp. 218–28.

27. Lie, p. 349; Truman, II, pp. 436–42; MacArthur, p. 389–96; Berger, pp. 550–51.

28. Beech, p. 207; Baillie, p. 261.

29. AP file, Dec. 5, 1952.

30. New York *Times,* April 9–11, 1953.

31. New York *Times,* Sept. 21, 1954; Dallin, p. 118.

32. Lie, pp. 35–36.

33. "W. L. Ryan," *E&P,* (Jan. 2, 1954), pp. 7–8.

34. New York *Journal-American,* Feb. 5–10, 1955.

35. The full text of the "secret speech" is in Basil Dmytryshyn, *USSR: A Concise History.* (New York, 1965), pp. 401–44, credited to the *Congressional Record,* 84th Cong. vol. 102, pt. 7, pp. 9389–9402.

36. Des Moines *Register,* Feb. 10, 1955.

37. Russell Jones, UP file, Oct. 29–Dec. 3, 1956; Morris, pp. 334–35.

38. Dallin, pp. 412–21 passim.

39. New York *Times,* Oct. 5, 1957.

40. Times Talk, New York *Times* "House Magazine," XIII, no. 3 (Nov. 1959).

41. Salisbury, Moscow, p. 61.

42. *Ibid.,* p. 262; New York *Times,* Sept, 15–20, 1959.

43. AP Log, Dec. 11–16, 1959. "Weary Reporters Puff but Ike Gets Lift." *E&P,* (June 18, 1960), p. 79.

44. New York *Times,* May 1–18, 1960.

45. AP Log, Aug. 11–17, 1969.

46. New York *Times,* Sept. 20–Oct. 13, 1960.

47. Earl J. Johnson, UPI Reporter, Dec. 21, 1960.

48. Matthews, Cuban, p. 15.

49. *Ibid.,* pp. 41–42.

50. New York *Times,* Feb. 24, 1957; Matthews, Cuban, pp. 77, 84, 290, 292.

51. New York *Times,* April 8–20, 1961; AP Log, April 20–26, 1962.

52. Halbertson to author.

53. New York *Times,* May 10, 1961. Ben H. Bagdikian, "Press Independence and the Cuban Crisis." *Columbia Journalism Review,* (Winter, 1963) pp. 9–11.

54. One such report was in the Miami *News* with Hal Hendrix, a correspondent, quoting unnamed sources to the general effect that Soviet experts were building missile sites in Cuba. The Washington *Post* also used such information without US confirmation.

55. Text of Kennedy address, broadcast from the White House, Oct. 22, 1962.

56. A. M. Schlesinger, Jr., *A Thousand Days* (Boston, 1965) pp. 820–21. This deeply

felt and detailed account of the missile crisis is by far the best on record because the author was a part of the Kennedy team in the White House that helped determine strategy.

57. Schlesinger, Jr., pp. 820–41. New York *Times,* Oct. 23, 24, 25 and Nov. 21, 1962.

58. *Pravda,* Oct. 17, 1964; Michel Tatu, *Power and the Kremlin* (New York, 1969), pp. 389, 398.

9. SURVIVING THE COLD WAR

1. Dwight David Eisenhower, *Mandate for Change* (Garden City, N.Y., 1963), p. 353.

2. *Ibid.,* pp. 353–54.

3. *Ibid.,* statement at White House news conference, April 29, 1954.

4. Ike made the point that one metropolitan paper he read didn't even have the fall of Dienbienphu on p. 1 the day the French lost the fortress and French Indochina to Ho Chi Minh, indicating support for his judgment as President not to intervene. See p. 356.

5. With the support of Winston Churchill, Ike carried out his program of keeping the United States out of Indochina once the Geneva Conference ended with Bao Dai's replacement, Ngo Dinh Diem, in charge of an independent anti-Communist South Vietnam and a Communist North Vietnam under Ho Chi Minh. See *Mandate for Change,* p. 371, report of Ike's news conference of July 21.

6. General Maxwell D. Taylor, *The Uncertain Trumpet* (New York, 1959), pp. 130–64. This strategy of "flexible response" was the beginning of the American involvement in Vietnam when President Kennedy was impressed by it.

7. Schlesinger, Jr., pp. 544–50. The Taylor mission to Vietnam resulted in the first shipment of troops to Vietnam.

8. Homer Bigart, "Bigart Tangles with Red Tape in Vietnam Jungle," Times Talk, New York *Times,* April 1962, pp. 1–8.

9. A sample of what the correspondents wrote at the time: "Foreign Correspondents — The View from Saigon," *Time* (Sept. 20, 1963), p. 44; "Foreign Correspondents — The Saigon Story," *Time* (Oct. 13, 1963), pp. 65–66; "Dateline, Saigon: War of Words," *Newsweek* (Oct. 7, 1963); David Halberstam, "The Best of All Possible Assignments," *ASNE Bulletin,* (Nov. 1, 1963), p. 15; "Halberstam Hits U.S., Diem Officials for Interfering in Vietnam Coverage," *Overseas Press Bulletin,* (Jan. 18, 1964), p. 3. As Halberstam said at a lecture at the Graduate School of Journalism at Columbia University on March 19, 1964, "We correspondents . . . had our duty . . . to tell the truth" about the Vietnam War.

10. Harkins, a spick-and-span general whose uniform and demeanor were always spotless, was the hero of another correspondents' jingle to the tune of "Twinkle, Twinkle, Little Star":

> We are winning, this we know,
> General Harkins tells us so . . .
> If you doubt that this is true,
> McNamara says so too.

11. Neil Sheehan, *A Bright and Shining Lie* (New York, 1988), p. 316.

12. See Halberstam's extended views of the war in his book *The Best and the Brightest* (New York, 1969, 1970, 1972).

13. Schlesinger, Jr., p. 989. Browne revisited Vietnam for a series of articles that was published in the New York *Times* beginning May 9, 1994. It was still a quagmire.

14. Sheehan, on Robinson's expulsion, p. 347.

15. The Battle of Ap Bac seemed to be a turning point in the view of the correspondents who reported, with few exceptions, from then on that the war was lost even before LBJ persuaded Congress to put the United States into it formally. See separate accounts by Sheehan, pp. 201–66; Halberstam in *The Making of a Quagmire* (New York, 1964–65), p. 80 et seq.; Robert Shaplen, *The Lost Revolution* (New York, 1965), p. 68 et seq. For the Kennedy administration view, see Schlesinger Jr., p. 982 et seq.

16. Sheehan, p. 352.

17. The substance of the views separately expressed by Miss Higgins and Joseph Alsop were a part of the record I collected and published in connection with my study of government-press relations in Vietnam and elsewhere in *Between Two Worlds*, pp. 39–43.

18. *Ibid.*, pp. 40–41.

19. Sheehan, p. 366.

20. Note to author.

21. Schlesinger, Jr., p. 995 et seq.

22. New York *Times* and Washington *Post*, Nov. 23–26, 1963.

23. LeMay was the commander of the Stretegic Air Command (SAC). At the time the bombing of North Vietnam was decided upon in Washington, General Westmoreland had reported that the Vietcong had overrun supposedly well-fortified bases in South Vietnam and that greater American participation in the war was a necessity. See a report of one of his inspection flights, on which I accompanied him in 1964, as recorded in a survey of American policy in the Asian Pacific conducted for the Ford Foundation, *New Era in the Pacific* (New York, 1972), pp. 230–31.

24. For changes in the Saigon government, see *New Era in the Pacific*, pp. 234–35. Some reports from Saigon had it that 1,000,000 South Vietnamese had been drafted; if so, there was no evidence of that many in the field on the basis of several inspection trips that I arranged with General Westmoreland. The graft in draft-deferment bribes must have been tremendous, even at that early date in the war.

25. For a description of how the bombing campaign against North Vietnam was conceived by President Johnson and his advisers and their reaction to the onset of "Rolling Thunder," see Charles Roberts, *LBJ's Inner Circle* (New York, 1965), pp. 19–31, entitled "A Victory for the Hawks."

26. LBJ news conference, July 28, 1965. For his view of the reporting from Vietnam, see James Reston, *Deadline: A Memoir* (New York, 1991), pp. 313–21. For a description of the protest riots, see Theodore H. White, *The Making of the President 1968* (1969), pp. 64–95, 210–23; Halberstam, *The Best and the Brightest*, pp. 572–73.

27. New York *Times*, Oct. 22, 1967.

28. Sheehan, p. 698; White, *1968*, p. 102.

29. My view of Tet was from the safety of my living room, sitting before a TV set, and viewing the devastating record of the events of Jan. 30–31, 1968. My impressions are in *New Era in the Pacific*, pp. 235–38. The inevitable result was the end of Westmoreland and McNamara in Vietnam.

30. The official figures, as reported from the Defense Department, came later, as recorded herein.

31. LBJ's March 22, 1968, news conference made Westmoreland's removal official. Clark Clifford succeeded McNamara on March 1, 1968.

32. LBJ's renunciation speech of March 31, 1968, and the atmosphere at the time, including the massive student protests, are summarized in White, pp. 161–63.

33. On Paris peace talks, see Hohenberg, *New Era in the Pacific,* pp. 228–30.

34. As late as April 28, 1994, on the op-ed page of the New York *Times,* Sheehan recalled Nixon's statement about not wanting to be the first President to lose a war. The funeral had been held the day before.

35. I was an observer at the Columbia riots, some of my classes having been shifted outdoors at the request of student protestors who wanted to prolong their strike. There was more noise than violence on the Columbia campus, however. I cannot testify as to others.

36. Miami *Herald,* Aug. 7–8, 1968, covered the black riots the night of Nixon's nomination at the Republican National Convention.

37. The violence began four days before the start of the Democratic National Convention in Chicago, and it didn't end until the day after the convention. Although the Chicago *Tribune,* editorially, was not a disinterested observer, its news reports are recommended for a picture of the total confusion they portrayed. Some of it is recorded in White, *1968,* pp. 302–13.

38. JoAnn Fogarty, who was not then Mrs. Hohenberg, supplied the account of the rioting at the University of Tennessee.

39. Reston, as the Executive Editor of the New York *Times,* recorded his performance in *Deadline,* pp. 353.

40. Hohenberg, *New Era in the Pacific,* pp. 251–53.

41. In addition to the demonstrations in Washington, South Vietnam itself was suffering from disillusionment with the war and the Nixon offensive in Cambodia was taking tens of thouands of Cambodian lives. When I returned to Saigon in 1970, I found an entirely different spirit—a cloud of defeat. I recorded my findings and my opinions in *New Era in the Pacific,* pp. 239–58.

42. The story of the Pentagon Papers is discussed to a greater extent in *The Pulitzer Prizes: A History* (New York, 1974), pp. 307–10.

43. Reston, *Deadline,* pp. 328–29.

44. *Ibid.,* p. 329.

45. *Ibid.,* p. 330.

46. See *The Pulitzer Prizes: A History,* pp. 311–13.

47. Sheehan's book, published in 1988, was awarded the Pulitzer Prize in General Non-Fiction in 1989, which also carries a $3,000 stipend. He wasn't on the scene in Vietnam at the time of the joint award for Halberstam and Browne. In the Pentagon Papers case, the Pulitzer Board invoked a seldom-used convention excluding reporters from sharing in a public service prize limited to newspapers.

48. *The Pulitzer Prizes: A History,* pp. 296–99.

49. *Ibid.,* pp. 299–300.

50. *Ibid.,* p. 301.

51. *Ibid.*

52. Arnett won the international reporting award in 1966.

53. North Vietnamese war casualties and costs are stated in *New Era in the Pacific,* pp. 254–56.

54. The AP covered the fall of Saigon, after which the correspondent left with the last Americans just before the North Vietnamese took over and unified the country.

55. President Clinton ordered the lifting of the trade embargo against Vietnam on Feb. 3, 1994, following a permissive 62–38 Senate vote supporting the move. Trade relations between the two countries were thereby resumed as a key step toward recognition.

56. Despite the Red Army's defeat in Afghanistan and the collapse of the Soviet Union, a leading Russian historian, Yuri N. Afanasyev, has concluded that this losing

conflict "taught the current leadership nothing." See his article in translation in *Foreign Affairs* (March–April 1994), p. 24. He concluded that attempts to revive an aggressive Russian empire are "doomed to failure."

57. The quotations from the Gorbachev-Bush news conference aboard the *Maxim Gorky* at the Malta summit are from the AP file for Dec. 3–4, 1989.

58. The liberation of Eastern Europe was reported at first hand when some of its principal actors visited President Bush at the White House. The account began with the visit of Vaclav Havel, the first elected President of the Czechoslovak parliament, on Dec. 29, 1989. Lech Walesa announced his succession to the presidency of Poland on April 10, 1990, at the White House. The Romanian and Yugoslav breakaway conflicts were bloody; however, by contrast, the collapse of the Berlin Wall was quiet.

59. Of all the challenges to Gorbachev and the Soviet system, Solzhenitsyn's was by far the most significant. His article, "How to Revitalize Russia," was published Sept. 18, 1990, in *Komsomolskaya Pravda,* and republished in English the next day in the New York *Times,* p. A-4. The rebuttal by Gorbachev and Solzhenitsyn's response followed in the AP and other wire service reports on succeeding days.

60. Food and other shortages in the Soviet Union were well documented before Congress in debate over humanitarian relief for the peoples of the breakaway Soviet republics. *Izvestia*'s comment was carried by the AP.

61. The story of the failed coup was put together from a variety of sources. Much that happened in those furious days from Aug. 18–21 still remains to be researched on the spot. For background, two *Foreign Affairs* articles were important: Dmitri K. Simes, "America and the Post-Soviet Republics" (Summer, 1992), pp. 75–89; and in the same issue, Adrian Karatnycky, "The Ukrainian Factor," pp. 90–107.

62. For the death of the Soviet Union on Christmas Eve, 1991, AP and other wire service reports provided the basis for this factual summation.

63. Clinton's troubles in the conduct of foreign policy came about primarily because of his prolonged attention to federal public health reform, to which he devoted his major effort in his first two years in office.

64. All American peacekeeping troops left Somalia on March 25, 1994, to comply with a congressional directive and a presidential order.

65. Both Congress and the White House were well aware of an inflexible public opinion that barred the use of ground troops in humanitarian peacekeeping efforts abroad after a murdered American pilot was dragged through the streets of Mogadishu in Somalia. It was of such incidents that a wavering White House and a newly-appointed Secretary of State, Warren Christopher, tried to fashion a foreign policy in the Balkans, where American interests were largely peripheral.

66. Nobody wanted to intervene in the bloody Rwandan civil war, even the country's neighbors in Africa, so that the most that the international community could do was to plead for a truce in the fighting and send in food and medical supplies to be distributed by the relatively few remaining UN peacekeepers while the fighting lasted. It was an abject confession that the civilized world had yet to devise a defense against such savage and inhumane outbreaks.

67. President Mandela took the oath of office and delivered his first address to his multiracial government and people on May 10, 1994, before an approving delegation of world leaders.

68. President Aristide's return to power in Haiti on Oct. 15, 1994, and the flight of the military junta leaders headed by Lt. Gen. Raoul Cedras led to renewed demands in Congress for the withdrawal of American forces. The Republican Senate leader, Bob Dole

of Kansas, argued that American forces had remained in Haiti the last time for more than a decade. The removal was contingent on the arrival of Latin-American peacekeepers.

69. I was among the correspondents who heard Sharett's response. The Palestinian attacks on Israelis in the Gaza Strip and the killing of Arab worshippers by a fanatical Israeli, among other incidents, showed how fragile any Middle East peace might be even if it was achieved. But late in 1994, some Arab boycotts of Israel had been lifted and Israel's recognition by Jordan as well as the PLO kept hope alive for the time being.

70. The United States and North Korean agreement on freezing North Korea's nuclear program was reported from Paris by the New York *Times* Oct. 17, 1994. The *Times* said the pact was based on a U.S. supply of light water nuclear reactors for peaceful uses at a cost estimated at $4,000,000,000. It was a deal that raised doubts of eventual fulfillment.

71. Bernard M. Baruch, *The Public Years* (New York, 1960), 369.

10. TOMORROW'S FOREIGN CORRESPONDENTS

1. "War Over, the Press Looks Back," *Presstime* magazine (April 1991), pp. 40–41.

2. Harrison E. Salisbury, *Behind the Lines — Hanoi* (New York, 1967), p. 209.

3. Professor Eliot A. Cohen, Johns Hopkins University, in *Foreign Affairs* (May–June, 1994), p. 142.

4. Frankel note, May 16, 1994.

5. "War Over . . . ," *Presstime,* pp. 40–41.

6. Moyers' *After the War* was aired June 18, 1991. It was among the broadcasts for which he received a Du Pont/Columbia award Jan. 30, 1992.

7. Henry A. Grunwald, "The Post-Cold War Press," *Foreign Affairs* (Summer, 1993), p. 16.

8. "Made in China," aired by CBS's *60 Minutes,* was honored with a Du Pont/Columbia award Jan. 28, 1993.

9. "China Will Yield on Trade Issue," New York *Times,* May 18, 1994, p. 1. On May 26, President Clinton abandoned the linkage between trade and human rights and renewed China's MFN trade status.

10. "Inside Gorbachev's U.S.S.R." received a Du Pont/Columbia award Jan. 29, 1991. Peter Jennings and the ABC program, *The Killing Fields,* were honored the same night.

11. Rather was honored Jan. 29, 1991; Chinoy and Koppel, on Jan. 25, 1990.

12. The Atlanta *Journal-Constitution* charges $6.95 a month for its electronic news service to home computers. The *Wall Street Journal* has a more elaborate financial service. Others vary with the degree of complexity and length of the offering. But the service appears to be popular among computer operators.

13. The AP is a membership organization and serves most of the existing American newspapers as well as others at home and abroad who buy the service's various types of offerings for the media.

14. The comment was in *TV Guide* (Oct. 2, 1993), p. 33.

15. Columbia University publishes a white book, a complete record of all the Pulitzer awards from their inception in 1917, that is updated from time to time. There is also a history of the awards that I was commissioned to research and write for the 60th anniversary of the prizes.

16. The Kristof-WuDunn prize was awarded in 1990.

17. Glenn Frankel's prize was awarded in 1989; Friedman's, in 1988; and, shared with Loren Jenkins of the Washington *Post,* in 1983.

18. Prizes were awarded as follows: Parks, 1987; Christian, 1981; three from *Newsday*, 1985; two from the Chicago *Tribune*, 1975.

19. Grunwald, p. 16.

20. David Gergen, "Adapting U.S. Foreign Policy Making to Changing Domestic Circumstances," in *Beyond the Beltway: Engaging the Public in U. S. Foreign Policy*, ed. Daniel Yankelovich and I. M. Destler (New York, 1994), p. 83.

21. "Issues of Foreign Ownership Cloud the Future of Fox TV," the New York *Times*, June 3, 1994, p. 1.

22. The prize for Ms. Amanpour and the CNN team was awarded Jan. 27, 1994.

23. The Murphy award was in 1991; House, in 1984; and Ellison and the San Jose team won in 1986.

24. "UN Panel Accuses the Serbs of Crimes Against Humanity," the New York *Times*, June 3, 1994, p. 1.

25. The President's week of memorials in Western Europe was climaxed on June 6, 1994, with his D-Day address.

26. Pope John Paul II visited the United States in August 1993 to celebrate a Roman Catholic Youth Festival before an audience of 90,000 in Denver. South of Denver on Aug. 15, he conducted a mass for 400,000 people.

27. "When the Press Shapes the News." *Saturday Rev.* (Jan. 11, 1964), pp. 75–85.

28. AP Log, Dec. 11–16, 1959.

29. AP Log, June 1–7, 1961.

30. AP Log, Nov. 20–26, 1963.

31. "The Pope in the Holy Land," AP Log, Jan. 1–7, 1964.

32. Letter of May 9, 1994, from François Giuliani, Director, Media Division, UN Department of Public Information. Most journalists who have worked at international conferences are familiar with the spectacle of huge requests for accreditation and relatively small numbers of the working press who actually cover the event. The explanation is not hard to find, for large delegations often use nonworking observers in the press section.

33. What Emanuel Freedman had to say about preparation for foreign correspondents in the spring of 1963, when my notes are dated, is as true today as it was then. The scope of most foreign correspondence still does not match the need.

34. May 1994, "Facts," an AP publication giving basic figures on the size and scope of the organization. Some figures are rounded off.

35. AP annual report, 1994, pp. 6 and 9.

36. My information is based on notes from conversations with editors and correspondents, the latter on several of my trips to the Indian subcontinent and the Far East. One of the few discussions of soaring costs in foreign correspondence that deal with specifics was in *Presstime* (April, 1980), pp. 18–19, in which a *Time* magazine editor estimated that his cost per correspondent abroad would exceed $200,000 annually at that time. A Los Angeles *Times* foreign editor put his cost per correspondent at $150,000. Since then, the field has grown even more expensive.

37. The McGraw-Hill survey was in the *Journalism Quarterly* (Spring, 1963), at a time when there were widespread complaints about the "vanishing foreign correspondent." The Ohio University survey of 1992 closely follows the count of almost 30 years before. Both contrast sharply with the great masses of foreign correspondents in the United States, as reported by the United Nations and the US Information Agency in Washington and *The Editor and Publisher International Year Book*, which is the most complete.

38. Frankel's opinions and figures were in his piece, "The Shroud," the New York *Times* Magazine (Nov. 27, 1994), pp. 42–44.

Bibliography

Abbot, Willis J. *Watching the World Go By*. Boston, 1933.

Abbott, Wilbur C. *New York in the American Revolution*. New York, 1929.

Acheson, Dean. *Present at the Creation*. New York, 1969.

Adam, George. *The Tiger*. New York. 1930.

Andrews, J. Cutler. *The North Reports the Civil War*. Pittsburgh, 1955.

————. *The South Reports the Civil War*. Princeton, 1970.

Atkins, J. B. *Life of Sir William Howard Russell*. 2 vols. 1911.

Baehr, Harry W., Jr. The New York Tribune *Since the Civil War*. New York, 1936.

Baillie, Hugh. *High Tension*. New York, 1959.

Baruch, Bernard M. *My Own Story*. New York, 1957.

————. *The Public Years*. New York, 1960.

Barrett, James W. *Joseph Pulitzer and His World*. New York, 1941.

Beatty, Richmond C. *Bayard Taylor, Laureate of the Gilded Age*. Norman, Okla., 1936.

Beech, Keyes. *Tokyo and Points East*. New York, 1954.

Berger, Meyer. *The Story of* The New York Times, *1851–1951*. New York, 1951.

Billington, James H. *The Icon and the Axe, An Interpretive History of Russian Culture*. New York, 1966.

Bonsal, Stephen. *Heydey in a Vanished World*. New York, 1937.

————. *Unfinished Business*. New York, 1944.

Brown, Cecil. *Suez to Singapore*. New York, 1942.

Brown, Lewis, and Elsa Wiehl *That Man Heine*. Boston, 1927.

Bullard, F. Lauriston. *Famous War Correspondents*. Boston, 1914.

Burleigh, Bennet. *Khartoum Campaign*. London, 1899. Sirdar and Khalifa London, 1898.

Burns, James McGregor. *John Kennedy*. New York, 1959.

Canham, Erwin D. *Commitment to Freedom: The Story of the* Christian Science Monitor. Boston, 1958.

349

Carlson, Oliver. *The Man Who Made News: James Gordon Bennett.* New York, 1942.

Cassidy, Henry C. *Moscow Dateline.* Boston, 1943.

Churchill, Winston S. His four early books covering his life as a soldier and war correspondent. New York, 1962.

——. *Ian Hamilton's March.* London, 1900.

——. *London to Ladysmith via Pretoria.* New York, 1900.

——. *My Early Life: A Roving Commission.* London, 1930.

——. *The River War.* 2 vols. London, 1899.

The above four volumes were republished as a unit in New York in 1962. The six volumes below were published over the five years beginning in 1953:

——. *The Second World War.* 6 vols. New York, 1948–53. Vol. 2: *Their Finest Hour,* 1949.

Coblentz, E. D. *William Randolph Hearst: A Portrait in His Own Words.* New York, 1952.

Coit, Margaret. *Mr. Baruch.* New York, 1957.

Compton, Arthur H. *Atomic Quest* New York, 1956.

Cooper, Kent. *Barriers Down.* New York, 1942.

——. *Kent Cooper and the Associated Press.* New York, 1959.

Copeland, Fayette. *Kendall of the* Picayune. Norman, Okla. 1948.

Creelman, James. *On the Great Highway.* Boston, 1901.

Crozier, Emmet. *American Reporters on the Western Front, 1914–1918.* New York, 1959.

Dallin, David J. *Foreign Policy After Stalin.* Philadelphia, 1961.

Davis, Elmer. *History of The New York* Times, *1851–1921.* New York, 1921.

Davis, Richard Harding. *Notes of a War Correspondent.* New York, 1910.

——. *With the Allies.* New York, 1914.

DeBlowitz, Henri George Stephan Adolphe. *Memoirs of M. DeBlowitz.* New York, 1903.

Dennis, Charles H. *Victor Lawson.* Chicago, 1935.

Desmond Robert W. *The Press and World Affairs.* New York, 1927.

Downey, Fairfax D. *Richard Harding Davis: His Day.* New York, 1933.

Duranty, Walter. *I Write as I Please.* New York, 1932.

Ebel, Gottfried. In the *Zürcher Zeitung,* dispatch from Paris dated July 17, 1789, about the storming of the Bastille.

Emery, Edwin, and Henry Ladd Smith. *The Press and America.* New York, 1954.

Ehrenburg, Ilya. *The Tempering of Russia.* New York, 1944.

Eisenhower, Dwight D. *Mandate for Change.* Garden City, N.Y., 1963.

Emerson, Ralph Waldo. *English Traits.* London, 1856.

Essary, J. Fred. *Covering Washington.* Boston, 1927.

Fenton, Charles A. *The Apprenticeship of Ernest Hemingway.* New York, 1954.

Fermi, Laura. *Mussolini.* Chicago, 1961.

Forbes, Archibald. *Memories and Studies of War and Peace.* London, 1895.

——. *My Experiences of the War Between France and Germany.* 2 vols. London, 1871.

————. *Souvenirs of Some Continents.* London, 1885.

Forrest, Wilbur. *Behind the Front Page.* New York, 1934.

Furneaux, Rupert. *The First War Correspondent: William Howard Russell of the* Times. London, 1944.

Gardener, Gilson. *Lusty Scripps.* New York, 1937.

Gelb, Arthur, and Barbara Gelb. *O'Neill.* New York, 1962.

Gibbons, Edward. *Floyd Gibbons.* New York, 1953.

Gibbs, Sir Philip. *Adventures in Journalism.* New York, 1922.

————. *Now It Can Be Told.* New York 1920.

Gipson, L.H. *Jared Ingersoll.* New Haven, 1920.

————. *The Triumphant Empire: Thunder Clouds Gather in the West, 1763–1766.* New York, 1961.

Gramling, Oliver. *AP: The Story of News.* New York, 1940.

————. *Free Men Are Fighting.* New York, 1942.

Groves, Leslie R. *Now It Can Be Told.* New York, 1968.

Halasz, Nicholas. *Captain Dreyfus: The Story of Mass Hysteria.* New York, 1955.

Halberstam, David. *The Best and the Brightest.* New York, 1969, 1970, 1972.

————. *The Making of a Quagmire.* New York, 1964–65.

Hartwelll'Dickson, and Andrew A.Rooney, eds. *Off the Record. Inside Stories by Members of the Overseas Press Club.* New York, 1952.

Heine, Heinrich. *Memoirs.* Edited by Gustav Karpeles. Translated by Gilbert Cannan. New York, 1910.

Hicks, Granville, with John Stuart. *John Reed: The Making of a Revolutionary.* New York, 1936.

Higgins, Marguerite. *War in Korea: Reports from Women Combat Correspondents.* New York, 1954.

Hohenberg, John. *Between Two Worlds.* New York, 1967.

————. *New Era in the Pacific.* New York, 1972.

————. *The Pulitzer Prizes: A History.* New York, 1974.

————. ed. *The Pulitzer Prize Story.* New York, 1959.

Hough, Richard. *The Fleet That Had to Die.* New York, 1958.

Huddleston, Sisley. *In My Time.* New York, 1938.

Hudson, Frederic. *Journalism in the United States from 1690 to 1872.* New York, 1873.

James, Lionel. *High Pressure.* London, 1929.

Johnson, Gerald and others. *The Sunpapers of Baltimore.* New York, 1937.

Jones, Sir Roderick. *A Life in Reuters.* London, 1951.

Kato, Masuo. *The Lost War.* New York, 1946.

Kennan, George F. *The Decision to Intervene.* Princeton, 1958.

————. *Memories.* Boston, 1967.

Kinglake, A. W. *The Invasions of the Crimea.* London, 1863–67.

Karnow, Stanley. *Mao and China.* New York, 1972.

Knollenberg, Bernhard. *Origin of the American Revolution, 1759–1766.* New York, 1960.

Kruglak, T. E. *The Foreign Correspondents.* Geneva, 1955.

————. *The Two Faces of Tass.* Minneapolis, 1962.

Laney, Al. *Paris* Herald. New York, 1947.

Langford, Gerald. *The Richard Harding Davis Years.* New York, 1961.

Laurence, William L. *Men and Atoms.* New York, 1946, 1959, 1962.

Lazareff, Pierre. *Deadline.* New York, 1942.

Leckie, Robert. *Conflict: The History of the Korean War.* New York, 1962.

Leech, Margaret. *In the Days of McKinley.* New York, 1959.

Levine, Isaac Don. *The Russian Revolution.* New York, 1917.

Lie, Trygve. *In the Cause of Peace.* New York, 1954.

Lindbergh, Charles A. *The Spirit of St.Louis.* New York, 1953.

Lochner, Louis. *Always the Unexpected.* New York, 1946.

Lord, Walter. *Day of Infamy.* New York, 1957.

Lucas, Reginald. *Lord Glenesk and the Morning Post.* N.p., 1910.

Lyons, Eugene. *Assignment in Utopia.* New York, 1937.

MacArthur, Gen. Douglas. *Reminiscences.* New York, 1964.

MacGahan, J. A. *Campaigning on the Oxus and the Fall of Khiva.* New York, 1874.

Mario, Jessie White. *The Birth of Modern Italy. The Posthumous Papers of Jessie White Mario.* New York, 1909.

Mathews, Joseph J. *Reporting the Wars.* Minneapolis, 1957.

Matthews, Herbert L. *The Cuban Story.* New York, 1961.

————. *The Education of a Foreign Correspondent.* New York, 1946.

Mehring, Franz. *Karl Marx.* Published in German in 1935 and translated into English in 1962 at Ann Arbor, University of Michigan Press.

Miller, Lee G. *The Story of Ernie Pyle.* New York, 1950.

Miller, Webb. *I Found No Peace.* New York, 1936.

Morin, Relman. *East Wind Rising.* New York, 1960.

Morison, Elting E. *Turmoil and Tradition: The Life and Times of Henry L. Stimson.* Boston, 1960.

Morison, S. E. *The Oxford History of the American People.* New York, 1967.

Morris, Joe Alex. *Deadline Every Minute: The Story of the United Press.* New York, 1957.

Mott, Frank Luther. *American Journalism,* 3d ed. New York, 1962.

Mowrer, Paul Scott. *The House of Europe.* Boston, 1945.

Murrow, Edward R. *This is London.* New York, 1941.

Nevinson, Henry W. *Fire of Life.* New York, 1936.

O'Brien, Frank M. *The Story of the Sun from 1833–1918.* New York, 1919.

Palmer, Frederick. *With My Own Eyes.* Indianapolis, 1933.

Patai, Josef. *Star Over Jordan: The Life and Calling of Theodore Herzl.* Translated by Frances Magyar. New York, 1946.

Pound, Reginald, and Geoffrey Harmsworth, *Northcliffe.* London, 1959.

Pray, Isaac C. *Memoirs of James Gordon Bennett and His Times.* New York, 1855.

Pringle, Henry F. *Theodore Roosevelt.* New York, 1931.

Reed, John. *Ten Days that Shook the World.* New York, 1939.

Reston, James. *Deadline*. New York, 1991.

Rich, Josephine. *Jean Henri Dunant*. N.p., 1956.

Ridgway, Gen. Matthew B. *The Korean War*. Garden City, N.Y., 1967.

Richardson, J. Hall. *From the City to Fleet Street*. London, 1927.

Roberts, Charles. *LBJ's Inner Circle*. New York, 1965.

Robinson, Henry Crabb. *Diary*. 3 vols. London, 1869.

Romulo, Carlos P. *I Saw the Fall of the Philippines*. New York, 1942.

Rosewater, Victor. *History of Cooperative Newsgathering in the United States*. New York, 1930.

Ross, Isabel. *Ladies of the Press*. New York, 1936.

Rothberg, Abraham. *The Heirs of Stalin*. Ithaca, N.Y., 1972.

Russell, W. H. *The British Expedition to the Crimea*. London, 1858.

———. *My Diary, North and South*. 2 vols. London, 1863.

Ryan, Cornelius. *The Longest Day*. New York, 1959.

Salisbury, Harrison E. *An American in Russia*. New York, 1955.

———. *Behind the Lines — Hanoi*. New York, 1967.

———. *To Moscow and Beyond*. New York, 1959.

Salmon, Lucy M. *The Newspaper and the Historian*. New York, 1923.

Schlesinger, A.M., Jr. *A Thousand Days*. Boston, 1965.

Seitz, Don C. *The James Gordon Bennetts, Father and Son*. Indianapolis, 1928.

———. *Joseph Pulitzer: His Life and Letters*. New York, 1924.

Sevareid, Eric. *Not So Wild a Dream*. New York, 1946.

Shaplen, Robert. *The Lost Revolution*. New York, 1955.

———. *Time out of Hand*. New York, 1965.

Sheehan, Neil. *A Bright and Shining Lie*. New York, 1988.

Shirer, William L. *Berlin Diary*. New York, 1941.

———. *The Rise and Fall of the Third Reich*. New York, 1960.

Shub, David. *Lenin*. New York, 1948.

Smalley, George W. *Anglo-American Memories*. London, 1911.

Smyth, Henry D. *Atomic Energy for Military Purposes*. Princeton, 1946.

Snow, Edgar. *Journey to the Beginning*. New York, 1958.

———. *Red Star over China*. New York, 1938.

Snyder, Louis L., and Richard B. Morris. *A Treasury of Great Reporting*. New York, 1949, 1962.

Stanley, Sir Henry Morton. *The Autobiography of Sir Henry Morton Stanley*. London, 1909.

———. *How I Found Livingstone*. New York, 1872.

———. *Through the Dark Continent*. 2 vols. London, 1899.

Starr, Louis M. *Bohemian Brigade: Civil War Newsmen in Action*. New York, 1954.

Steed, Wickham. *Through 30 Years*. 2 vols. London, 1924.

Stone, Melville E. *Fifty Years a Journalist*. New York, 1921.

Storey, Graham. *Reuters: The Story of a Century of Newsgathering*. New York, 1951.

Swanberg, W. A. *Citizen Hearst*. New York, 1961.

Swope, H.B. *Inside the German Empire.* New York, 1916.

Tatu, Michel. *Power and the Kremlin.* New York, 1969.

Taylor, Bayard. *A Visit to India, China and Japan in the Year 1853.* New York, 1855.

———. *The Poetical Works of Bayard Taylor.* Boston, 1880.

Taylor, Marie Hanson, and Horace Scudder. *The Life and Letters of Bayard Taylor.* Boston, 1884.

Times. *The History of the* 4 vols. New York & London, 1935–52.

Tolischus, Otto. *They Wanted War.* New York, 1940.

———. *Tokyo Record.* New York, 1943.

Truman, Harry S. *Memoirs.* 2 vols:

———. *Year of Decision.* Garden City, N.Y., 1946.

———. *Years of Trial and Hope.* Garden City, N.Y., 1956.

Tuchman, Barbara. *The Guns of August.* New York, 1962.

UNESCO. *News Agencies: Their Structure and Operation.* Paris, 1953.

Untermeyer, Louis. *Heinrich Heine: Paradox and Poet.* New York, 1937.

US State Department. *International Control of Atomic Energy: Growth of the Policy.* Washington, D.C., 1946.

Weigle, Clifford F. "The Rise and Fall of the Havas News Agency." *Journalism Quarterly,* vol. X, no.3 (Sept.1942), pp. 277–86.

Weizmann, Chaim. *Trial and Error.* New York, 1949

White, Theodore H. *The Making of the President 1964.* New York, 1965.

———. *The Making of the President 1968.* New York, 1969.

———. *The Making of the President 1972.* New York, 1973.

Wile, Frederick W. *News Is Where You Find It.* Indianapolis, 1939.

Williams, Wythe. *Dusk of Empire.* New York, 1937.

Willoughby, C. A. *Shanghai Conspiracy: The Sorge Spy Ring.* New York, 1952.

Windsor, Duke of. *A King's Story.* New York, 1947.

Wiskemann, Elizabeth. *A Great Swiss Newspaper: The Story of the* Neue Zürcher Zeitung. New York, 1959.

Wohlstetter, Roberta. *Pearl Harbor: Warning and Decision.* Palo Alto, Calif., 1962.

Young, Arthur. *Travels During the Years 1787–1794.* London, 1929.

Index